Programming Visual Basic .NET

Programming Visual Basic .NET

Dave Grundgeiger

O'REILLY®

Beijing • Cambridge • Farnham • Köln • Paris • Sebastopol • Taipei • Tokyo

Programming Visual Basic .NET
by Dave Grundgeiger

Printed in the United States of America.

Published by O'Reilly & Associates, Inc., 1005 Gravenstein Highway North, Sebastopol, CA 95472.

O'Reilly & Associates books may be purchased for educational, business, or sales promotional use. Online editions are also available for most titles (*safari.oreilly.com*). For more information contact our corporate/institutional sales department: (800) 998-9938 or *corporate@oreilly.com*.

Editor: Ron Petrusha

Production Editor: Darren Kelly

Cover Designer: Pam Spremulli

Interior Designer: Melanie Wang

Printing History:

January 2002: First Edition.

ISBN: 0-596-00093-6

[C]

Table of Contents

Preface

The purpose of this book is to provide experienced software developers with the means to quickly become productive in Microsoft's Visual Basic .NET development environment. The only assumption I make about you as a programmer is that you're comfortable with the concepts and processes of software development. This book will not teach you how to program. However, if you're currently a working Visual Basic, C++, or Java developer, this book will help you transfer your existing skills to this new environment.

Organization of This Book

This book contains eight chapters and four appendixes.

Chapter 1, *Introduction*, starts out with three short *hello, world* examples that show how to enter and compile a console app, a GUI app, and a browser app. This gives the reader immediate gratification. The chapter also provides an overview of the . NET Framework and Visual Basic .NET.

Chapter 2, *The Visual Basic .NET Language*, examines the syntax and use of the Visual Basic .NET language. This will not teach someone how to program, but it will teach a programmer how to program in Visual Basic .NET.

Chapter 3, *The .NET Framework*, explains the various components of the .NET Framework and explains why the .NET Framework is a Good Thing.

Chapter 4, *Windows Forms I: Developing Desktop Applications*, explains how to use the Windows Forms class library for building GUI applications.

Chapter 5, *Windows Forms II: Controls, Common Dialog Boxes, and Menus*, picks up where Chapter 4 left off by discussing individual controls, showing how to use the common dialog boxes available in the .NET Framework, and examining menu creation and use.

Chapter 6, *ASP.NET and Web Forms: Developing Browser-Based Applications*, explains how to use the Web Forms class library for building browser-based applications.

Chapter 7, *Web Services*, talks about building components that provide services over the Internet and how to consume those services.

Chapter 8, *ADO.NET: Developing Database Applications*, explains the distributed, stateless, disconnected data model encapsulated by ADO.NET.

Appendix A, *Custom Attributes Defined in the System Namespace*, provides a list of the types known as attributes. The concept of attributes is discussed in Chapter 2.

Appendix B, *Exceptions Defined in the System Namespace*, provides a list of system-generated exceptions. The concept of exceptions is discussed in Chapter 2.

Appendix C, *Cultures* provides a list of culture names and IDs for globalization.

Appendix D, *Resources for Developers*, provides a list of online resources where developers can get help and further information on Visual Basic .NET.

Appendix E, *Math Functions* lists the standard math functions that are available to the Visual Basic .NET programmer via the .NET Framework's Math class.

Conventions Used in This Book

Throughout this book, we've used the following typographic conventions:

`Constant width`
: Constant width in body text indicates a language construct, such as the name of a stored procedure, a SQL statement, a Visual Basic .NET statement, an enumeration, an intrinsic or user-defined constant, a structure (i.e., a user-defined type), or an expression (like `dblElapTime = Timer - dblStartTime`). Code fragments and code examples appear exclusively in constant-width text. In syntax statements and prototypes, text set in constant width indicates such language elements as the function or procedure name and any invariable elements required by the syntax.

`Constant width italic`
: Constant width italic in body text indicates parameter names. In syntax statements or prototypes, constant width italic indicates replaceable parameters. In addition, constant width italic is used in body text to denote variables.

Italic
: Italicized words in the text indicate intrinsic or user-defined function and procedure names. Many system elements, such as paths and filenames, are also italicized. URLs and email addresses are italicized. Finally, italics are used for new terms where they are defined.

This icon indicates a tip, suggestion, or general note.

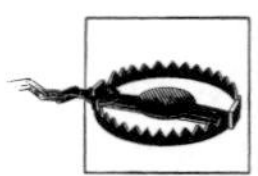

This icon indicates a warning or caution.

How to Contact Us

Please address comments and questions concerning this book to the publisher:

O'Reilly & Associates, Inc.
1005 Gravenstein Highway North
Sebastopol, CA 95472
(800) 998-9938 (in the United States or Canada)
(707) 829-0515 (international/local)
(707) 829-0104 (fax)

There is a web page for this book, where we list errata, examples, or any additional information. You can access this page at:

http://www.oreilly.com/catalog/progvbdotnet

To comment or ask technical questions about this book, send email to:

bookquestions@oreilly.com

For more information about our books, conferences, Resource Centers, and the O'Reilly Network, see our web site at:

http://www.oreilly.com

Acknowledgments

Thank you to the folks at Microsoft who were willing to answer my incessant questions, even in the midst of having to meet their own delivery deadlines. This list of top-notch people includes Brad Abrams, Alan Carter, Kit George, Scott Guthrie, Jim Hogg, Rob Howard, and Susan Warren. Several of these people also read major portions of the manuscript and offered constructive comments.

Thank you to my coworkers at Tara Software, Inc., for letting me use them as sounding boards and for assisting with technical issues. This includes Dan Boardman, Kevin Caswick, Varon Fugman, Anson Goldade, Karl Hauth, Garrett Peterson, Dan Phelps, Scott Rassbach, and Adam Steinert.

Thank you to Tara Software, Inc., and particularly to its principals, Roger Mills, Lynne Pilsner, and Larry Kleopping, for supporting this project (emotionally and financially).

Thank you to O'Reilly & Associates, Inc. for letting me write the book that I felt needed to be written. Thanks in particular to my editor, Ron Petrusha, who always knows what to mess with and what to leave alone. Thanks also to Budi Kurniawan for graciously granting me permission to use material that he had written on Windows controls.

And finally, thank you to my friend and wife, Annemarie Newman. Annemarie, you've supported all my endeavors—from shareware with lots of downloads and zero payments to books that take longer to write than they should. Thank you. I think you should start filling out that graduate school application, angel. It's your turn.

CHAPTER 1

Introduction

With its release for the .NET platform, the Visual Basic language has undergone dramatic changes. For example:

- The language itself is now fully object-oriented.
- Applications and components written in Visual Basic .NET have full access to the .NET Framework, an extensive class library that provides system and application services.
- All applications developed using Visual Basic .NET run within a managed runtime environment, the .NET common language runtime.

In this introduction, I briefly discuss these changes and other changes before showing you three very simple, but complete, Visual Basic .NET applications.

What Is the Microsoft .NET Framework?

The *.NET Framework* encompasses the following:

A new way to expose operating system and other APIs. For years, the set of Windows functionality that was available to developers and the way that functionality was invoked were dependent on the language environment being used. For example, the Windows operating system provides the ability to create windows (obviously). Yet, the way this feature was invoked from a C++ program was dramatically different from the way it was invoked from a Visual Basic program. With .NET, the way that operating system services are invoked is uniform across all languages (including code embedded in ASP.NET pages).

This portion of .NET is commonly referred to as the *.NET Framework class library*.

A new infrastructure for managing application execution. To provide a number of sophisticated new operating-system services—including code-level security, cross-language class inheritance, cross-language type compatibility, and hardware and operating-system independence, among others—Microsoft developed a new runtime environment known as the Common Language Runtime (CLR). The CLR includes the Common Type System (CTS) for cross-language type compatibility and the Common Language Specification (CLS) for ensuring that third-party libraries can be used from all .NET-enabled languages.

To support hardware and operating-system independence, Microsoft developed the Microsoft Intermediate Language (MSIL, or just IL). IL is a CPU-independent machine language–style instruction set into which .NET Framework programs are compiled. IL programs are compiled to the actual machine language on the target platform prior to execution (known as *just-in-time*, or JIT, compiling). IL is never interpreted.

A new web server paradigm. To support high-capacity web sites, Microsoft has replaced its Active Server Pages (ASP) technology with ASP.NET. While developers who are used to classic ASP will find ASP.NET familiar on the surface, the underlying engine is different, and far more features are supported. One difference, already mentioned in this chapter, is that ASP.NET web page code is now compiled rather than interpreted, greatly increasing execution speed.

A new focus on distributed-application architecture. Visual Studio .NET provides top-notch tools for creating and consuming *web services*—vendor-independent software services that can be invoked over the Internet.

The .NET Framework is designed top to bottom with the Internet in mind. For example, ADO.NET, the next step in the evolution of Microsoft's vision of "universal data access," assumes that applications will work with disconnected data by default. In addition, the ADO.NET classes provide sophisticated XML capabilities, further increasing their usefulness in a distributed environment.

An understanding of the .NET Framework is essential to developing professional Visual Basic .NET applications. The .NET Framework is explained in detail in Chapter 3.

What Is Visual Basic .NET?

Visual Basic .NET is the next generation of Visual Basic, but it is also a significant departure from previous generations. Experienced Visual Basic 6 developers will feel comfortable with Visual Basic .NET code and will recognize most of its constructs. However, Microsoft has made some changes to make Visual Basic .NET a better language and an equal player in the .NET world. These include such additions as a `Class` keyword for defining classes and an `Inherits` keyword for object inheritance, among others. Visual Basic 6 code can't be compiled by the Visual Basic .NET compiler without significant modification. The good news is that Microsoft has provided a migration tool to handle the task (mostly, anyway). Code migration is explained in Appendix A. The Visual Basic .NET language itself is detailed in Chapter 2.

Over the last several months I have spent almost all of my time playing with .NET and writing Visual Basic .NET programs. As a user of Visual Basic since Version 4, I can tell you that I am pleased with this new technology and with the changes that have been made to Visual Basic. In my opinion, Microsoft has done it right.

An Example Visual Basic .NET Program

> The first program to write is the same for all languages: Print the words hello, world
>
> —Brian W. Kernighan and Dennis M. Ritchie
> *The C Programming Language*

It has become a tradition for programming books to begin with a *hello, world* example. The idea is that entering and running a program—any program—may be the biggest hurdle faced by experienced programmers approaching a new platform or language. Without overcoming this hurdle, nothing else can follow. This chapter contains three such examples: one that creates a console application, one that creates a GUI application, and one that creates a browser-based application. Each example stands alone and can be run as is. The console and GUI applications can both be compiled from the command line (yes, Visual Basic .NET has a command-line compiler!). The browser-based application requires a computer running Internet Information Server (IIS).

hello, world

This is the world's favorite programming example, translated to Visual Basic .NET:

```
Imports System

Public Module Hello
   Public Sub Main( )
      Console.WriteLine("hello, world")
   End Sub
End Module
```

This version of *hello, world* is a *console application*—it displays its output in a Windows command-prompt window. To compile this program, enter it using any text editor, such as Windows's Notepad, save it in a file whose name ends with *.vb*, such as *Hello.vb*, and compile it from the Windows command line with this command:

```
vbc Hello.vb
```

The command `vbc` invokes the Visual Basic .NET command-line compiler, which ships with the .NET Framework SDK, and instructs it to compile the file named in the command-line argument. Compiling *Hello.vb* generates the file *Hello.exe*. After compiling, type `Hello` at the command line to run your program. Figure 1-1 shows the results of compiling and running this program.

Figure 1-1. Compiling and running hello, world

If you're accustomed to programming in Visual Basic 6, you can see even from this little program that Visual Basic has changed dramatically. Here's a breakdown of what's happening in this code.

The first line:

```
Imports System
```

indicates that the program may use one or more types defined in the System *namespace*. (Types are grouped into namespaces to help avoid name collisions and to group related types together.) Specifically, the *hello, world* program uses the Console class, which is defined in the System namespace. The `Imports` statement is merely a convenience. It is not needed if the developer is willing to qualify type names with their namespace names. For example, the *hello, world* program could have been written this way:

```
Public Module Hello
   Public Sub Main( )
      System.Console.WriteLine("hello, world")
   End Sub
End Module
```

However, it is customary to use the `Imports` statement to reduce keystrokes and visual clutter.

An important namespace for Visual Basic developers is Microsoft.VisualBasic. The types in this namespace expose members that form Visual Basic's intrinsic functions and subroutines. For example, the Visual Basic *Trim* function is a member of the Microsoft.VisualBasic.Strings class, while the *MsgBox* function is a member of the Microsoft.VisualBasic.Interaction class. In addition, Visual Basic's intrinsic constants come from enumerations within this namespace. Much of the functionality available in this namespace, however, is also duplicated within the .NET Framework's Base Class Library. Developers who are not familiar with Visual Basic 6 will likely choose to ignore this namespace, favoring the functionality provided by the .NET Framework. The .NET Framework is introduced later in this chapter and is explained in detail in Chapter 3.

Next, consider this line:

```
Public Module Hello
```

This line begins the declaration of a standard module named `Hello`. The standard-module declaration ends with this line:

```
End Module
```

In Visual Basic 6, various program objects were defined by placing source code in files having various filename extensions. For example, code that defined classes was placed in *.cls* files, code that defined standard modules was placed in *.bas* files, and so on. In Visual Basic .NET, all source files have *.vb* filename extensions, and program objects are defined with explicit syntax. For example, classes are defined with the `Class...End Class` construct, and standard modules are defined with the `Module... End Module` construct. Any particular *.vb* file can contain as many of these declarations as desired.

The purpose of standard modules in Visual Basic 6 was to hold code that was outside of any class definition. For example, global constants, global variables, and procedure libraries were often placed in standard modules. Standard modules in Visual Basic .NET serve a similar purpose and can be used in much the same way. However, in Visual Basic .NET they define datatypes that cannot be instantiated and whose members are all static. This will be discussed in more detail in Chapter 2.

The next line in the example begins the definition of a subroutine named *Main*:

```
Public Sub Main()
```

It ends with:

```
End Sub
```

This syntax is similar to Visual Basic 6. The `Sub` statement begins the definition of a *subroutine*—a method that has no return value.

The *Main* subroutine is the entry point for the application. When the Visual Basic .NET compiler is invoked, it looks for a subroutine named *Main* in one of the classes or standard modules exposed by the application. If *Main* is declared in a class rather than in a standard module, the subroutine must be declared with the `Shared` modifier. This modifier indicates that the class does not need to be instantiated for the subroutine to be invoked. In either case, the *Main* subroutine must be `Public`. An example of enclosing the *Main* subroutine in a class rather than in a standard module is given at the end of this section.

If no *Main* subroutine is found, or if more than one is found, a compiler error is generated. The command-line compiler has a switch (`/main:`*`location`*) that allows you to specify which class or standard module contains the *Main* subroutine that is to be used, in the case that there is more than one.

Lastly, there's the line that does the work:

```
Console.WriteLine("hello, world")
```

This code invokes the Console class's WriteLine method, which outputs the argument to the console. The WriteLine method is defined as a *shared* (also known as a *static*) method. Shared methods don't require an object instance in order to be invoked; nonshared methods do. Shared methods are invoked by qualifying them with their class name (in this case, Console).

Here is a program that uses a class instead of a standard module to house its *Main* subroutine. Note that *Main* is declared with the `Shared` modifier. It is compiled and run in the same way as the standard module example, and it produces the same output. There is no technical reason to choose one implementation over the other.

```
Imports System

Public Class Hello
   Public Shared Sub Main( )
      Console.WriteLine("hello, world")
   End Sub
End Class
```

Hello, Windows

Here's the GUI version of *hello, world*:

```
Imports System
Imports System.Drawing
Imports System.Windows.Forms

Public Class HelloWindows

   Inherits Form

   Private lblHelloWindows As Label

   Public Shared Sub Main( )
      Application.Run(New HelloWindows( ))
   End Sub

   Public Sub New( )

      lblHelloWindows = New Label( )
      With lblHelloWindows
         .Location = New Point(37, 31)
         .Size = New Size(392, 64)
         .Font = New Font("Arial", 36)
         .Text = "Hello, Windows!"
         .TabIndex = 0
         .TextAlign = ContentAlignment.TopCenter
      End With

      Me.Text = "Programming Visual Basic .NET"
      AutoScaleBaseSize = New Size(5, 13)
```

```
        FormBorderStyle = FormBorderStyle.FixedSingle
        ClientSize = New Size(466, 127)

        Controls.Add(lblHelloWindows)

    End Sub

End Class
```

This is similar to the *hello, world* console application, but with extra stuff required since this is a GUI application. Two additional `Imports` statements are needed for drawing the application's window:

```
Imports System.Drawing
Imports System.Windows.Forms
```

The HelloWindows class has something that Visual Basic programs have never seen before, the `Inherits` statement:

```
Inherits Form
```

The Visual Basic .NET language has class inheritance. The HelloWindows class inherits from the Form class, which is defined in the System.Windows.Forms namespace. Class inheritance and the `Inherits` statement are discussed in Chapter 2.

The next line declares a label control that will be used for displaying the text `Hello, Windows`:

```
Private lblHelloWindows As Label
```

The Label class is defined in the System.Windows.Forms namespace.

As is the case with console applications, GUI applications must have a shared subroutine called *Main*:

```
Public Shared Sub Main( )
   Application.Run(New HelloWindows( ))
End Sub
```

This Main method creates an instance of the HelloWindows class and passes it to the Run method of the Application class (defined in the System.Windows.Forms namespace). The Run method takes care of the housekeeping of setting up a Windows *message loop* and hooking the HelloWindows form into it.

Next is another special method:

```
Public Sub New( )
```

Like *Main*, *New* has special meaning to the Visual Basic .NET compiler. Subroutines named *New* are compiled into *constructors*. A constructor is a method that has no return value (but can have arguments) and is automatically called whenever a new object of the given type is instantiated. Constructors are explained further in Chapter 2.

The constructor in the HelloWindows class instantiates a Label object, sets some of its properties, sets some properties of the form, and then adds the Label object to the form's Controls collection. The interesting thing to note is how different this is from how Visual Basic 6 represented form design. In Visual Basic 6, form layout was represented by data in *.frm* files. This data was not code, but rather a listing of the properties and values of the various elements on the form. In Visual Basic .NET, this approach is gone. Instead, Visual Basic .NET statements must explicitly instantiate visual objects and set their properties. When forms are designed in Visual Studio .NET using its drag-and-drop designer, Visual Studio .NET creates this code on your behalf.

The command line to compile the *Hello, Windows* program is:

```
vbc HelloWindows.vb /reference:System.dll,System.Drawing.dll,
System.Windows.Forms.dll /target:winexe
```

(Note that there is no break in this line. The visual break here is required for printing in the book.)

The command line for compiling the *Hello, Windows* program has more stuff in it than the one for the console-based *hello, world* program. In addition to specifying the name of the *.vb* file, this command line uses the `/references` switch to specify three *.dll*s that contain the implementations of library classes used in the program (Form, Label, Point, etc.). The *hello, world* console application didn't require references when being compiled because all it used was the Console class, defined in the System namespace. The Visual Basic .NET command-line compiler includes two references implicitly: *mscorlib.dll* (which contains the System namespace) and *Microsoft.VisualBasic.dll* (which contains helper classes used for implementing some of the features of Visual Basic .NET).

Besides the `/references` switch, the command line for compiling the *Hello, Windows* program includes the `/target` switch. The `/target` switch controls what kind of executable code file is produced. The possible values of the `/target` switch are:

`exe`
: Creates a console application. The generated file has an extension of *.exe*. This is the default.

`winexe`
: Creates a GUI application. The generated file has an extension of *.exe*.

`library`
: Creates a class library. The generated file has an extension of *.dll*.

The output of *Hello, Windows* is shown in Figure 1-2.

GUI applications are explained in detail in Chapters 4 and 5.

Figure 1-2. Hello, Windows!

Hello, Browser

Here is a browser-based version of the *hello, world* application. Because the simplest version of such an application could be accomplished with only HTML, I've added a little spice. This web page includes three buttons that allow the end user to change the color of the text.

```
<script language="VB" runat="server">

      Sub Page_Load(Sender As Object, E As EventArgs)
         lblMsg.Text = "Hello, Browser!"
      End Sub

      Sub btnBlack_Click(Sender As Object, E As EventArgs)
         lblMsg.ForeColor = System.Drawing.Color.Black
      End Sub

      Sub btnGreen_Click(Sender As Object, E As EventArgs)
         lblMsg.ForeColor = System.Drawing.Color.Green
      End Sub

      Sub btnBlue_Click(Sender As Object, E As EventArgs)
         lblMsg.ForeColor = System.Drawing.Color.Blue
      End Sub

</script>

<html>

   <head>
      <title>Programming Visual Basic .NET</title>
   </head>

   <body>
      <form action="HelloBrowser.aspx" method="post" runat="server">
         <h1><asp:label id="lblMsg" runat="server"/></h1>
         <p>
            <asp:button type="submit" id="btnBlack" text="Black"
               OnClick="btnBlack_Click" runat="server"/>
            <asp:button id="btnBlue" text="Blue"
```

```
                OnClick="btnBlue_Click" runat="server"/>
             <asp:button id="btnGreen" text="Green"
                OnClick="btnGreen_Click" runat="server"/>
          </p>
       </form>
    </body>

</html>
```

To run this program, enter it using a text editor and save it in a file named *HelloBrowser.aspx*. Because the application is a web page that is meant to be delivered by a web server, it must be saved onto a machine that is running IIS and has the .NET Framework installed. Set up a virtual folder in IIS to point to the folder containing *HelloBrowser.aspx*. Finally, point a web browser to *HelloBrowser.aspx*. The output of the *Hello, Browser* application is shown in Figure 1-3.

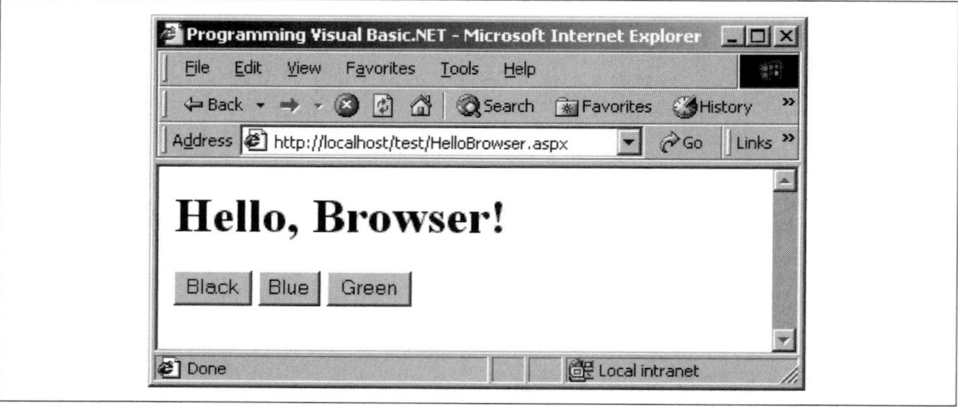

Figure 1-3. Hello, Browser!

Be sure to reference the file through the web server machine name or *localhost* (if the web server is on your local machine), so that the web server is invoked. For example, if the file is in a virtual directory called *Test* on your local machine, point your browser to *http://localhost/Test/HelloBrowser.aspx*. If you point your browser directly to the file using a filesystem path, the web server will not be invoked.

Going into detail on the *Hello, Browser* code would be too much for an introduction. However, I'd like to draw your attention to the `<asp:label>` and `<asp:button>` tags. These tags represent *server-side controls*. A server-side control is a class that is instantiated on the web server and generates appropriate output to represent itself on the browser. These classes have rich, consistent sets of properties and methods and can be referenced in code like controls on forms are referenced in GUI applications.

ASP.NET has many other nifty features, some of which are:

- Web pages are compiled, resulting in far better performance over classic ASP.
- Code can be pulled out of web pages entirely and placed in *.vb* files (called *code-behind files*) that are referenced by the web pages. This separation of web page layout from code results in pages that are easier to develop and maintain.
- ASP.NET automatically detects the capabilities of the end user's browser and adjusts its output accordingly.

Browser-based applications are discussed in detail in Chapter 6.

CHAPTER 2

The Visual Basic .NET Language

This chapter discusses the syntax of the Visual Basic .NET language, including basic concepts such as variables, operators, statements, classes, etc. Some material that you'd expect to find in this chapter will seem to be missing. For example, mathematical functions, file I/O, and form declarations are all very much a part of developing Visual Basic .NET applications, yet they are not introduced in this chapter because they are not intrinsic to the Visual Basic .NET language. They are provided by the .NET Framework and will be discussed in subsequent chapters. Additionally, Visual Basic .NET functions that exist merely for backward compatibility with Visual Basic 6 are not documented in this chapter.

Source Files

Visual Basic .NET source code is saved in files with a *.vb* extension. The exception to this rule is when Visual Basic .NET code is embedded in ASP.NET web page files. Such files have an *.aspx* extension.

Source files are plain-text files that can be created and edited with any text editor, including our old friend, Notepad. Source code can be broken into as many or as few files as desired. When you use Visual Studio .NET, source files are listed in the Solution Explorer window, and all source is included from these files when the solution is built. When you are compiling from the command line, all source files must appear as command-line arguments to the compile command. The location of declarations within source files is unimportant. As long as all referenced declarations appear somewhere in a source file being compiled, they will be found.

Unlike previous versions of Visual Basic, no special file extensions are used to indicate various language constructs (e.g., *.cls* for classes, *.frm* for forms, etc.). Syntax has been added to the language to differentiate various constructs. In addition, the pseudolanguage for specifying the graphical layout of forms has been removed. Form layout is specified by setting properties of form objects explicitly within code. Either this code can be written manually, or the WYSIWYG form designer in Visual Studio .NET can write it.

Identifiers

Identifiers are names given to namespaces (discussed later in this chapter), types (enumerations, structures, classes, standard modules, interfaces, and delegates), type members (methods, constructors, events, constants, fields, and properties), and variables. Identifiers must begin with either an alphabetic or underscore character (_), may be of any length, and after the first character must consist of only alphanumeric and underscore characters. Namespace declarations may be declared either with identifiers or *qualified identifiers*. Qualified identifiers consist of two or more identifiers connected with the dot character (.). Only namespace declarations may use qualified identifiers.

Consider this code fragment:

```
Imports System

Namespace ORelly.ProgVBNet

   Public Class Hello
      Public Shared Sub SayHello( )
         Console.WriteLine("hello, world")
      End Sub
   End Class

End Namespace
```

This code fragment declares three identifiers: OReilly.ProgVBNet (a namespace name), Hello (a class name), and SayHello (a method name). In addition to these, the code fragment uses three identifiers declared elsewhere: System (a namespace name), Console (a class name), and WriteLine (a method name).

Although Visual Basic .NET is not case sensitive, the case of identifiers is preserved when applications are compiled. When using Visual Basic .NET components from case-sensitive languages, the caller must use the appropriate case.

Ordinarily, identifiers may not match Visual Basic .NET keywords. If it is necessary to declare or use an identifier that matches a keyword, the identifier must be enclosed in square brackets ([ ]). Consider this code fragment:

```
Public Class [Public]
   Public Shared Sub SayHello( )
      Console.WriteLine("hello, world")
   End Sub
End Class

Public Class SomeOtherClass
   Public Shared Sub SomeOtherMethod( )
```

```
        [Public].SayHello( )
    End Sub
End Class
```

This code declares a class named Public and then declares a class and method that use the Public class. `Public` is a keyword in Visual Basic .NET. Escaping it with square brackets lets it be used as an identifier, in this case the name of a class. As a matter of style, using keywords as identifiers should be avoided, unless there is a compelling need. This facility allows Visual Basic .NET applications to use external components that declare identifiers matching Visual Basic .NET keywords.

Keywords

Keywords are words with special meaning in a programming language. In Visual Basic .NET, keywords are reserved; that is, they cannot be used as tokens for such purposes as naming variables and subroutines. The keywords in Visual Basic .NET are shown in Table 2-1.

Table 2-1. Visual Basic .NET keywords

Keyword	Description
`AddHandler`	Visual Basic .NET Statement
`AddressOf`	Visual Basic .NET Statement
`Alias`	Used in the `Declare` statement
`And`	Boolean operator
`AndAlso`	Boolean operator
`Ansi`	Used in the `Declare` statement
`Append`	Used as a symbolic constant in the *FileOpen* function
`As`	Used in variable declaration (`Dim`, `Friend`, etc.)
`Assembly`	Assembly-level attribute specifier
`Auto`	Used in the `Declare` statement
`Binary`	Used in the `Option Compare` statement
`Boolean`	Used in variable declaration (intrinsic data type)
`ByRef`	Used in argument lists
`Byte`	Used in variable declaration (intrinsic data type)
`ByVal`	Used in argument lists
`Call`	Visual Basic .NET statement
`Case`	Used in the `Select Case` construct
`Catch`	Visual Basic .NET statement
`CBool`	Data-conversion function
`CByte`	Data-conversion function
`CChar`	Data-conversion function
`CDate`	Data-conversion function

Table 2-1. Visual Basic .NET keywords (continued)

Keyword	Description
`CDec`	Data-conversion function
`CDbl`	Data-conversion function
`Char`	Used in variable declaration (intrinsic data type)
`CInt`	Data-conversion function
`Class`	Visual Basic .NET statement
`CLng`	Data-conversion function
`CObj`	Data-conversion function
`Compare`	Used in the `Option Compare` statement
`CShort`	Data-conversion function
`CSng`	Data-conversion function
`CStr`	Data-conversion function
`CType`	Data-conversion function
`Date`	Used in variable declaration (intrinsic data type)
`Decimal`	Used in variable declaration (intrinsic data type)
`Declare`	Visual Basic .NET statement
`Default`	Used in the `Property` statement
`Delegate`	Visual Basic .NET statement
`Dim`	Variable declaration statement
`Do`	Visual Basic .NET statement
`Double`	Used in variable declaration (intrinsic data type)
`Each`	Used in the `For Each...Next` construct
`Else`	Used in the `If...Else...ElseIf...End If` construct
`ElseIf`	Used in the `If...Else...ElseIf...End If` construct
`End`	Used to terminate a variety of statements
`EndIf`	Used in the `If...Else...ElseIf...End If` construct
`Enum`	Visual Basic .NET statement
`Erase`	Visual Basic .NET statement
`Error`	Used in the `Error` and `On Error` compatibility statements
`Event`	Visual Basic .NET statement
`Explicit`	Used in the `Option Explicit` statement
`False`	Boolean literal
`For`	Used in the `For...Next` and `For Each...Next` constructs
`Finally`	Visual Basic .NET statement
`For`	Visual Basic .NET statement
`Friend`	Statement and access modifier
`Function`	Visual Basic .NET statement
`Get`	Used in the `Property` construct

Table 2-1. Visual Basic .NET keywords (continued)

Keyword	Description
`GetType`	Visual Basic .NET operator
`GoTo`	Visual Basic .NET statement, used with the `On Error` statement
`Handles`	Defines an event handler in a procedure declaration
`If`	Visual Basic .NET statement
`Implements`	Visual Basic .NET statement
`Imports`	Visual Basic .NET statement
`In`	Used in the `For Each...Next` construct
`Inherits`	Visual Basic .NET statement
`Input`	Used in the *FileOpen* function
`Integer`	Used in variable declaration (intrinsic data type)
`Interface`	Visual Basic .NET statement
`Is`	Object comparison operator
`Let`	Reserved but unused in Visual Basic .NET
`Lib`	Used in the `Declare` statement
`Like`	Visual Basic .NET operator
`Lock`	Function name
`Long`	Used in variable declaration (intrinsic data type)
`Loop`	Used in a `Do` loop
`Me`	Statement referring to the current object instance
`Mid`	String-manipulation statement and function
`Mod`	Visual Basic .NET operator
`Module`	Visual Basic .NET statement
`MustInherit`	Used in the `Class` construct
`MustOverride`	Used in the `Sub` and `Function` statements
`MyBase`	Statement referring to an object's base class
`MyClass`	Statement referring to the current object instance
`Namespace`	Visual Basic .NET statement
`New`	Object-creation keyword, constructor name
`Next`	Used in the `For...Next` and `For Each...Next` constructs
`Not`	Visual Basic .NET operator
`Nothing`	Used to clear an object reference
`NotInheritable`	Used in the `Class` construct
`NotOverridable`	Used in the `Sub`, `Property`, and `Function` statements
`Object`	Used in variable declaration (intrinsic data type)
`Off`	Used in `Option` statements
`On`	Used in `Option` statements
`Option`	Used in `Option` statements

Table 2-1. Visual Basic .NET keywords (continued)

Keyword	Description
`Optional`	Used in the `Declare`, `Function`, `Property`, and `Sub` statements
`Or`	Boolean operator
`OrElse`	Boolean operator
`Output`	Used in the *FileOpen* function
`Overloads`	Used in the `Sub` and `Function` statements
`Overridable`	Used in the `Sub` and `Function` statements
`Overrides`	Used in the `Sub`, `Property`, and `Function` statements
`ParamArray`	Used in the `Declare`, `Function`, `Property`, and `Sub` statements
`Preserve`	Used with the `ReDim` statement
`Private`	Statement and access modifier
`Property`	Visual Basic .NET statement
`Protected`	Statement and access modifier
`Public`	Statement and access modifier
`RaiseEvent`	Visual Basic .NET statement
`Random`	Used in the *FileOpen* function
`Read`	Used in the *FileOpen* function
`ReadOnly`	Used in the `Property` statement
`ReDim`	Visual Basic .NET statement
`Rem`	Visual Basic .NET statement
`RemoveHandler`	Visual Basic .NET statement
`Resume`	Used in the `On Error` and `Resume` statements
`Return`	Visual Basic .NET statement
`Seek`	File-access statement and function
`Select`	Used in the `Select Case` construct
`Set`	Used in the `Property` statement
`Shadows`	Visual Basic .NET statement
`Shared`	Used in the `Sub` and `Function` statements
`Short`	Used in variable declaration (intrinsic data type)
`Single`	Used in variable declaration (intrinsic data type)
`Static`	Variable declaration statement
`Step`	Used in the `For...Next` construct
`Stop`	Visual Basic .NET statement
`String`	Used in variable declaration (intrinsic data type)
`Structure`	Visual Basic .NET statement
`Sub`	Visual Basic .NET statement
`SyncLock`	Visual Basic .NET statement
`Text`	Used in the `Option Compare` statement

Table 2-1. Visual Basic .NET keywords (continued)

Keyword	Description
`Then`	Used in the `If...Then...Else...EndIf` construct
`Throw`	Visual Basic .NET statement
`To`	Used in the `For...Next` and `Select Case` constructs
`True`	Boolean literal
`Try`	Visual Basic .NET statement
`TypeOf`	Used in variations of the `If...Then...EndIf` construct
`Unicode`	Used in the `Declare` statement
`Until`	Used in the `For...Next` construct
`Variant`	Reserved but unused in Visual Basic .NET
`When`	Used with the `Try...Catch...Finally` construct
`While`	Used with the `Do...Loop` and `While...End While` constructs
`With`	Visual Basic .NET statement
`WithEvents`	Used in variable declaration (`Dim`, `Public`, etc.)
`WriteOnly`	Used in the `Property` statement
`XOr`	Visual Basic .NET operator

Literals

Literals are representations of values within the text of a program. For example, in the following line of code, `10` is a literal, but `x` and `y` are not:

```
x = y * 10
```

Literals have data types just as variables do. The `10` in this code fragment is interpreted by the compiler as type Integer because it is an integer that falls within the range of the Integer type.

Numeric Literals

Any integer literal that is within the range of the Integer type (–2147483648 through 2147483647) is interpreted as type Integer, even if the value is small enough to be interpreted as type Byte or Short. Integer literals that are outside the Integer range but are within the range of the Long type (–9223372036854775808 through 9223372036854775807) are interpreted as type Long. Integer literals outside the Long range cause a compile-time error.

Numeric literals can also be of one of the floating point types—Single, Double, and Decimal. For example, in this line of code, `3.14` is a literal of type Double:

```
z = y * 3.14
```

In the absence of an explicit indication of type (discussed shortly), Visual Basic .NET interprets floating point literals as type Double. If the literal is outside the range of the Double type (–1.7976931348623157E308 through 1.7976931348623157E308), a compile-time error occurs.

Visual Basic .NET allows programmers to explicitly specify the types of literals. Table 2-2 (shown later in this chapter) lists Visual Basic .NET's intrinsic data types, along with the method for explicitly defining a literal of each type. Note that for some intrinsic types, there is no way to write a literal.

String Literals

Literals of type String consist of characters enclosed within quotation-mark characters. For example, in the following line of code, `"hello, world"` is a literal of type String:

```
Console.WriteLine("hello, world")
```

String literals are not permitted to span multiple source lines. In other words, this is not permitted:

```
' Wrong
Console.WriteLine("hello,
   world")
```

To write a string literal containing quotation-mark characters, type the character twice for each time it should appear. For example:

```
Console.WriteLine("So then Dave said, ""hello, world"".")
```

This line produces the following output:

```
So then Dave said, "hello, world".
```

Character Literals

Visual Basic .NET's Char type represents a single character. This is not the same as a one-character string; Strings and Chars are distinct types. Literals of type Char consist of a single character enclosed within quotation-mark characters, followed by the character `c`. For example, in the following code, `"A"c` is a literal of type Char:

```
Dim MyChar As Char
MyChar = "A"c
```

To emphasize that this literal is of a different data type than a single-character string, note that this code causes a compile-time error if `Option Strict` is `On`:

```
' Wrong
Dim MyChar As Char
MyChar = "A"
```

The error is:

```
Option Strict On disallows implicit conversions from 'String' to 'Char'.
```

Date Literals

Literals of type Date are formed by enclosing a date/time string within number-sign characters. For example:

```
Dim MyDate As Date
MyDate = #11/15/2001 3:00:00 PM#
```

Date literals in Visual Basic .NET code must be in the format `m/d/yyyy`, regardless of the regional settings of the computer on which the code is written.

Boolean Literals

The keywords `True` and `False` are the only Boolean literals. They represent the true and false Boolean states, respectively (of course!). For example:

```
Dim MyBoolean As Boolean
MyBoolean = True
```

Nothing

There is one literal that has no type: the keyword `Nothing`. `Nothing` is a special symbol that represents an uninitialized value of any type. It can be assigned to any variable and passed in any parameter. When used in place of a reference type, it represents a reference that does not reference any object. When used in place of a value type, it represents an empty value of that type. For numeric types, this is `0` or `0.0`. For the String type, this is the empty string (`""`). For the Boolean type, this is `False`. For the Char type, this is the Unicode character that has a numeric code of `0`. For programmer-defined value types, `Nothing` represents an instance of the type that has been created but has not been assigned a value.

Summary of Literal Formats

Table 2-2 shows all of Visual Basic .NET's intrinsic types, as well as the format for writing literals of those types in programs.

Table 2-2. Forming literals

Data type	Literal	Example
Boolean	`True`, `False`	`Dim bFlag As Boolean = False`
Char	`C`	`Dim chVal As Char = "X"C`
Date	`# #`	`Dim datMillen As Date = #01/01/2001#`
Decimal	`D`	`Dim decValue As Decimal = 6.14D`
Double	Any floating point number, or `R`	`Dim dblValue As Double = 6.142`
		`Dim dblValue As Double = 6.142R`

Table 2-2. Forming literals (continued)

Data type	Literal	Example

Integer	An integral value in the range of type Integer (–2,147,483,648 to 2,147,483,647), or `I`	`Dim iValue As Integer = 362`
		`Dim iValue As Integer = 362I`
		`Dim iValue As Integer = &H16AI` (hexadecimal)
		`Dim iValue As Integer = &O552I` (octal)

Long	An integral value outside the range of type Integer (–9,223,372,036,854,775,808 to –2,147,483,649, or 2,147,483,648 to 9,223,372,036,854,775,807), or `L`	`Dim lValue As Long = 362L` `Dim lValue As Long = &H16AL` (hexadecimal) `Dim lValue As Long = &O552L` (octal)
Short	`S`	`Dim shValue As Short = 362S` `Dim shValue As Short = &H16AS` (hexadecimal) `Dim shValue As Short = &O552S` (octal)
Single	`F`	`Dim sngValue As Single = 6.142F`
String	`" "`	`Dim strValue As String = "This is a string"`

Note the following facts about forming literals in Visual Basic .NET:

- There is no way to represent a literal of type Byte. However, this doesn't mean that literals cannot be used in situations where type Byte is expected. For example, the following code is fine:

  ```
  Dim MyByte As Byte = 100
  ```

  Even though the Visual Basic .NET compiler considers `100` to be of type Integer in this example, it recognizes that the number is small enough to fit into a variable of type Byte.
- Types not shown in Table 2-2 can't be expressed as literals.

Types

Types in Visual Basic .NET are divided into two categories: *value types* and *reference types*. Value types minimize memory overhead and maximize speed of access, but they lack some features of a fully object-oriented design (such as inheritance). Reference types give full access to object-oriented features, but they impose some memory and speed overhead for managing and accessing objects. When a variable holds a value type, the data itself is stored in the variable. When a variable holds a reference type, a *reference* to the data (also known as a *pointer*) is stored in the variable, and the data itself is stored somewhere else. Visual Basic .NET's primitive types include both value types and reference types (see "Fundamental Types" in this section). For extending the type system, Visual Basic .NET provides syntax for defining both new value types and new reference types (see "Custom Types" later in this section).

All reference types derive from the Object type. To unify the type system, value types can be treated as reference types when needed. This means that all types can derive from the Object type. Treating value types as reference types (a process known as *boxing*) is addressed later in this chapter, in the "Structures" section.

Fundamental Types

Visual Basic .NET has several built-in types. Each of these types is an alias for a type supplied by the .NET architecture. Because Visual Basic .NET types are equivalent to the corresponding underlying .NET-supplied types, there are no type-compatibility issues when passing arguments to components developed in other languages. In code, it makes no difference to the compiler whether types are specified using the keyword name for the type or using the underlying .NET type name. For example, the test in this code fragment succeeds:

```
Dim x As Integer
Dim y As System.Int32
If x.GetType() Is y.GetType( ) Then
   Console.WriteLine("They're the same type!")
Else
   Console.WriteLine("They're not the same type.")
End If
```

The fundamental Visual Basic .NET types are:

Boolean

The Boolean type is limited to two values: `True` and `False`. Visual Basic .NET includes many logical operators that result in a Boolean type. For example:

```
Public Shared Sub MySub(ByVal x As Integer, ByVal y As Integer)
   Dim b As Boolean = x > y
   ' other code
End Sub ' MySub
```

The result of the greater-than operator (>) is of type Boolean. The variable `b` is assigned the value `True` if the value in `x` is greater than the value in `y` and `False` if it is not. The underlying .NET type is System.Boolean.

Byte

The Byte type can hold a range of integers from 0 through 255. It represents the values that can be held in eight bits of data. The underlying .NET type is System. Byte.

Char

The Char type can hold any Unicode* character. The Char data type is new to Visual Basic .NET. The underlying .NET type is System.Char.

* Unicode is a 16-bit character-encoding scheme that is standard across all platforms, programs, and languages (human and machine). See *http://www.unicode.org* for information on Unicode.

Date

The Date type holds values that specify dates and times. The range of values is from midnight on January 1, 0001 (0001-01-01T00:00:00) through 1 second before midnight on December 31, 9999 (9999-12-31T23:59:59). The Date type contains many members for accessing, comparing, and manipulating dates and times. The underlying .NET type is System.DateTime.

Decimal

The Decimal type holds decimal numbers with a precision of 28 significant decimal digits. Its purpose is to represent and manipulate decimal numbers without the rounding errors of the Single and Double types. The Decimal type replaces Visual Basic 6's Currency type. The underlying .NET type is System.Decimal.

Double

The Double type holds a 64-bit value that conforms to IEEE standard 754 for binary floating point arithmetic. The Double type holds floating point numbers in the range –1.7976931348623157E308 through 1.7976931348623157E308. The smallest nonnegative number (other than zero) that can be held in a Double is 4.94065645841247E-324. The underlying .NET type is System.Double.

Integer

The Integer type holds integers in the range –2147483648 through 2147483647. The Visual Basic .NET Integer data type corresponds to the VB 6 Long data type. The underlying .NET type is System.Int32.

Long

The Long type holds integers in the range –9223372036854775808 through 9223372036854775807. In Visual Basic .NET, Long is a 64-bit integer data type. The underlying .NET type is System.Int64.

Object

The Object type is the base type from which all other types are derived. The Visual Basic .NET Object data type replaces the Variant in VB 6 as the universal data type. The underlying .NET type is System.Object.

Short

The Short type holds integers in the range –32768 through 32767. The Short data type corresponds to the VB 6 Integer data type. The underlying .NET type is System.Int16.

Single

The Single type holds a 32-bit value that conforms to IEEE standard 754 for binary floating point arithmetic. The Single type holds floating point numbers in the range –3.40282347E38 through 3.40282347E38. The smallest nonnegative number (other than zero) that can be held in a Double is 1.401298E-45. The underlying .NET type is System.Single.

String

The String type holds a sequence of Unicode characters. The underlying .NET type is System.String.

Of the fundamental types, Boolean, Byte, Char, Date, Decimal, Double, Integer, Long, Short, and Single (that is, all of them except Object and String) are value types. Object and String are reference types.

Custom Types

Visual Basic .NET provides rich syntax for extending the type system. Programmers can define both new value types and new reference types. Types declared with Visual Basic .NET's `Structure` and `Enum` statements are value types, as are all .NET Framework types that derive from System.ValueType. Reference types include Object, String, all types declared with Visual Basic .NET's `Class`, `Interface`, and `Delegate` statements, and all .NET Framework types that don't derive from System.ValueType.

Arrays

Array declarations in Visual Basic .NET are similar to those in Visual Basic 6 and other languages. For example, here is a declaration of an Integer array that has five elements:

```
Dim a(4) As Integer
```

The literal `4` in this declaration specifies the upper bound of the array. All arrays in Visual Basic .NET have a lower bound of `0`, so this is a declaration of an array with five elements, having indexes 0, 1, 2, 3, and 4.

The previous declaration is of a variable named `a`, which is of type "array of Integer." Array types implicitly inherit from the .NET Framework's Array type (defined in the System namespace) and, therefore, have access to the methods defined in that type. For example, the following code displays the lower and upper bounds of an array by calling the Array class's GetLowerBound and GetUpperBound methods:

```
Dim a(4) As Integer

Console.WriteLine("LowerBound is " & a.GetLowerBound(0).ToString( ))
Console.WriteLine("UpperBound is " & a.GetUpperBound(0).ToString( ))
```

The output is:

```
LowerBound is 0
UpperBound is 4
```

Note that the upper bound of the array is dynamic: it can be changed by methods available in the Array type.

Array elements are initialized to the default value of the element type. A type's default value is determined as follows:

- For numeric types, the default value is `0`.
- For the Boolean type, the default value is `False`.
- For the Char type, the default value is the character whose Unicode value is `0`.
- For structure types (described later in this chapter), the default value is an instance of the structure type with all of its fields set to their default values.
- For enumeration types (described later in this chapter), the default value is an instance of the enumeration type with its internal representation set to `0`, which may or may not correspond to a legal value in the enumeration.
- For reference types (including String), the default value is `Nothing`.

You can access array elements by suffixing the array name with the index of the desired element enclosed in parentheses, as shown here:

```
For i = 0 To 4
   Console.WriteLine(a(i))
Next
```

Arrays can be multidimensional. Commas separate the dimensions of the array when used in declarations and when accessing elements. Here is the declaration of a three-dimensional array, where each dimension has a different size:

```
Dim a(5, 10, 15) As Integer
```

As with single-dimensional arrays, array elements are initialized to their default values.

Initializing arrays

Arrays of primitive types can be initialized by enclosing the initial values in curly brackets ({}). For example:

```
Dim a( ) As String = {"First", "Second", "Third", "Fourth", "Fifth"}
```

Notice that when arrays are initialized in this manner, the array declaration is not permitted to specify an explicit size. The compiler infers the size from the number of elements in the initializer.

To initialize multidimensional arrays, include the appropriate number of commas in the array-name declaration and use nested curly brackets in the initializer. Here is a declaration of a two-dimensional array having three rows and two columns:

```
Dim a(,) As Integer = {{1, 2}, {3, 4}, {5, 6}}
```

This declaration produces the following array:

```
a(0,0)=1   a(0,1)=2
a(1,0)=3   a(1,1)=4
a(2,0)=5   a(2,1)=6
```

When initializing multidimensional arrays, the innermost curly brackets correspond to the rightmost dimension.

Dynamically allocating arrays

Use the New keyword to allocate arrays of any type. For example, this code creates an array of five Integers and initializes the elements as shown:

```
Dim a( ) As Integer
a = New Integer(4) {1, 2, 3, 4, 5}
```

If the array elements won't be initialized by the allocation, it is still necessary to include the curly brackets:

```
Dim a( ) As Integer
' allocates an uninitialized array of five Integers
a = New Integer(5) {}
```

Curly brackets are required so the compiler won't confuse the array syntax with constructor syntax.

Note also the meaning of this declaration by itself:

```
Dim a( ) As Integer
```

This is the declaration of a reference that could point to a single-dimensional array of Integers, but doesn't yet. Its initial value is Nothing.

Collections

A *collection* is any type that exposes the ICollection interface (defined in the System. Collections namespace). (Interfaces are explained later in this chapter. Briefly, an interface is an agreement in which the type will expose certain methods, properties, and other members. By exposing the ICollection interface, a type ensures that it can be used anywhere a collection is expected.) In general, collections store multiple values and provide a way for iterating through those values. Specialized collection types may also provide other means for adding and reading values. For example, the Stack type (defined in the System.Collections namespace) provides methods, such as Push and Pop, for performing operations that are appropriate for the stack data structure.

The Visual Basic .NET runtime provides a type called Collection (defined in the Microsoft.VisualBasic namespace) that mimics the behavior of Visual Basic 6 collections and exposes the ICollection interface. Example 2-1 shows its use.

Example 2-1. Using the Collection type

```
' Create a new collection object.
Dim col As New Collection( )

' Add some items to the collection.
col.Add("Some value")
col.Add("Some other value")
col.Add("A third value")

' Iterate through the collection and output the strings.
```

Example 2-1. Using the Collection type (continued)

```
Dim obj As Object
For Each obj In col
   Dim str As String = CType(obj, String)
   Console.WriteLine(str)
Next
```

The Collection type's Add method adds items to the collection. Although strings are added to the collection in Example 2-2, the Add method is defined to take items of type Object, meaning that any type can be passed to the method. After items are added to the collection, they can be iterated using the `For Each` statement (discussed later in this chapter, under "Statements"). Because the Collection class is defined to store items of type Object, the loop variable in the `For Each` statement must be of type Object. Because the items are actually strings, the code in Example 2-1 converts the Object references to String references using the *CType* function. Type conversions are discussed later in this section. The output of the code in Example 2-1 is:

```
Some value
Some other value
A third value
```

The items in a Collection object can also be iterated using a numerical index. The Collection object has a Count property, which indicates the number of items in the collection. Example 2-2 is precisely the same as Example 2-1, except that it iterates through the Collection object using a numerical index and a standard `For` loop.

Example 2-2. Using a numerical index on a collection object

```
' Create a new collection object.
Dim col As New Collection( )

' Add some items to the collection.
col.Add("Some value")
col.Add("Some other value")
col.Add("A third value")

' Iterate through the collection and output the strings.
Dim i As Integer
For i = 1 To col.Count
   Dim str As String = CType(col(i), String)
   Console.WriteLine(str)
Next
```

Note that to access an item by index, the index number is placed within parentheses following the name of the Collection reference variable, as shown again here:

```
col(i)
```

The syntax of the Add method is:

```
Public Sub Add( _
   ByVal Item As Object, _
```

```
        Optional ByVal Key As String = Nothing, _
        Optional ByVal Before As Object = Nothing, _
        Optional ByVal After As Object = Nothing _
    )
```

The parameters are:

Item
: The item to add to the collection.

Key
: An optional string value that can be used as an index to retrieve the associated item. For example, the following code adds an item to a collection and then uses the key value to retrieve the item:

```
Dim col As New Collection( )
col.Add("Some value", "Some key")
' ...
Dim str As String = CType(col("Some key"), String)
Console.WriteLine(str)
```

The output is:

```
Some value
```

Before
: The item before which the new item should be added.

After
: The item after which the new item should be added.

The .NET Framework class library provides several additional collection types, which are listed and briefly discussed in Chapter 3.

Type Conversions

Visual Basic .NET provides a variety of ways for values of one type to be converted to values of another type. There are two main categories of conversions: *widening conversions* and *narrowing conversions*. Widening conversions are conversions in which there is no possibility for data loss or incorrect results. For example, converting a value of type Integer to a value of type Long is a widening conversion because the Long type can accommodate every possible value of the Integer type. Narrowing is the reverse operation—converting from a Long to an Integer—because some values of type Long can't be represented as values of type Integer.

Visual Basic .NET performs widening conversions automatically whenever necessary. For example, a widening conversion occurs in the second line of the following code. The Integer value on the righthand side of the assignment is automatically converted to a Long value so it can be stored in the variable `b`:

```
Dim a As Integer = 5
Dim b As Long = a
```

A conversion that happens automatically is called an *implicit conversion*.

Now consider the reverse situation:

```
Dim a As Long = 5
Dim b As Integer = a
```

The second line of code here attempts to perform an implicit narrowing conversion. Whether the compiler permits this line of code depends on the value set for the `Option Strict` compiler option. When `Option Strict` is `On`, attempts to perform an implicit widening conversion result in a compiler error. When `Option Strict` is `Off`, the compiler automatically adds code behind the scenes to perform the conversion. At runtime, if the actual value being converted is out of the range that can be represented by the target type, a runtime exception occurs.

`Option Strict` can be set in either of two ways. First, it can be set in code at the top of a source file, like this:

```
Option Strict On
' ...
```

or:

```
Option Strict Off
' ...
```

The other way is to set a compiler switch, which affects all source files in the application. If you're compiling from the command line, specify `/optionstrict+` on the command line to set `Option Strict On`. Specify `/optionstrict-` to set `Option Strict Off`. For example:

```
vbc MySource.vb /optionstrict+
```

To set `Option Strict` in Visual Studio .NET:

1. Right-click on the project name in the Solution Explorer window and choose Properties. This brings up the Project Property Pages dialog box. (If the Solution Explorer window is not visible, choose View→Solution Explorer from the Visual Studio .NET main menu to make it appear.)
2. Within the Project Property Pages dialog box, choose the Common Properties folder. Within that folder, choose the Build property page. This causes the project-build options to appear on the right side of the dialog box.
3. Set the desired value for the `Option Strict` option.

By default, `Option Strict` is `Off`, meaning that implicit narrowing conversions are allowed. This matches the default setting of Visual Basic 6. However, most experienced developers consider it beneficial to set `Option Strict On` so the compiler can help detect coding errors before they become runtime errors. Attempting to assign a Long to an Integer, for example, is usually a sign either that something was mistyped or that there is a problem with the design of the program. Setting `Option Strict On` helps the developer discover such errors at compile time. On the other hand, there may sometimes be a legitimate need to perform a narrowing conversion. Perhaps the application is interfacing to another application that passes a value as a Long, but it is guaranteed that the actual value passed will never be outside the range of the Integer type. `Option Strict` could be set to `Off` to allow implicit narrowing conversions, but a better alternative is to have `Option Strict On` (so it can protect the majority of the program) and to specify an *explicit* narrowing conversion. For example:

```
Dim a As Long = 5
Dim b As Integer = CInt(a)
```

This is known as an *explicit conversion* because the programmer is explicitly requesting a conversion to Integer. If at runtime `a` contains a value that is outside the Integer range, an exception is thrown.

Table 2-3 shows Visual Basic .NET's conversion functions.

Table 2-3. Conversion functions

Conversion function	Converts its argument to
CBool	A Boolean
CByte	A Byte
CChar	A Char
CDate	A Date
CDbl	A Double
CDec	A Decimal
CInt	An Integer
CLng	A Long
CObj	An Object
CSng	A Single
CStr	A String

The functions shown in Table 2-3 all take a single argument. If the argument can't be converted to the given type, an exception is thrown. Note the following:

- When converting from any numeric value to Boolean, zero converts to `False` and nonzero converts to `True`.
- When converting from Boolean to a numeric value, `False` converts to `0` and `True` converts to `-1`.
- When converting from String to Boolean, the string must contain either the word `"false"`, which converts to `False`, or the word `"true"`, which converts to `True`. The case of the string is not important.
- When converting from Boolean to String, `True` converts to `"True"` and `False` converts to `"False"`.
- Anything can be converted to type Object.

It's also possible to convert between reference types. Any object-reference conversion of a derived type to a base type is considered a widening conversion and can therefore be done implicitly. Conversely, conversion from a base type to a derived type is a narrowing conversion. As previously discussed, in order for narrowing conversions to compile, either `Option Strict` must be `Off` or an explicit conversion must be performed. Explicit conversions of reference types are done with the *CType* function. The *CType* function takes two arguments. The first is a reference to some object, and the second is the name of the type to which the reference will convert. At runtime, if a conversion is possible, the return value of the function is an object reference of the appropriate type. If no conversion is possible, an exception is thrown.

Here is an example of converting between base and derived classes:

```
' This is a base class.
Public Class Animal
   ' ...
End Class

' This is a derived class.
Public Class Cat
   Inherits Animal
   ' ...
End Class

' This is another derived class.
Public Class Dog
   Inherits Animal
   ' ...
End Class

' This is a test class.
Public Class AnimalTest
   Public Shared Sub SomeMethod( )
      Dim myCat As New Cat( )
      Dim myDog As New Dog( )
      Dim myDog2 As Dog
      Dim myAnimal As Animal = myCat ' Implicit conversion OK
      myAnimal = myDog ' Implicit conversion OK
      myDog2 = CType(myAnimal, Dog) ' Explicit conversion required
   End Sub
End Class
```

Object references can also be implicitly converted to any interface exposed by the object's class.

Namespaces

Thousands of types are defined in the .NET Framework. In addition, programmers can define new types for use in their programs. With so many types, name clashes are inevitable. To prevent name clashes, types are considered to reside inside of *namespaces*. Often, this fact can be ignored. For example, in Visual Basic .NET a class may be defined like this:

```
Public Class SomeClass
   ' ...
End Class
```

This class definition might be in a class library used by third-party customers, or it might be in the same file or the same project as the client code. The client code that uses this class might look something like this:

```
Dim x As New SomeClass( )
x.DoSomething( )
```

Now consider what happens if the third-party customer also purchases another vendor's class library, which also exposes a SomeClass class. The Visual Basic .NET compiler can't know which definition of SomeClass will be used. The client must therefore use the *full name* of the type, also known as its *fully qualified name*. Code that needs to use both types might look something like this:

```
' The namespace is "FooBarCorp.SuperFoo2100".
Dim x As New FooBarCorp.SuperFoo2100.SomeClass( )
x.DoSomething( )
' ...
' The namespace is "MegaBiz.ProductivityTools.WizardMaster".
Dim y As New MegaBiz.ProductivityTools.WizardMaster.SomeClass( )
y.DoSomethingElse( )
```

Note that a namespace name can itself contain periods (.). When looking at a fully qualified type name, everything prior to the final period is the namespace name. The name after the final period is the type name.

Microsoft recommends that namespaces be named according to the format *CompanyName.TechnologyName*. For example, "Microsoft.VisualBasic".

The Namespace Statement

So how does a component developer specify a type's namespace? In Visual Basic .NET, this can be done several ways. One is to use the Namespace keyword, like this:

```
Namespace MegaBiz.ProductivityTools.WizardMaster

   Public Class SomeClass
      ' ...
   End Class

End Namespace
```

Note that it is permissible for different types in the same source file to have different namespaces.

A second way to provide a namespace is to use the /rootnamespace switch on the Visual Basic .NET command-line compiler. For example:

```
vbc src.vb /t:library /rootnamespace:MegaBiz.ProductivityTools.WizardMaster
```

All types defined within the compiled file(s) then have the given namespace.

If you're compiling in the Visual Studio .NET IDE, the root namespace is specified in the Project Property Pages dialog box, which can be reached by right-clicking the project name in the Solution Explorer window of the IDE, then choosing Properties (see Figure 2-1 for the resulting WizardMaster Property Pages dialog). By default, Visual Studio .NET sets the root namespace equal to the name of the project.

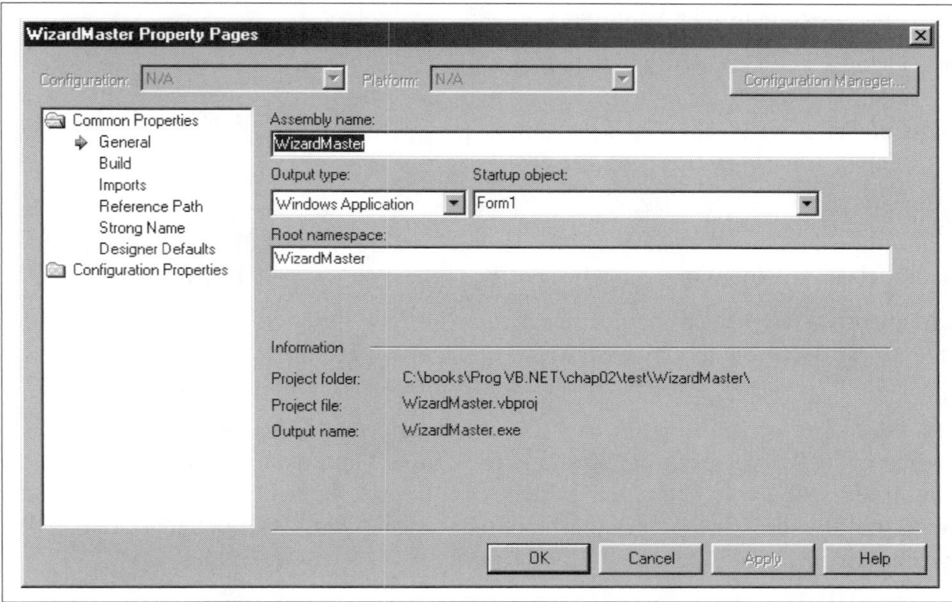

Figure 2-1. Setting the root namespace in the Visual Studio .NET IDE

Note that regardless of which compiler is used (command line or Visual Studio .NET), if a root namespace is specified *and* the `Namespace` keyword is used, the resulting namespace will be the concatenation of the root namespace name and the name specified using the `Namespace` keyword.

The Imports Statement

So far, the discussion has implied that it's not necessary for the user of a type to specify the type's full name unless there is a name clash. This isn't exactly true. The CLR deals with types only in terms of their full names. However, because humans don't like to deal with long names, Visual Basic .NET offers a shortcut. As an example, the .NET Framework provides a drawing library, in which a type called Point is defined. This type's namespace is called System.Drawing, so the type's fully qualified name is System.Drawing.Point. Code that uses this type might look like this:

```
Dim pt As System.Drawing.Point
pt.X = 10
```

```
pt.Y = 20
' ...
```

Typing the full name of every type whenever it is used would be too cumbersome, though, so Visual Basic .NET offers the Imports statement. This statement indicates to the compiler that the types from a given namespace will appear without qualification in the code. For example:

```
' At the top of the source code file:
Imports System.Drawing
' ...
' Somewhere within the source code file:
Dim pt As Point
pt.X = 10
pt.Y = 20
' ...
```

To import multiple namespaces, list each one in its own Imports statement. It's okay if multiple imported namespaces have some name clashes. For the types whose names clash, the full name must be specified wherever the type is used.

The Imports statement is just a convenience for the developer. It does not set a reference to the assembly in which the types are defined. See the discussion of assemblies in Chapter 3 to learn how to reference assemblies that contain the types you need.

Finally, note that namespaces, too, are just a convenience for the developer writing source code. To the runtime, a type is not "in" a namespace—a namespace is just another part of a type name. It is perfectly acceptable for any given assembly to have types in different namespaces, and more than one assembly can define types in a single namespace.

Symbolic Constants

Consider this function:

```
Public Shared Function RemainingCarbonMass( _
   ByVal InitialMass As Double, _
   ByVal Years As Long _
) As Double
   Return InitialMass * ((0.5 ^ (Years / 5730)))
End Function
```

What's wrong with this code? One problem is readability. What does it mean to divide Years by 5730? In this code, 5730 is referred to as a *magic number*—one whose meaning is not readily evident from examining the code. The following changes correct this problem:

```
Public Const CarbonHalfLifeInYears As Double = 5730

Public Shared Function RemainingCarbonMass( _
   ByVal InitialMass As Double, _
   ByVal Years As Long _
) As Double
```

```
    Return InitialMass * ((0.5 ^ (Years / CarbonHalfLifeInYears)))
End Function
```

There is now no ambiguity about the meaning of the divisor.

Another problem with the first code fragment is that a program filled with such code is hard to maintain. What if the programmer later discovers that the half-life of carbon is closer to 5730.1 years, and she wants to make the program more accurate? If this number is used in many places throughout the program, it must be changed in every case. The risk is high of missing a case or of changing a number that shouldn't be changed. With the second code fragment, the number needs to be changed in only one place.

See also the discussion of read-only fields later in this chapter, under the "Classes" section.

Variables

A *variable* is an identifier that is declared in a method and that stands for a value within that method. Its value is allowed to change within the method. Each variable is of a particular type, and that type is indicated in the declaration of the variable. For example, this line declares a variable named `i` whose type is Integer:

```
Dim i As Integer
```

The keyword `Dim` indicates a variable declaration. *Dim* is short for *dimension* and dates back to the original days of the BASIC programming language in the late 1960s. In that language, variables were not declared; they were just used where needed (except for arrays). Because of how arrays were laid out in memory, the BASIC language interpreter had to be told of the dimensions of an array before the array was used. This was the purpose of the `Dim` statement. In later years, when declaration of all variables was agreed upon to be a *good thing*, the use of the `Dim` statement was broadened to include all variable declarations.

Variable identifiers may be suffixed with *type characters* that serve to indicate the variable's type. For example, this line declares a variable of type Integer:

```
Dim x%
```

The effect is precisely the same as for this declaration:

```
Dim x As Integer
```

The set of type characters is shown in Table 2-4; note that not all data types have a type character.

Table 2-4. Type characters

Data type	Type character	Example
Decimal	@	`Dim decValue@ = 132.24`
Double	#	`Dim dblValue# = .0000001327`

Table 2-4. Type characters (continued)

Data type	Type character	Example
Integer	%	`Dim iCount% = 100`
Long	&	`Dim lLimit& = 1000000`
Single	!	`Dim sngValue! = 3.1417`
String	$	`Dim strInput$ = ""`

As a matter of style, type characters should be avoided in preference to spelling out type names and using descriptive variable names.

Variable Initializers

New to Visual Basic .NET is the ability to combine variable declaration and assignment. For example, this code declares an Integer `i` and gives it an initial value of `10`:

```
Dim i As Integer = 10
```

This is equivalent to the following code:

```
Dim i As Integer
i = 10
```

Scope

Scope refers to the so-called *visibility* of identifiers within source code. That is, given a particular identifier declaration, the *scope* of the identifier determines where it is legal to reference that identifier in code. For example, these two functions each declare a variable `CoffeeBreaks`. Each declaration is invisible to the code in the other method. The scope of each variable is the method in which it is declared.

```
Public Sub MyFirstMethod( )
   Dim CoffeeBreaks As Integer
   ' ...
End Sub

Public Sub MySecondMethod( )
   Dim CoffeeBreaks As Long
   ' ...
End Sub
```

Unlike previous versions of Visual Basic, Visual Basic .NET has *block scope*. Variables declared within a set of statements ending with `End`, `Loop`, or `Next` are local to that block. For example:

```
Dim i As Integer
For i = 1 To 100
   Dim j As Integer
   For j = 1 To 100
      ' ...
```

```
    Next
Next
' j is not visible here
```

Visual Basic .NET doesn't permit the same variable name to be declared at both the method level and the block level. Further, the life of the block-level variable is equal to the life of the method. This means that if the block is re-entered, the variable may contain an old value (don't count on this behavior, as it is not guaranteed and is the kind of thing that might change in future versions of Visual Basic).

Access Modifiers

Access modifiers control the accessibility of types (including enumerations, structures, classes, standard modules, and delegates) and type members (including methods, constructors, events, constants, fields [data members], and properties) to other program elements. They are part of the declarations of types and type members. In the following code fragment, for example, the keywords `Public` and `Private` are access modifiers:

```
Public Class SomeClass

   Public Sub DoSomething( )
      ' ...
   End Sub

   Private Sub InternalHelperSub( )
      ' ...
   End Sub

End Class
```

The complete list of access modifiers and their meanings is shown in Table 2-5.

Table 2-5. Access modifiers

Access modifier	Description
`Friend`	Defines a type that is accessible only from within the program in which it is declared.
`Private`	Defines a type that is accessible only from within the context in which it is declared. For instance, a Private variable declared within a class module is accessible only from within that class module. A Private class is accessible only from classes within which it is nested.
`Protected`	Applies to class members only. Defines a type that is accessible only from within its own class or from a derived class.
`Protected Friend`	Defines a type that is accessible from within the program in which it is declared as well as from derived classes.
`Public`	Defines a type that is publicly accessible. For example, a public method of a class can be accessed from any program that instantiates that class.

Assignment

In Visual Basic .NET, assignment statements are of the form:

```
variable, field, or property = expression
```

Either the type of the expression must be the same as that of the item receiving the assignment, or there must exist an appropriate implicit or explicit conversion from the type of the expression to the type of the item receiving the assignment. For information on implicit and explicit conversions, see "Type Conversions" earlier in this chapter.

When an assignment is made to a value type, the value of the expression is copied to the target. In contrast, when an assignment is made to a reference type, a reference to the value is stored in the target. This is an important distinction that is worth understanding well. Consider the code in Example 2-3.

Example 2-3. Value-type assignment versus reference-type assignment

```
Public Structure SomeStructure
   Public MyPublicMember As String
End Structure

Public Class SomeClass
   Public MyPublicMember As String
End Class

Public Class AssignmentTest

   Public Shared Sub TestValueAndReferenceAssignment( )

      Dim a, b As SomeStructure
      Dim c, d As SomeClass

      ' Test assignment to value type.
      a.MyPublicMember = "To be copied to 'b'"
      b = a
      a.MyPublicMember = "New value for 'a'"
      Console.WriteLine("The value of b.MyPublicMember is """ _
         & b.MyPublicMember & """")

      ' Test assignment to reference type.
      c = New SomeClass( )
      c.MyPublicMember = "To be copied to 'd'"
      d = c
      c.MyPublicMember = "New value for 'c'"
      Console.WriteLine("The value of d.MyPublicMember is """ _
         & d.MyPublicMember & """")

   End Sub

End Class
```

The output of the TestValueAndReferenceAssignment method in Example 2-3 is:

```
The value of b.MyPublicMember is "To be copied to 'b'"
The value of d.MyPublicMember is "New value for 'c'"
```

In Example 2-3, the SomeStructure structure and the SomeClass class have identical definitions, except that one is a structure and the other is a class. This leads to very different behavior during assignment. When a value type is copied, the actual value is copied. When a reference type is copied, only the reference is copied, resulting in two references to the same value. If the value is subsequently changed through one of the references, the new value is also seen through the other reference.

This difference is shown in the output from Example 2-3. The value type in variable `a` is copied to variable `b`. The value of `a.MyPublicMember` is then modified. Subsequently, the call to Console.WriteLine shows that this modification does not affect `b.MyPublicMember`. In contrast, the assignment of `c` to `d` copies only a reference, which means that after the assignment, both `c` and `d` reference the same object. The value of `c.MyPublicMember` is then modified. The subsequent call to Console.WriteLine shows that this modification *did* affect `d.MyPublicMember`. Indeed, `d.MyPublicMember` refers to the same memory as `c.MyPublicMember`.

Operators and Expressions

Operators are symbols (characters or keywords) that specify operations to be performed on one or two *operands* (or *arguments*). Operators that take one operand are called *unary operators*. Operators that take two operands are called *binary operators*. Unary operators use *prefix notation*, meaning that the operator precedes the operand (e.g., `-5`). Binary operators (except for one case) use *infix notation*, meaning that the operator is between the operands (e.g., `1 + 2`). The `TypeOf...Is` operator is a binary operator that uses a special form that is neither prefix nor infix notation.

Unary Operators

Visual Basic supports the following unary operators:

`+` *(unary plus)*
: The unary plus operator takes any numeric operand. It's not of much practical use because the value of the operation is equal to the value of the operand.

`-` *(unary minus)*
: The unary minus operator takes any numeric operand (except as noted later). The value of the operation is the negative of the value of the operand. In other words, the result is calculated by subtracting the operand from zero. If the operand type is Short, Integer, or Long, and the value of the operand is the maximum

negative value for that type, then applying the unary minus operator will cause a System.OverflowException error, as in the following code fragment:

```
Dim sh As Short = -32768
Dim i As Integer = -sh
```

`Not` *(logical negation)*

The logical negation operator takes a Boolean operand. The result is the logical negation of the operand. That is, if the operand is `False`, the result of the operation is `True`, and vice versa.

`AddressOf`

The `AddressOf` operator returns a reference to a method. Two different kinds of references can be obtained, depending on the context in which the operator is used:

- When the `AddressOf` operator is used within the argument list of a call to a method, which is made available via the `Declare` statement, it returns a function pointer that is suitable for such calls.
- When the `AddressOf` operator is used in any other context, a delegate object is returned. See the "Delegates" section later in this chapter for information.

Arithmetic Operators

The arithmetic operators perform the standard arithmetic operations on numeric values. The arithmetic operators supported by Visual Basic .NET are:

* *(multiplication)*

The multiplication operator is defined for all numeric operands. The result is the product of the operands.

/ *(regular division)*

The regular division operator is defined for all numeric operands. The result is the value of the first operand divided by the second operand.

\ *(integer division)*

The integer division operator is defined for integer operands (Byte, Short, Integer, and Long). The result is the value of the first operand divided by the second operand, then rounded to the integer nearest to zero.

`Mod` *(modulo)*

The modulo operator is defined for integer operands (Byte, Short, Integer, and Long). The result is the remainder after the integer division of the operands.

^ *(exponentiation)*

The exponentiation operator is defined for operands of type Double. Operands of other numeric types are converted to type Double before the result is calculated. The result is the value of the first operand raised to the power of the second operand.

+ *(addition)*
: The addition operator is defined for all numeric operands and operands of an enumerated type. The result is the sum of the operands. For enumerated types, the sum is calculated on the underlying type, but the return type is the enumerated type. See the discussion of enumerated types in the "Enumerations" section later in this chapter for more information on the types that can underlie an enumerated type. See also "String-Concatenation Operators" later in this section.

- *(subtraction)*
: The subtraction operator is defined for all numeric operands and operands of an enumerated type. The result is the value of the first operand minus the second operand. For enumerated types, the subtraction is calculated on the underlying type, but the return type is the enumerated type. See the discussion of enumerated types in the "Enumerations" section later in this chapter for more information on the types that can underlie an enumerated type.

Relational Operators

The relational operators all perform some comparison between two operands and return a Boolean value indicating whether the operands satisfy the comparison. The relational operators supported by Visual Basic .NET are:

= *(equality)*
: The equality operator is defined for all primitive value types and all reference types. For primitive value types and for the String type, the result is `True` if the values of the operands are equal; `False` if not. For reference types other than String, the result is `True` if the references refer to the same object; `False` if not. If the operands are of type Object and they reference primitive value types, value comparison is performed rather than reference comparison.

<> *(inequality)*
: The inequality operator is defined for all primitive value types and for reference types. For primitive value types and for the String type, the result is `True` if the values of the operands are not equal; `False` if equal. For reference types other than String, the result is `True` if the references refer to different objects; `False` if they refer to the same object. If the operands are of type Object and they reference primitive value types, value comparison is performed rather than reference comparison.

< *(less than)*
: The less-than operator is defined for all numeric operands and operands of an enumerated type. The result is `True` if the first operand is less than the second; `False` if not. For enumerated types, the comparison is performed on the underlying type.

> *(greater than)*
: The greater-than operator is defined for all numeric operands and operands that are of an enumerated type. The result is `True` if the first operand is greater than the second; `False` if not. For enumerated types, the comparison is performed on the underlying type.

<= *(less than or equal to)*
: The less-than-or-equal-to operator is defined for all numeric operands and operands of an enumerated type. The result is `True` if the first operand is less than or equal to the second operand; `False` if not.

>= *(greater than or equal to)*
: The greater-than-or-equal-to operator is defined for all numeric operands and operands of an enumerated type. The result is `True` if the first operand is greater than or equal to the second operand; `False` if not.

`TypeOf...Is`
: The `TypeOf...Is` operator is defined to take a reference as its first parameter and the name of a type as its second parameter. The result is `True` if the reference refers to an object that is type-compatible with the given type-name; `False` if the reference is `Nothing` or if it refers to an object that is not type-compatible with the given type name.

  Use the `TypeOf...Is` operator to determine whether a given object:

  - Is an instance of a given class
  - Is an instance of a class that is derived from a given class
  - Exposes a given interface

  In any of these cases, the `TypeOf` expression returns `True`.

`Is`
: The `Is` operator is defined for all reference types. The result is `True` if the references refer to the same object; `False` if not.

`Like`
: The `Like` operator is defined only for operands of type String. The result is `True` if the first operand matches the pattern given in the second operand; `False` if not.

  The rules for matching are:

  - The `?` (question mark) character matches any single character.
  - The `*` (asterisk) character matches zero or more characters.
  - The `#` (number sign) character matches any single digit.
  - A sequence of characters within `[]` (square brackets) matches any single character in the sequence.

    Within such a bracketed list, two characters separated by a `-` (hyphen) signify a range of Unicode characters, starting with the first character and ending with the second character. A `-` character itself can be matched by placing it at the beginning or end of the bracketed sequence.

Preceding the sequence of characters with an ! (exclamation mark) character matches any single character that does not appear in the sequence.

- The ?, *, #, and [characters can be matched by placing them within [] in the pattern string. Consequently, they cannot be used in their wildcard sense within [].
- The] character does not need to be escaped to be explicitly matched. However, it can't be used within [].

String-Concatenation Operators

The & (ampersand) and + (plus) characters signify string concatenation. String concatenation is defined for operands of type String only. The result is a string that consists of the characters from the first operand followed by the characters from the second operand.

Bitwise Operators

It is sometimes necessary to manipulate the individual bits that make up a value of one of the integer types (Byte, Short, Integer, and Long). This is the purpose of the bitwise operators. They are defined for the four integer types and for enumerated types. When the bitwise operators are applied to enumerated types, the operation is done on the underlying type, but the result is of the enumerated type.

The bitwise operators work by applying the given Boolean operation to each of the corresponding bits in the two operands. For example, consider this expression:

```
37 And 148
```

To calculate the value of this expression, consider the binary representation of each operand. It's helpful to write one above the other so that the bit columns line up:

```
00100101  (37)
10010100  (148)
```

Next, apply the Boolean And operation to the bits in each column:

```
       00100101  (37)
   And 10010100  (148)
   --------
       00000100  (4)
```

37 And 148, therefore, equals 4.

The bitwise operators are:

And

Performs a Boolean And operation on the bits. (The result bit is 1 if and only if both of the source bits are 1.)

`AndAlso`
: The result is `True` if and only if both the operands are `True`; otherwise, the result is `False`. `AndAlso` performs logical short-circuiting: if the first operand of the expression is `False`, the second operand is not evaluated.

`Or`
: Performs a Boolean `Or` operation on the bits. (The result bit is `1` if either or both of the source bits are `1`.)

`OrElse`
: The result is `True` if either or both the operands is `True`; otherwise, the result is `False`. `OrElse` performs logical short-circuiting: if the first operand of the expression is `True`, the second operand is not evaluated.

`Xor`
: Performs a Boolean *exclusive or* operation on the bits. (The result bit is `1` if either of the source bits is `1`, but not both.)

`Not`
: Performs a Boolean `Not` operation on the bits in the operand. This is a unary operator. (The result is `1` if the source bit is `0` and `0` if the source bit is `1`.)

Logical Operators

Logical operators are operators that require Boolean operands. They are:

`And`
: The result is `True` if and only if both of the operands are `True`; otherwise, the result is `False`.

`Or`
: The result is `True` if either or both of the operands is `True`; otherwise, the result is `False`.

`Xor`
: The result is `True` if one and only one of the operands is `True`; otherwise, the result is `False`.

`Not`
: This is a unary operator. The result is `True` if the operand is `False`; `False` if the operand is `True`.

Operator Precedence

Operator precedence defines the order in which operators are evaluated. For example, the expression `1 + 2 * 3` has the value `9` if the addition is performed first but has the value `7` if the multiplication is performed first. To avoid such ambiguity, languages must define the order in which operations are evaluated. Visual Basic .NET divides the operators into groups and defines each group's precedence relative to the others. Operators in higher-precedence groups are evaluated before operators in lower-precedence groups. Operators within each group have the same precedence relative to each other. When an expression contains multiple operators from a single group, those operators are evaluated from left to right.

Table 2-6 shows Visual Basic .NET's operators, grouped by precedence from highest to lowest order of evaluation.

Table 2-6. The precedence of Visual Basic .NET's operators

Category	Operator
Arithmetic and concatenation	Exponentiation
	Negation
	Multiplication and division
	Integer division
	Modulus arithmetic
	Addition and subtraction, string concatenation (+)
	String concatenation (&)
Comparison operators	Equality, inequality, greater than, less than, greater than or equal to, less than or equal to, `Is`, `TypeOf`, `Like`
Logical and bitwise operators	Negation (`Not`)
	Conjunction (`And`, `AndAlso`)
	Disjunction (`Or`, `OrElse`, `Xor`)

Parentheses override the default order of evaluation. For example, in the expression `1 + 2 * 3`, the multiplication is performed before the addition, yielding a value of `7`. To perform the addition first, the expression can be rewritten as `(1 + 2) * 3`, yielding a result of `9`.

Operator Overloading

Operator overloading is a feature that some languages (C#, for example) provide to allow developers to specify how the built-in operators (`+`, `-`, `*`, `/`, `=`, etc.) should behave when applied to programmer-defined types. For example, the developer of a type representing complex numbers could use operator overloading to specify appropriate functionality for the built-in arithmetic operators when applied to operands of the custom type.

The .NET Framework supports operator overloading, but .NET languages are not required to do so. The current version of Visual Basic .NET doesn't support operator overloading, although there's no reason that Microsoft couldn't add it in the future. Components that are written in other languages may overload operators, but Visual Basic .NET will not be aware of the overloads. Well-designed components provide an alternative mechanism for accessing the functionality provided by the overloads. For example, if a component written in C# provides a class that overloads the + operator, it should also provide a method that takes two parameters and returns their sum. Thus, what would be written as:

```
c = a + b
```

in a language that supports overloading would be written as:

```
c = MyCustomType.Add(a, b)
```

in Visual Basic .NET.

The name of the actual method would depend on the component's implementer.

Statements

Visual Basic .NET is a line-oriented language, in which line breaks generally indicate the ends of statements. However, there are times when a programmer may wish to extend a statement over several lines or have more than one statement on a single line.

To extend a statement over several lines, use the line-continuation character, an underscore (_). It must be the last character on its line, and it must be immediately preceded by a space character. Lines connected in this way become a single logical line. Here is an example:

```
Dim strSql As String = "SELECT Customers.CompanyName," _
   & " COUNT(Orders.OrderID) AS OrderCount" _
   & " FROM Customers INNER JOIN Orders" _
   & " ON Customers.CustomerID = Orders.CustomerID" _
   & " GROUP BY Customers.CompanyName" _
   & " ORDER BY OrderCount DESC"
```

A line break can occur only where whitespace is allowed.

To place two or more statements on a single line, use the colon (:) between the statements, like this:

```
i = 5 : j = 10
```

The remainder of this section discusses the statements in Visual Basic .NET.

Option Statements

There are three `Option` statements, which affect the behavior of the compiler. If used, they must appear before any declarations in the same source file. They control the compilation of the source code in the file in which they appear. They are:

`Option Compare`

The `Option Compare` statement controls the manner in which strings are compared to each other. The syntax is:

```
Option Compare [ Binary | Text ]
```

If `Binary` is specified, strings are compared based on their internal binary representation (i.e., string comparisons are case-sensitive). If `Text` is specified, strings are compared based on case-insensitive alphabetical order. The default is `Binary`.

`Option Explicit`

The `Option Explicit` statement determines whether the compiler requires all variables to be explicitly declared. The syntax is:

```
Option Explicit [ On | Off ]
```

If `On` is specified, the compiler requires all variables to be declared. If `Off` is specified, the compiler considers a variable's use to be an implicit declaration. It is considered good programming practice to require declaration of variables. The default is `On`.

`Option Strict`

The `Option Strict` statement controls the implicit type conversions that the compiler will allow. The syntax is:

```
Option Strict [ On | Off ]
```

If `On` is specified, the compiler only allows implicit widening conversions; narrowing conversions must be explicit. If `Off` is specified, the compiler allows implicit narrowing conversions as well. This could result in runtime exceptions not foreseen by the developer. It is considered good programming practice to require strict type checking. The default is `Off`.

See "Type Conversions" earlier in this chapter for the definitions of widening and narrowing conversions.

Branching Statements

Visual Basic .NET supports a number of branching statements that interrupt the sequential flow of program execution and instead allow it to jump from one portion of a program to another. These can be either conditional statements (such as `If` or `Select Case`) or unconditional (such as `Call` and `Exit`).

Call

The `Call` statement invokes a subroutine or function. For example:

```
Call SomeMethod( )
```

When the invoked subroutine or function finishes, execution continues with the statement following the `Call` statement. If a function is invoked, the function's return value is discarded.

The `Call` statement is redundant because subroutines and functions can be invoked simply by naming them:

```
SomeMethod( )
```

Exit

The `Exit` statement causes execution to exit the block in which the `Exit` statement appears. It is generally used to prematurely break out of a loop or procedure when some unusual condition occurs.

The `Exit` statement should be avoided when possible because it undermines the structure of the block in which it appears. For example, the exit conditions of a `For` loop should be immediately apparent simply by looking at the `For` statement. It should not be necessary to read through the entire loop to determine if there are additional circumstances under which the loop might exit. If a given `For` loop truly needs an `Exit` statement, investigate whether a different loop construct would be better suited to the task. If a given procedure truly needs an `Exit` statement, investigate whether the procedure is factored appropriately.

The `Exit` statement has a different form for each type of block in which it can be used, as listed here:

`Exit Do`
: Exits a `Do` loop. Execution continues with the first statement following the `Loop` statement.

`Exit For`
: Exits a `For` loop. Execution continues with the first statement following the `Next` statement.

`Exit Function`
: Exits a function. Execution continues with the first statement following the statement that called the function.

`Exit Property`
: Exits a property get or property set procedure. Execution continues with the first statement following the statement that invoked the property get or property set procedure.

`Exit Sub`
: Exits a subroutine. Execution continues with the first statement following the statement that called the subroutine.

`Exit Try`
: Exits the `Try` clause of a `Try` block. If the `Try` block has a `Finally` clause, execution continues with the first statement in the `Finally` clause. If the `Try` block does not have a `Finally` clause, execution continues with the first statement following the `Try` block.

Goto

The `Goto` statement transfers execution to the first statement following the specified label. For example:

```
    ' ...
    Goto MyLabel
    ' ...
MyLabel:
    ' ...
```

The label must be in the same procedure as the `Goto` statement.

The `Goto` statement is generally avoided in structured programming because it often leads to code that is difficult to read and debug.

If

The `If` statement controls whether a block of code is executed based on some condition. The simplest form of the `If` statement is:

```
If expression Then
   statements
End If
```

`expression` is any expression that can be interpreted as a Boolean value. If *`expression`* is `True`, the statements within the `If` block are executed. If *`expression`* is `False`, those statements are skipped.

To provide an alternative set of statements to execute when *`expression`* is `False`, add an `Else` clause, as shown here:

```
If expression Then
   statements
Else
   statements
End If
```

If *`expression`* is `True`, only the statements in the `If` clause are executed. If *`expression`* is `False`, only the statements in the `Else` clause are executed.

Finally, a sequence of expressions can be evaluated by including one or more `ElseIf` clauses, as shown here:

```
If expression Then
   statements
ElseIf expression Then
   statements
ElseIf expression Then
   statements
Else
   statements
End If
```

The first `If` or `ElseIf` clause whose expression evaluates to `True` will have its statements executed. Statements in subsequent `ElseIf` clauses will not be executed, even if their corresponding expressions are also `True`. If none of the expressions evaluate to `True`, the statements in the `Else` clause will be executed. The `Else` clause can be omitted if desired.

RaiseEvent

The RaiseEvent statement fires the given event. After the event has been fired to all listeners, execution continues with the first statement following the RaiseEvent statement. See "Events" later in this chapter for more information.

Return

The Return statement exits a function and provides a return value to the caller of the function. Execution continues with the first statement following the statement that called the function. Here is an example:

```
Public Shared Function MyFactorial(ByVal value As Integer) As Integer
   Dim retval As Integer = 1
   Dim i As Integer
   For i = 2 To value
      retval *= i
   Next
   Return retval
End Function
```

Another way to return a value to the caller of the function is to assign the value to the function name and then simply drop out of the bottom of the function. This is how it was done in Visual Basic 6 (and can still be done in Visual Basic .NET). Here is an example:

```
Public Shared Function MyFactorial(ByVal value As Integer) As Integer
   Dim retval As Integer = 1
   Dim i As Integer
   For i = 2 To value
      retval *= i
   Next
   MyFactorial = retval
End Function
```

In Visual Basic 6, the Return statement was used to return execution to the statement following a GoSub statement. In Visual Basic .NET, the GoSub statement no longer exists, and the Return statement is now used as described here.

Select Case

The Select Case statement chooses a block of statements to execute based on some value. For example:

```
Select Case strColor
   Case "red"
      ' ...
   Case "green"
      ' ...
   Case "blue"
      ' ...
```

```
    Case "yellow"
        ' ...
    Case Else
        ' ...
End Select
```

If strColor in this example contains "blue", only the statements in the Case "blue" clause are executed. If none of the Case clauses matches the value in the Select Case statement, the statements in the Case Else clause are executed. If more than one Case clause matches the given value, only the statements in the first matching Case clause are executed.

Case statements can include multiple values to be matched against the value given in the Select Case statement. For example:

```
Case "red", "green", "blue", strSomeColor
```

This case will be matched if the value in the Select Case statement is "red", "green", "blue", or the value contained in strSomeColor. The To keyword can be used to match a range of values, as shown here:

```
Case "apples" To "oranges"
```

This Case statement matches any string value that falls alphabetically within this range.

The Is keyword can be used for matching an open-ended range:

```
Case Is > "oranges"
```

Don't confuse this use of the Is keyword with the Is comparison operator.

Iteration Statements

Iteration statements, also known as *looping* statements, allow a group of statements to be executed more than once. The group of statements is known as the *body* of the loop. Three statements fall under this category in Visual Basic .NET: Do, For, and For Each.

Do

The Do loop executes a block of statements either until a condition becomes true or while a condition remains true. The condition can be tested at the beginning or at the end of each iteration. If the test is performed at the end of each iteration, the block of statements is guaranteed to execute at least once. The Do loop can also be written without any conditions, in which case it executes repeatedly until and unless an Exit Do statement is executed within the body of the loop. Here are some examples of Do loops:

```
Do While i < 10
    ' ...
Loop
```

```
Do Until i >= 10
   ' ...
Loop

Do
   ' ...
Loop While i < 10

Do
   ' ...
Loop Until i >= 10

Do
   ' ...
Loop
```

For

The For loop executes a block of statements a specified number of times. The number of iterations is controlled by a loop variable, which is initialized to a certain value by the For statement, then is incremented for each iteration of the loop. The statements in the body of the loop are repeatedly executed until the loop variable exceeds a given upper bound.

The syntax of the For loop is:

```
For variable = expression To expression [ Step expression ]
   statements
Next [ variable_list ]
```

The loop variable can be of any numeric type. The variable is set equal to the value of the first expression before entering the first iteration of the loop body. Prior to executing each iteration of the loop, the loop variable is compared with the value of the second expression. If the value of the loop variable is greater than the expression (or less than the expression if the step expression is negative), the loop exits and execution continues with the first statement following the Next statement.

The step expression is a numeric value that is added to the loop variable between loop iterations. If the Step clause is omitted, the step expression is taken to be 1.

The Next statement marks the end of the loop body. The Next keyword can either appear by itself in the statement or be followed by the name of the loop variable. If For statements are nested, a single Next statement can terminate the bodies of multiple loops. For example:

```
For i = 1 To 10
   For j = 1 To 10
      For k = 1 To 10
         ' ...
Next k, j, I
```

This code is equivalent to the following:

```
For i = 1 To 10
   For j = 1 To 10
      For k = 1 To 10
         ' ...
      Next
   Next
Next
```

I recommend the latter style, since it is considered more structured to terminate each block explicitly.

It is interesting to note that the `For` loop is equivalent to the following `Do` loop construction (assuming that *step_expression* is nonnegative):

```
loop_variable = from_expression
Do While loop_variable <= to_expression
   statements
   loop_variable += step_expression
Loop
```

If *step_expression* is negative, the `For` loop is equivalent to this (only the comparison in the `Do` statement is different):

```
loop_variable = from_expression
Do While loop_variable >= to_expression
   statements
   loop_variable += step_expression
Loop
```

For Each

The `For Each` statement is similar to the `For` statement, except that the loop variable need not be numeric, and successive iterations do not increment the loop variable. Instead, the loop variable takes successive values from a collection of values. Here is the syntax:

```
For Each variable In expression
   statements
Next [ variable ]
```

The loop variable can be of any type. The expression must be a reference to an object that exposes the `IEnumerable` interface (interfaces are discussed later in this chapter). Generally, types that are considered collections expose this interface. The .NET Framework class library provides several useful collection types, which are listed in Chapter 3. (See "Collections" earlier in this chapter for an explanation of what constitutes a collection type.) The type of the items in the collection must be compatible with the type of the loop variable. The statements in the body of the loop execute once for each item in the collection. During each iteration, the loop variable is set equal to each consecutive item in the collection.

Because all Visual Basic .NET arrays expose the IEnumerable interface, the For Each statement can be used to iterate through the elements of an array. For example:

```
Dim a( ) As Integer = {1, 2, 3, 4, 5}
Dim b As Integer
For Each b In a
   Console.WriteLine(b)
Next
```

This is equivalent to the following code:

```
Dim a( ) As Integer = {1, 2, 3, 4, 5}
Dim b As Integer
Dim i As Integer
For i = a.GetLowerBound(0) To a.GetUpperBound(0)
   b = a(i)
   Console.WriteLine(b)
Next
```

Because all arrays in Visual Basic .NET implicitly derive from the Array type (in the System namespace), the a array in this example has access to methods defined on the Array type (specifically GetLowerBound and GetUpperBound).

In case you're interested, here is the equivalent code using a Do loop. This is essentially what the For Each statement is doing under the covers, although the For Each construct is likely to compile to faster code.

```
Dim a( ) As Integer = {1, 2, 3, 4, 5}
Dim b As Integer
Dim e As Object = a.GetEnumerator( )
Do While CType(e.GetType( ).InvokeMember("MoveNext", _
   Reflection.BindingFlags.InvokeMethod, Nothing, e, Nothing), Boolean)
   b = CType(e.GetType( ).InvokeMember("Current", _
      Reflection.BindingFlags.GetProperty, Nothing, e, Nothing), Integer)
   Console.WriteLine(b)
Loop
```

Mathematical Functions

Mathematical functions are provided through the Math class (defined in the System namespace). The Math class constants and methods are listed in Appendix E.

Input/Output

File and Internet I/O features are provided by the .NET Framework class library and will be briefly touched on in Chapter 3. In addition, Visual Basic .NET provides its own class library that includes functions for opening, reading, and closing files. File access and network-protocol programming are not discussed in this book. Instead, preference is given to the much more common tasks of database access and web-service programming.

Classes

A *class* is one form of data type. As such, a class can be used in contexts where types are expected—in variable declarations, for example. In object-oriented design, classes are intended to represent the definition of real-world objects, such as *customer*, *order*, *product*, etc. The class is only the definition, not an object itself. An object would be *a* customer, *an* order, or *a* product. A class declaration defines the set of members—fields, properties, methods, and events—that each object of that class possesses. Together, these members define an object's state, as well as its functionality. An object is also referred to as an *instance* of a class. Creating an object of a certain class is called *instantiating* an object of the class.

Consider the class definition in Example 2-4.

Example 2-4. A class definition

```
Public Class Employee

   Public EmployeeNumber As Integer
   Public FamilyName As String
   Public GivenName As String
   Public DateOfBirth As Date
   Public Salary As Decimal

   Public Function Format( ) As String
      Return GivenName & " " & FamilyName
   End Function

End Class
```

The code in Example 2-4 defines a class called Employee. It has five public *fields* (also known as *data members*) for storing state, as well as one *member function*. The class could be used as shown in Example 2-5.

Example 2-5. Using a class

```
Dim emp As New Employee( )

emp.EmployeeNumber = 10
emp.FamilyName = "Rodriguez"
emp.GivenName = "Celia"
emp.DateOfBirth = #1/28/1965#
emp.Salary = 115000

Console.WriteLine("Employee Name: " & emp.Format( ))
Console.WriteLine("Employee Number: " & emp.EmployeeNumber)
Console.WriteLine("Date of Birth: " & emp.DateOfBirth.ToString("D", Nothing))
Console.WriteLine("Salary: " & emp.Salary.ToString("C", Nothing))
```

The resulting output is:

```
Employee Name: Celia Rodriguez
Employee Number: 10
Date of Birth: Thursday, January 28, 1965
Salary: $115,000.00
```

Object Instantiation and New

Object instantiation is done using the `New` keyword. The `New` keyword is, in effect, a unary operator that takes a type identifier as its operand. The result of the operation is a reference to a newly created object of the given type. Consider the following:

```
Imports System.Collections
' ...
Dim ht As Hashtable
ht = New Hashtable( )
```

The `Dim` statement declares a variable that is capable of holding a reference to an object of type Hashtable, but it doesn't actually create the object. The code in the line following the `Dim` statement instantiates an object of type Hashtable and assigns to the variable a reference to the newly created object. As with any other variable declaration, the assignment can be done on the same line as the declaration, as shown here:

```
Imports System.Collections
' ...
Dim ht As Hashtable = New Hashtable( )
```

Visual Basic .NET permits a typing shortcut that produces the same result:

```
Imports System.Collections
' ...
Dim ht As New Hashtable( )
```

Constructors

When a class is instantiated, some initialization often must be performed before the type can be used. To provide such initialization, a class may define a *constructor*. A constructor is a special kind of method. It is automatically run whenever an object of the class is instantiated. Constructor declarations use the same syntax as regular method declarations, except that in place of a method name, the constructor declaration uses the keyword `New`. For example:

```
Public Class SomeClass
   Public Sub New( )
      ' Do any necessary initialization of the object here.
   End Sub
End Class
```

To invoke the constructor, a new object must be instantiated:

```
Dim obj As New SomeClass( )
```

Note the parentheses (( )) following the name of the class. Until you get used to it, this method-style syntax following a class name may appear odd. However, the empty parentheses indicate that the class's constructor takes no arguments.

Constructors can take arguments, if they are necessary for the initialization of the object:

```
Public Class SomeClass

   Dim m_value As Integer

   Public Sub New(ByVal InitialValue As Integer)
      m_value = InitialValue
   End Sub

End Class
```

When objects of this class are instantiated, a value must be provided for the constructor's argument:

```
Dim obj As New SomeClass(27)
```

Constructors can be overloaded, if desired. For example:

```
Public Class SomeClass

   Dim m_value As Integer

   Public Sub New( )
      m_value = Date.Today.Day ' for example
   End Sub

   Public Sub New(ByVal InitialValue As Integer)
      m_value = InitialValue
   End Sub

End Class
```

The constructor that is called depends on the arguments that are provided when the class is instantiated, as shown here:

```
Dim obj1 As New SomeClass( ) ' calls parameterless constructor
Dim obj2 As New SomeClass(100) ' calls parameterized constructor
```

Constructors are usually marked `Public`. However, there are times when it may be desirable to mark a constructor as `Protected` or `Private`. Protected access prohibits the class from being instantiated by any class other than a class derived from this class. Private access prohibits the class from being instantiated by any code other than its own. For example, a particular class design might require that the class itself be in control of whether and when instances are created. Example 2-6 shows a class that implements a crude form of object pooling.

Example 2-6. Using a private constructor

```
Imports System.Collections
' ...
Public Class MyPooledClass

   ' This shared field keeps track of instances that can be handed out.
   Private Shared m_pool As New Stack( )

   ' This shared method hands out instances.
   Public Shared Function GetInstance( ) As MyPooledClass
      If m_pool.Count > 0 Then
         ' We have one or more objects in the pool. Remove one from the
         ' pool and give it to the caller.
         Return CType(m_pool.Pop( ), MyPooledClass)
      Else
         ' We don't have any objects in the pool. Create a new one.
         Return New MyPooledClass( )
      End If
   End Function

   ' This method must be called to signify that the client is finished
   ' with the object.
   Public Sub ImDone( )
      ' Put the object in the pool.
      m_pool.Push(Me)
   End Sub

   ' Declaring a private constructor means that the only way to
   ' instantiate this class is through the GetInstance method.
   Private Sub New( )
   End Sub

End Class
```

The class in Example 2-6 would be used like this:

```
Dim obj As MyPooledClass = MyPooledClass.GetInstance( )
' ...
obj.ImDone( )
```

Sometimes when constructors are overloaded, it makes sense to implement one constructor in terms of another. For example, here is a class that has a constructor that takes a SqlConnection object as a parameter. However, it also has a parameterless constructor that creates a SqlConnection object and passes it to the class's parameterized constructor. Note the use of the `MyClass` keyword to access members of the type:

```
Imports System.Data.SqlClient
' ...
Public Class SomeClass

   Public Sub New( )
      MyClass.New(New SqlConnection( ))
```

```
    End Sub

    Public Sub New(ByVal cn As SqlConnection)
       ' Do something with the connection object.
    End Sub

End Class
```

Similarly, `MyBase.New` can call a base-class constructor. If this is done, it must be done as the first statement in the derived class's constructor. Note that if no explicit call is made, the compiler creates a call to the base-class constructor's parameterless constructor. Even if the base class exposes a parameterized constructor having the same signature (i.e., the same number and types of parameters) as the derived class's constructor, by default the compiler generates code that calls the base class's *parameterless* constructor.

If a class has shared fields that must be initialized before access, and that initialization can't be performed by initializers in the fields' declarations, a shared constructor may be written to initialize the fields, as shown here:

```
Public Class SomeClass

    Public Shared SomeStaticField As Integer

    Shared Sub New( )
       SomeStaticField = Date.Today.Day
    End Sub

End Class
```

The shared constructor is guaranteed to run sometime before any members of the type are referenced. If any shared fields have initializers in their declarations, the initializers are assigned to the fields before the shared constructor is run.

Shared constructors may not be overloaded, nor may they have access modifiers (`Public`, `Private`, etc.). Neither feature is meaningful in the context of shared constructors.

Fields

Fields, also known as *data members*, hold the internal state of an object. Their declarations appear only within class and structure declarations. Field declarations include an *access modifier*, which determines how visible the field is from code outside the containing class definition. Access modifiers were discussed earlier in this chapter, under "Access Modifiers."

The value stored in a field is specific to a particular object instance. Two instances can have different values in their corresponding fields. For example:

```
Dim emp1 As New Employee( )
Dim emp2 As New Employee( )
```

```
emp1.EmployeeNumber = 10
emp2.EmployeeNumber = 20 ' Doesn't affect emp1.
```

Sometimes it is desirable to share a single value among all instances of a particular class. Declaring a field using the Shared keyword does this, as shown here:

```
Public Class X
   Public Shared a As Integer
End Class
```

Changing the field value through one instance affects what all other instances see. For example:

```
Dim q As New X( )
Dim r As New X( )

q.a = 10
r.a = 20

Console.WriteLine(q.a) ' Writes 20, not 10.
```

Shared fields are also accessible through the class name:

```
Console.WriteLine(X.a)
```

Read-only fields

Fields can be declared with the ReadOnly modifier, which signifies that the field's value can be set only in a constructor for the enclosing class. This gives the benefits of a constant when the value of the constant isn't known at compile time or can't be expressed in a constant initializer. Here's an example of a class that has a read-only field initialized in the class's constructor:

```
Public Class MyDataTier

   Public ReadOnly ActiveConnection As System.Data.SqlClient.SqlConnection

   Public Sub New(ByVal ConnectionString As String)
      ActiveConnection = _
         New System.Data.SqlClient.SqlConnection(ConnectionString)
   End Sub

End Class
```

The ReadOnly modifier applies only to the field itself—not to members of any object referenced by the field. For example, given the previous declaration of the MyDataTier class, the following code is legal:

```
Dim mydata As New MyDataTier(strConnection)
mydata.ActiveConnection.ConnectionString = strSomeOtherConnection
```

Handling Events

When a field is of an object type that exposes events, the field's enclosing class may define methods for handling those events. For an explanation of events, see "Events," later in this chapter.

Here is an example:

```
Imports System.Data.SqlClient

Public Class EventHandlingTest

   Private WithEvents m_cn As SqlConnection

   Public Sub MySqlInfoMessageEventHandler( _
      ByVal sender As Object, _
      ByVal e As SqlInfoMessageEventArgs _
   ) Handles m_cn.InfoMessage
      Dim sqle As SqlError
      For Each sqle In e.Errors
         Debug.WriteLine(sqle.Message)
      Next
   End Sub

   ' ...

End Class
```

This class has a field, m_cn, that holds a database connection. The field is declared with the `WithEvents` keyword, so the class is capable of receiving and handling events raised by the Connection object. In order to handle the Connection object's InfoMessage event, the class defines a method having the appropriate parameter list and a `Handles` clause:

```
Public Sub MySqlInfoMessageEventHandler( _
   ByVal sender As Object, _
   ByVal e As SqlInfoMessageEventArgs _
) Handles m_cn.InfoMessage
```

This declaration signifies that when the InfoMessage event is raised by the object referenced in m_cn, the MySQLInfoMessageEventHandler method should be called to handle it. The body of the event handler in this case simply outputs the messages received from SQL Server.

Inheritance

Inheritance is one way to reuse and extend previously written code. A program's design often requires several classes as variations of a common theme. Consider a drawing program that deals with many shapes. Such a program would probably define a class for each kind of shape. However, there would be much in common among such classes, including many of their fields, methods, and events. Inheritance allows these common features to be extracted into a *base class* from which the various specific shape classes are *derived*. Example 2-7 shows a base class called Shape, two utility classes used by Shape (Point and Extent), and two classes derived from Shape (Circle and Square).

Example 2-7. Class inheritance

```
' This structure represents a point on a plane.
Public Structure Point
   Public X As Integer
   Public Y As Integer
End Structure

' This structure represents a size or offset.
Public Structure Extent
   Public XExtent As Integer
   Public YExtent As Integer
End Structure

' This class represents the functionality that is common for
' all shapes. This class can't itself be instantiated, because
' of the "MustInherit" modifier.
Public MustInherit Class Shape

   ' The upper-left corner of the shape.
   Public Origin As Point

   ' The width and height of the shape.
   Public Size As Extent

   ' This forces all derived classes to implement a method
   ' called Draw. Notice that a method marked with MustInherit
   ' has no body in the base class.
   Public MustOverride Sub Draw( )

   ' This subroutine moves a shape.
   Public Sub Offset(ByVal Amount As Extent)
      Origin.X += Amount.XExtent
      Origin.Y += Amount.YExtent
   End Sub

   ' This property allows the class user to find or set the
   ' center of a shape.
   Public Property Center( ) As Point
      Get
         Dim retval As Point
         retval.X = Origin.X + (Size.XExtent \ 2)
         retval.Y = Origin.Y + (Size.YExtent \ 2)
         Return retval
      End Get
      Set
         Dim currentCenter As Point = Center
         Origin.X += Value.X - currentCenter.X
```

Example 2-7. Class inheritance (continued)

```
         Origin.Y += Value.Y - currentCenter.Y
      End Set
   End Property

End Class

Public Class Circle
   Inherits Shape
   Public Overrides Sub Draw( )
      ' Just a dummy statement for the example.
      Console.WriteLine("Circle.Draw( ) was called.")
   End Sub
End Class

Public Class Square
   Inherits Shape
   Public Overrides Sub Draw( )
      ' Just a dummy statement for the example.
      Console.WriteLine("Square.Draw( ) was called.")
   End Sub
End Class
```

Note the following:

- The `MustInherit` modifier in the Shape class declaration indicates that this class can't be instantiated—it can only be used as a base class in a derivation. In object-oriented design terminology, such a class is known as an *abstract* class.
- The Circle and Square classes inherit the public members declared in the Shape class.
- Using the `MustOverride` modifier on the Draw method declaration in the Shape class forces derived classes to provide an implementation for this method.
- Constructors aren't inherited. The Ellipse and Rectangle classes therefore declare their own constructors.

  When no constructor is explicitly provided in a class definition, the compiler automatically creates one. Therefore, all classes have at least one constructor. The autogenerated constructor (also known as the *default constructor*) created by the compiler is the same as if the following code were written in the class definition:

  ```
  Public Sub New( )
     MyBase.New( )
  End Sub
  ```

  That is, the default constructor simply calls the base class's parameterless constructor. If there is no parameterless constructor on the base class, the compiler generates an error. If a class defines a parameterized constructor, the compiler does not generate a default constructor. Therefore, if both parameterless and parameterized constructors are needed, both must be explicitly written in the class definition.

It is possible to define a class from which it is not possible to inherit. This is done with the `NotInheritable` keyword in the class declaration, as shown here:

```
Public NotInheritable Class SomeClass
   ' ...
End Class
```

Methods

Methods are members that contain code. They are either subroutines (which don't have a return value) or functions (which do have a return value).

Subroutine definitions look like this:

```
[ method_modifiers ] Sub [ attribute_list ] _
   method_name ( [ parameter_list ] ) [ handles_or_implements ]
[ method_body ]
End Sub
```

Function definitions look like this:

```
[ method_modifiers ] Function [ attribute_list ] _
   method_name ( [ parameter_list ] ) [ As type_name ] _
   [ handles_or_implements ]
[ method_body ]
End Function
```

The elements of method definitions are:

`method_modifiers`
: Keywords that affect the accessibility or use of the method. These include the following:

  Access modifiers
  : `Public`, `Protected`, `Friend`, `Protected Friend`, or `Private`, as described in Table 2-5. If no access-modifier keyword is given, `Public` is assumed.

  Override modifiers
  : `Overrides`, `MustOverride`, `Overridable`, or `NotOverridable`. See "Overriding inherited methods," later in this section.

  `Overloads` *keyword*
  : Specifies that this method is an overload. See "Overloading," later in this section.

  `Shared` *keyword*
  : Specifies that this method does not access object state. That means that the method does not access any nonshared members.

`Sub` *or* `Function` *keyword*
: Specifies whether this method is a subroutine or a function.

attribute_list
: An optional list of attributes to be applied to the method. See the "Attributes" section later in this chapter.

method_name
: The name of the method.

parameter_list
: An optional list of formal parameters for the method. See the next section, "Method parameters."

`As` *type_name*
: For functions only, the data type of the value returned from this function. If `Option Strict` is off, the `As` *type_name* clause is optional; otherwise, it is required. If it is omitted, the function's return type defaults to Object. Subroutine declarations do not have an `As` *type_name* clause.

handles_or_implements
: Either the `Handles` keyword followed by a list of events from the enclosing class's data members, or the `Implements` keyword followed by a list of methods from an interface implemented by the enclosing class. See the "Events" and "Interfaces" sections later in this chapter.

method_body
: Visual Basic .NET statements.

`End Sub` *or* `End Function` *keywords*
: Indicates the end of the method definition.

Method parameters

Methods can be defined to take arguments. As already shown, method definitions can take an optional parameter list. A parameter list looks like this:

```
parameter { , parameter }
```

That is, a parameter list is one or more parameters separated by commas. Each parameter in the list is of the form:

```
[ Optional ] [ ParamArray ] [ ByRef | ByVal ] [ attribute_list ] _
   parameter_name [ As type_name ] [ = constant_expression ]
```

The elements of each parameter declaration are:

`Optional` *keyword*
: Specifies that an actual argument may be omitted for this parameter in a call to this method. If `Optional` is specified, the `=` *constant_expression*, which defines the default value of an omitted argument, must also be specified. Nonoptional parameters can't follow optional parameters in a parameter list. `Optional` and `ParamArray` parameters can't appear in the same parameter list.

`ParamArray` *keyword*

Specifies that the caller can provide a variable number of arguments. The actual arguments are passed to the method in an array. Only the last parameter in a list may have the `ParamArray` keyword attached to it. `Optional` and `ParamArray` parameters can't appear in the same parameter list. Parameter arrays are discussed later in this section, under "Variable-length parameter lists."

`ByRef` *or* `ByVal` *keyword*

Specifies whether the actual argument will be passed to the method *by reference* or *by value*. When an argument is passed by reference, the address of the argument is passed to the routine; as a result, assignments to the parameter within the method affect the argument in the calling environment. When an argument is passed by value, a copy of the argument is passed to the routine; as a result, assignments to the parameter within the method do not affect the argument in the calling environment. Consider this code:

```
Public Shared Sub TestByRef(ByRef MyParameter As Integer)
   MyParameter += 1
End Sub

Public Shared Sub TestByVal(ByVal MyParameter As Integer)
   MyParameter += 1
End Sub

Public Shared Sub DoTest( )

   Dim x As Integer = 1
   TestByRef(x)
   Console.WriteLine("x = " & x)

   Dim y As Integer = 1
   TestByVal(y)
   Console.WriteLine("y = " & y)

End Sub
```

The output of the DoTest method is:

```
x = 2
y = 1
```

The TestByRef and TestByVal methods both increment the values of the arguments passed to them by one. However, because the parameter of the TestByRef method is `ByRef`, the new value is written back to the argument in the caller (in this case, the variable `x` in the DoTest method). In contrast, the TestByVal method's parameter is `ByVal`, so the assignment to the parameter doesn't affect the caller.

Be aware of the effects of `ByRef` and `ByVal` on arguments that are reference types. `ByRef` means that a reference to the reference is being passed; `ByVal` means that the reference itself is being passed. That means that inside the method, the reference could be used to modify the state of the object in the calling environment. For example:

```
Public Class SomeClass
   Public a As Integer
End Class

Public Class TestSomeClass

   Public Shared Sub TestByRef(ByRef MyParameter As SomeClass)
      MyParameter.a += 1
   End Sub

   Public Shared Sub TestByVal(ByVal MyParameter As SomeClass)
      MyParameter.a += 1
   End Sub

   Public Shared Sub DoTest( )

      Dim x As New SomeClass( )
      x.a = 1
      TestByRef(x)
      Console.WriteLine("x.a = " & x.a)

      Dim y As New SomeClass( )
      y.a = 1
      TestByRef(y)
      Console.WriteLine("y.a = " & y.a)

   End Sub

End Class
```

The output of the DoTest method in this code is:

```
x.a = 2
y.a = 2
```

Observe that even though the variable y is passed by value to the TestByVal method, one of its members nevertheless is updated. In this case, `ByVal` merely keeps the reference in y from being overwritten by another reference.

attribute_list
: Specifies a list of custom attributes to apply to the parameter. Attributes are discussed later in this chapter.

parameter_name
: Specifies the name of the parameter.

`As` *type_name*
: Specifies the data type of the parameter. When the method is called, the type of the actual argument must be compatible with the type of the parameter. The `As` *type_name* element is optional if `Option Strict` is off; otherwise, it is required. If it is omitted, Object is assumed.

constant_expression

Specifies a constant expression that specifies what value the parameter should take if no actual argument is provided. This is permitted only on optional parameters.

Passing arrays as parameters

To declare a parameter as able to receive an array, include parentheses after the parameter name in the declaration. The caller leaves off the parentheses when naming the actual argument. For example:

```
Public Shared Sub SomeMethod(ByVal x( ) As String)
   Dim str As String
   For Each str In x
      Console.WriteLine(str)
   Next
End Sub

Public Shared Sub TestSomeMethod( )
   Dim a(5) As String
   a(0) = "First"
   a(1) = "Second"
   a(2) = "Third"
   a(3) = "Fourth"
   a(4) = "Fifth"
   SomeMethod(a)
End Sub
```

In the SomeMethod method, parameter x represents an array of String objects. In the TestSomeMethod method, a String array is allocated, its elements are assigned, and the array as a whole is passed to the SomeMethod method, which then prints the array's contents.

All array types are reference types. That means that when passing an array as a parameter, only a reference to the array is passed. Because the target method receives a reference to the array, the array elements can be changed by the method, even if the array reference was passed by value. If the array reference is passed by reference, the array reference itself can be changed by the method. For example, the method could allocate a new array and return it through the `ByRef` parameter, like this:

```
Public Shared Sub DumpArray(ByVal x( ) As String)
   Dim str As String
   For Each str In x
      Console.WriteLine(str)
   Next
End Sub

Public Shared Sub CreateNewArray(ByRef x( ) As String)
   Dim newval(7) As String
   newval(0) = "1st"
   newval(1) = "2nd"
```

```
    newval(2) = "3rd"
    newval(3) = "4th"
    newval(4) = "5th"
    newval(5) = "6th"
    newval(6) = "7th"
    x = newval
End Sub

Public Shared Sub DoTest( )

    ' Set up a five-element string array and show its contents.
    Dim a(5) As String
    a(0) = "First"
    a(1) = "Second"
    a(2) = "Third"
    a(3) = "Fourth"
    a(4) = "Fifth"
    Console.WriteLine("a( ) before calling the CreateNewArray method:")
    DumpArray(a)

    ' Now pass it to the CreateNewArray method and then show its
    ' new contents.
    CreateNewArray(a)
    Console.WriteLine( )
    Console.WriteLine("a( ) after calling the CreateNewArray method:")
    DumpArray(a)

End Sub
```

In this code, the DoTest method creates a five-element string array and passes it to DumpArray to show the array's contents. The DoTest method then calls CreateNewArray, which allocates a new string array—this time with seven elements. It would not be possible, however, to pass back an array with a different number of dimensions, because the parameter is explicitly declared as one-dimensional. Visual Basic .NET considers the dimensionality of an array to be part of its type, but the size of any particular dimension is not part of the array's type.

Variable-length parameter lists

Some methods need to take a variable number of arguments. For example, a function to compute the average of the numbers passed to it should accommodate as few or as many numbers as needed. Visual Basic .NET provides this capability through *parameter arrays*. A parameter array is a parameter that to the method looks like an array but to the caller looks like a variable number of parameters. Here is the average-calculation method just mentioned:

```
Public Shared Function Avg(ParamArray ByVal Numbers( ) As Integer) As Double
    Dim sum As Integer = 0
    Dim count As Integer = 0
    Dim n As Integer
    For Each n In Numbers
```

```
        sum += n
        count += 1
    Next
    Return sum / count
End Function
```

This method declares only a single parameter—an array of Integers. However, it includes the ParamArray keyword in the declaration, which tells the compiler to allow calls such as this:

```
' Compute the average of some numbers.
Dim d As Double = Avg(31, 41, 59, 26, 53, 58)
```

It's worth noting that an actual array can be passed through the ParamArray parameter—something that wasn't possible in Visual Basic 6. For example:

```
' Compute the average of some numbers.
Dim args( ) As Integer = {31, 41, 59, 26, 53, 58}
Dim d As Double = Avg(args)
```

Main method

When an executable application is compiled, some code must be identified as the startup routine. This portion is what is executed when the application is run. The Visual Basic .NET compiler looks for a method named Main to fulfill this need. In .NET, all code exists as methods within classes, even the Main method. To make it accessible without having to instantiate a class, the Main method must be declared as shared. For example:

```
Public Class App
   Public Shared Sub Main( )
      ' ...
   End Sub
End Class
```

The name of the class is not important. At compile time, the Visual Basic .NET compiler looks for a public shared subroutine named Main somewhere in the code. If more than one class has such a method, the developer must specify which one to use by setting the *startup object* in the Project Properties dialog box. If you're using the command-line compiler, specify the desired startup object with the `/main:`*<class>* switch.

A program's Main method can also appear within a Visual Basic .NET *module* (not to be confused with .NET modules, which are described in Chapter 3). Because Visual Basic .NET modules are classes wherein everything is shared, the Shared keyword is not used in such a declaration:

```
Module App
   Public Sub Main( )
      ' ...
   End Sub
End Module
```

Implementing interface methods

Classes can be declared as implementing one or more interfaces. (See "Interfaces," later in this chapter.) To implement an interface, the class must expose methods that correspond to the methods defined by the interface. This is done by declaring the methods in the usual way, but with an `Implements` clause as part of the declaration. Note the `Implements` keyword added to the declaration of the CompareTo method in this example:

```
Public Class SomeClass
   Implements IComparable

   Public Function CompareTo( _
      ByVal obj As Object _
   ) As Integer Implements IComparable.CompareTo
      ' ...
   End Function

End Class
```

When appearing in a method declaration, the `Implements` keyword must be followed by the name of the interface and method that the given method implements. The class's method must have the same signature and return type as the interface's method, but they need not have the same name.

Overriding inherited methods

Example 2-7 showed how a base class can be written such that it forces derived classes to implement certain methods. In this case, the Shape class contains this declaration:

```
Public MustOverride Sub Draw( )
```

This declares the Draw method, which takes no arguments. The `MustOverride` keyword specifies that the base class does not provide an implementation for this method and that derived classes must do so.

It is sometimes preferable to allow the base class to provide a default implementation, yet allow derived classes to substitute their own implementations. Classes that don't provide their own implementations use the base class's implementation by default. Consider the following class definitions:

```
Class BaseClass
   Public Overridable Sub SomeMethod( )
      Console.WriteLine("BaseClass definition")
   End Sub
End Class ' BaseClass

Class DerivedClass
   Inherits BaseClass
   Public Overrides Sub SomeMethod( )
      Console.WriteLine("DerivedClass definition")
```

```
    End Sub
End Class ' DerivedClass

Class DerivedClass2
    Inherits BaseClass
End Class ' DerivedClass2
```

The BaseClass class defines a method called SomeMethod. In addition to providing an implementation of this method, the declaration specifies the `Overridable` keyword. This signals to the compiler that it's okay to override the method in derived classes. Without this modifier, derived classes cannot override the method. The DerivedClass class overrides this method by defining a method having the same name and signature and by specifying the `Overrides` keyword. The Visual Basic .NET compiler requires that the `Overrides` keyword be present to ensure that the developer actually meant to override a base-class method. The DerivedClass2 class does not override the SomeMethod method. Calls to SomeMethod through objects of type DerivedClass2 will invoke the BaseClass definition of SomeMethod. Here is an example:

```
Dim b As New BaseClass( )
Dim d As New DerivedClass( )
Dim d2 As New DerivedClass2( )

b.SomeMethod( )
d.SomeMethod( )
d2.SomeMethod( )
```

This code results in the following output:

```
BaseClass definition
DerivedClass definition
BaseClass definition
```

The SomeMethod implementation in the DerivedClass class can itself be overridden by a class deriving from DerivedClass. This can be prevented, if desired, by specifying the `NotOverridable` keyword in the definition of the SomeMethod method of the DerivedClass class, as shown here:

```
Class DerivedClass
    Inherits BaseClass
    Public NotOverridable Overrides Sub SomeMethod( )
        ' ...
    End Sub
End Class ' DerivedClass
```

Overloading

When two or more different methods conceptually perform the same task on arguments of different types, it is convenient to give the methods the same name. This technique is called *overloading* and is supported by Visual Basic .NET. For example, the following code defines an overloaded SquareRoot method that can take either a Long or a Double as a parameter:

```
Public Function SquareRoot( _
   ByVal Value As Long _
) As Double
   ' ...
End Function

Public Function SquareRoot( _
   ByVal Value As Double _
) As Double
   ' ...
End Function
```

When a call is made to the SquareRoot method, the version called is determined by the type of the parameter passed to it. For example, the following code calls the version of the method that takes a Long:

```
Dim result As Double = SquareRoot(10)
```

And this code calls the version that takes a Double:

```
Dim result As Double = SquareRoot(10.1)
```

Careful readers will note that in the first case the type of the argument is actually Integer, not Long. The Long version of the method is invoked because it is the closest match to the given argument. If there were also an Integer version of the method, that version would have been invoked, because it is a better match to the given argument. The .NET runtime (discussed in Chapter 3) always attempts to invoke the most appropriate version of an overloaded function, given the arguments provided. If no suitable overload is found, a compiler error occurs (if `Option Strict` is on) or a runtime exception occurs (if `Option Strict` is off).

The name of a method together with the number and types of its arguments are called the *signature* of the method. The signature uniquely identifies a specific overloaded version of a specific method. Note that the return type is not part of the signature. Two versions of an overloaded method are not permitted to differ only by return type.

Overloading inherited methods

A method can also overload a method in a base class. Be careful to note the difference between *overloading* a base-class method and *overriding* a base-class method. *Overriding* means that the base-class method and the derived-class method have the same signature and that the derived-class method is replacing the base-class method. In addition, the base-class method must be marked with the `Overridable` keyword. *Overloading* means that they have different signatures and that both methods exist as overloads in the derived class. When overloading a method defined in a base class, the derived-class method declaration must include the `Overloads` keyword, but the base-class method doesn't have any special keyword attached to it. Here's an example:

```
Public Class BaseClass
   Public Sub SomeMethod( )
      ' ...
   End Sub
End Class

Public Class DerivedClass
   Inherits BaseClass
   Public Overloads Sub SomeMethod(ByVal i As Integer)
      ' ...
   End Sub
End Class
```

The requirement for the `Overloads` keyword helps to document the fact that a base-class method is being overloaded. There is no technical reason that the compiler requires it, but it is required nevertheless to help prevent human error.

Shadowing

The `Shadows` keyword allows a derived-class method to hide all base-class methods with the same name. Consider the following code, which does not use the `Shadows` keyword:

```
Public Class BaseClass
   Public Overridable Sub SomeMethod( )
      ' ...
   End Sub
   Public Overridable Sub SomeMethod(ByVal i As Integer)
      ' ...
   End Sub
End Class

Public Class DerivedClass
   Inherits BaseClass
   Public Overloads Overrides Sub SomeMethod( )
      ' ...
   End Sub
End Class
```

The base class overloads the SomeMethod method, and the derived class overrides the version of the method having no parameters. Instances of the derived class not only possess the parameterless version defined in the derived class, but they also inherit the parameterized version defined in the base class. In contrast, consider the following code, which is the same except for the declaration of the SomeMethod method in the derived class:

```
Public Class BaseClass
   Public Overridable Sub SomeMethod( )
      ' ...
```

```
    End Sub
    Public Overridable Sub SomeMethod(ByVal i As Integer)
        ' ...
    End Sub
End Class

Public Class DerivedClass
    Inherits BaseClass
    Public Shadows Sub SomeMethod( )
        ' ...
    End Sub
End Class
```

In this version, instances of the derived class possess only the parameterless version declared in the derived class. Neither version in the base class can be called through a reference to the derived class.

Properties

Properties are members that are accessed like fields but are actually method calls. The idea is that a class designer may wish to expose some data values but needs to exert more control over their reading and writing than is provided by fields. Properties are also useful for exposing values that are calculated. This is demonstrated by the Center property in the Shape class of Example 2-7. The property can be read and written just like the Origin and Size fields. However, there is no actual data member called Center. When code reads the Center property, a call is generated to the Center property's *getter*. When a new value is assigned to the Center property, a call is generated to the property's *setter*.

Property declarations look like this:

```
[ property modifiers ] Property [ attributes ] Property_Name _
    ( [ parameter list ] ) [ As Type_Name ] [ implements list ]
[ getter ]
[ setter ]
End Property
```

The components of the declaration are:

property modifiers

Further defined as:

```
[ Default ][ access modifier ][ override modifier ] _
    [ overload modifier ] [ shared modifier ] [ read/write modifier ]
```

If the `Default` keyword is present, it specifies the property as the default property of the class. Only one property in a class can be the class's default property, and only parameterized (or *indexed*) properties can be default properties. So what is a default property? A default property is just a property that can be referenced without actually specifying the property's name. For example, if a class has a default property called Item, takes an Integer argument, and is of type String, the following two lines are equivalent to each other:

```
myObject.Item(3) = "hello, world"
myObject(3) = "hello, world"
```

Note that previous versions of Visual Basic did not constrain parameterized properties as the only possible default properties.

The *access modifier*, *override modifier*, *overload modifier*, and *shared modifier* clauses have the same meanings as discussed later in this chapter in relation to method definitions. The *read/write modifier* clause is defined as:

```
ReadOnly | WriteOnly
```

This clause determines whether the property is read/write (signified by the absence of `ReadOnly` and `WriteOnly`), read-only (signified by `ReadOnly`), or write-only (signified by `WriteOnly`).

`Property` *keyword*
: Identifies this as a property definition.

attributes
: Represents a comma-separated list of attributes to be stored as metadata with the property. Attributes are discussed earlier in this chapter.

Property_Name
: Represents the name of the property.

parameter list
: Permits properties to have parameters. Parameterized properties are also called indexed properties. See the discussion of parameter lists in the "Methods" section earlier in this chapter.

`As` *Type_Name*
: Indicates the data type of the property. This clause is optional if `Option Strict` is off; otherwise, it is required. If this clause is omitted, the property defaults to type Object.

implements list
: Has the same meaning as for method definitions.

getter
: Provides the method that is executed when the property is read. Its form is:

```
Get
   ' code
End Get
```

The value returned by the *getter* is returned as the value of the property. To return a value from the *getter*, either use the `Return` statement with an argument or assign a value to the property name. The value returned must be compatible with the data type of the property.

It is an error to provide a *getter* if the property has been marked `WriteOnly`.

setter

Provides the method that is executed when the property is written. Its form is:

```
Set [ ( ByVal Value [ As Type_Name ] ) ]
   ' code
End Set
```

The value assigned to the property is passed to the method through the parameter specified in the Set statement. The type specified in the Set statement must match the type specified in the Property statement. Alternatively, the parameter declaration can be omitted from the Set statement. In this case, the value assigned to the property is passed to the method through a special keyword called Value. For example, this *setter* copies the passed-in value to a class data member called MyDataMember:

```
Set
   MyDataMember = Value
End Set
```

The data type of Value is the same as the data type of the property.

End Property *keywords*

Indicates the end of the property definition.

Review the property definition from Example 2-7:

```
' This property allows the class user to find or set the
' center of a shape.
Public Property Center( ) As Point
   Get
      Dim retval As Point
      retval.X = Origin.X + (Size.XExtent \ 2)
      retval.Y = Origin.Y + (Size.YExtent \ 2)
      Return retval
   End Get
   Set
      Dim currentCenter As Point = Center
      Origin.X += Value.X - currentCenter.X
      Origin.Y += Value.Y - currentCenter.Y
   End Set
End Property
```

This is a public property called Center that has a type of Point. The *getter* returns a value of type Point that is calculated from some other members of the class. The *setter* uses the passed-in value to set some other members of the class.

The Me and MyClass Keywords

There are several ways for code to access members of the class in which the code is running. As long as the member being accessed is not hidden by a like-named declaration in a more immediate scope, it can be referenced without qualification:

```
Public Class SomeClass

   Public SomeValue As Integer
```

```
    Public Sub SomeMethod( )
        ' ...
        SomeValue = 5
        ' ...
    End Sub

End Class
```

If the member is hidden by a more immediate declaration, the `Me` keyword can be used to qualify the reference. Unqualified references refer to the more local declaration, as shown here:

```
Public Class SomeClass

    Public SomeValue As Integer

    Public Sub SomeMethod(ByVal SomeValue As Integer)
        ' ...
        ' Assign the passed-in value to a field.
        Me.SomeValue = SomeValue
        ' ...
    End Sub

End Class
```

The `Me` keyword is an implicit variable that holds a reference to the object instance running the code. Related to the `Me` keyword, but subtly different, is the `MyClass` keyword. While the `Me` keyword can be used in any context in which an object reference is expected, the `MyClass` keyword is used only for member access; it must always be followed by a period and the name of a member, as shown here:

```
Public Class SomeClass

    Public SomeValue As Integer

    Public Sub SomeMethod(ByVal SomeValue As Integer)
        ' ...
        ' Assign the passed-in value to a field.
        MyClass.SomeValue = SomeValue
        ' ...
    End Sub

End Class
```

As you can see, there is overlap in the contexts in which these two keywords can be used, and for most circumstances they can be considered synonymous. However, there are situations in which the two keywords differ:

- The `Me` keyword can't be used in shared methods because it represents a specific object instance of the class, yet shared methods can be executed when no instance exists.

- The keywords can behave differently when used in a class from which other classes are derived. Consider this code:

  ```
  Public Class BaseClass
     Public Sub Method1( )
        Console.WriteLine("Invoking Me.Method2...")
        Me.Method2( )
        Console.WriteLine("Invoking MyClass.Method2...")
        MyClass.Method2( )
     End Sub
     Public Overridable Sub Method2( )
        Console.WriteLine("BaseClass.Method2")
     End Sub
  End Class

  Public Class DerivedClass
     Inherits BaseClass
     Public Overrides Sub Method2( )
        Console.WriteLine("DerivedClass.Method2")
     End Sub
  End Class
  ```

  This code defines two classes: BaseClass and DerivedClass. BaseClass defines two methods: Method1 and Method2. DerivedClass inherits Method1 but provides its own implementation for Method2.

  Now consider the following instantiation of DerivedClass, as well as a call through it to the Method1 method:

  ```
  Dim d As New DerivedClass( )
  d.Method1( )
  ```

  This produces the following output:

  ```
  Invoking Me.Method2...
  DerivedClass.Method2
  Invoking MyClass.Method2...
  BaseClass.Method2
  ```

  The call to Method1 through the DerivedClass instance calls the Method1 implementation inherited from BaseClass. Method1 calls Method2 twice: once through the `Me` keyword and once through the `MyClass` keyword. The `Me` keyword is a reference to the actual object instance, which is of type DerivedClass. Therefore, `Me.Method2( )` invokes the DerivedClass class's implementation of Method2. In contrast, the `MyClass` keyword is used for referencing members in the class in which the code is defined, which in this case is the BaseClass class. Therefore, `MyClass.Method2( )` invokes the BaseClass class's implementation of Method2.

The MyBase Keyword

The `MyBase` keyword is used to access methods on the base class. This feature is commonly used when an overriding method needs to call the base-class implementation of the same method:

```
Public Class BaseClass
   Public Overridable Sub DoSomething( )
      ' ...
   End Sub
End Class

Public Class DerivedClass
   Inherits BaseClass
   Public Overrides Sub DoSomething( )
      ' Start by calling the base-class implemenation of DoSomething.
      MyBase.DoSomething( )
      ' Then continue on with additional stuff required by DerivedClass.
      ' ...
   End Sub
End Class
```

Nested Classes

Class definitions can be nested. The nested class is considered a member of the enclosing class. As with other members, dot notation is used for accessing the inner class definition. Consider this nested class definition:

```
Public Class OuterClass
   Public Class InnerClass
      Public Sub SomeMethod( )
         Console.WriteLine("Hello from InnerClass.SomeMethod!")
      End Sub
   End Class
End Class
```

Instantiating an object of type InnerClass requires qualifying the name with the name of the enclosing class:

```
Dim x As New OuterClass.InnerClass( )
x.SomeMethod( )
```

The accessibility of the inner-class declaration can be controlled with the class declaration's access modifier. For example, in the following definition, InnerClass has been declared with the `Private` modifier, making it visible only within the confines of the OuterClass class:

```
Public Class OuterClass
   Private Class InnerClass
      ' ...
   End Class
End Class
```

Classes can be nested as deeply as desired.

Destructors

Just as constructors are methods that run when objects are instantiated, it is often convenient to define methods that run when objects are destroyed (that is, when the memory that was allocated to them is returned to the pool of free memory). Such a method is called a *destructor*. Visual Basic .NET doesn't have special syntax for declaring destructors, as it does for constructors. Instead, Visual Basic .NET uses the specially named methods Finalize and Dispose to perform the work normally associated with destructors. Because this mechanism is actually part of the .NET Framework rather than Visual Basic .NET, it is explained in Chapter 3, under "Memory Management and Garbage Collection."

Early Versus Late Binding

Declarations permit the compiler to know the data type of the item being declared. Here is the declaration of a variable of type String:

```
Dim s As String
```

Knowing the data type of a variable (or parameter, field, etc.) allows the compiler to determine what operations are permitted on any object referenced by the variable. For example, given the previous declaration of s as String, the compiler knows that the expression `s.Trim( )` is permitted (because it is defined in the String class), while `s.Compact( )` is not (because there is no such method in the String class). During compilation, the Visual Basic .NET compiler complains if it encounters such errors.

There is, however, one case in which the developer is permitted to relax this constraint. If `Option Strict` is turned off, the compiler forgoes this kind of checking on variables of type Object. For example, the following code will compile without difficulty, even though the Object class doesn't have a method called "Whatever":

```
Option Strict Off
' ...
Dim obj As Object
obj.Whatever( )
```

With `Option Strict` off, the compiler compiles `obj.Whatever( )` to code that checks to see if the runtime type of the object referenced by `obj` is a type that possesses a Whatever method. If it does, the Whatever method is called. If not, a runtime exception is raised. Here is such a scenario:

```
Option Strict Off

Public Class WhateverClass
   Public Sub Whatever( )
      Console.WriteLine("Whatever!")
   End Sub
End Class

Public Class TestClass
```

```
   Public Shared Sub TestMethod( )
      Dim obj As Object
      obj = New WhateverClass( )
      obj.Whatever( )
   End Sub
End Class
```

Because `Option Strict` is off, this code compiles just fine. Because `obj` references an object at runtime that is of a class that implements a Whatever method, it also runs just fine. However, consider what happens if the Whatever method is removed from the WhateverClass class:

```
Option Strict Off

Public Class WhateverClass
End Class

Public Class TestClass
   Public Shared Sub TestMethod( )
      Dim obj As Object
      obj = New WhateverClass( )
      obj.Whatever( )
   End Sub
End Class
```

The code still compiles without a problem, because `Option Strict` is off. However, at runtime there is a problem, as shown in Figure 2-2.

Figure 2-2. A problem

The technique of accessing members through a generic object of type Object is called *late binding*. "Late" means that whether the desired member is really there is not known until the statement is actually executed. In contrast, leaving `Option Strict` on and accessing members only through variables that have been declared as the appropriate type is known as *early binding*. "Early" means that whether the member access is legitimate is known at compile time.

Late binding is less efficient than early binding because additional checks are needed at runtime to determine whether the requested member actually exists on the runtime object and, if it does, to access that member. The worst part of late binding is that it can mask certain program errors (such as mistyped member names) until runtime. In general, this is bad programming practice.

Interfaces

It is useful to make a distinction between a class's *interface* and its *implementation*. Conceptually, the interface of a class is the set of members that are visible to users of the class—i.e., the class's public members. The public members are thought of as comprising the class's interface because they are the only way that code outside of the class can interact (i.e., interface) with objects of that class. In contrast, the implementation is comprised of the class's code plus the set of members that are not public.

It is possible to take this interface concept further and separate interface definition from class definition altogether. This has benefits that will be shown shortly. To define an interface, use the `Interface` statement:

```
Public Interface ISomeInterface
   Sub SomeSub( )
   Function SomeFunction( ) As Integer
   Property SomeProperty( ) As String
   Event SomeEvent( _
      ByVal sender As Object, _
      ByVal e As SomeEventArgs _
   )
End Interface
```

An interface declaration defines methods, properties, and events that will ultimately be implemented by some class or structure definition. Because interfaces never include any implementation, the declarations are headers only—never any implementation code; `End Sub`, `End Function`, or `End Property` statements; or property get or set blocks. There are no access modifiers (`Public`, `Private`, etc.) because all members of an interface are public by definition. By convention, interface names start with the letter "I".

To provide an implementation for a given interface, it is necessary to define a class or structure. For example, the following class implements the interface defined earlier:

```
Public Class SomeClass
   ' This indicates that the class implements the methods,
   ' properties, and events of the ISomeInterface interface.
   Implements ISomeInterface

   ' This method implements the SomeSub method of the
   ' ISomeInterface interface.
   Private Sub SomeSub( ) Implements ISomeInterface.SomeSub
      ' ...
   End Sub

   ' This method implements the SomeFunction method of the
   ' ISomeInterface interface.
```

```
    Private Function SomeFunction( ) As Integer _
       Implements ISomeInterface.SomeFunction
       ' ...
    End Function

    ' This property implements the SomeProperty property of the
    ' ISomeInterface interface.
    Private Property SomeProperty( ) As String _
       Implements ISomeInterface.SomeProperty
       Get
          ' ...
       End Get
       Set
          ' ...
       End Set
    End Property

    ' This event implements the SomeEvent event of the
    ' ISomeInterface interface.
    Private Event SomeEvent( _
       ByVal sender As Object, _
       ByVal e As SomeEventArgs _
    ) Implements ISomeInterface.SomeEvent

End Class
```

The key elements of this class definition are:

- The class-declaration header is immediately followed by the `Implements` statement, indicating that this class will expose the `ISomeInterface` interface:

  ```
  Public Class SomeClass
     ' This indicates that the class implements the methods,
     ' properties, and events of the ISomeInterface interface.
     Implements ISomeInterface
  ```

  This information is compiled into the class. Class users can find out whether a given class implements a given interface by attempting to assign the object reference to a variable that has been declared of the interface type, like this:

  ```
  Dim obj As Object
  Dim ifce As ISomeInterface
  ' ...
  ' Get an object reference from somewhere.
  obj = New SomeClass( )
  ' ...
  ' Try to convert the object reference to a reference of type
  ' ISomeInterface. If the object implements the ISomeInterface
  ' interface, the conversion succeeds. If the object doesn't
  ' implement the ISomeInterface interface, an exception of
  ' type InvalidCastException (defined in the System namespace)
  ' is thrown.
  ifce = CType(obj, ISomeInterface)
  ```

- For each method, property, and event in the interface, there is a corresponding method, property, or event in the class that has precisely the same signature and return value. The names don't have to match, although they match in the example.

- The declaration header for each method, property, and event in the class that implements a corresponding item in the interface must have an *implements clause*. This is the keyword `Implements` followed by the qualified name of the interface method, property, or event being implemented.

Additional things to note about implementing interfaces include:

- The access modifiers in the class-member declarations need not be `Public`. Note that in the example all the members are marked as `Private`. This means that the members are accessible only when accessed *through* the `ISomeInterface` interface. This will be shown in a moment.
- The class definition can include members that are not part of the implemented interface. These can be public if desired. This results in a class that effectively has two interfaces: the *default interface*, which is the set of members defined as `Public` in the class definition; and the *implemented interface*, which is the set of members defined in the interface named in the `Implements` statement.
- Classes are permitted to implement multiple interfaces.

To access members defined by an interface, declare a variable as that interface type and manipulate the object through that variable. For example:

```
Dim x As ISomeInterface = New SomeClass( )
x.SomeFunction( )
```

This code declares `x` as a reference to an object of type ISomeInterface. That's right: interface definitions define new types. Declared in this way, `x` can take a reference to any object that implements the `ISomeInterface` interface and access all the members that `ISomeInterface` defines, confident that the underlying object can handle such calls. This is a powerful feature of defining and implementing explicit interfaces. Objects that explicitly implement an interface can be used in any context in which that interface is expected; objects that implement multiple interfaces can be used in any context in which any of the interfaces is expected.

Interface definitions can inherit from other interface definitions in the same way that classes can inherit from other classes. For example:

```
Public Interface ISomeNewInterface
   Inherits ISomeInterface
   Sub SomeNewSub( )
End Interface
```

This defines a new interface called `ISomeNewInterface` that has all the members of the `ISomeInterface` interface plus a new member, called SomeNewSub. Any class or structure that implements the `ISomeNewInterface` interface must implement all members in both interfaces. Any such class is then considered to implement both interfaces and could be used in any context where either `ISomeInterface` or `ISomeNewInterface` is required.

Structures

Structures define value types. Variables of a value type store an actual value, as opposed to a reference to a value stored elsewhere. Contrast this with classes, which define reference types. Variables of a reference type store a reference (a pointer) to the actual value. See the discussion of value types versus reference types in the "Types" section earlier in this chapter. Example 2-8 shows a structure definition.

Example 2-8. A structure definition

```
Public Structure Complex
   ' The IFormattable interface provides a generic mechanism for
   ' asking a value to represent itself as a string.
   Implements IFormattable

   ' These private members store the value of the complex number.
   Private m_RealPart As Double
   Private m_ImaginaryPart As Double

   ' These fields provide potentially useful values, similar to the
   ' corresponding values in the Double type. They are initialized
   ' in the shared constructor. The ReadOnly modifier indicates that
   ' they can be set only in a constructor.
   Public Shared ReadOnly MaxValue As Complex
   Public Shared ReadOnly MinValue As Complex

   ' This is a shared constructor. It is run once by the runtime
   ' before any other access to the Complex type occurs. Note again
   ' that this is run only once in the life of the program--not once
   ' for each instance. Note also that there is never an access
   ' modifier on shared constructors.
   Shared Sub New( )
      MaxValue = New Complex(Double.MaxValue, Double.MaxValue)
      MinValue = New Complex(Double.MinValue, Double.MinValue)
   End Sub

   ' The RealPart property gives access to the real part of the
   ' complex number.
   Public Property RealPart( ) As Double
      Get
         Return m_RealPart
      End Get
      Set(ByVal Value As Double)
         m_RealPart = Value
      End Set
   End Property

   ' The ImaginaryPart property gives access to the imaginary part
   ' of the complex number.
   Public Property ImaginaryPart( ) As Double
      Get
         Return m_ImaginaryPart
```

Example 2-8. A structure definition (continued)

```
      End Get
      Set(ByVal Value As Double)
         m_ImaginaryPart = Value
      End Set
   End Property

   ' This is a parameterized constructor allowing initialization of
   ' a complex number with its real and imaginary values.
   Public Sub New( _
      ByVal RealPart As Double, _
      ByVal ImaginaryPart As Double _
   )
      m_RealPart = RealPart
      m_ImaginaryPart = ImaginaryPart
   End Sub

   ' This function computes the sum of two Complex values.
   Public Shared Function Add( _
      ByVal Value1 As Complex, _
      ByVal Value2 As Complex _
   ) As Complex
      Dim retval As Complex
      retval.RealPart = Value1.RealPart + Value2.RealPart
      retval.ImaginaryPart = Value1.ImaginaryPart + Value2.ImaginaryPart
      Return retval
   End Function

   ' This function computes the difference of two Complex values.
   Public Shared Function Subtract( _
      ByVal Value1 As Complex, _
      ByVal Value2 As Complex _
   ) As Complex
      Dim retval As Complex
      retval.RealPart = Value1.RealPart - Value2.RealPart
      retval.ImaginaryPart = Value1.ImaginaryPart - Value2.ImaginaryPart
      Return retval
   End Function

   ' This function computes the product of two Complex values.
   Public Shared Function Multiply( _
      ByVal Value1 As Complex, _
      ByVal Value2 As Complex _
   ) As Complex
      Dim retval As Complex
      retval.RealPart = Value1.RealPart * Value2.RealPart _
         - Value1.ImaginaryPart * Value2.ImaginaryPart
      retval.ImaginaryPart = Value1.RealPart * Value2.ImaginaryPart _
         + Value1.ImaginaryPart * Value2.RealPart
      Return retval
   End Function

   ' This function computes the quotient of two Complex values.
```

Example 2-8. A structure definition (continued)

```
   Public Shared Function Divide( _
      ByVal Value1 As Complex, _
      ByVal Value2 As Complex _
   ) As Complex
      Dim retval As Complex
      Dim numerator1 As Double
      Dim numerator2 As Double
      Dim denominator As Double

      numerator1 = Value1.RealPart * Value2.RealPart _
         + Value1.ImaginaryPart * Value2.ImaginaryPart
      numerator2 = Value1.ImaginaryPart * Value2.RealPart _
         - Value1.RealPart * Value2.ImaginaryPart
      denominator = Value2.RealPart ^ 2 + Value2.ImaginaryPart ^ 2

      retval.RealPart = numerator1 / denominator
      retval.ImaginaryPart = numerator2 / denominator
      Return retval
   End Function

   ' This function implements IFormattable.ToString. Because it is
   ' declared Private, this function is not part of the Complex
   ' type's default interface. Note that the function name need
   ' not match the name as declared in the interface, nor need
   ' it be in the format shown here.
   Private Function IFormattable_ToString( _
      ByVal format As String, _
      ByVal formatProvider As IFormatProvider _
   ) As String Implements IFormattable.ToString
      Dim realFormatter As IFormattable = m_RealPart
      Dim imaginaryFormatter As IFormattable = m_ImaginaryPart
      Return realFormatter.ToString(format, formatProvider) & " + " _
         & imaginaryFormatter.ToString(format, formatProvider) & "i"
   End Function

   ' This function formats the Complex value as a string.
   Public Overrides Function ToString( ) As String
      Return CType(Me, IFormattable).ToString(Nothing, Nothing)
   End Function

End Structure ' Complex
```

Structure definitions can include fields, properties, methods, constructors, and more—any member, in fact, that a class definition can have. Unlike class definitions, however, structures are constrained in several ways:

- Structures are not permitted to inherit from any other type. (However, structures implicitly inherit from System.ValueType, which in turn inherits from Object.)
- Structures cannot override methods implicitly inherited from System.ValueType.

- No type can inherit from a structure.
- Structures are not permitted to have parameterless constructors. Consider this array declaration:

  ```
  Dim a(1000000) As SomeStructure
  ```

  When an array of value types is created, it is immediately filled with instances of the value type. This behavior corresponds to what you'd expect from an array holding a primitive type (such as Integer). If parameterless constructors were permitted for structures, this array declaration would result in 1,000,000 calls to the constructor. Ouch.
- Structures are not permitted to have destructors.
- Field members in structures are not permitted to be initialized in their declarations. This includes the special cases of using `As New` *type* in the declaration or specifying an initial size in an array declaration.

Boxing and Unboxing

Value types are optimized for size and speed. They don't carry around the same amount of overhead as reference types. It would not be very efficient if every four-byte integer also carried around a four-byte reference. There are times, however, when treating value types and reference types in a polymorphic way would be nice. Consider this method declaration, which takes any number of arguments of any type and processes them in some way:

```
Public Shared Sub Print(ParamArray ByVal objArray( ) As Object)

   Dim obj As Object

   For Each obj In objArray
      ' ...
   Next

End Sub
```

Clearly, `objArray` is an array of reference types, and `obj` is a reference type. Yet it would be nice to pass value types and reference types to the method, like this:

```
Print("hello, world", SomeObject, 4, True)
```

In fact, this is possible. When a value type is assigned to a variable of type Object or passed in a parameter of type Object, it goes through a process known as *boxing*. To box a value type means to allocate memory to hold a copy of the value, then copy the value into that memory, and finally manipulate or store a reference to the value. *Unboxing* is the opposite process: taking a reference to a value type and copying the referenced value into an actual value type.

Boxing and unboxing are done on your behalf by the .NET runtime—there is nothing you have to do to facilitate it. You should be aware of it, however, because the box and unbox operations aren't free.

Enumerations

An *enumeration* is a type whose values are explicitly named by the creator of the type. The .NET Framework and Visual Basic .NET define many enumerations for their and your use. In addition, Visual Basic .NET provides syntax for defining new enumerations. Here is an example:

```
Public Enum Rainbow
   Red
   Orange
   Yellow
   Green
   Blue
   Indigo
   Violet
End Enum
```

This declaration establishes a new type, called Rainbow. The identifiers listed within the body of the declaration become constant values that may be assigned to variables of the Rainbow type. Here is a declaration of a variable of type Rainbow and an initial assignment to it:

```
Dim myRainbow As Rainbow = Rainbow.Blue
```

Note that the value name is qualified by the type name.

Enumerations are value types that implicitly inherit from the .NET Framework's System.Enum type (which in turn inherits from System.ValueType). That means that every enumeration has access to the members defined by System.Enum. One such member is the ToString method, which returns a string containing the name of the value. This is handy for printing:

```
Dim myRainbow As Rainbow = Rainbow.Blue
Console.WriteLine("The value of myRainbow is: " & myRainbow.ToString( ))
```

This code results in the following output:

```
The value of myRainbow is: Blue
```

The values of an enumeration are considered as ordered. Thus, comparisons are permitted between variables of the enumeration type:

```
Dim myRainbow As Rainbow
Dim yourRainbow As Rainbow
' ...
If myRainbow < yourRainbow Then
   ' ...
End If
```

Variables of an enumeration type can be used as indexes in `For...Next` statements. For example:

```
For myRainbow = Rainbow.Red To Rainbow.Violet
   ' ...
Next
```

Internally, Visual Basic .NET and the .NET Framework use values of type Integer to represent the values of the enumeration. The compiler starts with 0 and assigns increasing Integer values to each name in the enumeration. It is sometimes useful to override the default Integer values that are assigned to each name. This is done by adding an initializer to each enumeration constant. For example:

```
Public Enum MyLegacyErrorCodes
   NoError = 0
   FileNotFound = -1000
   OutOfMemory = -1001
   InvalidEntry = -2000
End Enum
```

It is also possible to specify the type of the underlying value. For example:

```
Public Enum Rainbow As Byte
   Red
   Orange
   Yellow
   Green
   Blue
   Indigo
   Violet
End Enum
```

This could be an important space-saving measure if many values of the enumeration will be stored somewhere. The only types that can be specified for an enumeration are Byte, Short, Integer, and Long.

Sometimes enumerations are used as flags, with the idea that multiple flags can be combined in a single value. Such an enumeration can be defined by using the `Flags` attribute. (Attributes are discussed later in this chapter.) Here is an example:

```
<Flags( )> Public Enum Rainbow
   Red = 1
   Orange = 2
   Yellow = 4
   Green = 8
   Blue = 16
   Indigo = 32
   Violet = 64
End Enum
```

Note two important things in this definition:

- The first line of the definition starts with `<Flags( )>`. This indicates that values of this type can be composed of multiple items from the enumeration.
- The items in the enumeration have values that are powers of two. This ensures that each combination of items has a unique sum. For example, the combination of Yellow, Blue, and Violet has a sum of 84, which can't be attained with any other combination of items.

Individual values are combined using the `Or` operator.

The ToString method is smart enough to sort out the value names when creating a string representation of the value. For example, given the previous assignment, consider the following call to the ToString method:

```
Console.WriteLine(myRainbow.ToString( ))
```

This statement produces the following output:

```
Green, Blue
```

Exceptions

Sometimes errors or exceptional conditions prohibit a program from continuing its current activity. A classic example is division by zero:

```
Dim x As Integer = 0
Dim y As Integer = 1 \ x
```

When the process hits the line containing the integer division, an *exception* occurs. An exception is any occurrence that is not considered part of normal, expected program flow. The runtime detects, or *catches*, this exception and takes appropriate action, generally resulting in termination of the offending program. Figure 2-3 shows the message box that is displayed when this code is run within the Visual Studio .NET IDE.

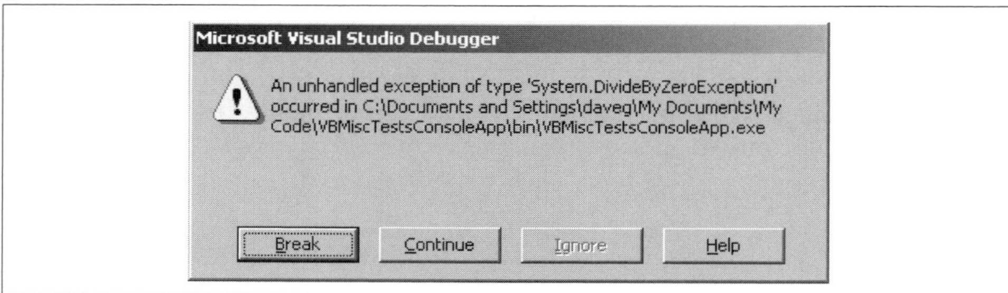

Figure 2-3. A divide-by-zero exception

Visual Basic .NET programs can and should be written to catch exceptions themselves. This is done by wrapping potentially dangerous code in `Try...End Try` blocks. Example 2-9 shows how to catch the divide-by-zero exception.

Example 2-9. Catching an exception

```
Try
   Dim x As Integer = 0
   Dim y As Integer = 1 \ x
Catch e As Exception
   Console.WriteLine(e.Message)
End Try
```

When the program attempts the division by zero, an exception occurs, and program execution jumps to the first statement in the Catch block. The Catch statement declares a variable of type Exception that receives information about the exception that occurred. This information can then be used within the Catch block to record or report the exception, or to take corrective action. The previous code merely displays the message associated with the exception that occurred, as shown here:

```
Attempted to divide by zero.
```

After executing the statements in the Catch block, program execution continues with whatever follows the End Try statement. In Try blocks in which no exception occurs, execution continues through to the last statement of the Try block and then skips the statements in the Catch block.

The variable declared in the Catch statement of Example 2-9 is of type Exception (defined in the System namespace). All exceptions are represented by types that derive, either directly or indirectly, from the Exception type. The As *type_name* clause of the Catch statement specifies the type of exception that the associated block of code can handle. Exceptions of the indicated type, or of any type derived (directly or indirectly) from the indicated type, are handled by the associated block of code.

Look again at the Catch statement from Example 2-9:

```
Catch e As Exception
```

Because all exceptions derive from the Exception type, any exception that occurs during execution of the Try block in Example 2-9 results in execution of the Catch block. This behavior can be modified by providing a more specific exception type in the Catch statement. Example 2-10 is identical to Example 2-9, except that it catches *only* divide by zero exceptions.

Example 2-10. Catching a specific exception

```
Try
   Dim x As Integer = 0
   Dim y As Integer = 1 \ x
Catch e As System.DivideByZeroException
   Console.WriteLine(e.Message)
End Try
```

If any exception other than DivideByZeroException were to occur in the Try block of Example 2-10, it would not be caught by the code shown. What happens in that case depends on the rest of the code in the program. Try...End Try blocks can be nested, so if there is a surrounding Try...End Try block with a suitable Catch statement, it will catch the exception. Alternatively, if the calling routine couches the method call within a Try...End Try block having a suitable Catch statement, execution jumps out of the current method and into the associated Catch block in the calling routine. If no suitable Catch block exists in the calling routine, the search for a suitable Catch continues up the call chain until one is found or until all callers have been examined. If no suitable `Catch` block exists anywhere in the call chain, the runtime environment catches the exception and terminates the application.

`Try...End Try` blocks can include multiple `Catch` blocks, which allows different exceptions to be handled in different ways. For example, the following code handles two specific exceptions, allowing all others to go unhandled:

```
Try
   ' ...
Catch e As System.DivideByZeroException
   ' ...
Catch e As System.OverflowException
   ' ...
End Try
```

Because all exception types are derived from the Exception type, the properties and methods of the Exception type are available on all exception types. In fact, most exception types don't define any additional properties or methods. The only reason they're defined as specific types is so that they can be specifically caught. The properties of the Exception class are:

HelpLink
: A URN or URL that links to a help-file topic that explains the error in further detail. The type is String.

HResult
: A COM HRESULT representing the exception. This is used for interoperating with COM components (a topic that is not discussed in this book). The type is integer.

InnerException
: Sometimes a method may choose to throw an exception because it has caught an exception from some other internal method call. The outer method throws an exception that is meaningful to it and its caller, but the exception thrown by the inner method should also be communicated to the caller. This is the purpose of the InnerException property. This property contains a reference to the internal exception (if any) that led to the current exception. The type is Exception.

Message
: The message associated with the exception. In general, this is a description of the condition that led to the exception and, where possible, an explanation of how to correct it. The type is String.

Source
: The name of the application or object in which the exception occurred. The type is String.

StackTrace
: A textual representation of the program call stack at the moment the exception occurred. The type is String.

TargetSite
: A reference to an object of type MethodBase (defined in the System.Reflection namespace) that represents the method in which the exception occurred. If the system cannot obtain this information, this property contains `Nothing`.

The methods of the Exception class are:

GetBaseException
: As discussed for the InnerException property, indicates that the current exception may be the end exception in a chain of exceptions. The GetBaseException method returns the first exception in the chain. This method takes no parameters. The return type is Exception.

GetObjectData
: Serializes the Exception object into a SerializationInfo object (a process not discussed in this book). The syntax is:

```
Overridable Public Sub GetObjectData( _
   ByVal info As SerializationInfo, _
   ByVal context As StreamingContext _
) Implements ISerializable.GetObjectData
```

ToString
: Returns a text representation of the Exception. This includes the exception type, the message, the stack trace, and similar information for any inner exceptions.

When an exception occurs, there is no facility for retrying the statement that caused the exception. If such behavior is desired, it must be explicitly coded. Here's one possibility:

```
Dim bSuccess As Boolean = False
Do
   Try
      ' Some code that is to be protected.
      ' ...
      bSuccess = True
   Catch e As Exception
      ' Some recovery action.
      ' ...
   End Try
Loop Until bSuccess
```

Sometimes you must ensure that certain code is executed regardless of whether there is an exception. For example, if a file is opened, the file should be closed even when an exception occurs. `Try...End Try` blocks can include `Finally` blocks for this purpose. Code appearing in a `Finally` block is executed regardless of whether an exception occurs. If no exception occurs, the statements in the `Finally` block are executed after the statements in the `Try` block have been executed. If an exception does occur, the statements in the `Finally` block are executed after the statements in the `Catch` block that handles the exception are executed. If the exception is not handled, or if there are no `Catch` blocks, the statements in the `Finally` block are executed prior to forwarding the exception to any enclosing exception handlers. Here's an example of using a Finally block:

```
Dim s As System.IO.Stream =_
   System.IO.File.Open("c:\test.txt", System.IO.FileMode.CreateNew)
Try
   ' Do something with the open stream.
   ' ...
Catch e As Exception
   ' Handle any exceptions.
   ' ...
Finally
   ' The stream should be closed whether or not there is an error.
   s.Close( )
End Try
```

Visual Basic .NET applications can intentionally *throw* exceptions to indicate errors or other unusual occurrences. For example, if a method is expecting an argument that is within a specific range and the actual value passed to the method is outside of that range, the method can throw an exception of type ArgumentOutOfRangeException (defined in the System namespace). This is done with the Throw statement, as shown in Example 2-11.

Example 2-11. Throwing an exception

```
Public Sub SomeMethod(ByVal MyParameter As Integer)
   ' Ensure that the argument is valid.
   If (MyParameter < 10) Or (MyParameter > 100) Then
      Throw New ArgumentOutOfRangeException( )
   End If
   ' Remainder of method.
   ' ...
End Sub
```

The Throw statement requires an instance of some type derived from the Exception type. When the Throw statement is reached, the runtime looks for an appropriate Catch block in the calling code to handle the exception. If no suitable Catch block is found, the runtime catches the exception itself and terminates the application. See Appendix B for a list of exception types defined in the System namespace.

Visual Basic .NET applications can create their own exception types simply by declaring types that derive from the Exception type. Example 2-12 shows how the exception handling of Example 2-11 can be made more specific to the actual error that occurs. In Example 2-12, a new exception type called MyParameterOutOfRangeException is declared. Next, a method is shown that throws this exception. Lastly, a method is shown that handles the exception.

Example 2-12. Defining and using a custom exception

```
' Define a custom exception class to represent a specific error condition.
Public Class MyParameterOutOfRangeException
```

Example 2-12. Defining and using a custom exception (continued)

```
   Inherits Exception
   Public Sub New( )
      ' The Exception type has a constructor that takes an error message
      ' as its argument. Because the Message property of the Exception
      ' type is read-only, using this constructor is the only way that
      ' the Message property can be set.
      MyBase.New("The value passed in the MyParameter parameter" _
         & " is out of range. The value must be in the range of" _
         & " 10 through 100.")
   End Sub
End Class

' ...

   ' Define a method that may throw a custom exception.
   Public Sub SomeMethod(ByVal MyParameter As Integer)
      ' Ensure that the argument is valid.
      If (MyParameter < 10) Or (MyParameter > 100) Then
         Throw New MyParameterOutOfRangeException( )
      End If
      ' Remainder of method.
      ' ...
   End Sub

' ...

   ' Call the SomeMethod method, catching only the
   ' MyParameterOutOfRangeException exception.
   Public Sub SomeCaller( )
      Try
         SomeMethod(500)
      Catch e As MyParameterOutOfRangeException
         ' ...
      End Try
   End Sub
```

Delegates

A *delegate* is a programmer-defined type that abstracts the ability to call a method. A delegate-type declaration includes the declaration of the signature and return type that the delegate encapsulates. Instances of the delegate type can then wrap any method that exposes the same signature and return type, regardless of the class on which the method is defined and whether the method is an instance method or shared method of the defining class. The method thus wrapped can be invoked through the delegate object. The delegate mechanism provides polymorphism for methods having the same signature and return type.

Delegates are often used to implement callback mechanisms. Imagine a class that will be used by a program you are writing. This class provides some useful functionality,

> ### What About On Error?
>
> Visual Basic 6 did not have exception objects and `Try...Catch` blocks. Instead, it used the `On Error` statement to specify a line within the current procedure to which execution should jump if an error occurred. The code at that point in the procedure could then examine the Err intrinsic object to determine the error that had occurred. For compatibility with previous versions, Visual Basic .NET continues to support the `On Error` and related statements, but they should not be used in new development, for the following reasons:
>
> - Structured exception handling is more flexible.
> - Structured exception handling does not use error codes. (Application-defined error codes often clashed with error codes defined by other applications.)
> - Structured exception handling exists at the .NET Framework level, meaning that regardless of the language in which each component is written, exceptions can be thrown and caught across component boundaries.
>
> Error handling with the `On Error` and related statements are not discussed in this book.

including the ability to call in to a method that you must implement within your program. Perhaps this callback mechanism is provided to feed your program data as it becomes available in the class you are using. One way to achieve this capability is through the use of delegates. Here's how:

1. The writer of the class you're using (call it a server class) declares a public delegate type that defines the signature and return value of the method that you will implement.
2. The writer of the server class exposes a method for clients of the class to pass in an instance of the delegate type.
3. You implement a method having the appropriate signature and return value.
4. You instantiate a new object of the delegate type.
5. You connect your method to your delegate instance.
6. You call the method defined in Step 2, passing in your delegate instance.
7. The server class now has a delegate instance that wraps your method. The class can call your method through the delegate at any time.
8. Depending on the application, it might be appropriate for the writer of the server class to provide a method that allows the client application to disconnect its delegate from the server to stop receiving callbacks.

Example 2-13 shows an example of this mechanism.

Example 2-13. Defining and using a delegate type to implement a callback mechanism

```
' This class is defined in the server component.
Public Class ServerClass

   ' Even though the following declaration looks similar to a
   ' method declaration, it is actually a type declaration. It
   ' compiles to a type that ultimately derives from the
   ' System.Delegate type. The purpose of the method syntax in
   ' this declaration is to define the signature and return type
   ' of the methods that instances of this delegate type are able
   ' to wrap.
   Public Delegate Sub MessageDelegate(ByVal msg As String)

   ' The following is a private field that will hold an instance of
   ' the delegate type. The instance will be provided by the client
   ' by calling the RegisterForMessages method. Even though this
   ' field can hold only a single delegate instance, the
   ' System.Delegate class itself is designed such that a
   ' delegate instance can refer to multiple other delegate
   ' instances. This feature is inherited by all delegate types.
   ' Therefore, the client will be able to register multiple
   ' delegates, if desired. See the RegisterForMessages and
   ' UnregisterForMessages methods in the current class to see
   ' how multiple delegates are saved.
   Private m_delegateHolder As MessageDelegate = Nothing

   ' The client calls the RegisterForMessages method to give the
   ' server a delegate instance that wraps a suitable method on
   ' the client.
   Public Sub RegisterForMessages(ByVal d As MessageDelegate)
      ' The System.Delegate class's Combine method takes two
      ' delegates and returns a delegate that represents them
      ' both. The return type is System.Delegate, which must be
      ' explicitly converted to the appropriate delegate type.
      Dim sysDelegate As System.Delegate = _
         System.Delegate.Combine(m_delegateHolder, d)
      m_delegateHolder = CType(sysDelegate, MessageDelegate)
   End Sub

   ' The client calls the UnregisterForMessages method to tell
   ' the server not to send any more messages through a
   ' particular delegate instance.
   Public Sub UnregisterForMessages(ByVal d As MessageDelegate)
      ' The System.Delegate class's Remove method takes two
      ' delegates. The first is a delegate that represents a list
      ' of delegates. The second is a delegate that is to be
      ' removed from the list. The return type is
      ' System.Delegate, which must be explicitly converted to
      ' the appropriate delegate type.
      Dim sysDelegate As System.Delegate = _
         System.Delegate.Remove(m_delegateHolder, d)
      m_delegateHolder = CType(sysDelegate, MessageDelegate)
   End Sub
```

Example 2-13. Defining and using a delegate type to implement a callback mechanism (continued)

```
   ' The DoSomethingUseful method represents the normal
   ' processing of the server object. At some point during normal
   ' processing, the server object decides that it is time to
   ' send a message to the client(s).
   Public Sub DoSomethingUseful( )
      ' ...
      ' Some processing has led up to a decision to send a
      ' message. However, do so only if a delegate has been
      ' registered.
      If Not (m_delegateHolder Is Nothing) Then
         ' The delegate object's Invoke method invokes the
         ' methods wrapped by the delegates represented by
         ' the given delegate.
         m_delegateHolder.Invoke("This is the msg parameter.")
      End If
      ' ...
   End Sub

End Class ' ServerClass

' This class is defined in the client component.
Public Class ClientClass

   ' This is the callback method. It will handle messages
   ' received from the server class.
   Public Sub HandleMessage(ByVal msg As String)
      Console.WriteLine(msg)
   End Sub

   ' This method represents the normal processing of the client
   ' object. As some point during normal processing, the client
   ' object creates an instance of the server class and passes it
   ' a delegate wrapper to the HandleMessage method.
   Public Sub DoSomethingUseful( )
      ' ...
      Dim server As New ServerClass( )
      ' The AddressOf operator in the following initialization
      ' is a little misleading to read. It's not returning an
      ' address at all. Rather, a delegate instance is being
      ' created and assigned to the myDelegate variable.
      Dim myDelegate As ServerClass.MessageDelegate _
         = AddressOf HandleMessage
      server.RegisterForMessages(myDelegate)
      ' ...
      ' This represents other calls to the server object, which
      ' might somehow trigger the server object to call back to
      ' the client object.
      server.DoSomethingUseful( )
      ' ...
      ' At some point, the client may decide that it doesn't want
      ' any more callbacks.
      server.UnregisterForMessages(myDelegate)
```

Example 2-13. Defining and using a delegate type to implement a callback mechanism (continued)

```
   End Sub

End Class ' ClientClass
```

Delegates are central to event handling in the .NET Framework. See the next section for more information.

Delegates don't provide any capabilities that can't be achieved in other ways. For example, the solution in Example 2-13 could have been achieved in at least two ways that don't involve delegates:

- The server component could define an abstract base class defining the method to be implemented by the client. The client would then define a class that inherits from the server's abstract base class, providing an implementation for the class's one method. The server would then provide methods for registering and unregistering objects derived from the abstract base class.
- The server component could define an interface that includes the definition of the method to be implemented by the client. The client would then define a class that implemented this interface, and the server would provide methods for registering and unregistering objects that expose the given interface.

Any of these methods (including delegates) could be a reasonable solution to a given problem. Choose the one that seems to fit best.

Delegates are sometimes characterized as *safe function pointers*. I don't think that this characterization aids the learning process, because delegates aren't any sort of pointer—safe or otherwise. They are objects that encapsulate method access. Delegate objects can invoke methods without knowing where the actual methods are implemented. In effect, this allows individual methods to be treated in a polymorphic way.

Events

An *event* is a callback mechanism. With it, objects can notify users that something interesting has happened. If desired, data can be passed from the object to the client as part of the notification. Throughout this section, I use the terms *event producer*, *producer class*, and *producer object* to talk about a class (and its instances) capable of raising events. I use the terms *event consumer*, *consumer class*, and *consumer object* to talk about a class (and its instances) capable of receiving and acting on events raised by an event producer.

Here is a class that exposes an event:

```
Public Class EventProducer

   Public Event SomeEvent( )
```

```
    Public Sub DoSomething( )
       ' ...
       RaiseEvent SomeEvent( )
       ' ...
    End Sub

End Class
```

The Event statement in this code fragment declares that this class is capable of raising an event called SomeEvent. The empty parentheses in the declaration indicate that the event will not pass any data. An example later in this section will show how to define events that pass data.

The RaiseEvent statement in the DoSomething method raises the event. Any clients of the object that have registered their desire to receive this event will receive it at this time. Receiving an event means that a method will be called on the client to handle the event. Here is the definition of a client class that receives and handles events from the EventProducer class:

```
Public Class EventConsumer

   Private WithEvents producer As EventProducer

   Public Sub producer_SomeEvent( ) Handles producer.SomeEvent
      Console.WriteLine("Hey, an event happened!!")
   End Sub

   Public Sub New( )
      producer() = New EventProducer( )
   End Sub

   Public Sub DoSomething( )
      ' ...
      producer().DoSomething( )
      ' ...
   End Sub

End Class
```

The key aspects here are:

- The consumer object has a field that contains a reference to the producer object.
- The consumer object has a method capable of handling the event. A method is capable of handling an event if the method and event have the same signature. The name of the method is not important.
- The handler-method declaration has a *handles clause*.
- The handles clause specifies the event to be handled. The identifier before the dot indicates the field with the object to generate events. The identifier after the dot indicates the name of the event.

The handler method is called synchronously, which means that the statement following the RaiseEvent statement in the event producer does not execute until after the method handler in the consumer completes. If an event has multiple consumers, each consumer's event handler is called in succession. The order in which the multiple consumers are called is not specified.

Here's a class that exposes an event with parameters:

```
Public Class EventProducer

   Public Event AnotherEvent(ByVal MyData As Integer)

   Public Sub DoSomething( )
      ' ...
      RaiseEvent AnotherEvent(42)
      ' ...
   End Sub

End Class
```

And here's a class that consumes it:

```
Public Class EventConsumer

   Private WithEvents producer As EventProducer

   Public Sub New( )
      producer = New EventProducer( )
   End Sub

   Public Sub producer_AnotherEvent(ByVal MyData As Integer) _
      Handles producer.AnotherEvent
      Console.WriteLine("Received the 'AnotherEvent' event.")
      Console.WriteLine("The value of MyData is {0}.", Format(MyData))
   End Sub

   Public Sub DoSomething( )
      ' ...
      producer().DoSomething( )
      ' ...
   End Sub

End Class
```

The result of calling the EventConsumer class's DoSomething method is:

```
Received the 'AnotherEvent' event.
The value of MyData is 42.
```

Using Events and Delegates Together

Under the covers, .NET uses delegates as part of its events architecture. Delegates are necessary in this architecture because they enable hooking up the consumer class's event-handler method to the event producer (recall that delegates encapsulate method invocation). The Visual Basic .NET compiler hides the details of this mechanism, quietly creating delegates as needed under the surface. However, the programmer is free to make this process explicit. The following definition of the EventProducer class is semantically equivalent to the previous one:

```
Public Class EventProducer

   Public Delegate Sub SomeDelegate(ByVal MyData As Integer)

   Public Event AnotherEvent As SomeDelegate

   Public Sub DoSomething( )
      ' ...
      RaiseEvent AnotherEvent(42)
      ' ...
   End Sub

End Class
```

Note here that the declaration of SomeDelegate defines a delegate capable of wrapping any subroutine whose signature matches the signature given in the declaration. The subsequent declaration of AnotherEvent defines an event that will use the signature defined by SomeDelegate. Regardless of which syntax is being used, events are actually fields whose type is some delegate type.

Variations in syntax are possible on the consumer side, too. When the `WithEvents` and `Handles` keywords are used, Visual Basic .NET creates a delegate that wraps the given handler method and then registers that delegate with the object and event given in the `Handles` clause. The `WithEvents` and `Handles` keywords can be omitted, and the delegate declaration and hookup can be done explicitly, as shown here:

```
Public Class EventConsumer

   Private producer As EventProducer

   Public Sub New( )
      producer = New EventProducer( )
      AddHandler producer.AnotherEvent, _
         New EventProducer.SomeDelegate(AddressOf producer_AnotherEvent)
   End Sub

   Public Sub producer_AnotherEvent(ByVal MyData As Integer)
      Console.WriteLine("Received the 'AnotherEvent' event.")
      Console.WriteLine("The value of MyData is {0}.", Format(MyData))
   End Sub

   Public Sub DoSomething( )
      ' ...
      producer.DoSomething( )
      ' ...
   End Sub

End Class
```

The hookup of the handler method to the event producer is done with this statement in the EventConsumer class's constructor:

```
AddHandler producer.AnotherEvent, _
   New EventProducer.SomeDelegate(AddressOf producer_AnotherEvent)
```

The `AddHandler` statement and its companion, the `RemoveHandler` statement, allow event handlers to be dynamically registered and unregistered. The `RemoveHandler` statement takes exactly the same parameters as the `AddHandler` statement.

Standard Modules

A *standard module* is a type declaration. It is introduced with the `Module` statement, as shown here:

```
Public Module ModuleTest
   ' ...
End Module
```

Don't confuse the Visual Basic .NET term, *standard module*, with the .NET term, *module*. They are unrelated to each other. See Chapter 3 for information about .NET modules.

Standard module definitions are similar to class definitions, with these differences:

- Standard module members are implicitly shared.
- Standard modules cannot be inherited.
- The members in a standard module can be referenced without being qualified with the standard module name.

Standard modules are a good place to put global variables and procedures that aren't logically associated with any class.

Attributes

An *attribute* is a program element that modifies some declaration. Here is a simple example:

```
<SomeAttribute( )> Public Class SomeClass
   ' ...
End Class
```

This example shows a fictitious `SomeAttribute` attribute that applies to a class declaration. Attributes appear within angle brackets (<>) and are following by parentheses (( )), which may contain a list of arguments. To apply multiple attributes to a single declaration, separate them with commas within a single set of angle brackets, like this:

```
<SomeAttribute(), SomeOtherAttribute( )> Public Class SomeClass
   ' ...
End Class
```

Attributes can be placed on the following kinds of declarations:

Types
: This includes classes, delegates, enumerations, events, interfaces, Visual Basic .NET standard modules, and structures.

The attribute is placed at the beginning of the first line of the type declaration:

```
<SomeAttribute( )> Public Class SomeClass
   ' ...
End Class
```

Constructors
: The attribute is placed at the beginning of the first line of the constructor declaration:

```
<SomeAttribute()> Public Sub New( )
   ' ...
End Sub
```

Fields
: The attribute is placed at the beginning of the field declaration:

```
<SomeAttribute( )> Public SomeField As Integer
```

Methods
: The attribute is placed at the beginning of the first line of the method declaration:

```
<SomeAttribute()> Public Sub SomeMethod( )
' ...
End Sub
```

Parameters
: The attribute is placed immediately prior to the parameter declaration. Each parameter can have its own attributes:

```
Public Sub SomeMethod(<SomeAttribute( )> ByVal SomeParameter As Integer)
```

Properties
: An attribute that applies to a property is placed at the beginning of the first line of the property declaration. An attribute that applies specifically to one or both of a property's Get or Set methods is placed at the beginning of the first line of the respective method declaration:

```
<SomeAttribute()> Public Property SomeProperty( ) As Integer
Get
   ' ...
End Get
<SomeOtherAttribute( )> Set(ByVal Value As Integer)
   ' ...
End Set
End Property
```

Return values

The attribute is placed after the As keyword and before the type name:

```
Public Function SomeFunction() As <SomeAttribute( )> Integer
   ' ...
End Function
```

Assemblies

The attribute is placed at the top of the Visual Basic .NET source file, following any Imports statements and preceding any declarations. The attribute must be qualified with the Assembly keyword so that the compiler knows to apply the attribute to the assembly rather than the module. Assemblies and modules are explained in Chapter 3.

```
Imports ...
<Assembly: SomeAttribute( )>
Public Class ...
```

Modules

The attribute is placed at the top of the Visual Basic .NET source file, following any Imports statements and preceding any declarations. The attribute must be qualified with the Module keyword so that the compiler knows to apply the attribute to the module rather than the assembly. Assemblies and modules are explained in Chapter 3.

```
Imports ...
<Module: SomeAttribute( )>
Public Class ...
```

Some attributes are usable only on a subset of this list.

The .NET Framework supplies several standard attributes. For example, the Obsolete attribute provides an indication that the flagged declaration should not be used in new code. This allows component developers to leave obsolete declarations in the component for backward compatibility, while still providing a hint to component users that certain declarations should no longer be used. Here's an example:

```
<Obsolete("Use ISomeInterface2 instead.")> Public Interface ISomeInterface
   ' ...
End Interface
```

When this code is compiled, the Obsolete attribute and the associated message are compiled into the application. Tools or other code can make use of this information. For example, if the compiled application is a code library referenced by some project in Visual Studio .NET, Visual Studio .NET warns the developer when she tries to make use of any items that are flagged as Obsolete. Using the previous example, if the developer declares a class that implements ISomeInterface, Visual Studio .NET displays the following warning:

```
Obsolete: Use ISomeInterface2 instead.
```

See Appendix A for the list of attributes defined by the .NET Framework.

Creating Custom Attributes

The attribute mechanism is extensible. A new attribute is defined by declaring a class that derives from the Attribute type (in the System namespace) and that provides an indication of what declarations the attribute should be allowed to modify. Here's an example:

```
<AttributeUsage(AttributeTargets.All)> Public Class SomeAttribute
   Inherits System.Attribute
End Class
```

This code defines an attribute called `SomeAttribute`. The SomeAttribute class itself is modified by the `AttributeUsage` attribute. The `AttributeUsage` attribute is a standard .NET Framework attribute that indicates which declarations can be modified by the new attribute. In this case, the value of `AttributeTargets.All` indicates that the `SomeAttribute` attribute can be applied to any and all declarations. The argument of the `AttributeUsage` attribute is of type AttributeTargets (defined in the System namespace). The values in this enumeration are: `Assembly`, `Module`, `Class`, `Struct`, `Enum`, `Constructor`, `Method`, `Property`, `Field`, `Event`, `Interface`, `Parameter`, `Delegate`, `ReturnValue`, and `All`.

To create an attribute that takes one or more arguments, add a parameterized constructor to the attribute class. Here's an example:

```
<AttributeUsage(AttributeTargets.Method)> _
Public Class MethodDocumentationAttribute
   Inherits System.Attribute

   Public ReadOnly Author As String
   Public ReadOnly Description As String

   Public Sub New(ByVal Author As String, ByVal Description As String)
      Me.Author = Author
      Me.Description = Description
   End Sub

End Class
```

This code defines an attribute that takes two parameters: *`Author`* and *`Description`*. It could be used to modify a method declaration like this:

```
<MethodDocumentation("Dave Grundgeiger", "This is my method.")> _
Public Sub SomeMethod( )
   ' ...
End Sub
```

By convention, attribute names end with the word `Attribute`. Visual Basic .NET references attributes either by their full names—for example, `MethodDocumentationAttribute`—or by their names less the trailing `Attribute`—for example, `MethodDocumentation`. Attributes whose names do not end with the word `Attribute` are simply referenced by their full names.

Reading Attributes

Compiled applications can be programmatically examined to determine what attributes, if any, are associated with the applications' various declarations. For example, it is possible to write a Visual Basic .NET program that searches a compiled component for the `Obsolete` attribute and produces a report. This is done by using the .NET Framework's *reflection* capability. Reflection is the ability to programmatically examine type information. The .NET Framework provides a great deal of support for reflection in the Type class (in the System namespace) and in the types found in the System.Reflection namespace.

Reflection deserves a book of its own, but here's a brief look to get you started:

```
Imports System
Imports System.Reflection
' ...
Dim typ As Type = GetType(System.Data.SqlClient.SqlConnection)
Dim objs( ) As Object = typ.GetCustomAttributes(False)
Dim obj As Object

For Each obj In objs
   Console.WriteLine(obj.GetType( ).FullName)
Next
```

This code fragment does the following:

- Uses the *GetType* function to get a Type object that represents the SqlConnection type (defined in the System.Data.SqlClient namespace). You can experiment with putting any type name here (including the types that you create). I chose SqlConnection because I know that it happens to have an attribute associated with it.
- Calls the GetCustomAttributes method of the Type object to get an array of objects that represent the attributes associated with the type. Each object in the array represents an attribute.
- Loops through the object array and prints the type name of each object. The type name is the name of the attribute.

The output is shown here:

```
System.ComponentModel.DefaultEventAttribute
```

Reflection is not discussed further in this book. Review the .NET documentation for the System.Reflection namespace for more information.

Conditional Compilation

Conditional compilation is the ability to specify that a certain block of code will be compiled into the application only under certain conditions. Conditional compilation uses precompiler directives to affect which lines are included in the compilation process. This feature is often used to wrap code used only for debugging. For example:

```
#Const DEBUG = True

Public Sub SomeMethod( )

#If DEBUG Then
   Console.WriteLine("Entering SomeMethod( )")
#End If

   ' ...

#If DEBUG Then
   Console.WriteLine("Exiting SomeMethod( )")
#End If

End Sub
```

The `#Const` directive defines a symbolic constant for the compiler. This constant is later referenced in the `#If` directives. If the constant evaluates to `True`, the statements within the `#If` block are compiled into the application. If the constant evaluates to `False`, the statements within the `#If` block are ignored.

The scope of constants defined by the `#Const` directive is the source file in which the directive appears. However, if the constant is referenced prior to the definition, its value is `Nothing`. It is therefore best to define constants near the top of the file. Alternatively, compiler constants can be defined on the command line or within the Visual Studio .NET IDE. If you're compiling from the command line, use the `/define` compiler switch, like this:

```
vbc MySource.vb /define:DEBUG=True
```

You can set multiple constants within a single `/define` switch by separating the *`symbol=value`* pairs with commas, like this:

```
vbc MySource.vb /define:DEBUG=True,SOMECONSTANT=42
```

To assign compiler constants in Visual Studio .NET:

1. Right-click on the project name in the Solution Explorer window and choose Properties. This brings up the Project Property Pages dialog box. (If the Solution Explorer window is not visible, choose View→Solution Explorer from the Visual Studio .NET main menu to make it appear.)
2. Within the Project Property Pages dialog box, choose the Configuration Properties folder. Within that folder, choose the Build property page. This causes the configuration build options to appear on the right side of the dialog box.
3. Add values to the Custom constants text box on the right side of the dialog box.

Summary

This chapter provided an overview of the syntax of the Visual Basic .NET language. In Chapter 3, you'll learn about the .NET Framework—an integral part of developing in any .NET language. Subsequent chapters will teach you how to accomplish specific programming tasks in Visual Basic .NET.

CHAPTER 3

The .NET Framework

The .NET Framework is the next iteration of Microsoft's platform for developing component-based software. It provides fundamental advances in runtime services for application software. It also supports development of applications that can be free of dependencies on hardware, operating system, and language compiler.

This chapter provides an overview of the architecture of the .NET Framework and describes the base features found in the core of its class library.

Common Language Infrastructure (CLI) and Common Language Runtime (CLR)

At the heart of the .NET Framework is a new mechanism for loading and running programs and managing their interactions. This mechanism is described in the *Common Language Infrastructure* (CLI), a specification for a runtime environment that allows software components to:

- Pass data between each other without regard to the programming language in which each component is written
- Execute on different operating systems and on different hardware platforms without having to recompile the high-level source code (a low-level compilation still automatically occurs on the target platform, as will be discussed in this chapter)

Although the CLI specification was created by Microsoft, it has since been submitted to the *ECMA* standards organization (*http://www.ecma.ch*), which now has responsibility and control over it.

The CLI is just a specification—it has to be implemented in order to be useful. An implementation of the CLI is known as a *Common Language Runtime* (CLR). Microsoft's CLR implementation on the Windows platform is not under ECMA's control, but it is Microsoft's intention that the CLR be a fully compliant implementation of the CLI. As of this writing, the CLI has not been implemented on non-Windows platforms, but Microsoft and others have announced intentions to do so.

The CLI specifies how executable code is loaded, run, and managed. The portion of the CLR that performs the tasks of loading, running, and managing .NET applications is called the *virtual execution system* (VES). Code run by the VES is called *managed code*.

The CLI greatly expands upon concepts that exist in Microsoft's *Component Object Model* (COM). As its core feature, COM specifies how object interfaces are laid out in memory. Any component that can create and consume this layout can share data with other components that do the same. COM was a big step forward when it was introduced (circa 1992), but it has its shortcomings. For example, in spite of its name, COM actually has no concept of an object—only object interfaces. Therefore, COM can't support passing native types from one component to another.

Common Type System (CTS)

The CLI specification defines a rich type system that far surpasses COM's capabilities. It's called the *Common Type System* (CTS). The CTS defines at the runtime level how types are declared and used. Previously, language compilers controlled the creation and usage of types, including their layout in memory. This led to problems when a component written in one language tried to pass data to a component written in a different language. Anyone who has written Visual Basic 6 code to call Windows API functions, for instance, or who has tried to pass a JavaScript array to a component written either in Visual Basic 6 or C++, is aware of this problem. It was up to the developer to translate the data to be understandable to the receiving component. The CTS obliterates this problem by providing the following features:

- Primitive types (Integer, String, etc.) are defined at the runtime level. Components can easily pass instances of primitive types between each other because they all agree on how that data is formatted.
- Complex types (structures, classes, enumerations, etc.) are constructed in a way that is defined at the runtime level. Components can easily pass instances of complex types between each other because they all agree on how complex types are constructed from primitive types.
- All types carry rich type information with them, meaning that a component that is handed an object can find out the definition of the type of which the object is an instance. This is analogous to type libraries in COM, but the CTS is different because the type information is much richer and is guaranteed to be present.

Namespaces

Namespaces were introduced in Chapter 2 as a way to group related types. They are mentioned again here because they aren't just a Visual Basic .NET concept; they are also used by the CLR and by other languages that target the .NET platform. It's important to keep in mind that to the CLR, a namespace is just part of a fully qualified type name, and nothing more. See "Comparison of Assemblies, Modules, and Namespaces" later in this chapter for more information.

Portions of the CLI

The CLI specification recognizes that the CLR can't be implemented to the same extent on all platforms. For example, the version of the CLR implemented on a cell phone won't be as versatile as the one implemented on Windows 2000 or Windows XP. To address this issue, the CLI defines a set of *libraries*. Each library contains a set of classes that implement a certain portion of the CLI's functionality. Further, the CLI defines *profiles*. A profile is a set of libraries that must be implemented on a given platform.

The libraries defined by the CLI are:

Runtime Infrastructure Library
: This library provides the core services that are needed to compile and run an application that targets the CLI.

Base Class Library
: This library provides the runtime services that are needed by most modern programming languages. Among other things, the primitive data types are defined in this library.

Network Library
: This library provides simple networking services.

Reflection Library
: This library provides the ability to examine type information at runtime and to invoke members of types by supplying the member name at runtime, rather than at compile time.

XML Library
: This library provides a simple XML parser.

Floating Point Library
: This library provides support for floating point types and operations.

Extended Array Library
: This library provides support for multidimensional arrays.

The profiles defined by the CLI at this time are:

Kernel Profile
: This profile defines the minimal functionality of any system claimed as an implementation of the CLI. CLRs that conform to the Kernel Profile must implement the Base Class Library and the Runtime Infrastructure Library.

Compact Profile
: This profile includes the functionality of the Kernel Profile, plus the Network Library, the Reflection Library, and the XML Library. It is intended that an implementation of the Compact Profile can be lightweight, yet provide enough functionality to be useful.

Additional profiles will be defined in future versions of the CLI specification. Any given implementation of the CLI is free to implement more than the functionality specified by these minimal profiles. For example, a given implementation could support the Compact Profile but also support the Floating Point Library. The .NET Framework on Windows 2000 supports all the CLI libraries, plus additional libraries not defined by the CLI.

Note that the CLI does not include such major class libraries as Windows Forms, ASP.NET, and ADO.NET. These are Microsoft-specific class libraries for developing applications on Windows platforms. Applications that depend on these libraries will not be portable to other implementations of the CLI unless Microsoft makes those class libraries available on those other implementations.

Modules and Assemblies

A *module* is an *.exe* or *.dll* file. An *assembly* is a set of one or more modules that together make up an application. If the application is fully contained in an *.exe* file, fine—that's a one-module assembly. If the *.exe* is always deployed with two *.dll* files and one thinks of all three files as comprising an insepa rable unit, then the three modules together form an assembly, but none of them does so by itself. If the product is a class library that exists in a *.dll* file, then that single *.dll* file is an assembly. To put it in Microsoft's terms, the assembly is the unit of deployment in .NET.

An assembly is more than just an abstract way to think about sets of modules. When an assembly is deployed, one (and only one) of the modules in the assembly must contain the *assembly manifest*, which contains information about the assembly as a whole, including the list of modules contained in the assembly, the version of the assembly, its culture, etc. The command-line compiler and the Visual Studio .NET compiler create single-module assemblies by default. Multiple-module assemblies are not used in this book.

Assembly boundaries affect type resolution. When a source file is compiled, the compiler must resolve type names used in the file to the types' definitions. For types that are defined in the same source project, the compiler gets the definitions from the code it is compiling. For types that are defined elsewhere, the compiler must be told where to find the definitions. This is done by referencing the assemblies that contain the compiled type definitions. When the command-line compiler is used, the `/reference` switch identifies assemblies containing types used in the project being compiled. An assembly has the same name as the module that contains the assembly manifest, except for the file extension. In some cases, however, an assembly is specified by giving the full name of the module that contains the assembly manifest. For example, to compile an application that uses the System.Drawing.Point class, you could use the following command line:

```
vbc MySource.vb /reference:System.Drawing.dll
```

The documentation for the command-line compiler states that the argument to the reference switch is an assembly. This is not quite accurate. The argument is the name of the module that contains the assembly manifest for an assembly.

If more than one assembly needs to be referenced, you can list them all in the same `/reference` switch, separated by commas, like this:

```
vbc MySource.vb /reference:System.Drawing.dll,System.Windows.Forms.dll
```

The Visual Basic .NET command-line compiler automatically references two assemblies: *mscorlib.dll*, which contains most of the types found in the System namespace; and *Microsoft.VisualBasic.dll*, which contains the types found in the Microsoft.VisualBasic namespace.

When you're working within the Visual Studio .NET IDE, external assemblies are referenced by doing the following:

1. In the Solution Explorer window, right-click on References, then click on Add Reference. The Add Reference dialog box appears, as shown in Figure 3-1.
2. Scroll down to find the desired assembly.
3. Double-click or highlight the assembly name, and press the Select button. The assembly name appears in the Selected Components frame of the dialog box.
4. Select additional assemblies, or click OK.

Global Assembly Cache (GAC)

By default, assemblies are not shared. When one assembly is dependent on another, the two assemblies are typically deployed into a single application directory. This makes it easy to install and remove an application. To install an application, simply create the application directory and copy the files into it. To delete the application, just delete the application directory. The Windows Registry is not used at all.

If an assembly must be shared among more than one program, either it can be copied into each appropriate application directory or it can be installed into the *global assembly cache* (GAC). The GAC is an area on disk (typically, it's the *assembly* subdirectory of the Windows directory) that holds assemblies to be shared among all applications. All of the .NET Framework assemblies reside in the GAC. (See Figure 3-2 for a partial view of the assemblies in a typical GAC.) Placing an assembly into the GAC should be avoided if possible: it makes application installation and removal more difficult. This is because the Windows Installer or *gacutil.exe* must be

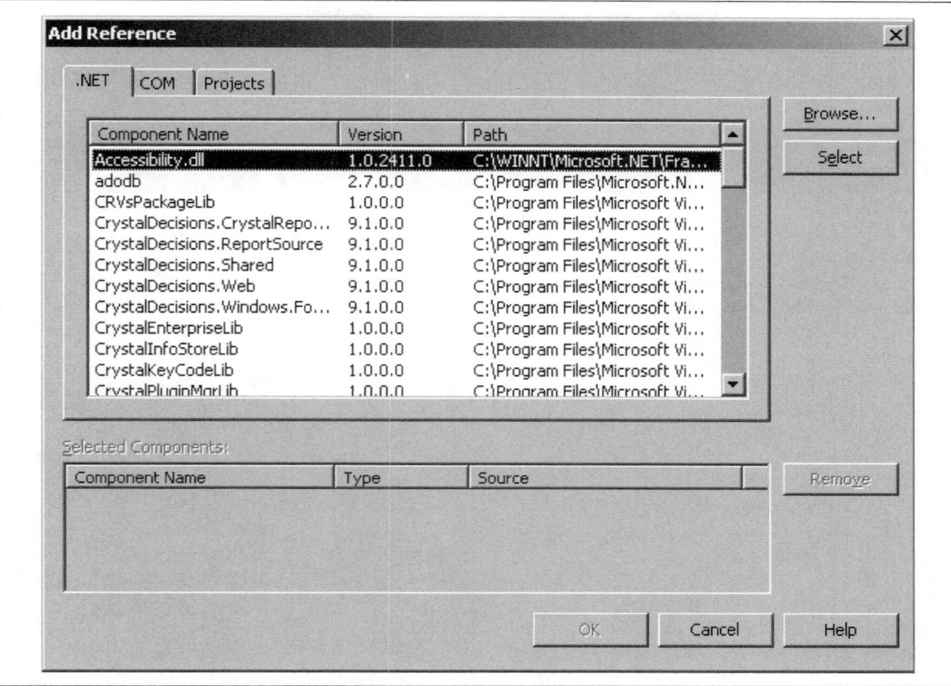

Figure 3-1. The Add Reference dialog box

used to manipulate the GAC—you can no longer simply copy or remove the application directory. Installing assemblies into the GAC is not covered in this book. For information, point your browser to *http://msdn.microsoft.com* and perform a search for "Deploying Shared Components."

Comparison of Assemblies, Modules, and Namespaces

It's easy to confuse the three concepts of *namespace*, *module*, and *assembly*. Here is a recap:

Namespace
: A portion of a type name. Specifically, it is the portion that precedes the final period in a fully qualified type name.

Module
: A file that contains executable code (*.exe* or *.dll*).

Assembly
: A set of one or more modules that are deployed as a unit. The assembly name is the same as the name of the module that contains the assembly manifest, minus the filename extension.

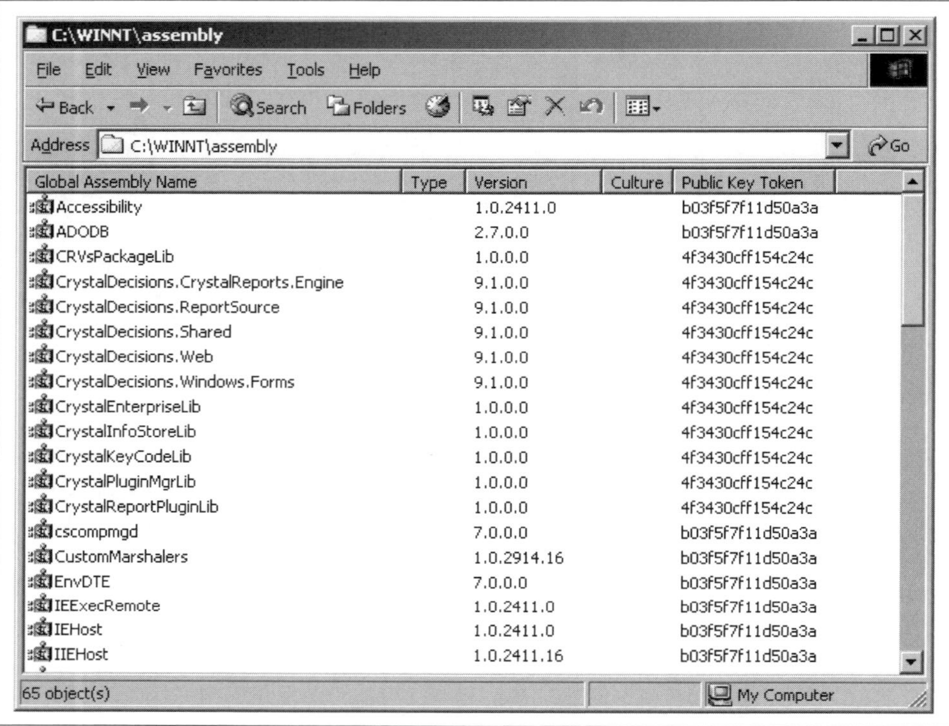

Figure 3-2. Partial view of a typical GAC

Depending on how things are named, it can seem like these three terms are interchangeable. For example, *System.Drawing.dll* is the name of a module that is deployed as part of the .NET Framework. As it happens, this module is part of a single-module assembly. Because assemblies are named after the module that contains the assembly manifest, the assembly is called System.Drawing. A compiler will reference this assembly as *System.Drawing.dll*. Many (but not all) of the types in this assembly have a namespace of System.Drawing. (Other types in the System.Drawing assembly have namespaces of System.Drawing.Design, System.Drawing.Drawing2D, System.Drawing.Imaging, System.Drawing.Printing, and System.Drawing.Text.) Note that even though the namespace, module, and assembly are similarly named in this case, they are distinct concepts. Note in particular that importing a namespace and referencing an assembly are different operations with different purposes. The statement:

```
Imports System.Drawing
```

allows the developer to avoid typing the fully qualified names of the types in the System.Drawing namespace. It does *not* reference the assembly in which those types are defined. To use the types, the System.Drawing assembly (contained in the *System.Drawing.dll* module) must be referenced as described earlier in this section. The `Imports` statement was introduced in Chapter 2.

In other cases, namespace and assembly names *don't* correspond. One example is the System namespace. Some types with this namespace are found in the mscorlib assembly, and others are found in the System assembly. In addition, each of those assemblies has types with other namespaces. For example, the System assembly contains types with the Microsoft.VisualBasic namespace, even though most of the types with that namespace are found in the Microsoft.VisualBasic assembly. (The reason for this apparent inconsistency is actually quite sound. Namespaces group types according to functionality, while assemblies tend to group types according to which types are most likely to be used together. This improves performance because it minimizes the number of assemblies that have to be loaded at runtime.)

When thinking about namespaces, just remember that types can have any namespace at all, regardless of where they're defined—the namespace is just part of the type name.

Application Domains

Application domains are to the CLR what processes are to an operating system. It may be surprising to note that the CLR can run multiple .NET applications within a single process, without any contention or security difficulties. Because the CLR has complete control over loading and executing programs, and because of the presence of type information, the CLR guarantees that .NET applications cannot read or write each other's memory, even when running in the same process. Because there is less performance overhead in switching between application domains than in switching between processes, this provides a performance gain. This is especially beneficial to web applications running in Internet Information Services (IIS), where scalability is an issue.

Common Language Specification (CLS)

The CLI defines a runtime that is capable of supporting most, if not all, of the features found in modern programming languages. It is not intended that all languages that target the CLR will support all CLR features. This could cause problems when components written in different languages attempt to interoperate. The CLI therefore defines a subset of features that are considered compatible across language boundaries. This subset is called the *Common Language Specification* (CLS).

Vendors creating components for use by others need to ensure that all externally visible constructs (e.g., public types, public and protected methods, parameters on public and protected methods, etc.) are CLS-compliant. This ensures that their components will be usable within a broad array of languages, including Visual Basic . NET. Developers authoring components in Visual Basic .NET have an easy job because all Visual Basic .NET code is CLS-compliant (unless the developer explicitly exposes a public or protected type member or method parameter that is of a non-CLS-compliant type).

Because Visual Basic .NET automatically generates CLS-compliant components, this book does not describe the CLS rules. However, to give you a sense of the kind of thing that the CLS specifies, consider that some languages support a feature called *operator overloading*. This allows the developer to specify actions that should be taken if the standard operator symbols (+, -, *, /, =, etc.) are used on user-defined classes. Because it is not reasonable to expect that all languages should implement such a feature, the CLS has a rule about it. The rule states that if a CLS-compliant component has public types that provide overloaded operators, those types must provide access to that functionality in another way as well (usually by providing a public method that performs the same operation).

Intermediate Language (IL) and Just-In-Time (JIT) Compilation

All compilers that target the CLR compile source code to *Intermediate Language* (IL), also known as *Common Intermediate Language* (CIL). IL is a machine language that is not tied to any specific machine. Microsoft designed it from scratch to support the CLI's programming concepts. The CLI specifies that all CLR implementations can compile or interpret IL on the machine on which the CLR is running. If the IL is compiled (versus interpreted), compilation can occur at either of two times:

- Immediately prior to a method in the application being executed
- At deployment time

In the first case, each method is compiled only when it is actually needed. After the method is compiled, subsequent calls bypass the compilation mechanism and call the compiled code directly. The compiled code is not saved to disk, so if the application is stopped and restarted, the compilation must occur again. This is known as *just-in-time* (JIT) compilation and is the most common scenario.

In the second case, the application is compiled in its entirety at deployment time.

IL is saved to *.exe* and *.dll* files. When such a file containing IL is executed, the CLR knows how to invoke the JIT compiler and execute the resulting code.

Note that on the Microsoft Windows platforms, IL is always compiled—never interpreted.

Metadata

Source code consists of some constructs that are *procedural* in nature and others that are *declarative* in nature. An example of a procedural construct is:

```
someObject.SomeMember = 5
```

This is procedural because it compiles into executable code that performs an action at runtime. Namely, it assigns the value 5 to the SomeMember member of the someObject object.

In contrast, here is a declarative construct:

```
Dim someObject As SomeClass
```

This is declarative because it doesn't perform an action. It states that the symbol someObject is a variable that holds a reference to an object of type SomeClass.

In the past, declarative information typically was used only by the compiler and did not compile directly into the executable. In the CLR, however, declarative information is everything! The CLR uses type and signature information to ensure that memory is always referenced in a safe way. The JIT compiler uses type and signature information to resolve method calls to the appropriate target code at JIT compile time. The only way for this to work is for this declarative information to be included alongside its associated procedural information. Compilers that target the CLR therefore store both procedural and declarative information in the resulting *.exe* or *.dll* file. The procedural information is stored as IL, and the declarative information is stored as *metadata*. Metadata is just the CLI's name for declarative information.

The CLI has a mechanism that allows programmers to include arbitrary metadata in compiled applications. This mechanism is known as *custom attributes* and is available in Visual Basic .NET. Custom attributes were discussed in detail in Chapter 2.

Memory Management and Garbage Collection

In any object-oriented programming environment, there arises the need to instantiate and destroy objects. Instantiated objects occupy memory. When objects are no longer in use, the memory they occupy should be reclaimed for use by other objects. Recognizing when objects are no longer being used is called *lifetime management*, which is not a trivial problem. The solution the CLR uses has implications for the design and use of the components you write, so it is worth understanding.

In the COM world, the client of an object notified the object whenever a new object reference was passed to another client. Conversely, when any client of an object was finished with it, the client notified the object of that fact. The object kept track of how many clients had references to it. When that count dropped to zero, the object was free to delete itself (that is, give its memory back to the memory heap). This method of lifetime management is known as *reference counting*. Visual Basic programmers were not necessarily aware of this mechanism because the Visual Basic compiler automatically generated the low-level code to perform this housekeeping. C++ developers had no such luxury.

Reference counting has some drawbacks:

- A method call is required every time an object reference is copied from one variable to another and every time an object reference is overwritten.
- Difficult-to-track bugs can be introduced if the reference-counting rules are not precisely followed.
- Care must be taken to ensure that circular references are specially treated (because circular references can result in objects that never go away).

The CLR mechanism for lifetime management is quite different. Reference counting is not used. Instead, the memory manager keeps a pointer to the address at which free memory (known as the *heap*) starts. To satisfy a memory request, it just hands back a copy of the pointer and then increments the pointer by the size of the request, leaving it in a position to satisfy the next memory request. This makes memory allocation very fast. No action is taken at all when an object is no longer being used. As long as the heap doesn't run out, memory is not reclaimed until the application exits. If the heap is large enough to satisfy all memory requests during program execution, this method of memory allocation is as fast as is theoretically possible, because the only overhead is incrementing the heap pointer on memory allocations.

If the heap runs out of memory, there is more work to do. To satisfy a memory request when the heap is exhausted, the memory manager looks for any previously allocated memory that can be reclaimed. It does this by examining the application variables that hold object references. The objects that these variables reference (and therefore the associated memory) are considered in use because they can be reached through the program's variables. Furthermore, because the runtime has complete access to the application's type information, the memory manager knows whether the objects contain members that reference other objects, and so on. In this way, the memory manager can find all of the memory that is in use. During this process, it consolidates the contents of all this memory into one contiguous block at the start of the heap, leaving the remainder of the heap free to satisfy new memory requests. This process of freeing up memory is known as *garbage collection* (GC), a term that also applies to this overall method of lifetime management. The portion of the memory manager that performs garbage collection is called the *garbage collector*.

The benefits of garbage collection are:

- No overhead is incurred unless the heap becomes exhausted.
- It is impossible for applications to cause memory leaks.
- The application need not be careful with circular references.

Although the process of garbage collection is expensive (on the order of a fraction of a second when it occurs), Microsoft claims that the total overhead of garbage collection is on average much less than the total overhead of reference counting (as shown by their benchmarks). This, of course, is highly dependent on the exact pattern of object allocation and deallocation that occurs in any given program.

Finalize

Many objects require some sort of cleanup (i.e., *finalization*) when they are destroyed. An example might be a business object that maintains a connection to a database. When the object is no longer in use, its database connection should be released. The .NET Framework provides a way for objects to be notified when they are about to be released, thus permitting them to release nonmemory resources. (Memory resources held by the object can be ignored because they will be handled automatically by the garbage collector.) Here's how it works: the Object class (defined in the System namespace) has a method called Finalize that can be overridden. Its default implementation does nothing. If it is overridden in a derived class, however, the garbage collector automatically calls it on an instance of that class when that instance is about to be reclaimed. Here's an example of overriding the Finalize method:

```
Public Class SomeClass
   Protected Overrides Sub Finalize( )
      ' Release nonmanaged resources here.
      MyBase.Finalize( ) ' Important
   End Sub
End Class
```

The Finalize method should release any nonmanaged resources that the object has allocated. *Nonmanaged resources* are any resources other than memory (for example, database connections, file handles, or other OS handles). In contrast, *managed resources* are object references. As already mentioned, it is not necessary to release managed resources in a Finalize method—the garbage collector will handle it. After releasing resources allocated by the class, the Finalize method must always call the base class's Finalize implementation so that it can release any resources allocated by base-class code. If the class is derived directly from the Object class, technically this could be omitted (because the Object class's Finalize method doesn't do anything). However, calling it doesn't hurt anything, and it's a good habit to get into.

An object's Finalize method should not be called by application code. The Finalize method has special meaning to the CLR and is intended to be called only by the garbage collector. If you're familiar with *destructors* in C++, you'll recognize that the Finalize method is the identical concept. The only difference between the Finalize method and C++ destructors is that C++ destructors automatically call their base class destructors, whereas in Visual Basic .NET, the programmer must remember to put in the call to the base class's Finalize method. It is interesting to note that C#—another language on the .NET platform—actually has destructors (as C++ does), but they are automatically compiled into Finalize methods that work as described here.

Dispose

The downside of garbage collection and the Finalize method is the loss of *deterministic finalization*. With reference counting, finalization occurs as soon as the last reference to an object is released (this is *deterministic* because object finalization is controlled by program flow). In contrast, an object in a garbage-collected system is not destroyed until garbage collection occurs or until the application exits. This is *nondeterministic* because the program has no control over when it happens. This is a problem because an object that holds scarce resources (such as a database connection) should free those resources as soon as the object is no longer needed. If this is not done, the program may run out of such resources long before it runs out of memory.

Unfortunately, no one has discovered an elegant solution to this problem. Microsoft does have a recommendation, however. Objects that hold nonmanaged resources should implement the `IDisposable` interface (defined in the System namespace). The `IDisposable` interface exposes a single method, called Dispose, which takes no parameters and returns no result. Calling it tells the object that it is no longer needed. The object should respond by releasing all the resources it holds, both managed and nonmanaged, and should call the Dispose method on any subordinate objects that also expose the `IDisposable` interface. In this way, scarce resources are released as soon as they are no longer needed.

This solution requires that the user of an object keep track of when it is done with the object. This is often trivial, but if there are multiple users of an object, it may be difficult to know which user should call Dispose. At the time of this writing, it is simply up to the programmer to work this out. In a sense, the Dispose method is an alternate destructor to address the issue of nondeterministic finalization when nonmanaged resources are involved. However, the CLR itself never calls the Dispose method. It is up to the client of the object to call the Dispose method at the appropriate time, based on the client's knowledge of when it is done using the object. This implies responsibilities for both the class author and client author. The class author must document the presence of the Dispose method so that the client author knows that it's necessary to call it. The client author must make an effort to determine whether any given class has a Dispose method and, if so, to call it at the appropriate time.

Even when a class exposes the `IDisposable` interface, it should still override the Finalize method, just in case the client neglects to call the Dispose method. This ensures that nonmanaged resources are eventually released, even if the client forgets to do it. A simple (but incomplete) technique would be to place a call to the object's Dispose method in its Finalize method, like this:

```
' Incomplete solution. Don't do this.
Public Sub Dispose( ) Implements IDisposable.Dispose
   ' Release resources here.
End Sub

Protected Overrides Sub Finalize( )
   Dispose( )
   MyBase.Finalize( )
End Sub
```

In this way, if the client of the object neglects to call the Dispose method, the object itself will do so when the garbage collector destroys it. Microsoft recommends that the Dispose method be written so it is not an error to call it more than once. This way, even if the client calls it at the correct time, it's OK for it to be called again in the Finalize method.

If the object holds references to other objects that implement the `IDisposable` interface, the code just shown may cause a problem. This is because the order of object destruction is not guaranteed. Specifically, if the Finalize method is executing, it means that garbage collection is occurring. If the object holds references to other objects, the garbage collector may have already reclaimed those other objects. If the object attempts to call the Dispose method on a reclaimed object, an error will occur. This situation exists only during the call to Finalize—if the client calls the Dispose method, subordinate objects will still be there. (They can't have been reclaimed by the garbage collector because they are reachable from the application's code.)

To resolve this race condition, it is necessary to take slightly different action when finalizing than when disposing. Here is the modified code:

```
Public Sub Dispose( ) Implements IDisposable.Dispose
   DisposeManagedResources( )
   DisposeUnmanagedResources( )
End Sub

Protected Overrides Sub Finalize( )
   DisposeUnmanagedResources( )
   MyBase.Finalize( )
End Sub

Private Sub DisposeManagedResources( )
   ' Call subordinate objects' Dispose methods.
End Sub

Private Sub DisposeUnmanagedResources( )
   ' Release unmanaged resources, such as database connections.
End Sub
```

Here, the Finalize method only releases unmanaged resources. It doesn't worry about calling the Dispose method on any subordinate objects, assuming that if the subordinate objects are also unreachable, they will be reclaimed by the garbage collector and their finalizers (and hence their Dispose methods) will run.

An optimization can be made to the Dispose method. When the Dispose method is called by the client, there is no longer any reason for the Finalize method to be called when the object is destroyed. Keeping track of and calling objects' Finalize methods imposes overhead on the garbage collector. To remove this overhead for an object with its Dispose method called, the Dispose method should call the SuppressFinalize shared method of the GC class, like this:

```
Public Sub Dispose( ) Implements IDisposable.Dispose
   DisposeManagedResources( )
```

```
      DisposeUnmanagedResources( )
      GC.SuppressFinalize(Me)
   End Sub
```

The type designer must decide what will occur if the client attempts to use an object after calling its Dispose method. If possible, the object should automatically reacquire its resources. If this is not possible, the object should throw an exception. Example 3-1 shows the latter.

Example 3-1. A complete Finalize/Dispose example

```
Public Class SomeClass
   Implements IDisposable

   ' This member keeps track of whether the object has been disposed.
   Private disposed As Boolean = False

   ' The Dispose method releases the resources held by the object.
   ' It must be called by the client when the client no longer needs
   ' the object.
   Public Sub Dispose( ) Implements IDisposable.Dispose
      If Not disposed Then
         DisposeManagedResources( )
         DisposeUnmanagedResources( )
         GC.SuppressFinalize(Me)
         disposed = True
      End If
   End Sub

   ' The Finalize method releases nonmanaged resources in the case
   ' that the client neglected to call Dispose. Because of the
   ' SuppressFinalize call in the Dispose method, the Finalize method
   ' will be called only if the Dispose method is not called.
   Protected Overrides Sub Finalize( )
      DisposeUnmanagedResources( )
      MyBase.Finalize( )
   End Sub

   Private Sub DisposeManagedResources( )
      ' Call subordinate objects' Dispose methods.
   End Sub

   Private Sub DisposeUnmanagedResources( )
      ' Release unmanaged resources, such as database connections.
   End Sub

   Private Sub DoSomething( )
      ' Call the EnsureNotDisposed method at the top of every method that
      ' needs to access the resources held by the object.
      EnsureNotDisposed( )
      ' ...
   End Sub
```

Example 3-1. A complete Finalize/Dispose example (continued)

```
   Private Sub EnsureNotDisposed( )
      ' Make sure that the object hasn't been disposed.
      ' Instead of throwing an exception, this method could be written
      ' to reacquire the resources that are needed by the object.
      If disposed Then
         Throw New ObjectDisposedException(Me.GetType( ).Name)
      End If
   End Sub

End Class
```

A Brief Tour of the .NET Framework Namespaces

The .NET Framework provides a huge class library—something on the order of 6,000 types. To help developers navigate though the huge hierarchy of types, Microsoft has divided them into namespaces. However, even the number of namespaces can be daunting. Here are the most common namespaces and an overview of what they contain:

Microsoft.VisualBasic
: Runtime support for applications written in Visual Basic .NET. This namespace contains the functions and procedures included in the Visual Basic .NET language.

Microsoft.Win32
: Types that access the Windows Registry and provide access to system events (such as low memory, changed display settings, and user logout).

System
: Core system types, including:

  - Implementations for Visual Basic .NET's fundamental types (see "Types" in Chapter 2 for a list of fundamental types and the .NET classes that implement them).
  - Common custom attributes used throughout the .NET Framework class library (see Appendix A), as well as the Attribute class, which is the base class for most (although not all) custom attributes in .NET applications.
  - Common exceptions used throughout the .NET Framework class library (see Appendix B), as well as the Exception class, which is the base class for all exceptions in .NET applications.
  - The Array class, which is the base class from which all Visual Basic .NET arrays implicitly inherit.
  - The Convert class, which contains methods for converting values between various types.

- The Enum class, from which all enumerations implicitly derive.
- The Delegate class, from which all delegates implicitly derive.
- The Math class, which has many shared methods for performing common mathematical functions (e.g., Abs, Min, Max, Sin, and Cos). This class also defines two constant fields, E and PI, that give the values of the numbers `e` and `pi`, respectively, within the precision of the Double data type.
- The Random class, for generating pseudorandom numbers.
- The Version class, which encapsulates version information for .NET assemblies.

System.CodeDom
: Types for automatically generating source code (used by tools such as the wizards in Visual Studio .NET and by the ASP.NET page compiler).

System.Collections
: Types for managing collections, including:

  ArrayList
  : Indexed like a single-dimensional array and iterated like an array, but much more flexible than an array. With an ArrayList, it is possible to add elements without having to worry about the size of the list (the list grows automatically as needed), insert and remove elements anywhere in the list, find an element's index given its value, and sort the elements in the list.

  BitArray
  : Represents an array of bits. Each element can have a value of `True` or `False`. The BitArray class defines a number of bitwise operators that operate on the entire array at once.

  Hashtable
  : Represents a collection of key/value pairs. Both the key and value can be any object.

  Queue
  : Represents a queue, which is a *first-in-first-out* (FIFO) list.

  SortedList
  : Like a Hashtable, represents a collection of key/value pairs. When enumerated, however, the items are returned in sorted key order. In addition, items can be retrieved by index, which the Hashtable cannot do. Not surprisingly, SortedList operations can be slower than comparable Hashtable operations because of the increased work that must be done to keep the structure in sorted order.

  Stack
  : Represents a stack, which is a *last-in-first-out* (LIFO) list.

Be aware that in addition to these types, there is also the Array type, defined in the System namespace, and the Collection type, defined in the Microsoft.Visual-

Basic namespace. The latter is a collection type that mimics the behavior of Visual Basic 6 collection objects.

System.ComponentModel
: Support for building components that can be added to Windows Forms and Web Forms.

System.Configuration
: Support for reading and writing program configuration.

System.Data
: Support for data access. The types in this namespace constitute ADO.NET.

System.Diagnostics
: Support for debugging and tracing.

System.Drawing
: Graphics-drawing support.

System.EnterpriseServices
: Transaction-processing support.

System.Globalization
: Internationalization support.

System.IO
: Support for reading and writing streams and files.

System.Net
: Support for communicating over networks, including the Internet.

System.Reflection
: Support for runtime type discovery.

System.Resources
: Support for reading and writing program resources.

System.Security
: Support for accessing and manipulating security information.

System.ServiceProcess
: Types for implementing system services.

System.Text
: Types for manipulating text and strings.

  Note in particular the StringBuilder type. When strings are built from smaller parts, the methods on the StringBuilder class are more efficient than similar methods on the String class. This is because the instances of the String class can't be modified in place; every time a change is made to a String object, a new String object is actually created to hold the new value. In contrast, the methods in StringBuilder that modify the string actually modify the string in place.

System.Threading
: Support for multithreaded programming.

System.Timers
: Provides the Timer class, which can generate an event at predetermined intervals. This addresses one of the limitations of the Visual Basic 6 Timer control: it had to be hosted in a container and therefore could be used only in an application with a user interface.

System.Web
: Support for building web applications. The types in this namespace constitute Web Forms and ASP.NET.

System.Windows.Forms
: Support for building GUI (fat client) applications. The types in this namespace constitute Windows Forms.

System.Xml
: Support for parsing, generating, transmitting, and receiving XML.

Configuration

System and application configuration is managed by XML files with a *.config* extension. Configuration files exist at both the machine and application level. There is a single machine-level configuration file, located at *runtime_install_path\CONFIG\machine.config*. For example, *C:\WINNT\Microsoft.NET\Framework\v1.0.2914\CONFIG\machine.config*. Application-configuration files are optional. When they exist, they reside in the application's root folder and are named *application_file_name.config*. For example, *myApplication.exe.config*. Web application–configuration files are always named *web.config*. They can exist in the web application's root folder and in subfolders of the application. Settings in subfolders' configuration files apply only to pages retrieved from the same folder and its child folders and override settings from configuration files in higher-level folders.

Configuration files should be used for all application-configuration information; the Windows Registry should no longer be used for application settings.

Configuration File Format

Configuration files are XML documents, where the root element is `<configuration>`. For example:

```
<?xml version="1.0" encoding="UTF-8"?>

<configuration>
   <!-- More stuff goes in here. -->
</configuration>
```

To be as flexible as possible, .NET configuration files use a scheme in which the application developer can decide on the names of the subelements within the `<configuration>` element. This is done using the `<configSections>`, `<section>`, and

<sectionGroup> elements. Example 3-2 shows how this is done using the <configSections> and <section> elements; the <sectionGroup> element is discussed later in this section.

Example 3-2. Defining a section in a configuration file

```
<?xml version="1.0" encoding="UTF-8"?>

<configuration>

   <configSections>
      <section
         name="mySectionName"
         type="System.Configuration.SingleTagSectionHandler" />
   </configSections>

   <mySectionName
      someSetting="SomeValue"
      anotherSetting="AnotherValue" />

</configuration>
```

The name attribute of the <section> element specifies the name of an element that will (or could) appear later in the file. The type attribute specifies the name of a *configuration section handler*, which is a class that knows how to read an XML section that's formatted in a particular way. The .NET Framework provides stock configuration section handlers (notably the SingleTagSectionHandler and the NameValueSectionHandler classes, both of which will be discussed later in this section), which are sufficient for the majority of cases. Although it's beyond the scope of this book, a custom configuration section handler can be created by writing a class that implements the IConfigurationSectionHandler interface.

The SingleTagSectionHandler configuration section handler reads XML sections that are of the form:

```
<sectionName key1Name="Value1" key2Name="Value2" etc... />
```

The element can contain any number of key/value pairs.

The configuration section handler class is not used directly in code. To read information from an application's configuration file, use the GetConfig method in the ConfigurationSettings class (defined in the System.Configuration namespace). The syntax of the GetConfig method is:

```
Public Shared Function GetConfig(ByVal sectionName As String) As Object
```

Here's how the mechanism works (an example will follow):

1. The application calls the GetConfig method, passing it the name of the configuration section that is to be read.
2. Internally, the GetConfig method instantiates the configuration section handler class that is appropriate for reading that section. (Recall that it is the values

found in the <configSections> portion of the configuration file that identify the appropriate configuration section handler class to use.)

3. The Create method of the configuration section handler is called and is passed the XML from the requested configuration section.
4. The configuration section handler's Create method returns an object containing the values read from the configuration section.
5. The object returned from the Create method is passed back to the caller of the GetConfig method.

The type of object returned from GetConfig is determined by the specific configuration section handler that handles the given configuration section. The caller of the GetConfig method must have enough information about the configuration section handler to know how to use the object that is returned. Two stock configuration section handlers—and the objects they create—will be discussed in this section.

Example 3-3 shows how to read the configuration file shown in Example 3-2. To run this example, do the following:

1. Create a new directory for the application.
2. Save the code from Example 3-3 into a file named *ConfigurationTest.vb*.
3. Compile the code with this command line:

   ```
   vbc ConfigurationTest.vb /reference:System.dll
   ```

   The reference to the System assembly is required because the System assembly contains the definition of the ConfigurationSettings class.

   The compiler creates an executable file named *ConfigurationTest.exe*.
4. Save the configuration file from Example 3-2 into a file named *ConfigurationTest.exe.config*. Run the executable from the command prompt. The application prints the configuration values to the command window.

Example 3-3. Reading the configuration file shown in Example 3-2

```
Imports System
Imports System.Collections
Imports System.Configuration

Public Module SomeModule

   Public Sub Main( )

      Dim cfg As Hashtable
      Dim strSomeSetting As String
      Dim strAnotherSetting As String

      cfg = CType(ConfigurationSettings.GetConfig("mySectionName"), _
         Hashtable)
      If Not (cfg Is Nothing) Then
         strSomeSetting = CType(cfg("someSetting"), String)
         strAnotherSetting = CType(cfg("anotherSetting"), String)
```

Example 3-3. Reading the configuration file shown in Example 3-2 (continued)

```
      End If

      Console.WriteLine(strSomeSetting)
      Console.WriteLine(strAnotherSetting)

   End Sub

End Module
```

To read the configuration settings, the code in Example 3-3 calls the GetConfig method of the ConfigurationSettings class. The SingleTagSectionHandler configuration section handler creates a Hashtable object (defined in the System.Collections namespace) to hold the key/value pairs found in the configuration file. That is why the code in Example 3-3 calls the *CType* function to convert the reference returned by the GetConfig method to a Hashtable reference. After that is done, the code can do anything appropriate for a Hashtable object, including retrieving specific values by key (as shown in Example 3-3) or iterating through the Hashtable object's items. Also note that because Hashtable objects store values of type Object, the object references retrieved from the Hashtable have to be converted to the appropriate reference type, which in this case is String. The Visual Basic *CStr* function could have been used here, although in this case the Visual Basic *CType* function is called instead.

The application does not specify the name of the configuration file in which to look for the configuration information. The system automatically looks in the *application_file_name.config* file found in the application's directory. If the requested section is not found in that file, the system automatically looks for it in the machine-configuration file.

Another stock configuration section handler is the NameValueSectionHandler class. This handler also reads key/value pairs, but in a different format. Example 3-4 is the same as Example 3-2, but rewritten to use NameValueSectionHandler.

Example 3-4. Using the NameValueSectionHandler configuration section handler

```
<?xml version="1.0" encoding="UTF-8"?>

<configuration>

   <configSections>
      <section
         name="mySectionName"
         type="System.Configuration.NameValueSectionHandler" />
   </configSections>

   <mySectionName>
      <add key="someSetting" value="SomeValue" />
      <add key="anotherSetting" value="AnotherValue" />
   </mySectionName>

</configuration>
```

Example 3-5 shows the code that reads this configuration section.

Example 3-5. Reading the configuration file shown in Example 3-4

```
Imports System
Imports System.Collections.Specialized
Imports System.Configuration

Public Module SomeModule

   Public Sub Main( )

      Dim cfg As NameValueCollection
      Dim strSomeSetting As String
      Dim strAnotherSetting As String

      cfg = CType(ConfigurationSettings.GetConfig("mySectionName"), _
         NameValueCollection)
      If Not (cfg Is Nothing) Then
         strSomeSetting = CType(cfg("someSetting"), String)
         strAnotherSetting = CType(cfg("anotherSetting"), String)
      End If

      Console.WriteLine(strSomeSetting)
      Console.WriteLine(strAnotherSetting)

   End Sub

End Module
```

The main difference to note in Example 3-5 is that the NameValueSectionHandler creates an object of type NameValueCollection (defined in the System.Collections. Specialized namespace).

Configuration Section Groups

If application-configuration information is to be stored in the machine-configuration file, it is a good idea to introduce *configuration section groups* into the picture. (Recall that if the runtime doesn't find the requested section in the application-configuration file, it automatically looks for it in the machine-configuration file.) This simply groups an application's settings into an enclosing group element in the configuration file, so that the contained elements won't potentially conflict with like-named elements for other applications. Example 3-6 shows how to introduce a section group. It is identical to the configuration file shown in Example 3-2, except that a section group is defined.

Example 3-6. Creating a section group

```
<?xml version="1.0" encoding="UTF-8"?>

<configuration>
```

Example 3-6. Creating a section group (continued)

```
   <configSections>
      <sectionGroup name="myGroupName">
         <section
            name="mySectionName"
            type="System.Configuration.SingleTagSectionHandler" />
      </sectionGroup>
   </configSections>

   <myGroupName>
      <mySectionName
         someSetting="SomeValue"
         anotherSetting="AnotherValue" />
   </myGroupName>

</configuration>
```

Example 3-7 shows how to read this configuration file in code.

Example 3-7. Reading the configuration file shown in Example 3-6

```
Imports System
Imports System.Collections
Imports System.Configuration

Public Module SomeModule

   Public Sub Main( )

      Dim cfg As Hashtable
      Dim strSomeSetting As String
      Dim strAnotherSetting As String

      cfg = CType( _
         ConfigurationSettings.GetConfig("myGroupName/mySectionName"), _
         Hashtable)
      If Not (cfg Is Nothing) Then
         strSomeSetting = CType(cfg("someSetting"), String)
         strAnotherSetting = CType(cfg("anotherSetting"), String)
      End If

      Console.WriteLine(strSomeSetting)
      Console.WriteLine(strAnotherSetting)

   End Sub

End Module
```

The only difference between Example 3-7 and Example 3-3 is the path-style syntax in Example 3-7 used to specify the section name: `"myGroupName/mySectionName"`. Group definitions can be nested, if desired.

The <appSettings> Section

Most applications just need a simple way to store key/value pairs. To support this, the *machine.config* file contains a predefined section definition called <appSettings>. It is always legal to include an <appSettings> section in any configuration file. The configuration section handler for the <appSettings> section is the NameValueSectionHandler class, so the section should be in this form:

```
<appSettings>
   <add key="setting1" value="value1" />
   <add key="setting2" value="value2" />
   <add key="setting3" value="value3" />
</appSettings>
```

Although the <appSettings> section can be read using the GetConfig method just like any other section, the ConfigurationSettings class has a property that is specifically intended to assist with reading the <appSettings> section. The read-only AppSettings property of the ConfigurationSettings class returns a NameValueCollection object that contains the key/value pairs found in the <appSettings> section. Example 3-8 shows how to read the settings shown in the previous code listing.

Example 3-8. Reading the <appSettings> section

```
Imports System
Imports System.Collections.Specialized
Imports System.Configuration

Public Module SomeModule

   Public Sub Main( )

      Dim cfg As NameValueCollection
      Dim strSetting1 As String
      Dim strSetting2 As String
      Dim strSetting3 As String

      cfg = CType(ConfigurationSettings.AppSettings, NameValueCollection)
      If Not (cfg Is Nothing) Then
         strSetting1 = CType(cfg("setting1"), String)
         strSetting2 = CType(cfg("setting2"), String)
         strSetting3 = CType(cfg("setting3"), String)
      End If

      Console.WriteLine(strSetting1)
      Console.WriteLine(strSetting2)
      Console.WriteLine(strSetting3)

   End Sub

End Module
```

The name/value pairs in the `<appSettings>` section are developer-defined. The CLR doesn't attribute any intrinsic meaning to any particular name/value pair.

Summary

The .NET Framework is a broad and deep new foundation for application development. At its core is a runtime that provides services that were previously found in compiler libraries. This runtime eliminates the application's need to possess knowledge of the underlying operating system and hardware, while providing performance on par with natively compiled code.

CHAPTER 4

Windows Forms I: Developing Desktop Applications

Windows Forms is a set of classes that encapsulates the creation of the graphical user interface (GUI) portion of a typical desktop application. Previously, each programming language had its own way of creating windows, text boxes, buttons, etc. This functionality has all been moved into the .NET Framework class library—into the types located in the System.Windows.Forms namespace. Closely related is the System.Drawing namespace, which contains several types used in the creation of GUI applications. The capabilities provided by the types in the System.Drawing namespace are commonly referred to as GDI+ (discussed more fully later in this chapter).

In this chapter, we'll examine the form (or window) as the central component in a classic desktop application. We'll look at how forms are programmatically created and how they're hooked to events. We'll also examine how multiple forms in a single application relate to one another and how you handle forms in an application that has one or more child forms. Finally, we'll discuss two topics, printing and 2-D graphics, that are relevant to desktop application development.

Creating a Form

The easiest way to design a form is to use the Windows Forms Designer in Visual Studio .NET. The developer can use visual tools to lay out the form, with the designer translating the layout into Visual Basic .NET source code. If you don't have Visual Studio .NET, you can write the Visual Basic .NET code directly and not use the designer at all. This section will demonstrate both methods.

Programmatically, a form is defined by deriving a class from the Form class (defined in System.Windows.Forms). The Form class contains the know-how for displaying an empty form, including its title bar and other amenities that we expect from a Windows form. Adding members to the new class and overriding members inherited from the Form class add visual elements and behavior to the new form.

Creating a Form Using Visual Studio .NET

To create a GUI application in Visual Studio .NET:

1. Select File→New→Project. The New Project dialog box appears, as shown in Figure 4-1.

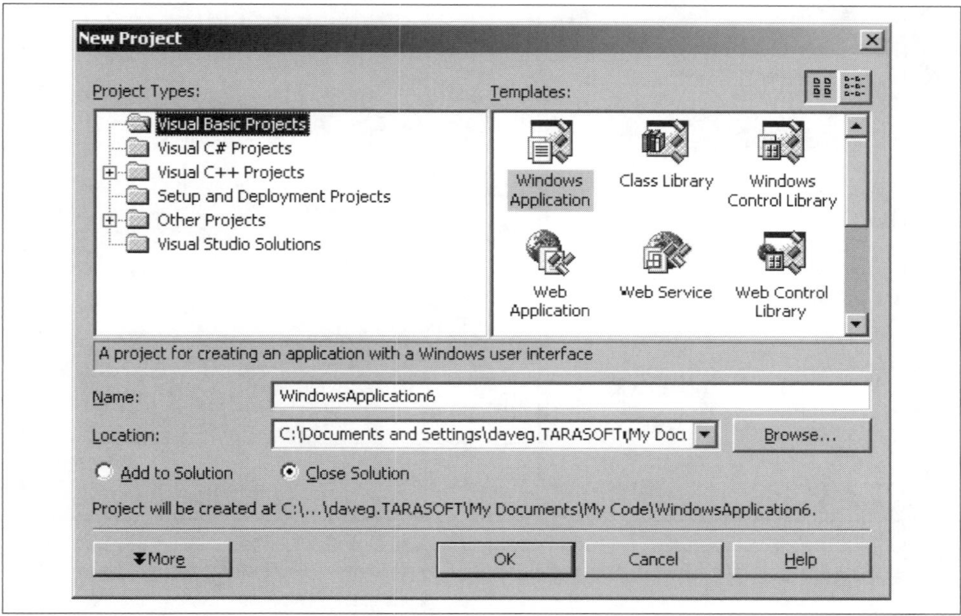

Figure 4-1. The New Project dialog box

2. Select Visual Basic Projects in the Project Types pane on the left side of the dialog box.
3. Select Windows Application in the Templates pane on the right side of the dialog box.
4. Enter a name in the Name text box.
5. Click OK. Visual Studio .NET creates a project with a form in it and displays the form in a designer, as shown in Figure 4-2.

To see the code created by the form Windows Forms Designer, right-click on the form, then select View Code. Doing this for the blank form shown in Figure 4-2 reveals the code shown here:

```
Public Class Form1
    Inherits System.Windows.Forms.Form

 Windows Form Designer generated code

End Class
```

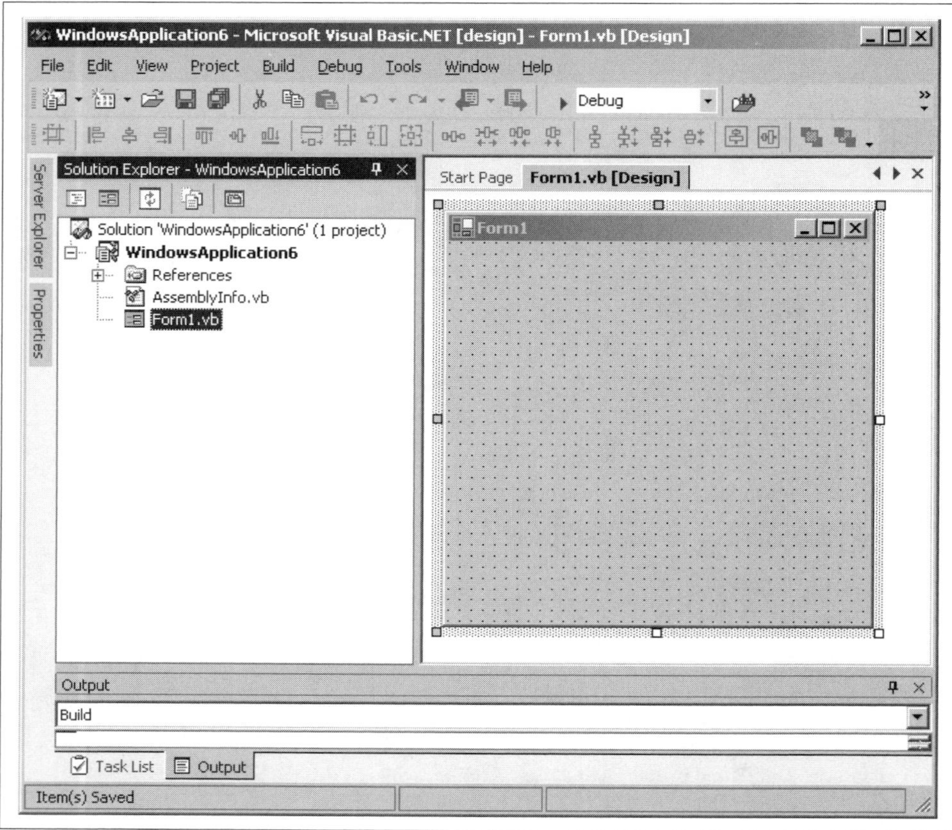

Figure 4-2. The Windows Forms Designer

This shows the definition of a class named Form1 that inherits from the Form class. The Windows Forms Designer also creates a lot of boilerplate code that should not be modified by the developer. By default, it hides this code from view. To see the code, click on the "+" symbol that appears to the left of the line that says "Windows Form Designer generated code." Doing so reveals the code shown in Example 4-1.

Example 4-1. The Windows Forms Designer–generated code for a blank form

```
Public Class Form1
   Inherits System.Windows.Forms.Form

#Region " Windows Form Designer generated code "

   Public Sub New( )
      MyBase.New( )

      'This call is required by the Windows Form Designer.
      InitializeComponent( )
```

Example 4-1. The Windows Forms Designer–generated code for a blank form (continued)

```
      'Add any initialization after the InitializeComponent( ) call

   End Sub

   'Form overrides dispose to clean up the component list.
   Protected Overloads Overrides Sub Dispose(ByVal disposing As Boolean)
      If disposing Then
         If Not (components Is Nothing) Then
            components.Dispose( )
         End If
      End If
      MyBase.Dispose(disposing)
   End Sub

   'Required by the Windows Form Designer
   Private components As System.ComponentModel.Container

   'NOTE: The following procedure is required by the Windows Form Designer
   'It can be modified using the Windows Form Designer.
   'Do not modify it using the code editor.
   <System.Diagnostics.DebuggerStepThrough( )> Private Sub InitializeComponent( )
      components = New System.ComponentModel.Container( )
      Me.Text = "Form1"
   End Sub

#End Region

End Class
```

The Windows Forms Designer autogenerates the code for four class members:

New method (the class constructor)
: The constructor calls the base class's constructor and then invokes the InitializeComponent method. Developer-supplied initialization code should follow the call to InitializeComponent. After the constructor is generated, the designer doesn't touch it again.

Dispose method
: The Dispose method is where the object gets rid of any expensive resources. In this case, it calls the base class's Dispose method to give it a chance to release any expensive resources that it may hold, then it calls the components field's Dispose method. (For more on the components field, see the next item.) This in turn calls the Dispose methods on each individual component in the collection. If the derived class uses any expensive resources, the developer should add code here to release them. When a form is no longer needed, all code that uses the form should call the form's Dispose method. After the Dispose method is generated, the designer doesn't touch it again.

Components field
The components field is an object of type IContainer (defined in the System. ComponentModel namespace). The designer-generated code uses the components field to manage finalization of components that may be added to a form (for example, the Timer component).

InitializeComponent method
The code in this method should not be modified or added to by the developer in any way. The Windows Forms Designer automatically updates it as needed. When controls are added to the form using the designer, code is added to this method to instantiate the controls at runtime and set their initial properties. Note also in Example 4-1 that properties of the form itself (such as Text and Name) are initialized in this method.

One thing missing from this class definition is a Main method. Recall from Chapter 2 that .NET applications must expose a public, shared Main method. This method is called by the CLR when an application is started. So why doesn't the designer-generated form include a Main method? It's because the Visual Basic .NET compiler in Visual Studio .NET automatically creates one as it compiles the code. In other words, the compiled code has a Main method in it even though the source code does not. The Main method in the compiled code is a member of the Form1 class and is equivalent to this:

```
<System.STAThreadAttribute( )> Public Shared Sub Main( )
   System.Threading.Thread.CurrentThread.ApartmentState = _
      System.Threading.ApartmentState.STA
   System.Windows.Forms.Application.Run(New Form1( ))
End Sub
```

Note that the Visual Basic .NET command-line compiler doesn't automatically generate the Main method. This method must appear in the source code if the command-line compiler is to be used.

The next steps in designing the form are to name the code file something meaningful and to set some properties on the form, such as the title-bar text. To change the name of the form's code file, right-click on the filename in the Solution Explorer window and select Rename. If you're following along with this example, enter *HelloWindows.vb* as the name of the file.

Changing the name of the file doesn't change the name of the class. To change the name of the class, right-click the form in the designer and choose Properties. In the Properties window, change the value of the Name property. For this example, change the name to "HelloWindows".

To change the form's caption, set the form's Text property to a new value. Set the Text property in this example to "Programming Visual Basic .NET".

Next, controls can be added to the form from the Visual Studio .NET toolbox. To display the toolbox, select View→Toolbox from the Visual Studio .NET main menu.

For this example, double-click on the Label control in the toolbox to add a Label control on the form. Use the Properties window to change the label's Text property to "Hello, Windows!" and its Font property to Arial 24pt.

Next, double-click on the Button control in the toolbox to add a Button control to the form. Use the Properties window to change the button's Name property to "OkButton" and its Text property to "OK".

Finally, position the controls as desired, size the Label control and the form to be appealing, and set the form's FormBorderStyle property to "FixedToolWindow". The resulting form should look something like the one shown in Figure 4-3.

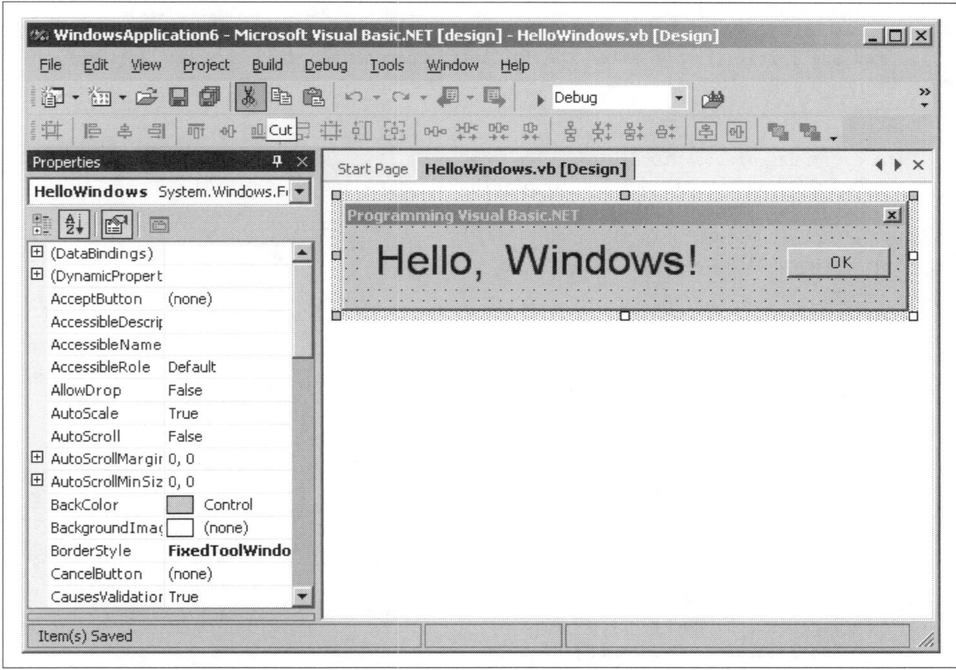

Figure 4-3. A form with controls

Press the F5 key to build and run the program. The result should look something like Figure 4-4.

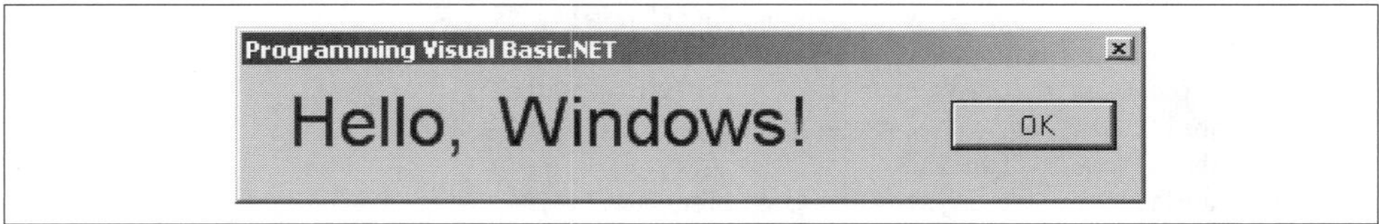

Figure 4-4. Hello, Windows!, as created by the Windows Forms Designer

The code generated by the designer is shown in Example 4-2.

Example 4-2. Hello, Windows! code, as generated by the Windows Forms Designer

```
Public Class HelloWindows
   Inherits System.Windows.Forms.Form

#Region " Windows Form Designer generated code "

   Public Sub New( )
      MyBase.New( )

      'This call is required by the Windows Form Designer.
      InitializeComponent( )

      'Add any initialization after the InitializeComponent( ) call

   End Sub

   'Form overrides dispose to clean up the component list.
   Protected Overloads Overrides Sub Dispose(ByVal disposing As Boolean)
      If disposing Then
         If Not (components Is Nothing) Then
            components.Dispose( )
         End If
      End If
      MyBase.Dispose(disposing)
   End Sub
   Friend WithEvents Label1 As System.Windows.Forms.Label
   Friend WithEvents OkButton As System.Windows.Forms.Button

   'Required by the Windows Form Designer
   Private components As System.ComponentModel.Container

   'NOTE: The following procedure is required by the Windows Form Designer
   'It can be modified using the Windows Form Designer.
   'Do not modify it using the code editor.
   <System.Diagnostics.DebuggerStepThrough( )> _
   Private Sub InitializeComponent( )
      Me.Label1 = New System.Windows.Forms.Label( )
      Me.OkButton = New System.Windows.Forms.Button( )
      Me.SuspendLayout( )
      '
      'Label1
      '
      Me.Label1.Font = New System.Drawing.Font("Arial", 24!, _
         System.Drawing.FontStyle.Regular, _
         System.Drawing.GraphicsUnit.Point, CType(0, Byte))
      Me.Label1.Location = New System.Drawing.Point(8, 8)
      Me.Label1.Name = "Label1"
      Me.Label1.Size = New System.Drawing.Size(264, 48)
      Me.Label1.TabIndex = 0
      Me.Label1.Text = "Hello, Windows!"
      '
```

Example 4-2. Hello, Windows! code, as generated by the Windows Forms Designer (continued)

```
      'OkButton
      '
      Me.OkButton.Location = New System.Drawing.Point(280, 16)
      Me.OkButton.Name = "OkButton"
      Me.OkButton.TabIndex = 1
      Me.OkButton.Text = "OK"
      '
      'HelloWindows
      '
      Me.AutoScaleBaseSize = New System.Drawing.Size(5, 13)
      Me.ClientSize = New System.Drawing.Size(362, 58)
      Me.Controls.AddRange(New System.Windows.Forms.Control( ) _
         {Me.OkButton, Me.Label1})
      Me.FormBorderStyle = _
         System.Windows.Forms.FormBorderStyle.FixedToolWindow
      Me.Name = "HelloWindows"
      Me.Text = "Programming Visual Basic .NET"
      Me.ResumeLayout(False)

   End Sub

#End Region

End Class
```

Note that the designer made the following modifications to the code:

- Two Friend fields were added to the class, one for each of the controls that were added to the form:

  ```
  Friend WithEvents Label1 As System.Windows.Forms.Label
  Friend WithEvents OkButton As System.Windows.Forms.Button
  ```

  The `Friend` keyword makes the members visible to other code within the project, but it hides them from code running in other assemblies.

  The `WithEvents` keyword allows the HelloWindows class to handle events generated by the controls. In the code shown, no event handlers have been added yet, but you'll see how to do that later in this section.

  Note that the field names match the control names as shown in the Properties window.

- Code was added to the InitializeComponent method to instantiate the two controls and assign their references to the member fields:

  ```
  Me.Label1 = New System.Windows.Forms.Label( )
  Me.OkButton = New System.Windows.Forms.Button( )
  ```

- Code was added to the InitializeComponent method to set various properties of the label, button, and form. Some of these assignments directly correspond to the settings made in the Properties window, while others are the implicit result of other actions taken in the designer (such as sizing the form).

Adding event handlers

The *Hello, Windows!* application built thus far has an OK button, but the application doesn't yet respond to button clicks. To add a Click event handler for the OK button, double-click on the button in the Windows Forms Designer. The designer responds by switching to the form's code view and inserting a subroutine that handles the Click event (i.e., it will be called when the user of the running application clicks the OK button). The subroutine the designer creates looks like this (note that I added the line-continuation character for printing in this book):

```
Private Sub OkButton_Click(ByVal sender As System.Object, _
   ByVal e As System.EventArgs) Handles OkButton.Click

End Sub
```

The body of the subroutine can then be added. This would be a likely implementation for this event handler:

```
Private Sub OkButton_Click(ByVal sender As System.Object, _
   ByVal e As System.EventArgs) Handles OkButton.Click
   Me.Close( )
   Me.Dispose( )
End Sub
```

An alternative way to add an event handler is to use the drop-down lists at the top of the form's code-view window. In the lefthand drop-down list, choose the object for which you would like to add an event handler. Then, in the righthand drop-down list, choose the desired event. See Figure 4-5.

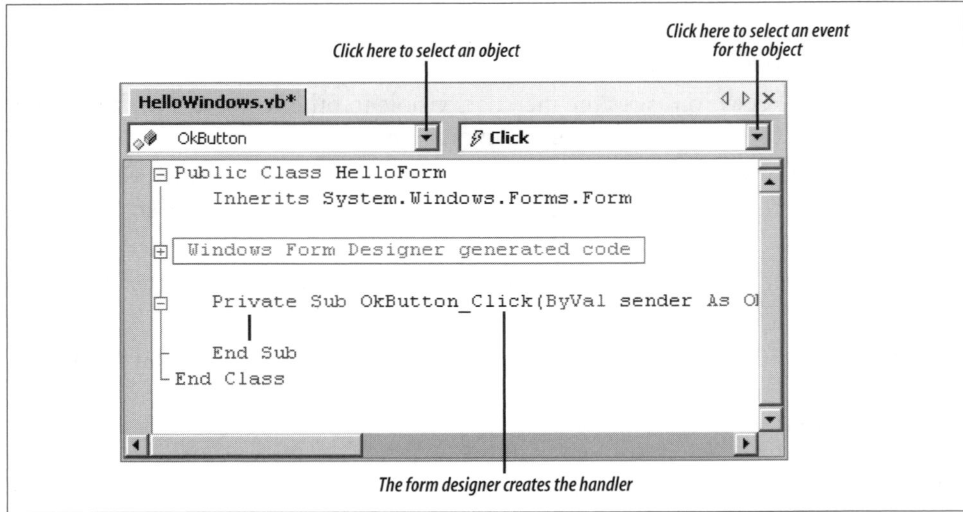

Figure 4-5. Adding an event handler using the code view's drop-down lists

Event handlers can be typed directly into the form's code if you know the correct signature for the handler. Event-handler signatures are documented in the Microsoft Developer Network (MSDN) Library.

Creating a Form in Code

Although form designers are convenient, it is certainly possible to code a form directly. To do so, follow these steps:

1. Define a class that is derived from the Form class (defined in the System.Windows.Forms namespace). If the form is to be the startup form for an application, include a public, shared Main method. For example:

```
Imports System.Windows.Forms

Public Class HelloWindows
   Inherits Form

   ' Include this method only if this is the application's startup form.
   ' Alternatively, place this method in a separate module in the
   ' application. If it is placed in a separate module, remove the
   ' Shared keyword.
   <System.STAThreadAttribute( )> Public Shared Sub Main( )
      System.Threading.Thread.CurrentThread.ApartmentState = _
         System.Threading.ApartmentState.STA
      Application.Run(New HelloWindows( ))
   End Sub ' Main

End Class
```

2. Declare a data member for each control that is to appear on the form. If you want to handle events from the control, use the `WithEvents` keyword in the declaration. For example:

```
Imports System.Windows.Forms

Public Class HelloWindows
   Inherits Form

   Private lblHelloWindows As Label
   Private WithEvents btnOK As Button

   <System.STAThreadAttribute( )> Public Shared Sub Main( )
      System.Threading.Thread.CurrentThread.ApartmentState = _
         System.Threading.ApartmentState.STA
      Application.Run(New HelloWindows( ))
   End Sub ' Main

End Class
```

The visibility (`Private`, `Friend`, `Protected`, or `Public`) of these data members is a design issue that depends on the project and on the developer's preferences. My own preference is to make all data members private. If code external to the class needs to modify the data held by these members, specific accessor methods can be added for the purpose. This prevents internal design changes from affecting external users of the class.

3. Declare a constructor. Perform the following operations in the constructor:
   a. Instantiate each control.
   b. Set properties for each control and for the form.
   c. Add all controls to the form's Controls collection.

   For example:

```
Imports System.Drawing
Imports System.Windows.Forms

Public Class HelloWindows
   Inherits Form

   Private lblHelloWindows As Label
   Private WithEvents btnOK As Button

   Public Sub New

      ' Instantiate a label control and set its properties.
      lblHelloWindows = New Label( )
      With lblHelloWindows
         .Font = New Font("Arial", 24)
         .Location = New Point(16, 8)
         .Size = New Size(248, 40)
         .TabIndex = 0
         .Text = "Hello, Windows!"
      End With

      ' Instantiate a button control and set its properties.
      btnOK = New Button( )
      With btnOK
         .Location = New Point(320, 16)
         .TabIndex = 1
         .Text = "OK"
      End With

      ' Set properties on the form.
      FormBorderStyle = FormBorderStyle.FixedToolWindow
      ClientSize = New Size(405, 61)
      Text = "Programming Visual Basic .NET"

      ' Add the controls to the form's Controls collection.
      Controls.Add(lblHelloWindows)
      Controls.Add(btnOK)

   End Sub

   <System.STAThreadAttribute( )> Public Shared Sub Main( )
      System.Threading.Thread.CurrentThread.ApartmentState = _
```

```
            System.Threading.ApartmentState.STA
        Application.Run(New HelloWindows( ))
    End Sub ' Main

End Class
```

An Imports statement was added to give access to types in the System.Drawing namespace, such as Point and Size.

Adding event handlers

Define event handlers directly in code for any events that you wish to handle. For example:

```
Private Sub btnOK_Click(ByVal sender As Object, _
   ByVal e As System.EventArgs) Handles btnOK.Click
   Close( )
   Dispose( )
End Sub
```

The complete code for a standalone Windows Forms application is shown in Example 4-3. Compile it from the command line with this command:

```
vbc HelloWindows.vb /r:System.dll,System.Drawing.dll,System.Windows.Forms.dll /t:
winexe
```

(Note that the command should be typed on a single line. It is wrapped here only for printing in the book.)

Example 4-3. Hello, Windows! code generated outside of Visual Studio

```
Imports System.Drawing
Imports System.Windows.Forms
Public Class HelloWindows
   Inherits Form
   Private lblHelloWindows As Label
   Private WithEvents btnOK As Button

   Private Sub btnOK_Click(ByVal sender As Object, _
      ByVal e As System.EventArgs) Handles btnOK.Click
      Close( )
      Dispose( )
   End Sub
   Public Sub New
      ' Instantiate a label control and set its properties.
      lblHelloWindows = New Label( )
      With lblHelloWindows
         .Font = New Font("Arial", 24)
         .Location = New Point(16, 8)
         .Size = New Size(248, 40)
         .TabIndex = 0
         .Text = "Hello, Windows!"
      End With
```

Example 4-3. Hello, Windows! code generated outside of Visual Studio (continued)

```
      ' Instantiate a button control and set its properties.
      btnOK = New Button( )
      With btnOK
         .Location = New Point(320, 16)
         .TabIndex = 1
         .Text = "OK"
      End With
      ' Set properties on the form.
      FormBorderStyle = FormBorderStyle.FixedToolWindow
      ClientSize = New Size(405, 61)
      Text = "Programming Visual Basic .NET"
      ' Add the controls to the form's Controls collection.
      Controls.Add(lblHelloWindows)
      Controls.Add(btnOK)
   End Sub

   <System.STAThreadAttribute( )> Public Shared Sub Main( )
      System.Threading.Thread.CurrentThread.ApartmentState = _
         System.Threading.ApartmentState.STA
      Application.Run(New HelloWindows( ))
   End Sub ' Main
End Class
```

Handling Form Events

The base Form class may at times raise events. These events can be handled by the derived Form class. One way to do this is to define a handler subroutine that uses the `MyBase` keyword in the `Handles` clause, like this:

```
' This is not the preferred technique.
Private Sub Form_Closing( _
   ByVal sender As Object, _
   ByVal e As System.ComponentModel.CancelEventArgs _
) Handles MyBase.Closing
   ' ...
End Sub
```

However, a better technique is to override the protected methods, which are provided by the Form class for this purpose. For example, the following method could be placed in the derived class's definition, providing a way to respond to the form's imminent closing:

```
' Assumes Imports System.ComponentModel
Protected Overrides Sub OnClosing( _
   ByVal e As CancelEventArgs _
)
   ' ...
   MyBase.OnClosing(e) ' Important
End Sub
```

Note that the implementation of the OnClosing method includes a call to the base class's implementation. This is important. If this is not done, the Closing event won't be raised, which will affect the behavior of any other code that has registered for the event.

Following is the list of events the Form class defines, including a brief description of each event and the syntax for overriding the protected method that corresponds to each event. Note also that the Form class indirectly derives from the Control class and that the Control class also exposes events and overridable methods that aren't shown here.

Activated
Fired when the form is activated. Its syntax is:

```
Protected Overrides Sub OnActivated(ByVal e As System.EventArgs)
```

Closed
Fired when the form has been closed. Its syntax is:

```
Protected Overrides Sub OnClosed(ByVal e As System.EventArgs)
```

Closing
Fired when the form is about to close. Its syntax is:

```
Protected Overrides Sub OnClosing( _
   ByVal e As System.ComponentModel.CancelEventArgs)
```

The CancelEventArgs.Cancel property can be set to `True` to prevent the form from closing; its default value is `False`.

Deactivate
Fired when the form is deactivated. Its syntax is:

```
Protected Overrides Sub OnDeactivate(ByVal e As System.EventArgs)
```

InputLanguageChanged
Fired when the form's input language has been changed. Its syntax is:

```
Protected Overrides Sub OnInputLanguageChanged( _
   ByVal e As System.Windows.Forms.InputLanguageChangedEventArgs)
```

The InputLanguageChangedEventArgs class has three properties that identify the new language: CharSet, which defines the character set associated with the new input language; Culture, which contains the culture code (see Appendix C) of the new input language; and InputLanguage, which contains a value indicating the new language.

InputLanguageChanging
Fired when the form's input language is about to be changed. Its syntax is:

```
Protected Overrides Sub OnInputLanguageChanging( _
   ByVal e As System.Windows.Forms.InputLanguageChangingEventArgs)
```

The InputLanguageChangingEventArgs class has a Culture property that identifies the proposed new language and locale. It also has a Cancel property that can be set to `True` within the event handler to cancel the change of input language; the default value of the Cancel property is `False`.

Load

Fired when the form is loaded. Its syntax is:

```
Protected Overrides Sub OnLoad(ByVal e As System.EventArgs)
```

MaximizedBoundsChanged

Fired when the value of the form's MaximizedBounds property (which determines the size of the maximized form) is changed. Its syntax is:

```
Protected Overrides Sub OnMaximizedBoundsChanged( _
   ByVal e As System.EventArgs)
```

MaximumSizeChanged

Fired when the value of the form's MaximumSize property (which defines the maximum size to which the form can be resized) is changed. Its syntax is:

```
Protected Overrides Sub OnMaximumSizeChanged(ByVal e As System.EventArgs)
```

MdiChildActivate

Fired when an MDI child window is activated. Its syntax is:

```
Protected Overrides Sub OnMdiChildActivate(ByVal e As System.EventArgs)
```

MenuComplete

Fired when menu selection is finished. Its syntax is:

```
Protected Overrides Sub OnMenuComplete(ByVal e As System.EventArgs)
```

MenuStart

Fired when a menu is displayed. Its syntax is:

```
Protected Overrides Sub OnMenuStart(ByVal e As System.EventArgs)
```

MinimumSizeChanged

Fired when the value of the form's MinimumSize property (which defines the minimum size to which the form can be resized) is changed. Its syntax is:

```
Protected Overrides Sub OnMinimumSizeChanged(ByVal e As System.EventArgs)
```

Relationships Between Forms

The Form class has two properties that control a form's relationship to other forms: the Parent property (inherited from the Control class) and the Owner property. Setting the Parent property causes the constrained form to appear only within the bounds of the parent—and always to appear on top of the parent. This gives an effect similar to MDI applications (which have other features as well and are discussed later in this chapter). When a form has a parent, it can be docked to the parent's edges, just like any other control. The code in Example 4-4 demonstrates this. It can be compiled from the command line with this command:

```
vbc filename.vb /r:System.dll,System.Drawing.dll,System.Windows.Forms.dll /t:winexe
```

The result is displayed in Figure 4-6.

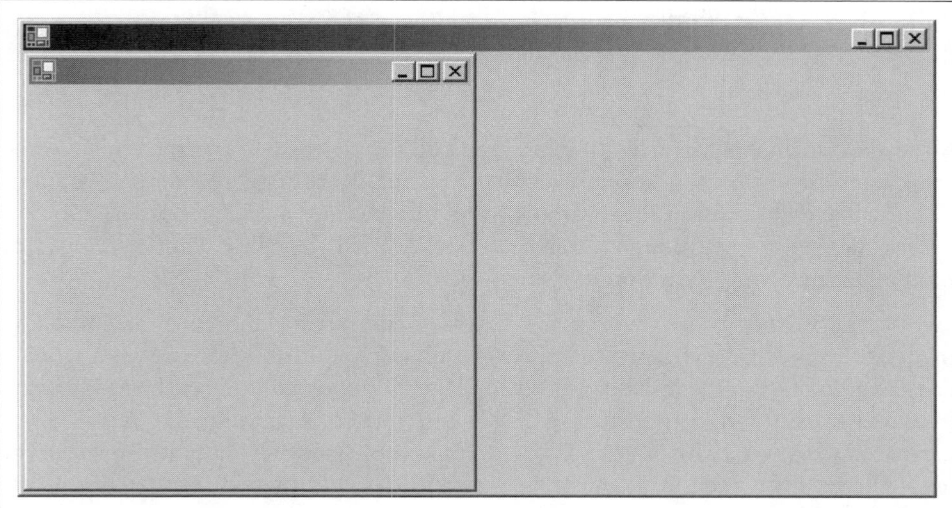

Figure 4-6. A form with a parent

Example 4-4. Creating a form with a parent

```
Imports System.Drawing
Imports System.Windows.Forms

Module modMain
   <System.STAThreadAttribute( )> Public Sub Main( )
      System.Threading.Thread.CurrentThread.ApartmentState = _
         System.Threading.ApartmentState.STA
      System.Windows.Forms.Application.Run(New MyParentForm( ))
   End Sub
End Module

Public Class MyParentForm
   Inherits Form
   Public Sub New( )
      ' Set my size.
      Me.ClientSize = New System.Drawing.Size(600, 400)
      ' Create and show a child form.
      Dim frm As New MyChildForm(Me)
      frm.Show( )
   End Sub
End Class

Public Class MyChildForm
   Inherits Form
   Public Sub New(ByVal Parent As Control)
      ' TopLevel must be False for me to have a parent.
      Me.TopLevel = False
      ' Set my parent.
      Me.Parent = Parent
      ' Dock to my parent's left edge.
```

Example 4-4. Creating a form with a parent (continued)

```
      Me.Dock = DockStyle.Left
   End Sub
End Class
```

If the child form is maximized, it expands to fill the parent form. If the child form is minimized, it shrinks to a small rectangle at the bottom of the parent window. Because the child form in this example has a title bar and a sizable border, it can be moved and sized even though it has been docked. This behavior can be changed by modifying the form's FormBorderStyle property.

Setting the Owner property of a form causes another form to own the first. An owned form is not constrained to appear within the bounds of its owner, but when it does overlay its owner, it is always on top. Furthermore, the owned form is always minimized, restored, or destroyed when its owner is minimized, restored, or destroyed. Owned forms are good for floating-tool windows or Find/Replace-type dialog boxes. The code in Example 4-5 creates an owner/owned relationship. Compile it with this command:

```
vbc filename.vb /r:System.dll,System.Drawing.dll,System.Windows.Forms.dll /t:winexe
```

Example 4-5. Creating a form with an owner

```
Imports System.Drawing
Imports System.Windows.Forms

Module modMain
   <System.STAThreadAttribute( )> Public Sub Main( )
      System.Threading.Thread.CurrentThread.ApartmentState = _
         System.Threading.ApartmentState.STA
      System.Windows.Forms.Application.Run(New MyOwnerForm( ))
   End Sub
End Module

Public Class MyOwnerForm
   Inherits Form
   Public Sub New( )
      ' Set my size.
      Me.ClientSize = New System.Drawing.Size(600, 450)
      ' Create and show an owned form.
      Dim frm As New MyOwnedForm(Me)
      frm.Show( )
   End Sub
End Class

Public Class MyOwnedForm
   Inherits Form
   Public Sub New(ByVal Owner As Form)
      ' Set my owner.
      Me.Owner = Owner
   End Sub
End Class
```

MDI Applications

Multiple document interface (MDI) applications permit more than one document to be open at a time. This is in contrast to *single document interface* (SDI) applications, which can manipulate only one document at a time. Visual Studio .NET is an example of an MDI application—many source files and design views can be open at once. In contrast, Notepad is an example of an SDI application—opening a document closes any previously opened document.

There is more to MDI applications than their ability to have multiple files open at once. The Microsoft Windows platform SDK specifies several UI behaviors that MDI applications should implement. The Windows operating system provides support for these behaviors, and this support is exposed through Windows Forms as well.

Parent and Child Forms

MDI applications consist of a main form, which does not itself display any data, and one or more child forms, which appear only within the main form and are used for displaying documents. The main form is called the *MDI parent*, and the child forms are called the *MDI children*.

The Form class has two properties that control whether a given form is an MDI parent, MDI child, or neither. The Boolean IsMdiContainer property determines whether a form behaves as an MDI parent. The MdiParent property (which is of type Form) controls whether a form behaves as an MDI child. Setting the MdiParent property of a form to reference the application's MDI parent form makes the form an MDI child form. Example 4-6 shows the minimum amount of code required to display an MDI parent form containing a single MDI child form.

Example 4-6. A minimal MDI application

```
Imports System
Imports System.Windows.Forms

Public Module AppModule
   Public Sub Main( )
      Application.Run(New MainForm( ))
   End Sub
End Module

Public Class MainForm
   Inherits Form

   Public Sub New( )
      ' Set the main window caption.
      Text = "My MDI Application"
      ' Set this to be an MDI parent form.
      IsMdiContainer = True
      ' Create a child form.
```

Example 4-6. A minimal MDI application (continued)

```
      Dim myChild As New DocumentForm("My Document", Me)
      myChild.Show
   End Sub

End Class

Public Class DocumentForm
   Inherits Form

   Public Sub New(ByVal name As String, ByVal parent As Form)
      ' Set the document window caption.
      Text = name
      ' Set this to be an MDI child form.
      MdiParent = parent
   End Sub

End Class
```

Assuming that the code in Example 4-6 is saved in a file named *MyApp.vb*, it can be compiled from the command line with this command:

```
vbc MyApp.vb /r:System.dll,System.Windows.Forms.dll
```

Running the resulting executable produces the display shown in Figure 4-7.

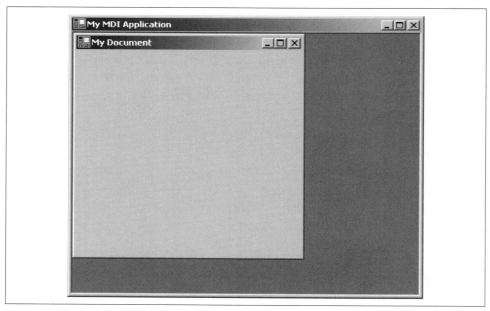

Figure 4-7. A minimal MDI application (the output of the code in Example 4-6)

The Form class has two read-only properties related to MDI behavior. The IsMdiChild property returns a Boolean value that indicates whether the form is an MDI child. The MdiChildren property of a parent form contains a collection of references to the form's child forms. The IsMdiChild and MdiChildren properties are both automatically maintained in response to setting the child forms' MdiParent properties.

Creating a Window Menu

MDI applications usually have a main-menu item called Window. On this menu appear standard items for cascading, tiling, and activating child windows and arranging the icons of minimized child windows. Figure 4-8 shows a typical example.

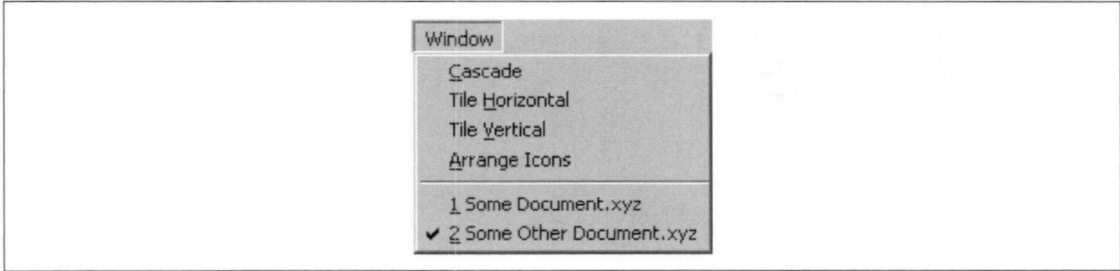

Figure 4-8. A typical Window menu

Such a menu is easy to create using the support in Windows Forms. Assuming that you were to do it programmatically, Example 4-7 shows a revised version of Example 4-6 that has been modified to include a Window menu; the added code is shown in boldface. For details on how to work with menus from the Visual Studio IDE, as well as programmatically, see the "Menus" section in Chapter 5.

Example 4-7. An MDI application with a Window menu

```
Imports System
Imports System.Windows.Forms

Public Module AppModule
   Public Sub Main( )
      Application.Run(New MainForm( ))
   End Sub
End Module

Public Class MainForm
   Inherits Form

   ' Declare MainForm's main menu
   Private myMainMenu As MainMenu

   ' Declare Windows menu
   Protected WithEvents mnuWindow As MenuItem
```

Example 4-7. An MDI application with a Window menu (continued)

```
    Protected WithEvents mnuTileHoriz As MenuItem
    Protected WithEvents mnuCascade As MenuItem
    Protected WithEvents mnuTileVert As MenuItem
    Protected WithEvents mnuArrangeAll As MenuItem

    Public Sub New( )
       ' Set the main window caption.
       Text = "My MDI Application"
       ' Set this to be an MDI parent form.
       IsMdiContainer = True
       ' Create main menu
       MyMainMenu = New MainMenu( )
       ' Define menu items
       mnuWindow = New MenuItem( )
       mnuTileHoriz = New MenuItem( )
       mnuTileVert = New MenuItem( )
       mnuCascade = New MenuItem( )
       mnuArrangeAll = New MenuItem( )
       ' Set menu properties
       mnuWindow.Text = "&Window"
       mnuWindow.MdiList = True
       mnuTileHoriz.Text = "Tile Horizontally"
       mnuTileVert.Text = "Tile Vertically"
       mnuCascade.Text = "Cascade"
       mnuArrangeAll.Text = "Arrange Icons"
       ' Add items to menu
       MyMainMenu.MenuItems.Add(mnuWindow)
       mnuWindow.MenuItems.Add(mnuCascade)
       mnuWindow.MenuItems.Add(mnuTileHoriz)
       mnuWindow.MenuItems.Add(mnuTileVert)
       mnuWindow.MenuItems.Add(mnuArrangeAll)
       ' Assign menu to form
       Me.Menu = MyMainMenu
       ' Create a child form.
       Dim myChild As New DocumentForm("My Document", Me)
       myChild.Show
    End Sub

    Public Sub mnuCascade_Click(o As Object, e As EventArgs) _
             Handles mnuCascade.Click
       LayoutMdi(MdiLayout.Cascade)
    End Sub

    Public Sub mnuTileHoriz_Click(o As Object, e As EventArgs) _
             Handles mnuTileHoriz.Click
       LayoutMdi(MdiLayout.TileHorizontal)
    End Sub

    Public Sub mnuTileVert_Click(o As Object, e As EventArgs) _
             Handles mnuTileVert.Click
       LayoutMdi(MdiLayout.TileVertical)
    End Sub
```

Example 4-7. An MDI application with a Window menu (continued)

```
   Public Sub mnuArrangeAll_Click(o As Object, e As EventArgs) _
            Handles mnuArrangeAll.Click
      LayoutMdi(MdiLayout.ArrangeIcons)
   End Sub

End Class

Public Class DocumentForm
   Inherits Form

   Public Sub New(ByVal name As String, ByVal parent As Form)
      ' Set the document window caption.
      Text = name
      ' Set this to be an MDI child form.
      MdiParent = parent
   End Sub

End Class
```

To add a Window menu to the parent form of an MDI application, perform the following steps. First, add a menu item to the MDI parent form's main menu, setting its Text property to anything desired (usually `Window`) and its MdiList property to `True`. It is the MdiList property that makes the Window menu a Window menu. Setting the MdiList property to `True` causes the Windows Forms framework to add and delete menu items to and from this menu item as necessary. This in turn will always display the current list of MDI child windows in the menu.

Next, add menu items for Cascade, Tile Horizontally, Tile Vertically, and Arrange Icons. In the Click event handler for each of these menu items, call the Form class's LayoutMdi method, passing the appropriate parameter value for the desired action.

The syntax of the LayoutMdi method is:

```
Public Sub LayoutMdi(ByVal value As MdiLayout)
```

The method's single argument must be a value from the MdiLayout enumeration (defined in the System.Windows.Forms namespace). The values in this enumeration are:

`ArrangeIcons`
: Indicates that the icons for the minimized MDI child windows should be neatly arranged.

`Cascade`
: Indicates that the MDI child windows should be cascaded (displayed overlapping each other).

`TileHorizontal`
: Indicates that the MDI child windows should be tiled (displayed without overlapping), with each child window filling the width of the MDI parent.

`TileVertical`
: Indicates that the MDI child windows should be tiled, with each child window filling the height of the MDI parent.

Merging Menus

Often, the items that should appear on an MDI application's main menu are dependent on the type of document being displayed or on whether any document is displayed at all. Of course, this effect could be achieved in code by dynamically adding and removing menu items each time a child window is activated. However, the Windows Forms framework provides an easier way.

If an MDI child form has a main menu of its own, it and the MDI parent form's main menu are merged to produce the menu that is shown to the user when the child form is displayed. Two properties of the MenuItem class affect how the menu items are merged. First, the MergeOrder property determines the order in which the menu items are displayed. This property can be set to any Integer value, and the values don't have to be contiguous. The menu items from the two menus are sorted on this value to determine the order in which the menu items are displayed on screen.

For example, consider an MDI parent form that has a main menu with three menu items representing File, Window, and Help menus. Further, say that the MergeOrder properties of these menu items are 10, 20, and 30, respectively. Now, if an MDI child form is displayed and its main menu has, for example, an Edit item with a MergeOrder property value of 15, the menu displayed to the user will have four items: File, Edit, Window, and Help, in that order. Example 4-8 shows a revised version of Example 4-6 that contains the code necessary to create such a menu; lines shown in boldface have been added to define the main menu and its menu items.

Example 4-8. An MDI application with merged menus

```
Imports System
Imports System.Windows.Forms

Public Module AppModule
   Public Sub Main( )
      Application.Run(New MainForm( ))
   End Sub
End Module

Public Class MainForm
   Inherits Form

   ' Declare MainForm's main menu.
   Private myMainMenu As MainMenu

   ' Declare the Window menu.
   Protected WithEvents mnuFile As MenuItem
   Protected WithEvents mnuWindow As MenuItem
```

Example 4-8. An MDI application with merged menus (continued)

```
   Protected WithEvents mnuHelp As MenuItem

   Public Sub New( )
      ' Set the main window caption.
      Text = "My MDI Application"
      ' Set this to be an MDI parent form.
      IsMdiContainer = True
      ' Create main menu
      MyMainMenu = New MainMenu( )
      ' Define menu items
      mnuFile = New MenuItem( )
      mnuWindow = New MenuItem( )
      mnuHelp = New MenuItem( )
      ' Set menu properties
      mnuFile.Text = "&File"
      mnuFile.MergeOrder = 10
      mnuWindow.Text = "&Window"
      mnuWindow.MergeOrder = 20
      mnuWindow.MdiList = True
      mnuHelp.Text = "&Help"
      mnuHelp.MergeOrder = 30
      ' Add items to menu
      MyMainMenu.MenuItems.Add(mnuFile)
      MyMainMenu.MenuItems.Add(mnuWindow)
      MyMainMenu.MenuItems.Add(mnuHelp)
      ' Assign menu to form
      Me.Menu = MyMainMenu
      ' Create a child form.
      Dim myChild As New DocumentForm("My Document", Me)
      myChild.Show
   End Sub

End Class

Public Class DocumentForm
   Inherits Form

   ' Declare menu
   Private mdiMenu As New MainMenu
   ' Declare menu items
   Protected WithEvents mnuEdit As MenuItem

   Public Sub New(ByVal name As String, ByVal parent As Form)
      ' Set the document window caption.
      Text = name
      ' Set this to be an MDI child form.
      MdiParent = parent
      ' Instantiate menu and menu items
      mdiMenu = New MainMenu( )
      mnuEdit = New MenuItem( )
      ' Set menu properties
      mnuEdit.Text = "&Edit"
```

Example 4-8. An MDI application with merged menus (continued)

```
      mnuEdit.MergeOrder = 15
      ' Add item to main menu
      mdiMenu.MenuItems.Add(mnuEdit)
      ' Add menu to child window
      Me.Menu = mdiMenu
   End Sub

End Class
```

If a menu item in the MDI child form menu has the same MergeOrder value as a menu item in the MDI parent form menu, a second property comes into play. The MergeType property of both MenuItem objects is examined, and the behavior is determined by the combination of their values. The MergeType property is of type MenuMerge (an enumeration defined in the System.Windows.Forms namespace) and can have one of the following values:

`Add`
: The menu item appears as a separate item in the target menu, regardless of the setting of the other menu item's MergeType property.

`MergeItems`
: If the other menu item's MergeType property is also set to `MergeItems`, the two menu items are merged into a single item in the target menu. Merging is then recursively applied to the subitems of the source menus, using their MergeOrder and MergeType properties.

  If the other menu item's MergeType property is set to `Add`, both menu items appear in the target menu (just as though both had specified `Add`).

  If the other menu item's MergeType property is set to `Remove`, only this menu item appears in the target menu (again, the same as specifying `Add` for this menu item).

  If the other menu item's MergeType property is set to `Replace`, only the child form's menu item is displayed, regardless of which one is set to `MergeItems` and which one is set to `Replace`. (This seems like inconsistent behavior and may be a bug.)

`Remove`
: The menu item isn't shown in the target menu, regardless of the setting of the other menu item's MergeType property.

`Replace`
: If the other menu item's MergeType property is set to `Add`, both menu items appear in the target menu (just as though both had specified `Add`).

  If the other menu item's MergeType property is set to `MergeItems` or `Replace`, only the child form's menu item is shown. (This seems like inconsistent behavior and may be a bug.)

If the other menu item's MergeType property is also set to Replace, only the child form's menu item is shown.

Detecting MDI Child Window Activation

Code in the MDI parent form class can be notified when an MDI child form becomes active inside an MDI parent form. ("Active" means that the child form receives the input focus after another MDI child form or the MDI parent form had the input focus.) To receive such notification, the MDI parent form must override the OnMdiChildActivate method (defined in the Form class). For example:

```
' Place this within the class definition of the MDI parent form.
Protected Overrides Sub OnMdiChildActivate(ByVal e As EventArgs)
   MyBase.OnMdiChildActivate(e) ' Important
   ' ...
End Sub
```

It is important to call the base-class implementation of OnMdiChildActivate within the overriding function, so that any necessary base-class processing (including raising of the MdiChildActivate event) can occur.

The *e* parameter carries no information. To find out which MDI child form became active, read the ActiveMdiChild property of the MDI parent form. This property is of type Form. Convert it to the MDI child form's type to gain access to any public members that are specific to that type. For example:

```
Protected Overrides Sub OnMdiChildActivate(ByVal e As EventArgs)
   MyBase.OnMdiChildActivate(e)
   ' Assumes that SomeFormType is defined elsewhere and inherits
   ' from Form. Also assumes that the MDI child forms in the
   ' application are always of this type.
   Dim childForm As SomeFormType = _
      CType(ActiveMdiChild, SomeFormType)
   ' Do something with childForm here.
   ' ...
End Sub
```

To have code outside of the MDI parent form class notified when an MDI child form becomes active, write a handler for the MDI parent form's MdiChildActivate event. This event is defined in the Form class as:

```
Public Event MdiChildActivate( _
   ByVal sender As Object, _
   ByVal e As EventArgs _
)
```

The *sender* parameter is the MDI parent form, not the MDI child form that has been activated. The *e* parameter does not contain any additional information about the event. As when overriding the OnMdiChildActivate method, read the MDI parent form's ActiveMdiChild property to discover which MDI child form has been activated.

Component Attributes

As explained in Chapter 2, attributes can be added to code elements to provide additional information about those elements. The System.ComponentModel namespace defines several attributes for use in component, control, and form declarations. These attributes don't affect component behavior. Rather, they provide information that is used or displayed by the Visual Studio .NET IDE. The following is a description of each attribute:

`AmbientValueAttribute`

For ambient properties, specifies the property value that will mean "get this property's actual value from wherever ambient values come from for this property." *Ambient properties* are properties able to get their values from another source. For example, the BackColor property of a Label control can be set either to a specific Color value or to the special value Color.Empty, which causes the Label's background color to be the same as the background color of the form on which it is placed.

Putting this attribute on a property definition isn't what causes the property to behave as an ambient property: the control itself must be written such that when the special value is written to the property, the control gets the actual value from the appropriate location. This attribute simply provides the Windows Forms Designer with a way to discover what the special value is.

When specifying this attribute, pass the special value to the attribute's constructor. For example, `<AmbientValue(0)>`.

`BindableAttribute`

Indicates whether a property is typically usable for data binding. Specify `<Bindable(True)>` to indicate that the property can be used for data binding or `<Bindable(False)>` to indicate that the property typically is not used for data binding. This attribute affects how a property is displayed in the IDE, but does not affect whether a property can be bound at runtime. By default, properties are considered not bindable.

`BrowsableAttribute`

Indicates whether a property should be viewable in the IDE's Properties window. Specify `<Browsable(True)>` to indicate that the property should appear in the Properties window or `<Browsable(False)>` to indicate that it should not. By default, properties are considered browsable.

`CategoryAttribute`

Indicates the category to which a property or event belongs ("Appearance," "Behavior," etc.). The IDE uses this attribute to sort the properties and events in the Properties window. Specify the category name as a string argument to the attribute. For example, `<Category("Appearance")>`. The argument can be any string. If it is not one of the standard strings, the Properties window will add a new group for it. The standard strings are:

`Action`
: Used for events that indicate a user action, such as the Click event.

`Appearance`
: Used for properties that affect the appearance of a component, such as the BackColor property.

`Behavior`
: Used for properties that affect the behavior of a component, such as the AllowDrop property.

`Data`
: Used for properties that relate to data, such as the DecimalPlaces property of the NumericUpDown control.

`Design`
: Used for properties that relate to the design-time appearance or behavior of a component.

`DragDrop`
: Used for properties and events that relate to drag and drop. No Windows Forms components have any properties or events marked with this category.

`Focus`
: Used for properties and events that relate to input focus, such as the CanFocus property and the GotFocus event.

`Format`
: Used for properties and events that relate to formats. No Windows Forms components have any properties or events marked with this category.

`Key`
: Used for events that relate to keyboard input, such as the KeyPress event.

`Layout`
: Used for properties and events that relate to the visual layout of a component, such as the Height property and the Resize event.

`Mouse`
: Used for events that relate to mouse input, such as the MouseMove event.

`WindowStyle`
: Used for properties and events that relate to the window style of top-level forms. No Windows Forms components have any properties or events marked with this category.

If no `CategoryAttribute` is specified, the property is considered to have a category of `Misc`.

`DefaultEventAttribute`
: Indicates the name of the event that is to be considered the default event of a component. For example, `<DefaultEvent("Click")>`. When a component is double-clicked in the Windows Forms Designer, the designer switches to code

view and displays the event handler for the default event. This attribute can be used only on class declarations.

`DefaultPropertyAttribute`
: Indicates the name of the property that is to be considered the default property of a component. For example, `<DefaultProperty("Text")>`. This attribute can be used only on class declarations. The default property is the property that the Windows Forms Designer highlights in the Properties window when a component is clicked in design view.

Don't confuse this usage of the term default property with the usage associated with the Default modifier of a property declaration. The two concepts are unrelated. Refer to Chapter 2 for details on the Default modifier.

`DefaultValueAttribute`
: Indicates the default value of a property. For example, `<DefaultValue(0)>`. If the IDE is used to set a property value to something other than the default value, the code generator will generate the appropriate assignment statement in code. However, if the IDE is used to set a property to the default value, no assignment statement is generated.

`DescriptionAttribute`
: Provides a description for the code element. For example, `<Description("The text contained in the control.")>`. The IDE uses this description in tool tips and IntelliSense.

`DesignerAttribute`
: Identifies the class that acts as the designer for a component. For example, `<Designer("MyNamespace.MyClass")>`. The designer class must implement the `IDesigner` interface. This attribute can be used only on class declarations and is needed only if the built-in designer isn't sufficient. Creating custom designers is not discussed in this book.

`DesignerCategoryAttribute`
: Used with custom designers to specify the category to which the class designer belongs.

`DesignerSerializationVisibilityAttribute`
: Used with custom designers to specify how a property on a component is saved by the designer.

`DesignOnlyAttribute`
: Indicates when a property can be set. Specify `<DesignOnly(True)>` to indicate that the property can be set at design time only or `<DesignOnly(False)>` to indicate that the property can be set at both design time and runtime (the default).

`EditorAttribute`
: Identifies the "editor" to use in the IDE to allow the user to set the values of properties that have the type on which the `EditorAttribute` attribute appears. In this way, a component can declare new types and can declare properties having those types, yet still allow the user to set the values of the properties at design time. Creating custom type editors is not discussed in this book.

`EditorBrowsableAttribute`
: Indicates whether a property is viewable in an editor. The argument to the attribute's constructor must be one of the values defined by the EditorBrowsableState enumeration (defined in the System.ComponentModel namespace). The values of this enumeration are:

  `Advanced`
  : Only advanced users should see the property. It is up to the editor to determine when it's appropriate to display advanced properties.

  `Always`
  : The property should always be visible within the editor.

  `Never`
  : The property should never be shown within the editor.

`ImmutableObjectAttribute`
: Indicates whether a type declaration defines a state that can change after an object of that type is constructed. Specify `<ImmutableObject(True)>` to indicate that an object of the given type is immutable. Specify `<ImmutableObject(False)>` to indicate that an object of the given type is not immutable. The IDE uses this information to determine whether to render a property as read-only.

`InheritanceAttribute`
: Used to document an inheritance hierarchy that can be read using the `IInheritanceService` interface. This facility is not discussed in this book.

`InstallerTypeAttribute`
: Used on type declarations to specify the installer for the type. Installers are not discussed in this book.

`LicenseProviderAttribute`
: Indicates the license provider for a component.

`ListBindableAttribute`
: Indicates whether a property can be used as a data source. (A *data source* is any object that exposes the `IList` interface.) Specify `<ListBindable(True)>` to indicate that the property can be used as a data source. Specify `<ListBindable(False)>` to indicate that the property can't be used as a data source.

`LocalizableAttribute`
: Indicates whether a property's value should be localized when the application is localized. Specify `<Localizable(True)>` to indicate that the property's value

should be localized. Specify <Localizable(False)> or omit the LocalizableAttribute attribute to indicate that the property's value should not be localized. The values of properties declared with <Localizable(True)> are stored in a resource file, which can be localized.

MergablePropertyAttribute

Indicates where property attributes can be merged. By default, when two or more components are selected in the Windows Forms Designer, the Properties window typically shows the properties that are common to all of the selected components. If the user changes a value in the Properties window, the value is changed for that property in all of the selected components. Placing <MergableProperty(False)> on a property declaration changes this behavior. Any property declared in this way is omitted from the Properties window when two or more components are selected. Specifying <MergableProperty(True)> is the same as omitting the attribute altogether.

NotifyParentPropertyAttribute

Indicates whether the display of a property's *parent property* should be refreshed when the given property changes its value.

ParenthesizePropertyNameAttribute

Indicates whether the property name should be parenthesized in the Properties window. Specify <ParenthesizePropertyName(True)> to indicate that the property name should appear within parentheses. Specify <ParenthesizePropertyName(False)> to indicate that the property name should not appear within parentheses. Omitting the attribute is the same as specifying <ParenthesizePropertyName(False)>.

The only benefit to parenthesizing property names in the property window is that they are sorted to the top of the list. Microsoft has no specific recommendations for when to parenthesize a property name.

PropertyTabAttribute

Specifies a type that implements a custom property tab (or tabs) for a component. This facility is not discussed in this book.

ProvidePropertyAttribute

Used with *extender providers*—i.e., classes that provide properties for *other* objects. Extender providers are not discussed in this book.

ReadOnlyAttribute

Indicates whether a property is read-only at design time. Specify <ReadOnly(True)> to indicate that the property is read-only at design time. Specify <ReadOnly(False)> to indicate that the property's ability to be modified at design time is determined by whether a Set method is defined for the property. Omitting the attribute is the same as specifying <ReadOnly(False)>.

`RecommendedAsConfigurableAttribute`
: Indicates whether a property is configurable. Configurable properties aren't discussed in this book.

`RefreshPropertiesAttribute`
: Determines how the Properties window is refreshed when the value of the given property changes.

`RunInstallerAttribute`
: Indicates whether an installer should be invoked during installation of the assembly that contains the associated class. This attribute can be used only on class declarations, and the associated class must inherit from the Installer class (defined in the System.Configuration.Install namespace). Installers are not discussed in this book.

`ToolboxItemAttribute`
: Specifies a type that implements a toolbox item related to the declaration on which the attribute is placed. This facility is not discussed in this book.

`ToolboxItemFilterAttribute`
: Specifies a filter string for a toolbox-item filter. This facility is not discussed in this book.

`TypeConverterAttribute`
: Indicates the type converter to be used with the associated item. Type converters are not discussed in this book.

2-D Graphics Programming with GDI+

The Windows operating system has always included support for drawing two-dimensional graphics. This support is known as the Graphics Device Interface (GDI) library. The GDI library is now easier to use and provides additional features. The new capabilities are known collectively as GDI+. GDI+ features are exposed in the .NET Framework through classes in the System.Drawing, System.Drawing.Drawing2D, System.Drawing.Imaging, and System.Drawing.Text namespaces. This section discusses some of those capabilities.

The Graphics Class

Objects of type Graphics (defined in the System.Drawing namespace) represent two-dimensional surfaces on which to draw. A Graphics object must be obtained before any drawing can be done. A common way to obtain a Graphics object is to override the OnPaint method of a form or user control, as shown in the following code fragment:

```
Public Class MyControl
   Inherits UserControl
```

```
    Protected Overrides Sub OnPaint(ByVal e As PaintEventArgs)
       e.Graphics.FillEllipse(New SolidBrush(Me.ForeColor), _
          Me.ClientRectangle)
    End Sub

    Public Sub New( )
       Me.ResizeRedraw = True
    End Sub

End Class
```

The single argument passed to the OnPaint method, *e*, is of type PaintEventArgs. This class has a property called Graphics, which holds a reference to the Graphics object to be used for drawing on the user control or form. The PaintEventArgs class is defined in the System.Windows.Forms namespace. It has two properties:

ClipRectangle
: Defines the area that needs to be drawn. Drawing done outside the limits of the clip rectangle will not be displayed. The coordinates of the rectangle are relative to the client rectangle of the user control or form.

  The syntax of the ClipRectangle property is:

  ```
  Public ReadOnly Property ClipRectangle( ) As System.Drawing.Rectangle
  ```

Graphics
: Defines the graphics surface on which to draw. The syntax of the Graphics property is:

  ```
  Public ReadOnly Property Graphics( ) As System.Drawing.Graphics
  ```

The following list shows some of the Graphics class's many methods that are available for drawing various lines and shapes, and Example 5-7 in Chapter 5 gives an example of drawing a filled ellipse. This list is just to get you started; it is beyond the scope of this book to document the syntax of each of these methods.

DrawArc
: Draws an arc (that is, a portion of an ellipse).

DrawBezier
: Draws a Bezier curve.

DrawBeziers
: Draws a series of Bezier curves.

DrawClosedCurve
: Is the same as the DrawCurve method (see the next item in this list), except that the last point in the curve is connected back to the first point.

DrawCurve
: Draws a smooth, curved figure that passes through a given array of points.

DrawEllipse
: Draws an ellipse.

DrawIcon
: Draws an icon. Icons are represented by objects of type Icon (defined in the System.Drawing namespace). The Icon class defines various methods for loading icons.

DrawIconUnstretched
: Is the same as the DrawIcon method, but does not stretch the icon to fit the clipping rectangle.

DrawImage
: Draws an image. Images are represented by objects of type Image (defined in the System.Drawing namespace). The Image class defines various methods for loading images in standard formats, such as bitmaps and JPEGs.

DrawImageUnscaled
: Is the same as DrawImage, except that the DrawImageUnscaled method ignores any width and height parameters passed to it.

DrawLine
: Draws a line.

DrawLines
: Draws a series of lines.

DrawPath
: Draws a series of lines and curves that are defined by a GraphicsPath object. The GraphicsPath class is beyond the scope of this book.

DrawPie
: Draws a pie section.

DrawPolygon
: Draws lines to connect a series of points.

DrawRectangle
: Draws a rectangle.

DrawRectangles
: Draws a series of rectangles.

DrawString
: Draws text.

FillClosedCurve
: Draws a filled, closed curve.

FillEllipse
: Draws a filled ellipse.

FillPath
: Draws a filled figure whose shape is given by a GraphicsPath object. The GraphicsPath class is beyond the scope of this book.

FillPie
: Draws a filled pie section.

FillPolygon
: Draws a filled polygon (see the DrawPolygon method earlier in this list).

FillRectangle
: Draws a filled rectangle.

FillRectangles
: Draws a series of filled rectangles.

FillRegion
: Draws a filled figure whose shape is given by a Region object.

The Pen Class

Pen objects hold the settings used when drawing lines. All of the Graphics class's Draw...methods (DrawArc, DrawBezier, etc.) require that the caller supply a Pen object. The supplied Pen object determines the properties of the line used for drawing (for example, its color, width, etc.). Example 4-9 shows an OnPaint method that can be used to draw an ellipse on a user control or a form. It is similar to the code in Example 5-6 in Chapter 5, but displays the ellipse a little smaller, and with only a border. The resulting display is shown in Figure 4-9.

Example 4-9. Drawing an ellipse on a form

```
Protected Overrides Sub OnPaint(ByVal e As PaintEventArgs)
   Dim pn As New Pen(Me.ForeColor)
   Dim rect As Rectangle

   rect.X = Me.ClientRectangle.X + (Me.ClientRectangle.Width \ 4)
   rect.Y = Me.ClientRectangle.Y + (Me.ClientRectangle.Height \ 4)
   rect.Width = Me.ClientRectangle.Width \ 2
   rect.Height = Me.ClientRectangle.Height \ 2

   e.Graphics.DrawEllipse(pn, rect)
   pn.Dispose( )
End Sub
```

In Example 4-9, the Graphics class's DrawEllipse method is passed a Pen object, which determines the appearance of the line used for drawing the ellipse, and a rectangle, which defines the shape of the ellipse. The Pen class has four constructors. The constructor used in Example 4-9 takes a parameter of type Color (defined in System.Drawing). The color passed to the Pen class constructor in Example 4-9 is the foreground color of the form (Me.ForeColor). This is a nice touch ensuring that the ellipse will be drawn using whatever color is set as the foreground color of the form on which the ellipse is drawn. See "The Color Structure" later in this chapter for information on choosing and manipulating colors. Finally, note this line in Example 4-9:

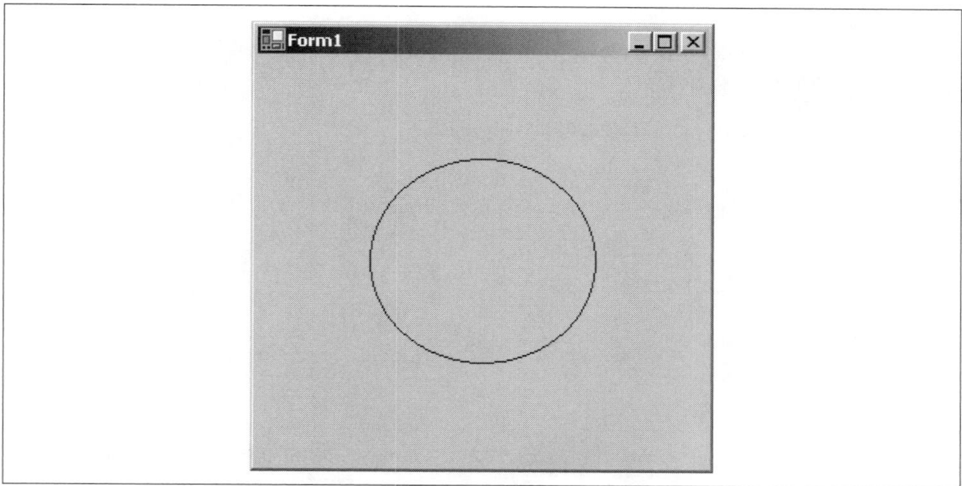

Figure 4-9. The ellipse drawn by the code in Example 4-9

```
pn.Dispose( )
```

By convention, objects that allocate scarce resources expose a Dispose method to allow the object client to tell the object to release its resources. When using any object that exposes a Dispose method (as the Pen object does), the Dispose method must be called when the client code is finished using the object. If the Dispose method isn't called (or if it isn't implemented), resources will be held longer than necessary, which may in turn result in resources being unavailable for other code that needs them.

The .NET Framework provides a number of predefined pens through the properties of the Pens and SystemPens classes (defined in the System.Drawing namespace). For example, the Blue property of the Pens class returns a Pen object whose color is set to `Color.Blue`. Thus, the following line of code draws a blue ellipse:

```
e.Graphics.DrawEllipse(Pens.Blue, rect)
```

Similarly, the SystemPens class's WindowText property returns a Pen object whose color is set to the system's window text color. Using the standard pens provided by the Pens and SystemPens classes can be more efficient than instantiating new Pen objects. However, their properties (such as line width) cannot be altered.

See Table 4-1, later in this chapter, for the list of Pen objects available through the Pens class. See "System colors" in the section titled "The Color Structure" later in this chapter for the list of Pen objects available through the SystemPens class.

When working with a user-instantiated pen, you can modify the line that is drawn by setting properties of the Pen object. The code in Example 4-10 sets the Pen object's Width property to widen the outline of the ellipse. The lines of code that differ from Example 4-9 are shown in bold. The resulting display is shown in Figure 4-10.

Example 4-10. Setting Pen properties

```
Protected Overrides Sub OnPaint(ByVal e As PaintEventArgs)
   Dim pn As New Pen(Me.ForeColor)
   pn.Width = 10
   pn.DashStyle = Drawing.Drawing2D.DashStyle.Dash
   Dim rect As Rectangle

   rect.X = Me.ClientRectangle.X + (Me.ClientRectangle.Width \ 4)
   rect.Y = Me.ClientRectangle.Y + (Me.ClientRectangle.Height \ 4)
   rect.Width = Me.ClientRectangle.Width \ 2
   rect.Height = Me.ClientRectangle.Height \ 2

   e.Graphics.DrawEllipse(pn, rect)
   pn.Dispose( )
End Sub
```

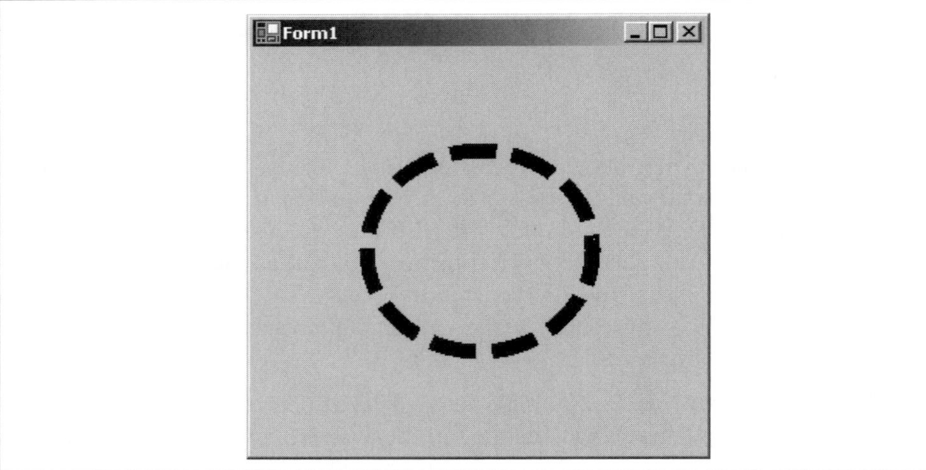

Figure 4-10. The ellipse drawn by the code in Example 4-10

Example 4-10 sets the Pen object's Width and DashStyle properties to attain the effect shown in Figure 4-10. The Width property is a value of type Single that determines the width of lines drawn with this pen. The default is 1. The unit of measurement is determined by the PageUnit property of the Graphics object in which the lines are drawn. The PageUnit property is of the enumeration type GraphicsUnit (defined in the System.Drawing namespace). The values of GraphicsUnit that are appropriate for assignment to the PageUnit property are:

`Display`
: Units are specified in 1/75 of an inch.

`Document`
: Units are specified in 1/300 of an inch.

`Inch`
: Units are specified in inches.

`Millimeter`
: Units are specified in millimeters.

`Pixel`
: Units are specified in pixels.

`Point`
: Units are specified in points (1/72 of an inch).

The DashStyle property of the Pen object determines the whether the line is solid or dashed, as well as the style of the dash. The DashStyle property is of the enumeration type DashStyle (defined in the System.Drawing.Drawing2D namespace), which defines the following values:

`Custom`
: Specifies a programmer-defined dash style. If this value is used, other properties of the Pen object control the exact appearance of the dashes in the line. Creating custom dash styles is not discussed in this book.

`Dash`
: Specifies a dashed line.

`DashDot`
: Specifies a line consisting of alternating dashes and dots.

`DashDotDot`
: Specifies a line consisting of alternating dashes and two dots.

`Dot`
: Specifies a dotted line.

`Solid`
: Specifies a solid line.

The standard dash styles are shown in Figure 4-11.

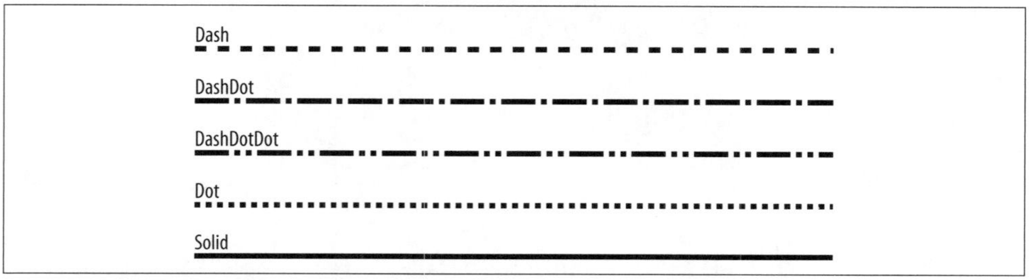

Figure 4-11. The standard DashStyle values

The Brush Class

Brush objects hold the settings used when filling graphics areas. All of the Graphics class's Fill...methods (FillClosedCurve, FillEllipse, etc.) require that the caller supply a Brush object. The supplied Brush object determines how the interior of the figure will be painted. Example 4-11 shows an OnPaint method that can be used to draw an ellipse on a user control or a form. It is similar to Example 4-9, but draws a filled ellipse rather than an outline. The lines that differ from Example 4-9 are shown in bold. The resulting display is shown in Figure 4-12.

Example 4-11. Drawing a filled ellipse on a form

```
Protected Overrides Sub OnPaint(ByVal e As PaintEventArgs)
   Dim br As New SolidBrush(Me.ForeColor)
   Dim rect As Rectangle

   rect.X = Me.ClientRectangle.X + (Me.ClientRectangle.Width \ 4)
   rect.Y = Me.ClientRectangle.Y + (Me.ClientRectangle.Height \ 4)
   rect.Width = Me.ClientRectangle.Width \ 2
   rect.Height = Me.ClientRectangle.Height \ 2

   e.Graphics.FillEllipse(br, rect)
   br.Dispose( )
End Sub
```

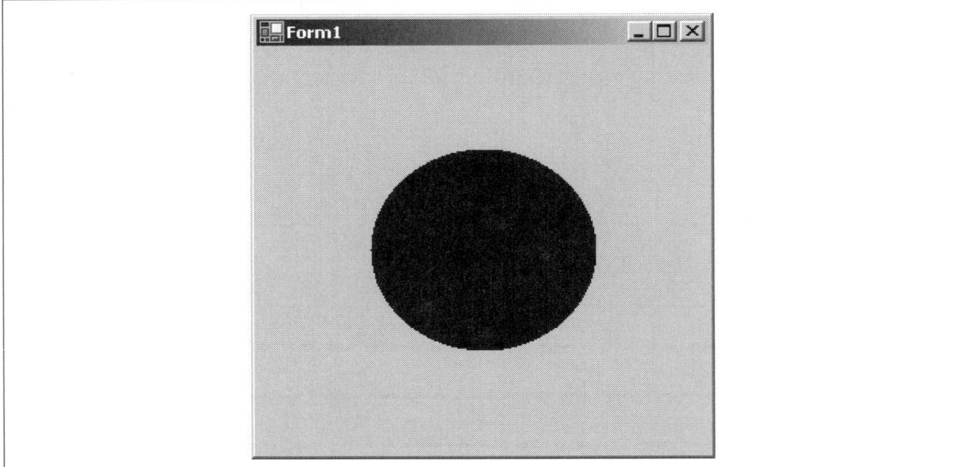

Figure 4-12. The ellipse drawn by the code in Example 4-11

Note that Example 4-11 is not entirely parallel to Example 4-9. Specifically, Example 4-9 instantiated a Pen object directly, but Example 4-11 instantiates an object from a class that derives from the Brush class rather than directly from the Brush class. Objects can't be directly instantiated from the Brush class. The classes that derive from Brush are:

HatchBrush
Fills an area with a hatch pattern. Hatch patterns are patterns of lines and spaces. The HatchBrush class's HatchStyle property determines the exact pattern of the hatch. It is defined in the System.Drawing.Drawing2D namespace.

LinearGradientBrush
Fills an area with a gradient blend of two or more colors. It is defined in the System.Drawing.Drawing2D namespace.

PathGradientBrush
Fills the internal area of a GraphicsPath object with a gradient blend of two or more colors. It is defined in the System.Drawing.Drawing2D namespace.

SolidBrush
Fills an area with a solid color. It is defined in the System.Drawing namespace.

TextureBrush
Fills an area with an image. It is defined in the System.Drawing namespace.

The .NET Framework provides a number of predefined brushes through the properties of the Brushes and SystemBrushes classes (defined in the System.Drawing namespace). For example, the Blue property of the Brushes class returns a Brush object that fills areas with solid blue. Thus, the following line of code draws a solid blue ellipse:

```
e.Graphics.FillEllipse(Brushes.Blue, rect)
```

Similarly, the SystemBrushes class's Window property returns a Brush object whose color is set to the background color of the system's window client area. Using the standard brushes provided by the Brushes and SystemBrushes classes can be more efficient than instantiating new Brush objects. However, their properties cannot be altered.

See Table 4-1 for the list of Brush objects available through the Brushes class. See "System colors" in the next section for the list of Brush objects available through the SystemBrushes class.

The Color Structure

Colors are represented by values of type Color. The Color structure defines 141 named colors and exposes them as shared read-only properties whose values are of type Color. They serve the purpose of color constants. For example, the following code fragment sets the background color of the form `frm` to white:

```
frm.BackColor = Color.White
```

The color properties exposed by the Color structure have the same names as the pen properties exposed by the Pens class and the brush properties exposed by the Brushes class. The list is lengthy, so it is printed here only once, in Table 4-1.

Table 4-1. Properties common to the Color, Pens, and Brushes classes

AliceBlue	AntiqueWhite	Aqua
Aquamarine	Azure	Beige
Bisque	Black	BlanchedAlmond
Blue	BlueViolet	Brown
BurlyWood	CadetBlue	Chartreuse
Chocolate	Coral	CornflowerBlue
Cornsilk	Crimson	Cyan
DarkBlue	DarkCyan	DarkGoldenrod
DarkGray	DarkGreen	DarkKhaki
DarkMagenta	DarkOliveGreen	DarkOrange
DarkOrchid	DarkRed	DarkSalmon
DarkSeaGreen	DarkSlateBlue	DarkSlateGray
DarkTurquoise	DarkViolet	DeepPink
DeepSkyBlue	DimGray	DodgerBlue
Firebrick	FloralWhite	ForestGreen
Fuchsia	Gainsboro	GhostWhite
Gold	Goldenrod	Gray
Green	GreenYellow	Honeydew
HotPink	IndianRed	Indigo
Ivory	Khaki	Lavender
LavenderBlush	LawnGreen	LemonChiffon
LightBlue	LightCoral	LightCyan
LightGoldenrodYellow	LightGray	LightGreen
LightPink	LightSalmon	LightSeaGreen
LightSkyBlue	LightSlateGray	LightSteelBlue
LightYellow	Lime	LimeGreen
Linen	Magenta	Maroon
MediumAquamarine	MediumBlue	MediumOrchid
MediumPurple	MediumSeaGreen	MediumSlateBlue
MediumSpringGreen	MediumTurquoise	MediumVioletRed
MidnightBlue	MintCream	MistyRose
Moccasin	NavajoWhite	Navy
OldLace	Olive	OliveDrab
Orange	OrangeRed	Orchid
PaleGoldenrod	PaleGreen	PaleTurquoise
PaleVioletRed	PapayaWhip	PeachPuff
Peru	Pink	Plum

Table 4-1. Properties common to the Color, Pens, and Brushes classes (continued)

PowderBlue	Purple	Red
RosyBrown	RoyalBlue	SaddleBrown
Salmon	SandyBrown	SeaGreen
SeaShell	Sienna	Silver
SkyBlue	SlateBlue	SlateGray
Snow	SpringGreen	SteelBlue
Tan	Teal	Thistle
Tomato	Transparent	Turquoise
Violet	Wheat	White
WhiteSmoke	Yellow	YellowGreen

System colors

It is useful to discover the colors that Windows uses to draw specific window elements, such as the active window's title bar. If the color itself is required, it can be obtained from the SystemColors class. If a pen or brush of the appropriate color is needed, the pen or brush can be obtained from the corresponding property of the Pens or Brushes class, respectively. The property names exposed by these three classes overlap and, therefore, are presented here in a single list:

ActiveBorder
: The color of the filled area of the border of the active window. (Not available on the Pens class.)

ActiveCaption
: The background color of the title bar of the active window. (Not available on the Pens class.)

ActiveCaptionText
: The text color in the title bar of the active window.

AppWorkspace
: The background color of MDI parent windows. (Not available on the Pens class.)

Control
: The background color of controls.

ControlDark
: The shadow color of controls (for 3-D effects).

ControlDarkDark
: The very dark shadow color of controls (for 3-D effects).

ControlLight
: The highlight color of controls (for 3-D effects).

ControlLightLight
The very light highlight color of controls (for 3-D effects).

ControlText
The color of text on controls.

Desktop
The color of the Windows desktop. (Not available on the Pens class.)

GrayText
The text color of disabled controls or other disabled visual elements. (Not available on the Brushes class.)

Highlight
The background color of highlighted (selected) text.

HighlightText
The text color of highlighted (selected) text.

HotTrack
The background color of a *hot tracked* item. Hot tracking is highlighting an item as the mouse moves over it. Windows menus use hot tracking. (Not available on the Pens class.)

InactiveBorder
The color of the filled areas of the borders of inactive windows. (Not available on the Pens class.)

InactiveCaption
The background color of the title bars of inactive windows. (Not available on the Pens class.)

InactiveCaptionText
The text color in the title bars of inactive windows. (Not available on the Brushes class.)

Info
The background color of tool tips. (Not available on the Pens class.)

InfoText
The text color of tool tips. (Not available on the Brushes class.)

Menu
The background color of menus. (Not available on the Pens class.)

MenuText
The text color of menus. (Not available on the Brushes class.)

ScrollBar
The color of scroll bars in the area not occupied by the scroll box (or *thumb*). (Not available on the Pens class.)

Window
: The background color of the client areas of windows. (Not available on the Pens class.)

WindowFrame
: The color of the frames surrounding windows. (Not available on the Brushes class.)

WindowText
: The color of the text in the client areas of windows.

Note that some of these properties aren't available on either the Pens class or the Brushes class. In such cases, it is still possible to get a Pen or Brush object of the appropriate color by instantiating a new Pen or Brush object, passing to its constructor the desired color value, like this:

```
Dim br As New SolidBrush(SystemColors.InfoText)
```

Alpha Blending

Alpha blending is a process that allows a Graphics object to appear transparent, causing Graphics objects beneath it to be seen through the object. The degree of transparency can be controlled in steps from completely transparent (invisible) to completely opaque (obscuring any objects beneath it). To draw a transparent object, instantiate Pen and Brush objects having colors whose *alpha* component is less than the maximum value of 255. A color's alpha component is given by the A property of the Color structure. This property is a Byte, so it can take values from 0 (invisible) to 255 (completely opaque).

Example 4-12 shows an OnPaint method that draws text and then draws two overlapping, transparent ellipses in the same space as the text. Normally, the ellipses would obscure the text, and the second ellipse would obscure the first. In this case, however, the text can be seen through the ellipses because the ellipses are transparent, and the first ellipse can be seen through the second. The result is shown in Figure 4-13.

Example 4-12. Drawing transparent figures

```
Protected Overrides Sub OnPaint(ByVal e As PaintEventArgs)

   ' Determine the text to display and its font.
   Dim str As String = "Here is some text to display in a form."
   Dim fnt As New Font("Arial", 10, FontStyle.Regular, GraphicsUnit.Point)

   ' Determine the X and Y coordinates at which to draw the text so
   ' that it is centered in the window.
   Dim szf As SizeF = e.Graphics.MeasureString(str, fnt)
   Dim xText As Single = (Me.DisplayRectangle.Width - szf.Width) / 2
   Dim yText As Single = (Me.DisplayRectangle.Height - szf.Height) / 2
```

Example 4-12. Drawing transparent figures (continued)

```
    ' Draw the text.
    e.Graphics.DrawString(str, fnt, Brushes.Black, xText, yText)

    ' Create a blue brush that is mostly transparent.
    Dim br As New SolidBrush(Color.FromArgb(160, Color.Blue))

    ' Determine the bounding rectangle for the first ellipse.
    Dim rect As Rectangle
    rect.X = Me.DisplayRectangle.X + (Me.DisplayRectangle.Width \ 8)
    rect.Y = Me.DisplayRectangle.Y + (Me.DisplayRectangle.Height \ 8)
    rect.Width = Me.DisplayRectangle.Width \ 2
    rect.Height = Me.DisplayRectangle.Height \ 2

    ' Draw the first ellipse.
    e.Graphics.FillEllipse(br, rect)

    ' Release the brush.
    br.Dispose( )

    ' Create a red brush that is mostly transparent.
    br = New SolidBrush(Color.FromArgb(160, Color.Red))

    ' Determine the bounding rectangle for the second ellipse.
    rect.X += (Me.DisplayRectangle.Width \ 4)
    rect.Y += (Me.DisplayRectangle.Height \ 4)

    ' Draw the second ellipse.
    e.Graphics.FillEllipse(br, rect)

    ' Release the brush.
    br.Dispose( )

End Sub
```

Antialiasing

Antialiasing is a technique for making the edges of graphics figures appear less jagged. To turn on antialiasing, set the Graphics object's SmoothingMode property to `SmoothingMode.AntiAlias`. (SmoothingMode is an enumeration defined in the System.Drawing.Drawing2D namespace.) Compare the arcs shown in Figure 4-14. Both arcs were drawn by calling the DrawArc method of the Graphics class, but the arc on the left was drawn with the SmoothingMode property set to `SmoothingMode.None` (the default), and the arc on the right was drawn with the SmoothingMode property set to `SmoothingMode.AntiAlias`. Figure 4-15 shows a close-up comparison view of the upper portion of both arcs.

As Figure 4-15 shows, antialiasing appears to improve pixel resolution by using gradient shades of the color being rendered and of the background color (in this case, black and white, respectively).

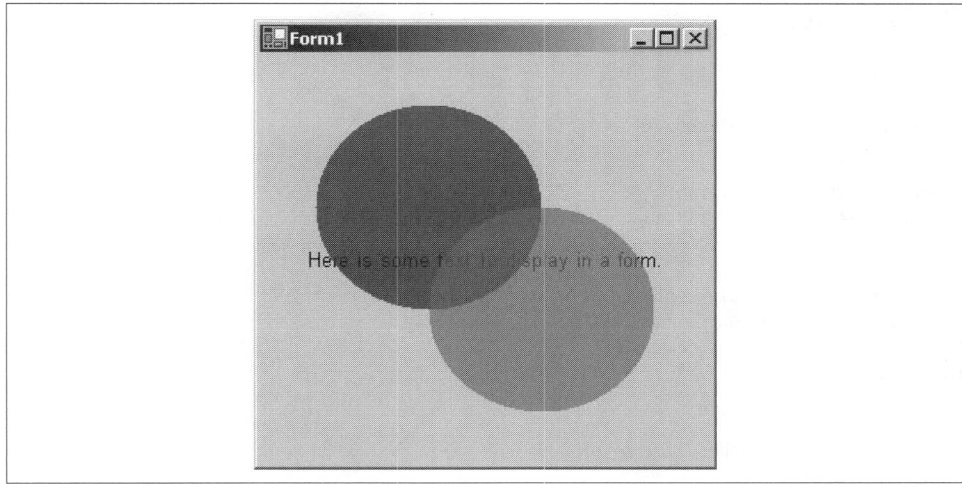

Figure 4-13. The display drawn by the code in Example 4-12

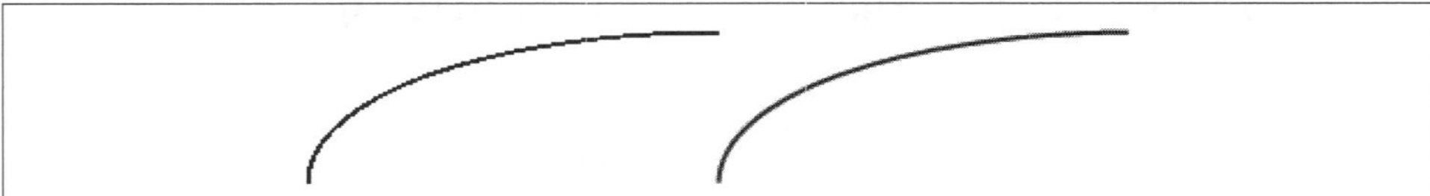

Figure 4-14. Nonantialiased versus antialiased arcs

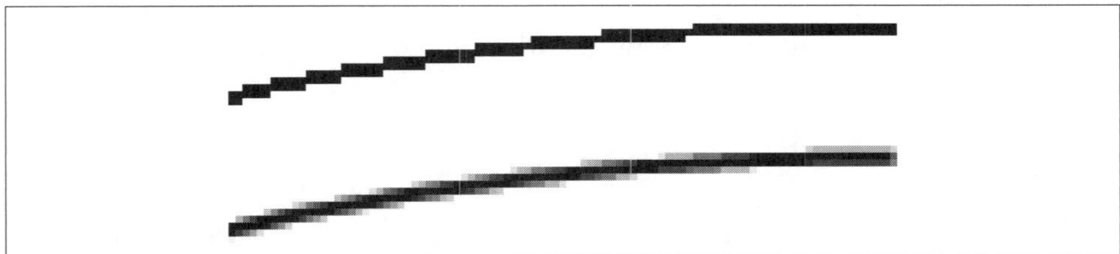

Figure 4-15. Close-up view of nonantialiased and antialiased arcs

The downside to antialiasing is that it takes more time to render.

Printing

Most Visual Basic .NET programs will never need to use the .NET Framework's native printing capabilities. Reporting tools such as Crystal Reports, as well as RAD tools for laying out reports, provide most of the printing facilities that typical Visual Basic .NET programs need. However, for the cases in which a reporting tool is not flexible enough, this section describes the .NET Framework's support for outputting text and graphics directly to a printer.

Hello, Printer!

Example 4-13 shows a minimal printing example.

Example 4-13. Hello, Printer!

```
Imports System.Drawing
Imports System.Drawing.Drawing2D
Imports System.Drawing.Printing

' ...
' These two lines initiate printing. Place this code in an
' appropriate place in the application.
Dim pd As New HelloPrintDocument( )
pd.Print( )
' ...

' This class manages the printing process.
Public Class HelloPrintDocument
   Inherits PrintDocument

   Protected Overrides Sub OnPrintPage(ByVal e As PrintPageEventArgs)
      MyBase.OnPrintPage(e)

      ' Draw text to the printer graphics device.
      Dim fnt As New Font("Arial", 10, FontStyle.Regular, _
         GraphicsUnit.Point)
      e.Graphics.DrawString("Hello, Printer!", fnt, Brushes.Black, 0, 0)
      fnt.Dispose( )

      ' Indicate that there are no more pages.
      e.HasMorePages = False
   End Sub

End Class
```

Printing is managed by defining a class that inherits from the PrintDocument class (defined in the System.Drawing.Printing namespace). Printing is initiated by instantiating the derived class and calling its Print method (inherited from the PrintDocument class). The Print method repeatedly calls the OnPrintPage method, until the HasMorePages property of the PrintPageEventArgs parameter is set to `False`. It is the job of the OnPrintPage method to generate each page of output that is sent to the printer.

Take a closer look at the OnPrintPage method in Example 4-13, starting with the first line:

```
MyBase.OnPrintPage(e)
```

This line of code calls the OnPrintPage method implemented by the base PrintDocument class, passing it the same argument that was passed into the derived class's OnPrintPage method. This call is important because the PrintDocument class's

OnPrintPage method is responsible for firing the PrintDocument object's PrintPage event. If this is not done, any code that has registered for this event will not receive it. This is not an issue in this small example, but it's nevertheless good programming practice.

The next three lines of code are responsible for handling the printing:

```
' Draw text to the printer graphics device.
Dim fnt As New Font("Arial", 10, FontStyle.Regular, _
   GraphicsUnit.Point)
e.Graphics.DrawString("Hello, Printer!", fnt, Brushes.Black, 0, 0)
fnt.Dispose( )
```

This code draws some text to the Graphics object provided through the PrintPageEventArgs parameter. Everything you learned in the previous section about the Graphics object is applicable here.

Finally, since we're printing just one page in our example program, PrintPageEventArgs.HasMorePages is set to `False`:

```
' Indicate that there are no more pages.
e.HasMorePages = False
```

This line indicates to the Print method that the end of the document has been reached. If more pages need to be printed, the OnPrintPage method should set the HasMorePages property to `True`.

The PrintPageEventArgs Class

The PrintPageEventArgs class is declared in the System.Drawing.Printing namespace as:

```
Public Class PrintPageEventArgs
   Inherits System.EventArgs
```

Its properties are:

Cancel
: An indication of whether the print job is being canceled. This property is set to `True` by the printing system if the user cancels the print job. Code in the OnPrintPage method can read this value and take any appropriate action. However, programmatically setting this property back to `False` does not resume the print job. On the other hand, programmatically setting it to `True` does cancel the print job, even if the user has not clicked the Cancel button. The syntax of the Cancel property is:

```
Public Property Cancel( ) As Boolean
```

Graphics
: The Graphics object that represents the page surface. The syntax of the Graphics property is:

```
Public ReadOnly Property Graphics( ) As System.Drawing.Graphics
```

HasMorePages

The mechanism for the OnPrintPage method to indicate to the printing system whether there are more pages to be printed after the current page. The OnPrintPage method should set this property to True when there are more pages to print and to False when there are no more pages to print. The syntax of the HasMorePages property is:

```
Public Property HasMorePages( ) As Boolean
```

MarginBounds

A rectangle that specifies the area of the page that is within the document margins (i.e., the area of the page on which rendering should occur). The syntax of the MarginBounds property is:

```
Public ReadOnly Property MarginBounds( ) As System.Drawing.Rectangle
```

PageBounds

A rectangle that specifies the full area of the page, including the area outside the margins. The syntax of the PageBounds property is:

```
Public ReadOnly Property PageBounds( ) As System.Drawing.Rectangle
```

PageSettings

The page settings that apply to the page currently being printed. The syntax of the PageSettings property is:

```
Public ReadOnly Property PageSettings( ) As _
   System.Drawing.Printing.PageSettings
```

The PageSettings class is described later in this section.

The OnBeginPrint and OnEndPrint Methods

The PrintDocument class provides the OnBeginPrint and OnEndPrint methods for managing the start and finish of print jobs. The OnBeginPrint method is called prior to the first call to OnPrintPage, and the OnEndPrint method is called after the final call to OnPrintPage. The OnBeginPrint method is a good place to set up objects that will be used throughout the life of the print job—pens, brushes, and fonts, for example. The HelloPrintDocument class in Example 4-13 instantiates a Font object during the OnPrintPage method. This is acceptable here because only one page is being printed. However, in practice documents may contain many pages, so it is better to move this code to the OnBeginPrint method. Example 4-14 shows how the HelloPrintDocument looks when modified in this way.

Example 4-14. Using OnBeginPrint and OnEndPrint to set up and tear down objects used during printing

```
Public Class HelloPrintDocument
   Inherits PrintDocument

   ' Private member to hold the font that will be used for printing.
   Private m_fnt As Font
```

Example 4-14. Using OnBeginPrint and OnEndPrint to set up and tear down objects used during printing (continued)

```
   Protected Overrides Sub OnBeginPrint(ByVal e As PrintEventArgs)
      MyBase.OnBeginPrint(e)

      ' Create the font that will be used for printing.
      m_fnt = New Font("Arial", 10, FontStyle.Regular, _
         GraphicsUnit.Point)
   End Sub

   Protected Overrides Sub OnEndPrint(ByVal e As PrintEventArgs)
      MyBase.OnEndPrint(e)

      ' Release the font.
      m_fnt.Dispose( )
   End Sub

   Protected Overrides Sub OnPrintPage(ByVal e As PrintPageEventArgs)
      MyBase.OnPrintPage(e)

      ' Draw text to the printer graphics device.
      Dim rect As Rectangle = e.MarginBounds
      e.Graphics.DrawString("Hello, Printer!", m_fnt, Brushes.Black, 0, 0)

      ' Indicate that there are no more pages.
      e.HasMorePages = False
   End Sub

End Class
```

Choosing a Printer

The code given in Examples 4-13 and 4-14 merely prints to the default printer. To allow the user to select a specific printer and set other printer options, pass the PrintDocument object to a PrintDialog object and call the PrintDialog object's ShowDialog method. The ShowDialog method displays a PrintDialog dialog box (shown in Figure 5-19 in Chapter 5). When the user clicks OK in the PrintDialog dialog box, the ShowDialog method sets the appropriate values in the given PrintDocument object. The PrintDocument object's Print method can then be called to print the document to the selected printer. Here is the code:

```
' Create the PrintDocument object and the dialog box object.
Dim pd As New HelloPrintDocument( )
Dim dlg As New PrintDialog( )
' Pass the PrintDocument object to the dialog box object.
dlg.Document = pd
' Show the dialog box. Be sure to test the result so that printing
' occurs only if the user clicks OK.
If dlg.ShowDialog = DialogResult.OK Then
   ' Print the document.
   pd.Print( )
End If
```

This code assumes the presence of the HelloPrintDocument class defined in Example 4-13 or Example 4-14. Note that the HelloPrintDocument class itself does not need to be modified to support choosing a printer.

The PageSettings Class

As mentioned earlier, the PrintPageEventArgs object passed to the OnPrintPage method has a PageSettings property that holds a PageSettings object. This object holds the settings applicable to printing a single page. The properties of the PageSettings class are:

Bounds
: Represents a rectangle that specifies the full area of the page, including the area outside the margins. This is the same value found in the PageBounds property of the PrintPageEventArgs class. The syntax of the Bounds property is:

```
Public ReadOnly Property Bounds( ) As System.Drawing.Rectangle
```

Color
: Indicates whether the page should be printed in color. The syntax of the Color property is:

```
Public Property Color( ) As Boolean
```

Landscape
: Indicates whether the page is being printed in landscape orientation. The syntax of the Landscape property is:

```
Public Property Landscape( ) As Boolean
```

Margins
: Indicates the size of the margins. The syntax of the Margins property is:

```
Public Property Margins( ) As System.Drawing.Printing.Margins
```

The Margins class has four properties, Left, Top, Right, and Bottom, each of which is an Integer expressing the size of the respective margin.

PaperSize
: Indicates the size of the paper. The syntax of the PaperSize property is:

```
Public Property PaperSize( ) As System.Drawing.Printing.PaperSize
```

The PaperSize class has four properties:

Width
: An Integer expressing the width of the paper. This is the same value found in the Width member of the Bounds property of the PageSettings object.

Height
: An Integer expressing the height of the paper. This is the same value found in the Height member of the Bounds property of the PageSettings object.

Kind

An enumeration of type PaperKind expressing the size of the paper in terms of standard named sizes, such as `Letter` and `Legal`.

PaperName

A string giving the name of the paper size, such as `"Letter"` and `"Legal"`.

PaperSource

Indicates the paper tray from which the page will be printed. The syntax of the PaperSource property is:

```
Public Property PaperSource( ) As System.Drawing.Printing.PaperSource
```

The PaperSource class has two properties:

Kind

An enumeration of type PaperSourceKind expressing the paper source in terms of standard names, such as `Lower` and `Upper`.

SourceName

A string giving the name of the paper source, such as `"Lower"` and `"Upper"`.

PrinterResolution

Indicates the resolution capability of the printer. The syntax of the PrinterResolution property is:

```
Public Property PrinterResolution( ) As _
   System.Drawing.Printing.PrinterResolution
```

The PrinterResolution class has three properties:

X

An Integer expressing the horizontal resolution of the printer in dots per inch.

Y

An Integer expressing the vertical resolution of the printer in dots per inch.

Kind

An enumeration of type PrinterResolutionKind expressing the resolution mode. The values of this enumeration are `Draft`, `Low`, `Medium`, `High`, and `Custom`.

PrinterSettings

Indicates the settings applicable to the printer being used. The syntax of the PrinterSettings property is:

```
Public Property PrinterSettings( ) As _
   System.Drawing.Printing.PrinterSettings
```

The PrinterSettings class is described in the next section.

The PrinterSettings Class

The PrinterSettings class holds values that describe the capabilities and settings of a specific printer. It exposes these properties:

CanDuplex
: Indicates whether the printer can print on both sides of the paper. The syntax of the CanDuplex property is:

```
Public ReadOnly Property CanDuplex( ) As Boolean
```

Collate
: Indicates whether the document being printed will be collated. The syntax of the Collate property is:

```
Public Property Collate( ) As Boolean
```

Copies
: Indicates the number of copies to print. The syntax of the Copies property is:

```
Public Property Copies( ) As Short
```

DefaultPageSettings
: Indicates the default page settings for this printer. The syntax of the DefaultPageSettings property is:

```
Public ReadOnly Property DefaultPageSettings( ) As _
   System.Drawing.Printing.PageSettings
```

The PageSettings class was described in the previous section.

Duplex
: Indicates whether the print job is to print on both sides of the paper. The syntax of the Duplex property is:

```
Public Property Duplex( ) As System.Drawing.Printing.Duplex
```

The Duplex type is an enumeration with the following values:

`Simplex`
: The document will print only on one side of each page.

`Horizontal`
: The document will print using both sides of each page.

`Vertical`
: The document will print using both sides of each page, and the second side will be inverted to work with vertical binding.

`Default`
: The document will print using the printer's default duplex mode.

FromPage
: Specifies the first page to print if the PrintRange property is set to `SomePages`. The syntax of the FromPage property is:

```
Public Property FromPage( ) As Integer
```

InstalledPrinters

Indicates the names of the printers installed on the computer. This list includes only the printers physically connected to the machine (if any), not necessarily all printers set up in the Control Panel. The syntax of the InstalledPrinters property is:

```
Public Shared ReadOnly Property InstalledPrinters( ) As _
   System.Drawing.Printing.PrinterSettings.StringCollection
```

The StringCollection class is a collection of strings. It can be iterated using code such as this:

```
' Assume pts is of type PrinterSettings.
Dim str As String
For Each str In pts.InstalledPrinters
   Console.WriteLine(str)
Next
```

IsDefaultPrinter

Indicates whether this printer is the user's default printer. The syntax of the IsDefaultPrinter property is:

```
Public ReadOnly Property IsDefaultPrinter( ) As Boolean
```

If the PrinterName property is explicitly set to anything other than `Nothing`, this property always returns `False`.

IsPlotter

Indicates whether this printer is a plotter. The syntax of the IsPlotter property is:

```
Public ReadOnly Property IsPlotter( ) As Boolean
```

IsValid

Indicates whether the PrinterName property designates a valid printer. The syntax of the IsValid property is:

```
Public ReadOnly Property IsValid( ) As Boolean
```

This property is useful if the PrinterName property is being set explicitly. If the PrinterName is set as a result of allowing the user to select a printer through the PrintDialog dialog box, this property will always be `True`.

LandscapeAngle

Indicates the angle (in degrees) by which portrait orientation is rotated to produce landscape orientation. The syntax of the LandscapeAngle property is:

```
Public ReadOnly Property LandscapeAngle( ) As Integer
```

This value can only be 90 or 270. If landscape orientation is not supported, this value can only be 0.

MaximumCopies

Indicates the maximum number of copies that the printer can print at one time. The syntax of the MaximumCopies property is:

```
Public ReadOnly Property MaximumCopies( ) As Integer
```

MaximumPage

Indicates the highest page number that can be entered in a PrintDialog dialog box. The syntax of the MaximumPage property is:

```
Public Property MaximumPage( ) As Integer
```

Set this value prior to calling the PrintDialog object's ShowDialog method to prohibit the user from entering a page number that is too high.

MinimumPage

Indicates the lowest page number that can be entered in a PrintDialog dialog box. The syntax of the MinimumPage property is:

```
Public Property MinimumPage( ) As Integer
```

Set this value prior to calling the PrintDialog object's ShowDialog method to prohibit the user from entering a page number that is too low.

PaperSizes

Indicates the paper sizes that are supported by this printer. The syntax of the PaperSizes property is:

```
Public ReadOnly Property PaperSizes( ) As _
   System.Drawing.Printing.PrinterSettings+PaperSizeCollection
```

The PaperSizeCollection is a collection of objects of type PaperSize. The PaperSize type was described in the previous section, under the description for the PaperSize property of the PageSettings class. The PaperSizeCollection can be iterated using the following code:

```
' Assume pts is of type PrinterSettings.
Dim pprSize As PaperSize
For Each pprSize In pts.PaperSizes
   Console.WriteLine(pprSize.PaperName)
Next
```

PaperSources

Indicates the paper sources that are available on the printer. The syntax of the PaperSources property is:

```
Public ReadOnly Property PaperSources( ) As _
   System.Drawing.Printing.PrinterSettings+PaperSourceCollection
```

The PaperSourceCollection is a collection of objects of type PaperSource. The PaperSource type was described in the previous section, under the description for the PaperSource property of the PageSettings class. The PaperSourceCollection can be iterated using the following code:

```
' Assume pts is of type PrinterSettings.
Dim pprSource As PaperSource
For Each pprSource In pts.PaperSources
   Console.WriteLine(pprSource.SourceName)
Next
```

PrinterName

Indicates the name of the printer. The syntax of the PrinterName property is:

```
Public Property PrinterName( ) As String
```

Unless a string has been explicitly assigned to the property, its value is `Null`.

PrinterResolutions

Indicates the resolution supported by this printer. The syntax of the PrinterResolutions property is:

```
Public ReadOnly Property PrinterResolutions( ) As _
   System.Drawing.Printing.PrinterSettings.PrinterResolutionCollection
```

The PrinterResolutionCollection is a collection of objects of type PrinterResolution. The PrinterResolution type was described in the previous section, under the description for the PrinterResolution property of the PageSettings class. The PrinterResolutionCollection can be iterated using the following code:

```
' Assume pts is of type PrinterSettings.
Dim ptrResolution As PrinterResolution
For Each ptrResolution In pts.PrinterResolutions
   Console.WriteLine(ptrResolution.Kind.ToString( ))
Next
```

PrintRange

Indicates the range of pages that are to be printed. The syntax of the PrintRange property is:

```
Public Property PrintRange( ) As System.Drawing.Printing.PrintRange
```

The PrintRange type is an enumeration having the following values:

`AllPages`
: Prints the entire document.

`Selection`
: Prints only the selected portion of the document.

`SomePages`
: Prints the pages starting at the page specified in the FromPage property and ending at the page specified in the ToPage property.

SupportsColor

Indicates whether the printer supports color printing. The syntax of the SupportsColor property is:

```
Public ReadOnly Property SupportsColor( ) As Boolean
```

ToPage

Specifies the final page to print if the PrintRange property is set to `SomePages`. The syntax of the ToPage property is:

```
Public Property ToPage( ) As Integer
```

The methods of the PrinterSettings class are:

Clone

Creates a copy of the PrinterSettings object. The syntax of the Clone method is:

```
Public NotOverridable Function Clone( ) As Object _
   Implements System.ICloneable.Clone
```

GetHdevmode

Returns a handle to a Windows DEVMODE (device mode) structure corresponding to this PrinterSettings object. The GetHdevmode method has two forms:

```
Public Overloads Function GetHdevmode( ) As System.IntPtr
```

and:

```
Public Overloads Function GetHdevmode( _
   ByVal pageSettings As System.Drawing.Printing.PageSettings _
) As System.IntPtr
```

The DEVMODE structure is part of the Windows API and is not discussed further in this book.

GetHdevnames

Returns a handle to a Windows DEVNAMES structure corresponding to this PrinterSettings object. The syntax of the GetHdevnames method is:

```
Public Function GetHdevnames( ) As System.IntPtr
```

The DEVNAMES structure is part of the Windows API and is not discussed further in this book.

SetHdevmode

Sets properties of this PrinterSettings object based on values in the given DEVMODE structure. The syntax of the SetHdevmode method is:

```
Public Sub SetHdevmode(ByVal hdevmode As System.IntPtr)
```

The DEVMODE structure is part of the Windows API and is not discussed further in this book.

SetHdevnames

Sets properties of this PrinterSettings object based on values in the given DEVNAMES structure. The syntax of the SetHdevnames method is:

```
Public Sub SetHdevnames(ByVal hdevnames As System.IntPtr)
```

The DEVNAMES structure is part of the Windows API and is not discussed further in this book.

Page Setup Dialog Box

Windows Forms provides a common dialog box for page setup (shown in Figure 5-18 in Chapter 5). Settings entered by the user in this dialog box are saved to a PageSettings object. This PageSettings object can be saved by the application and passed to the PrintDocument object prior to calling the PrintDocument object's Print method. The PrintDocument object will then use the given settings for printing. Here's the code that displays the dialog box:

```
Private Sub ShowPageSetup( )
   ' Display the page settings dialog box. This assumes that there is
   ' a class-level variable of type PageSettings called m_pgSettings.
   Dim pgSetupDlg As New PageSetupDialog( )
   pgSetupDlg.PageSettings = m_pgSettings
```

```
        pgSetupDlg.ShowDialog( )
    End Sub
```

This code depends on the existence of a class-level variable of type PageSettings called m_pgSettings. Here is a suitable definition for this variable:

```
    ' Private member to hold the application's page settings.
    ' This could be placed in an application's main form or in another
    ' class that is accessible to the code that will need to print.
    Private m_pgSettings As New PageSettings( )
```

Note the use of the New keyword to ensure that the PageSettings object is instantiated as soon as the enclosing class is instantiated.

All that remains is to hand the PageSettings object to the PrintDocument object when it's time to print. Here is the code:

```
    Private Sub PrintTheDocument( )
        ' Create the PrintDocument object.
        Dim pd As New HelloPrintDocument( )
        ' Hand it the PageSettings object.
        pd.DefaultPageSettings = m_pgSettings
        ' Create the dialog box object.
        Dim dlg As New PrintDialog( )
        ' Pass the PrintDocument object to the dialog box object.
        dlg.Document = pd
        ' Show the dialog box. Be sure to test the result so that printing
        ' occurs only if the user clicks OK.
        If dlg.ShowDialog = DialogResult( ).OK Then
            ' Print the document.
            pd.Print( )
        End If
    End Sub
```

Print Preview

Generating a print preview is trivial. An instance of the PrintDocument object is created and passed to a PrintPreviewDialog object, whose ShowDialog method is then called to show the print preview. Here is the code:

```
    Private Sub ShowPrintPreview( )
        ' Create the PrintDocument object.
        Dim pd As New HelloPrintDocument( )
        ' Hand it the PageSettings object.
        pd.DefaultPageSettings = m_pgSettings
        ' Create the print preview dialog box object.
        Dim dlg As New PrintPreviewDialog( )
        ' Pass the PrintDocument object to the dialog box object.
        dlg.Document = pd
        ' Show the dialog box.
        dlg.ShowDialog( )
    End Sub
```

The result is shown in Figure 4-16.

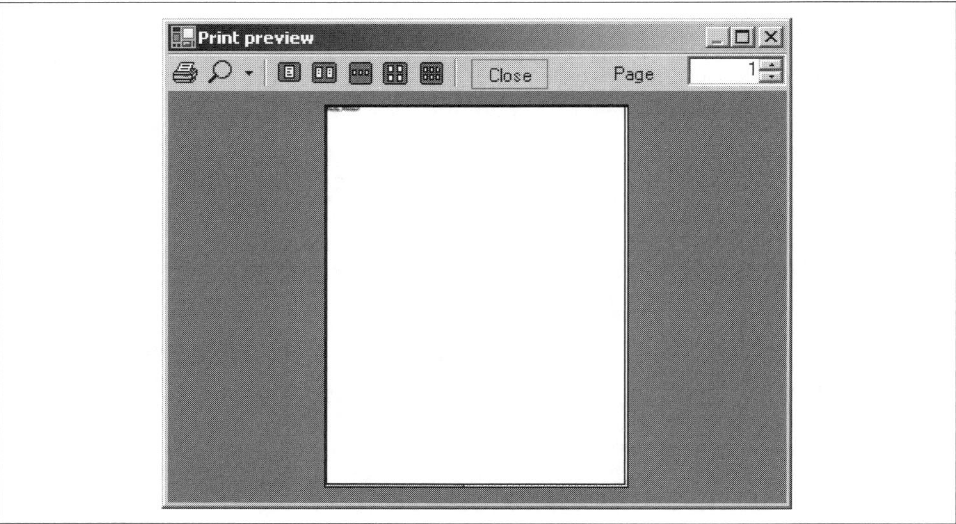

Figure 4-16. Hello, Printer! in a print preview window

Summary of Printing

The .NET Framework hides the mechanics of printing. Applications don't have to know how to find printers, they don't have to know what a given printer's capabilities are, and they don't have to know how to issue commands that are meaningful to a given brand of printer. The Framework abstracts all of this away. However, the Framework doesn't know anything about a given application's documents. It is up to the application developer to know how to paginate the application's documents and render each page in response to each call to the PrintDocument class's OnPrintPage method.

Summary

In this chapter, you've seen how to work with Windows forms in creating a desktop application. A Windows form, however, is simply a container for the application's user interface components. In the next chapter, you'll round out your examination of desktop application development by looking at controls, common dialogs, and menus.

CHAPTER 5

Windows Forms II: Controls, Common Dialog Boxes, and Menus

By themselves, one or more forms provide very little functionality to most desktop applications. For the most part, forms are valuable insofar as they serve as containers for controls. In this chapter, we'll complete our discussion of building desktop applications by focusing on the objects that forms contain—in particular, controls and components, common dialogs, and menus.

Common Controls and Components

This section contains a summary of the controls and components defined in the System.Windows.Forms namespace. *Components* are classes derived from the Component class (defined in the System.ComponentModel namespace). They may or may not provide a visual interface. They are often used as elements of forms but don't have to be. *Controls* are classes derived from the Control class (defined in the System.Windows.Forms namespace). Controls generally are used to build the visual appearance of a form. The Control class itself is derived from the Component class, so controls are also components.

The common dialog boxes are not listed here, even though they all derive from the Component class. They are given their own section, "Common Dialog Boxes," later in this chapter.

The Button Class

This class represents a button control, which is one of the most commonly used controls in Windows applications. The Button class's Click event, which it inherits from Control, is its most commonly used event.

The Button class inherits two important properties from ButtonBase: FlatStyle and Image. The first determines the appearance of the button and can take any value of the FlatStyle enumeration: `Flat`, `Popup`, `Standard` (the default), and `System`. Buttons with these four settings are shown in Figure 5-1. Assigning `FlatStyle.System` as the value of the FlatStyle property makes the appearance of the button dependent on the operating system.

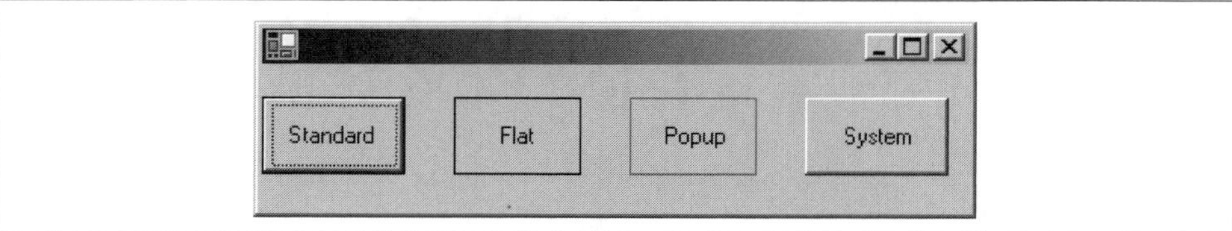

Figure 5-1. Various appearances of the Button control

The Image property allows you to embed an image into a button. The following code shows how to programmatically set the Image property of Button:

```
Button1.Image = New System.Drawing.Bitmap(filepath)
```

The CheckBox Class

The CheckBox class represents a checkbox control. Its appearance is determined by its Appearance property, which can take either value of the Appearance enumeration: `Button` or `Normal` (the default). The `Button` value is rarely used because this setting makes the checkbox look like a Button control.

The CheckBox class's Checked property can be set to `True` to make the checkbox checked or `False` to uncheck it.

The ComboBox Class

Both the ComboBox and ListBox classes derive from the ListControl class; therefore, the ComboBox class is very similar to the ListBox class and has properties and methods similar to those of the ListBox class. Refer to the later section "The ListBox Class" for information on these common properties and methods.

The following properties are specific to the ComboBox class:

DropDownStyle
: Defines the drop-down style of the ComboBox. It can take any value of the ComboBoxStyle enumeration: `DropDown` (the default value), `DropDownList`, and `Simple`. Both `DropDown` and `DropDownList` require the user to click the arrow button to display the drop-down portion of the ComboBox; however, `DropDown` allows the user to edit the text portion of the ComboBox. `Simple` makes a ComboBox's text portion editable and its drop-down portion always visible.

DroppedDown
: Specifies whether the drop-down portion of a ComboBox is visible.

The DateTimePicker Class

The DateTimePicker class represents a control that allows users to select a date in the calendar, just like the MonthCalendar control. Unlike MonthCalendar, however, the DateTimePicker control only displays a box, which looks like a combo box, containing the selected date. When the user clicks the arrow, the control displays a drop-down calendar similar to the MonthCalendar control, from which the user can select a date. This drop-down portion closes as soon as the user selects a date. The user can also click on the day, date, month, or year portion of the control for editing.

The DateTimePicker class has MinDate and MaxDate properties that are similar to the ones in the MonthCalendar class. To set the current date or to obtain the selected date, use the Value property of the DateTimePicker class. The selected date is readily available as a DateTime data type.

The GroupBox Class

As the name implies, a GroupBox control is used for grouping other controls, such as radio buttons or checkboxes; it corresponds to the Frame control in Visual Basic 6.0. A GroupBox grouping two radio buttons is shown in Figure 5-2.

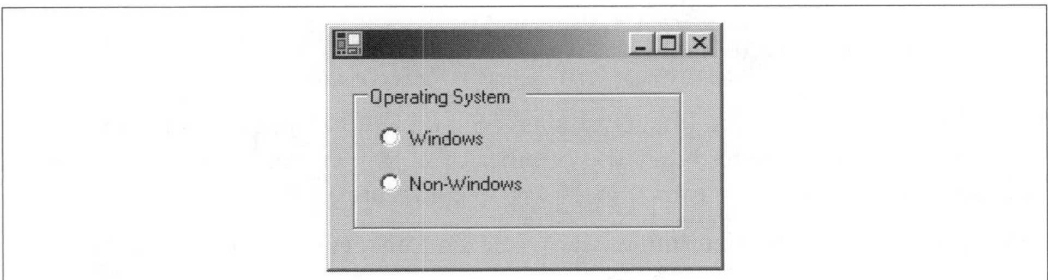

Figure 5-2. A GroupBox grouping two radio buttons

The Controls property of GroupBox represents a Control.ControlCollection class. It has methods such as Add, AddRange, Clear, GetEnumerator, and Remove, which behave exactly as do the same methods in Form.ControlCollection. For example, you can add several controls at once to a GroupBox using its AddRange method, as demonstrated by the following code that adds two radio buttons to a GroupBox named groupBox1:

```
groupBox1.Controls.AddRange(New Control( ) {radioButton1, radioButton2})
```

The ImageList Class

The ImageList class allows you to manage a collection of images. The most important property of this class is Images, which returns an ImageList.ImageCollection object. The ImageList.ImageCollection class has methods to add and remove images from the collection.

The Add method of the ImageList.ImageCollection class adds a bitmap image or an icon to the ImageList's image collection. The Add method has three overloads, whose signatures are given as follows:

```
Overloads Public Sub Add( ByVal value As System.Drawing.Icon)
Overloads Public Sub Add( ByVal value As System.Drawing.Image)
Overloads Public Sub Add( ByVal value As System.Drawing.Image, _
  ByVal transparentColor as System.Drawing.Color)
```

The first overload allows you to add an icon, and the second overload is used to add an object of type System.Drawing.Image. The third overload is used to add an image and make a color of that image transparent. For example, if you have an image with a blue background color, you can make the added image transparent by passing a blue color as the second argument to the third overload of the Add method.

The RemoveAt method of the ImageList.ImageCollection class allows you to remove an image.

Once you instantiate an ImageList object, you can start adding images or icons. The following code, for example, adds three images and icons using three different overloads of the Add method:

```
Imports System.Drawing
Dim imageList1 As ImageList1 = New ImageList( )
ImageList1.Images.Add(New Icon("C:\Palm.ico"))
ImageList1.Images.Add(New Bitmap("C:\TV.bmp"))
ImageList1.Images.Add(New Bitmap("C:\Dog.bmp"), Color.White)
```

Important properties of the ImageList class include ColorDepth and ImageSize. The ColorDepth property determines the number of colors available for the ImageList. For example, a value of 4 means that 2^4 = 16 colors are available.

The ImageSize property determines the sizes of all images in the list. By default, the value is System.Drawing.Size(16, 16).

You can assign an ImageList object to the ImageList property of controls such as Label, Button, and ListView. You can then select an image from the ImageList to be displayed on the control using the control's ImageIndex property. For example, the following code uses an ImageList for a button and selects the first image as the background image for the button:

```
button1.ImageList = imageList1
button1.ImageIndex = 0
```

The Label Class

This class represents a Label control. Its appearance is determined by two properties: BorderStyle and FlatStyle. The BorderStyle property defines the appearance of the control's border and takes any of the three members of the BorderStyle enumeration: `None` (the default), `FixedSingle`, and `Fixed3D`. Figure 5-3 shows three labels with three different values of BorderStyle.

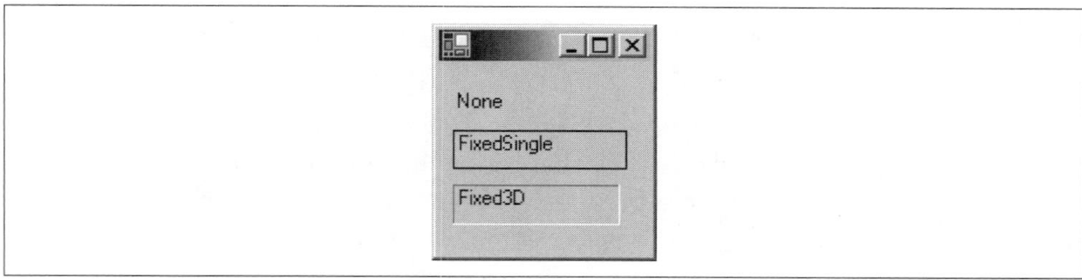

Figure 5-3. Three labels with different BorderStyle values

The FlatStyle property defines the appearance of the control and can take as its value any member of the FlatStyle enumeration: `Flat`, `Popup`, `Standard`, and `System`. However, if the value of the BorderStyle property is set to `None`, the label's FlatStyle property can take no other value than `FlatStyle.Standard`. For more information on the FlatStyle property, see "The Button Class" earlier in this chapter.

You normally assign a String to the label's Text property. However, you can also assign an image to its Image property. For example, the following code programmatically sets the Image property of a label:

```
Label1.Image = New System.Drawing.Bitmap(filepath)
```

Another important property is TextAlign, which determines how the label's text is aligned. This property can take any member of the ContentAlignment enumeration, including `BottomCenter`, `BottomLeft`, `BottomRight`, `MiddleCenter`, `MiddleLeft`, `MiddleRight`, `TopCenter`, `TopLeft` (the default value), and `TopRight`.

The UseMnemonic property can be set to `True` so that the label accepts an ampersand character in the Text property as an access-key prefix character.

The LinkLabel Class

The LinkLabel class represents a label that can function as a hyperlink, which is a URL to a web site. Its two most important properties are Text and Links. The Text property is a String that defines the label of the LinkLabel object. You can specify that some or all of the Text property value is a hyperlink. For example, if the Text property has the value "Click here for more details", you can make the whole text a hyperlink, or you can make part of it (e.g., the word "here") a hyperlink. How to do this will become clear after the second property is explained.

For a LinkLabel to be useful, it must contain at least one hyperlink. The Links property represents a LinkLabel.LinkCollection class of the LinkLabel object. You use the Add method of the LinkLabel.LinkCollection class to add a LinkLabel.Link object. The Add method has two overloads; the one that will be used here has the following signature:

```
Overloads Public Function Add( _
  ByVal start As Integer, _
  ByVal length As Integer, _
```

```
  ByVal linkData As Object _
) As Link
```

The start argument is the first character of the Text property's substring that you will turn into a hyperlink. The `length` argument denotes the length of the substring. The `linkData` argument is normally a String containing a URL, such as "www.oreilly.com". For example, if your Text property contains "Go to our web site", and you want "web site" to be the hyperlink, here is how you would use the Add method:

```
linkLabel1.Links.Add(10, 8, "www.oreilly.com")
```

`10` is the position of the character `w` in the Text property, and `8` is the length of the substring "web site".

The LinkLabel class has a LinkClicked event that you can capture so that you can run code when a LinkLabel object is clicked. The following example creates a LinkLabel object that is linked to the URL *www.oreilly.com* and starts and directs the default browser to that URL when the LinkLabel is clicked:

```
Dim WithEvents linkLabel1 As LinkLabel = new LinkLabel( )
linkLabel1.Text = "Go to our web site"
linkLabel1.Links.Add(10, 8, "www.oreilly.com")
linkLabel1.Location = New System.Drawing.Point(64, 176)
linkLabel1.Name = "LinkLabel1"
linkLabel1.Size = New System.Drawing.Size(120, 16)
' Add to a form.
Me.Controls.Add(linkLabel1)

Private Sub LinkLabel1_LinkClicked( _
  ByVal sender As Object, _
  ByVal e As LinkLabelLinkClickedEventArgs) _
  Handles linkLabel1.LinkClicked
  ' Start the default browser and direct it to "www.oreilly.com".
  System.Diagnostics.Process.Start(e.Link.LinkData.ToString( ))
End Sub
```

The LinkLabel class has a number of properties that are related to the appearance of a LinkLabel object:

ActiveLinkColor
: Represents the color of the LinkLabel when it is being clicked (i.e., when you press your mouse button but before you release it). By default, the value of ActiveLinkColor is System.Drawing.Color.Red.

DisabledLinkColor
: Represents the color of the LinkLabel when it is disabled.

LinkColor
: Represents the color of the LinkLabel in its normal condition. By default, the value is System.Drawing.Color.Blue.

VisitedLinkColor
: Represents the color of a LinkLabel that has been visited. By default, this property value is System.Drawing.Color.Purple. The LinkLabel does not automatically

display in its VisitedLinkColor after it is clicked. You must change its LinkVisited property to True. Normally, you do this inside the LinkClicked event handler of the LinkLabel object. Therefore, in the previous example, if you want the LinkLabel to change color after it is clicked, you can modify its LinkClicked event handler with the following:

```
Private Sub LinkLabel1_LinkClicked( _
  ByVal sender As Object, _
  ByVal e As LinkLabelLinkClickedEventArgs) _
  Handles linkLabel1.LinkClicked

  LinkLabel1.LinkVisited = True

  ' Start the default browser and direct it to "www.oreilly.com".
  System.Diagnostics.Process.Start(e.Link.LinkData.ToString( ))
End Sub
```

LinkBehavior
: Determines how the LinkLabel is displayed. This property can take any member of the LinkBehavior enumeration: `AlwaysUnderline`, `HoverUnderline`, `NeverUnderline`, and `SystemDefault` (the default value).

The ListBox Class

The ListBox class represents a box that contains a list of items. The following are its more important properties:

MultiColumn
: This is a Boolean that indicates whether the listbox has more than one column. Its default value is `False`.

ColumnWidth
: In a multicolumn listbox, this property represents the width of each column in pixels. By default, the value of this property is zero, which makes each column have a default width.

Items
: This is the most important property of the ListBox class. It returns the ListBox. ObjectCollection class, which is basically the Items collection in the ListBox. You can programmatically add an item using the Add method or add a range of items using the AddRange method of the ListBox.ObjectCollection class. For example, the following code adds the names of vegetables and fruits to a ListBox object named listBox1:

```
listBox1.Items.AddRange(New Object( ) _
  {"apple", "avocado", "banana", "carrot", _
  "mandarin", "orange"})
```

For more information about the ListBox.ObjectCollection class, see the next section, "The ListBox.ObjectCollection Class."

SelectionMode

This property determines whether multi-item selection is possible in a ListBox object. It can be assigned any member of the SelectionMode enumeration: `None`, `One` (the default value), `MultiSimple`, and `MultiExtended`. Both `MultiSimple` and `MultiExtended` allow the user to select more than one item. However, `MultiExtended` allows the use of the Shift, Ctrl, and arrow keys to make a selection.

SelectedIndex

This is the index of the selected item. The index is zero-based. If more than one item is selected, this property represents the lowest index. If no item is selected, the property returns –1.

SelectedIndices

This read-only property returns the indices to all items selected in a ListBox object in the form of a ListBox.SelectedIndexCollection object. The ListBox.SelectedIndexCollection class has a Count property that returns the number of selected indices and an Item property that returns the index number. For example, the following code returns the index number of all selected items in a ListBox control named listBox1:

```
Dim selectedIndices As ListBox.SelectedIndexCollection
' Obtain the selected indices.
selectedIndices = listBox1.SelectedIndices
' Get the number of indices.
Dim count As Integer = selectedIndices.Count
Dim i As Integer
For i = 0 To count - 1
  Console.WriteLine(selectedIndices(i))
Next
```

SelectedItem

This read-only property returns the selected item as an object of type Object. You must cast the returned value to an appropriate type, which is normally String. If more than one item is selected, the property returns the item with the lowest index.

SelectedItems

This read-only property returns all items selected in a ListBox object in the form of a ListBox.SelectedObjectCollection object. The ListBox.SelectedObjectCollection class has a Count property that returns the number of items in the collection and an Item property that you can use to obtain the selected item. For example, the following code displays all the selected items of a ListBox control called listBox1:

```
Dim selectedItems As ListBox.SelectedObjectCollection
selectedItems = listBox1.SelectedItems
Dim count As Integer = selectedItems.Count
Dim i As Integer
For i = 0 To count - 1
  Console.WriteLine(selectedItems(i))
Next
```

Sorted

A value of `True` means that the items are sorted. Otherwise, the items are not sorted. By default, the value of this property is `False`.

Text

This is the currently selected item's text.

TopIndex

This is the index of the first visible item in the ListBox. The value changes as the user scrolls through the items.

The ListBox.ObjectCollection Class

This class represents all the items in a ListBox object. It has a Count property that returns the number of items in the ListBox and an Item property that returns the item object in a certain index position.

The following sample code reiterates all the items in a ListBox control named listBox1:

```
Dim items As ListBox.ObjectCollection
items = ListBox1.Items
Dim count As Integer = items.Count
Dim i As Integer
For i = 0 To count - 1
  Console.WriteLine(items(i))
Next
```

In addition, the ListBox.ObjectCollection class has the following methods:

Add

Adds an item to the ListBox object. Its syntax is:

```
ListBox.ObjectCollection.Add(item)
```

where *`item`* is data of type Object that is to be added to the collection. The method returns the zero-based index of the new item in the collection.

AddRange

Adds one or more items to the ListBox object. Its most common syntax is:

```
ListBox.ObjectCollection.AddRange(items())
```

where *`items`* is an array of objects containing the data to be added to the ListBox.

Clear

Clears the ListBox, removing all the items. Its syntax is:

```
ListBox.ObjectCollection.Clear()
```

Contains

Checks whether an item can be found in the list of items. Its syntax is:

```
ListBox.ObjectCollection.Contains(value)
```

where *`value`* is an Object containing the value to locate in the ListBox. The method returns `True` if *`value`* is found; otherwise, it returns `False`.

CopyTo

Copies all items to an object array. Its syntax is:

```
ListBox.ObjectCollection.CopyTo(dest( ), arrayIndex)
```

where *dest* is the Object array to which the ListBox items are to be copied, and *arrayIndex* is the starting position within *dest* at which copying is to begin.

IndexOf

Returns the index of a particular item. Its syntax is:

```
ListBox.ObjectCollection.IndexOf(value)
```

where *value* is an Object representing the item to locate in the collection. The method returns the item's index. If the item cannot be found, the method returns –1.

Insert

Inserts an item into the ListBox at the specified index position. Its syntax is:

```
ListBox.ObjectCollection.Insert(index, item)
```

where *index* is the zero-based ordinal position at which the item is to be inserted, and *item* is an Object containing the data to be inserted into the collection.

Remove

Removes the item that is passed as an argument to this method from the ListBox. Its syntax is:

```
ListBox.ObjectCollection.Remove(value)
```

where *value* is an Object representing the item to remove from the collection.

RemoveAt

Removes an item at the specified index position. Its syntax is:

```
ListBox.ObjectCollection.RemoveAt(index)
```

where *index* is the zero-based ordinal position in the collection of the item to be removed.

The ListView Class

A ListView is a container control that can hold a collection of items. Each item in a ListView can have descriptive text and an image, and the items can be viewed in four modes. The righthand pane of Windows Explorer is a ListView control.

An item in a ListView is represented by an object of type ListViewItem. The various constructors of the ListViewItem class permit a ListViewItem to be constructed with a String or with a String and an index number. If an index number is used, it represents the index of the item's image in the ImageList referenced by the ListView.

The following code constructs two ListViewItem objects. The first has the text "Item1" and uses the first image in the ImageList. The second has the text "Item2" and uses the second image of the ImageList:

```
Dim listViewItem1 As ListViewItem = New ListViewItem("Item1", 0)
Dim listViewItem2 As ListViewItem = New ListViewItem("Item2", 1)
```

Once you have references to one or more ListViewItem objects, you can add the items to your ListView object. To add an item or a group of items, you first need to reference the ListView.ListViewItemCollection collection of the ListView object. This collection can easily be referenced using the Items property of the ListView class. The ListView.ListViewItemCollection has Add and AddRange methods that you can use to add one item or a group of items. For instance, the following code uses the AddRange method to add two ListViewItem objects to a ListView object:

```
listView1.Items.AddRange(New ListViewItem( ) _
  {listViewItem1, listViewItem2})
```

The Add method of the ListView.ListViewItemCollection has three overloads, two of which allow you add to a ListViewItem without first creating a ListViewItem object.

To add a ListViewItem object to the collection, you can use the following overload of the Add method:

```
Overridable Overloads Public Function Add _
  (ByVal value As ListViewItem) _
  As ListViewItem
```

Or, to add a String and convert it into a ListViewItem object, use the following overload:

```
Overridable Overloads Public Function Add _
  (ByVal text As String) _
  As ListViewItem
```

Alternatively, you can pass a String and an image index to the third overload:

```
Overridable Overloads Public Function Add _
  (ByVal text As String, _
   ByVal imageIndex As Integer) _
  As ListViewItem
```

The following code demonstrates how to add two ListViewItem objects to a ListView. The ListView is linked to an ImageList that has two images in its collection. When the code is run, it produces something similar to Figure 5-4.

```
' Declare and instantiate an ImageList called imageList1.
Dim imageList1 As ImageList = New ImageList( )
' Set the ColorDepth and ImageSize properties of imageList1.
imageList1.ColorDepth = ColorDepth.Depth8Bit
imageList1.ImageSize = New System.Drawing.Size(48, 48)
' Add two images to imageList1.
imageList1.Images.Add(New Icon("c:\Spotty.ico"))
imageList1.Images.Add(New Bitmap("c:\StopSign.bmp"))

' Declare and instantiate two ListViewItem objects named
' listViewItem1 and listViewItem2.
' The text for listItem1 is "Item1", and the image is the first
' image in the imageList1.
' The text for listItem1 is "Item2", and the image is the second
' image in the imageList1.
Dim listViewItem1 As ListViewItem = New ListViewItem("Item1", 0)
```

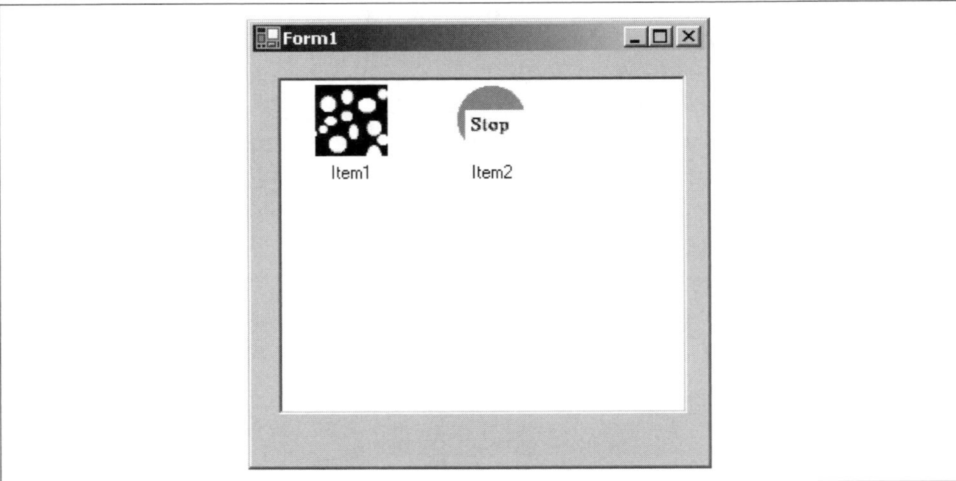

Figure 5-4. A ListView control with two ListViewItem objects

```
Dim listViewItem2 As ListViewItem = New ListViewItem("Item2", 1)

' Declare and instantiate a ListView called listView1.
Dim listView1 As ListView = New ListView( )
' Set its properties.
listView1.View = View.LargeIcon
listView1.LargeImageList = imageList1
listView1.Location = New System.Drawing.Point(16, 16)
listView1.Name = "ListView1"
listView1.Size = New System.Drawing.Size(264, 224)
listView1.SmallImageList = Me.ImageList1

' Add listViewItem1 and listViewItem2.
listView1.Items.AddRange(New ListViewItem( ) _
  {listViewItem1, listViewItem2})

' Add listView1 to the form.
Me.Controls.AddRange(New Control( ) {listView1})
```

Two properties of the ListView class tell you which item(s) are selected: SelectedIndices and SelectedItems. The first returns a ListView.SelectedIndexCollection object, and the second returns a ListView.SelectedListViewItemCollection object.

The ListView.SelectedIndexCollection class has a Count property that tells you how many items are selected and an Item property that returns the index of the designated item. For example, you can retrieve the index of the first selected item by passing 0 to the Item property, as follows:

```
Index = ListView1.SelectedIndices.Item(0)
```

The ListView.SelectedListViewItemCollection class is very similar to ListView.SelectedIndexCollection. Its Count property indicates how many items are selected. However, its Item property returns the item itself, not an index number.

The MonthCalendar Class

The MonthCalendar class represents a control that displays days of a month. A MonthCalendar control is shown in Figure 5-5. By default, when first displayed, the control displays the current month on the user's computer system. Users can select a day by clicking on it or select a range of dates by holding the Shift key while clicking the date at the end of the desired range. Users can also scroll backward and forward to previous or upcoming months, or they can click on the month part and more quickly select one of the 12 months. To change the year, users can click on the year part and click the scrollbar that appears.

Figure 5-5. A MonthCalendar control

Two properties determine the date range that users can select: MinDate and MaxDate. The MinDate property is a DateTime value representing the minimum date permitted; its default is January 1, 1753. The MaxDate property determines the maximum date allowed. By default, the value of MaxDate is December 31, 9998.

If you want your MonthCalendar to display a certain range of dates, you need to change these two properties. For instance, the following code allows the user to select a date between January 1, 1980 and December 14, 2010:

```
MonthCalendar1.MinDate = New DateTime(1980, 1, 1)
MonthCalendar1.MaxDate = New DateTime(2010, 12, 14)
```

The MonthCalendar class has a TodayDate property that represents today's date. The user selecting a new date does not automatically change the value of TodayDate. If you want the date selected by the user to be reflected as today's date, you can use the Date_Changed event handler to change its value explicitly, as shown in the following code:

```
Private Sub MonthCalendar1_DateChanged( _
  ByVal sender As System.Object, _
  ByVal e As DateRangeEventArgs) _
  Handles MonthCalendar1.DateChanged
```

```
    MonthCalendar1.TodayDate = e.Start
End Sub
```

A DateRangeEventArgs object is passed as an argument to the DateChanged event handler. Its members include a Start property, which represents the beginning of the range of selected dates, and an End property, which represents the end of the range of selected dates. The previous code simply assigns the value of the Start property to TodayDate. Later, if you need to know the value of the user-selected date, you can query the TodayDate property.

Note that the MonthCalendar control has a fixed size. It will ignore any attempt to change its Size property. If you need more flexibility in terms of the space it occupies, use a DateTimePicker control.

The Panel Class

A panel is a container that can hold other controls. Panels are typically used to group related controls in a form. Like the PictureBox class, the Panel class has a BorderStyle property that defines the panel's border and can take as its value any member of the BorderStyle enumeration: `None` (the default value), `FixedSingle`, and `Fixed3D`.

You can add controls to a Panel object using the Add method or the AddRange method of the Control.ControlCollection class. The following code adds a button and a text box to a Panel control called panel1:

```
Dim panel1 As Panel = New Panel( )
Dim textBox1 As TextBox = New TextBox( )
Dim WithEvents button1 As Button

button1 = New Button( )

' button1
button1.Location = New System.Drawing.Point(104, 72)
button1.Name = "button1"
button1.Size = New System.Drawing.Size(64, 48)
button1.TabIndex = 0
button1.Text = "Button1"

' textBox1
textBox1.Location = New System.Drawing.Point(128, 48)
textBox1.Name = "textBox1"
textBox1.TabIndex = 1

panel1.Controls.AddRange(New Control( ) {textBox1, button1})
panel1.Location = New System.Drawing.Point(24, 24)
panel1.Name = "Panel1"
panel1.Size = New System.Drawing.Size(336, 216)
Me.Controls.Add(panel1)
```

The PictureBox Class

The PictureBox class represents a control to display an image. Loading an image into this control is achieved by assigning a System.Drawing.Bitmap object to its Image property, as the following code does:

```
Dim pictureBox1 As PictureBox = New PictureBox( )
pictureBox1.Image = New System.Drawing.Bitmap("c:\tv.bmp")
pictureBox1.Location = New System.Drawing.Point(72, 64)
pictureBox1.Size = New System.Drawing.Size(144, 128)
Me.Controls.Add(pictureBox1)
```

In addition, the PictureBox class has the BorderStyle and SizeMode properties. The BorderStyle property determines the PictureBox object's border and can take as its value any member of the BorderStyle enumeration: `None` (the default value), `FixedSingle`, and `Fixed3D`.

The SizeMode property determines how the image assigned to the Image property is displayed. The SizeMode property can take any of the members of the PictureBoxSizeMode enumeration: `AutoSize`, `CenterImage`, `Normal` (the default value), and `StretchImage`.

The RadioButton Class

The RadioButton class represents a radio button. When you add more than one radio button to a form, those radio buttons automatically become one group, and you can select only one button at a time. If you want to have multiple groups of radio buttons on a form, you need to use a GroupBox or Panel control to add radio buttons in the same group to a single GroupBox or Panel.

The following code shows how you can add two radio buttons to a GroupBox and then add the GroupBox to a form. Notice that you don't need to add each individual radio button to a form:

```
' Declare and instantiate a GroupBox and two radio buttons.
Dim groupBox1 As GroupBox = New GroupBox( )
Dim radioButton1 As RadioButton = new RadioButton( )
Dim radioButton2 As RadioButton = new RadioButton( )

' Set the Size and Location of each control.
groupBox1.Size = New System.Drawing.Size(248, 88)
groupBox1.Location = New System.Drawing.Point(112, 168)
radioButton1.Location = New System.Drawing.Point(16, 10)
radioButton1.Size = New System.Drawing.Size(104, 20)
radioButton2.Location = New System.Drawing.Point(16, 50)
radioButton2.Size = New System.Drawing.Size(104, 20)
' Add radioButton1 and radioButton2 to the GroupBox.
groupBox1.Controls.AddRange(New Control( ) {radioButton1, radioButton2})

' Add the GroupBox to the form.
Me.Controls.Add(groupBox1)
```

Like a checkbox, the appearance of a radio button is determined by its Appearance property, which can take one of two members of the Appearance enumeration: `Normal` (the default) and `Button`. You don't normally use `Appearance.Button` because it will make your radio button look like a button.

The CheckAlign property determines the text alignment of the radio button. Its value is one of the members of the ContentAlignment enumeration: `BottomCenter`, `BottomLeft`, `BottomRight`, `MiddleCenter`, `MiddleLeft` (the default), `MiddleRight`, `TopCenter`, `TopLeft`, and `TopRight`. The Checked property takes a Boolean. Setting this property to `True` selects the radio button (and deselects others in the group); setting it to `False` unselects it.

The TextBox Class

This class represents a text-box control, a control that can accept text as user input. Its major properties are:

Multiline
: This property can be set to `True` (indicating that multiple lines are permitted) or `False` (single-line mode). By default, the value for this property is `False`.

AcceptsReturn
: If `True` (its default value), and if the Multiline property is also `True`, pressing the Enter key will move to the next line in the text box. Otherwise, pressing Enter will have the same effect as clicking the form's default button.

CharacterCasing
: This property determines how characters that are input by the user appear in the text box. It can take any member of the CharacterCasing enumeration: `Normal` (the default), `Upper`, and `Lower`. Setting this property to `CharacterCasing.Upper` translates all input characters to uppercase. Assigning `CharacterCasing.Lower` to this property converts all input to lowercase. `CharacterCasing.Normal` means that no conversion is performed on the input.

PasswordChar
: This property defines a mask character to be displayed in place of each character input by the user, thereby turning the text box into a password box. This property applies only to a single-line text box (i.e., a text box whose Multiline property is `False`). It affects the display, but not the value of the Text property.

ScrollBars
: In a multiline text box, this property determines whether scrollbars are shown on the control. The property can take any member of the ScrollBars enumeration: `None` (the default), `Horizontal`, `Vertical`, and `Both`.

TextAlign
: This property determines how text is aligned in the text box. It can take any member of the HorizontalAlignment enumeration: `Center`, `Left`, and `Right`.

The Timer Class

The Timer class represents a timer that can trigger an event at a specified interval. At each interval, a Timer object raises its Tick event. You can write code in the Tick event handler that runs regularly.

The Timer will raise its Tick event only after you call its Start method. To stop the timer, call its Stop method.

The interval for the Timer is set by assigning a value to its Interval property. It accepts a number representing the interval in milliseconds. The following code, which prints an incremented integer from 1 to 20 to the console, shows how to use a timer:

```
Dim i As Integer
Friend WithEvents timer1 As Timer
timer1 = New Timer( )
timer1.Interval = 1000
timer1.Start( )

' The event handler for Tick.
Private Sub Timer1_Tick( _
  ByVal sender As System.Object, _
  ByVal e As System.EventArgs) _
  Handles Timer1.Tick

  If i < 20 Then
    i = i + 1
    Console.WriteLine(i)
  Else
    timer1.Stop( )
  End If
End Sub
```

Other Controls and Components

In addition to the controls we've discussed in some detail in the preceding sections, the .NET Framework includes a number of other controls and components for Windows application development. These include:

AxHost
: Wraps ActiveX controls to let them be used within Windows Forms.

CheckedListBox
: The same as the ListBox control, except that checkboxes are displayed to the left of each item. The CheckedListBox control derives from the ListBox control.

ContainerControl
: A container for other controls. The emphasis of this control is on managing the focus state of contained controls. For example, it has a method that can be called to force activation of a given contained control (ActivateControl) and an overrid-

able method that is invoked when the user tabs between contained controls (ProcessTabKey).

The ContainerControl control provides automatic support for scrolling because it derives from ScrollableControl.

When contained controls are anchored or docked, they anchor or dock to the edges of the containing control.

ContextMenu
: Provides a method for displaying a context menu (also known as a pop-up menu). Context menus are usually displayed in response to the user right-clicking the mouse. See "Menus" later in this chapter for details.

DataGrid
: A grid control for displaying ADO.NET data. See Chapter 8 for examples.

DomainUpDown
: A Windows up-down control (also known as a spin button) that allows the user to select from a list of text values by clicking the control's up and down arrows. See also NumericUpDown, later in this list.

HScrollBar
: A standard Windows horizontal scrollbar.

MainMenu
: Provides a method for displaying an application's main menu. See "Menus" later in this chapter for details.

MenuItem
: Represents a menu item within a menu. See "Menus" later in this chapter for details.

NotifyIcon
: Provides a way to put an icon into the Windows System Tray.

NumericUpDown
: A Windows up-down control (also known as a spin button) that allows the user to select from a list of numeric values by clicking the control's up and down arrows. See also DomainUpDown, earlier in this list.

PrintPreviewControl
: Displays a preview image of a document to be printed. The PrintPreviewControl is not usually used directly. It is found on the PrintPreviewDialog form discussed later in this chapter, in the "Common Dialog Boxes" section.

ProgressBar
: A standard Windows progress bar.

PropertyGrid
: A user interface for viewing and setting the properties of any object.

RichTextBox
: A standard Windows rich text box (also known as a rich edit control). The RichTextBox control can manipulate text in Rich Text Format (RTF).

ScrollableControl
: Not used directly. The ScrollableControl control serves as the base class for controls that need to provide automatic support for scrolling. The ContainerControl control and the Panel control are both derived from ScrollableControl.

Splitter
: Provides the user with a way to resize docked controls using the mouse. This will be discussed later in this chapter, under "Form and Control Layout."

StatusBar
: A standard Windows status bar.

TabControl
: A container that provides pages to contain other controls and tabs to click to move between the pages. The pages are instances of the TabPage control, which is derived from the Panel control.

ToolBar
: A standard Windows toolbar.

TrackBar
: A standard Windows trackbar (also known as a slider)

TreeView
: A standard Windows tree view.

UserControl
: Not used directly. UserControl serves as the base class for developer-created container controls. See "Creating a Control" later in this chapter.

VScrollBar
: A standard Windows vertical scrollbar.

Control Events

Controls on a form are represented in code as fields—one field for each control. For example, when the Visual Studio .NET Windows Forms Designer is used to add a text box to a form, the following declaration is added to the form class:

```
Private WithEvents TextBox1 As System.Windows.Forms.TextBox
```

This declaration doesn't instantiate the control; it only defines a field that can hold a reference to a control of type TextBox. The control is instantiated in the InitializeComponent subroutine, which is called in the Form class's constructor. The code that instantiates the control looks like this:

```
Me.TextBox1 = New System.Windows.Forms.TextBox( )
```

As discussed in Chapter 2, when a field declaration includes the `WithEvents` keyword, the parent class can handle events that the referenced object raises. To do so, the parent class must define a handler method having the appropriate signature, and the definition of the method must include a `Handles` clause to link the method to the appropriate event on the appropriate object. For example, here is the definition of a handler method for the Click event of TextBox1:

```
Private Sub TextBox1_Click( _
   ByVal sender As Object, _
   ByVal e As System.EventArgs _
) Handles TextBox1.Click
   ' ...
End Sub
```

The event-handler method can be given any name, but it is a common convention to use a name of the form *`FieldName_EventName`*. The event-handler method's signature must correspond to the signature of the event being handled. By convention, event signatures have two parameters: *`sender`* and *`e`*. The *`sender`* parameter is always of type Object and holds a reference to the object that raised the event. The *`e`* parameter is of type EventArgs—or of a type that inherits from EventArgs—and holds a reference to an object that provides any extra information needed for the event. Events that pass a generic EventArgs argument have no event information to pass. Events that pass an argument of an EventArgs-derived type pass additional information within the fields of the passed object.

The correct signature for handling a specific event can be determined either by referring to the control's documentation or by using Visual Studio .NET's built-in object browser. In addition, the Visual Studio .NET Windows Forms Designer can automatically generate a handler-method declaration for any event exposed by any control on a given form.

Form and Control Layout

Windows Forms allows developers to lay out sophisticated user interfaces that are capable of intelligently resizing without writing a line of code. Previously, developers writing desktop applications for Windows typically spent a good deal of time writing resizing code to handle the placement of controls on the form when the user resized the form. The .NET platform, however, allows you to define a control's layout and size by setting a few properties.

The Anchor Property

The Anchor property lets a control anchor to any or all sides of its container. Each anchored side of the control is kept within a constant distance from the corresponding side of its container. When the container is resized, its anchored controls are repositioned and resized as necessary to enforce this rule. The Anchor property is defined by the Control class (in the System.Windows.Forms namespace) and so is inherited by all controls and forms. Its syntax is:

```
Public Overridable Property Anchor( ) As System.Windows.Forms.AnchorStyles
```

The AnchorStyles type is an enumeration that defines the values `Left`, `Top`, `Right`, `Bottom`, and `None`. To anchor a control on more than one edge, combine the values with the `Or` operator, as shown here:

```
' Assumes Imports System.Windows.Forms
SomeControl.Anchor = AnchorStyles.Top Or AnchorStyles.Right
```

By default, controls are anchored on the top and left sides. This means that if a form is resized, its controls maintain a constant distance from the top and left edges of the form. This behavior matches the behavior of Visual Basic 6 forms.

For example, Figure 5-6 shows a common button configuration, where the OK and Cancel buttons should track the right edge of the form as the form is resized. In previous versions of Visual Basic, it was necessary to add code to the form's Resize event handler to reposition the buttons as the form was resized. In Visual Basic .NET, however, it is necessary only to set the button's Anchor property appropriately. This can be done either in Visual Studio .NET's Properties window or in code (in the form's constructor).

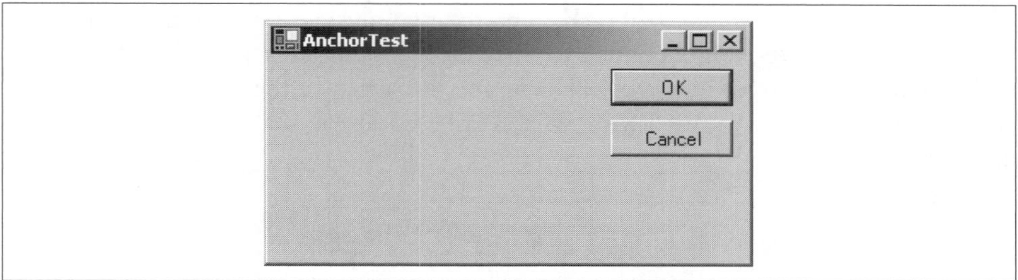

Figure 5-6. A sizable form with controls that should be anchored on the top and right edges

The code to anchor a button on the top and right edges looks like this:

```
' Assumes Imports System.Windows.Forms
btnOk.Anchor = AnchorStyles.Top Or AnchorStyles.Right
```

Sometimes a control should stretch as the form is resized. This is accomplished by anchoring the control to two opposite sides of the form. For example, the text box in Figure 5-7 should always fill the space between the left edge of the form and the OK button on the right side of the form.

To accomplish this, lay out the form as shown, anchor the buttons on the top and right edges as already discussed, then anchor the text box on the top, left, and right edges. By default, the label in the form is already anchored on the top and left edges. The code looks like this:

```
' Assumes Imports System.Windows.Forms
```

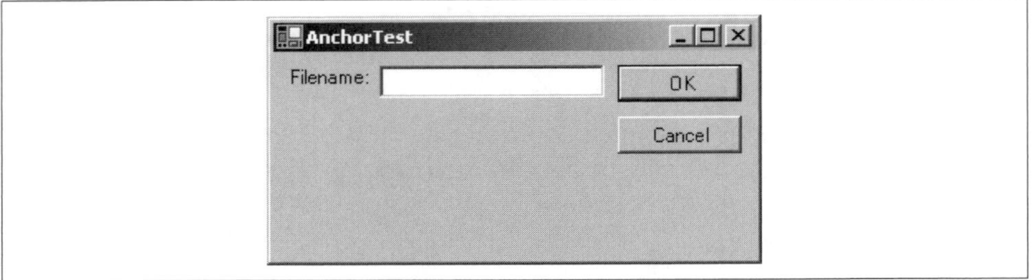

Figure 5-7. In this form, the text box should expand and shrink to fill the available space

```
' Anchor the OK and Cancel buttons on the top and right edges.
btnOk.Anchor = AnchorStyles.Top Or AnchorStyles.Right
btnCancel.Anchor = AnchorStyles.Top Or AnchorStyles.Right

' Anchor the Filename text box on the top, left, and right edges.
' This causes the text box to resize itself as needed.
txtFilename.Anchor = AnchorStyles.Top Or AnchorStyles.Left _
   Or AnchorStyles.Right
```

The Dock Property

The Dock property lets a control be docked to any one side of its container or lets it fill the container. Docking a control to one side of a container resembles laying out the control with three of its edges adjacent and anchored to the three corresponding edges of its container. Figure 5-8 shows a text box control docked to the left side of its form.

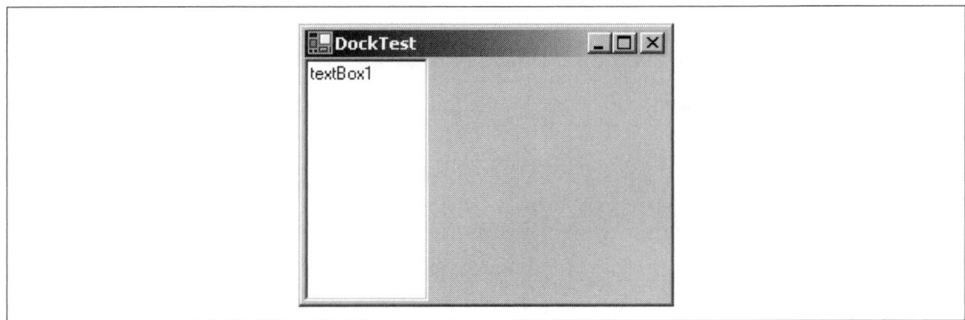

Figure 5-8. A TreeView docked to the left side of a form

The Dock property is defined by the Control class (in the System.Windows.Forms namespace) and so is inherited by all controls and forms. Its syntax is:

```
Public Overridable Property Dock( ) As System.Windows.Forms.DockStyle
```

The DockStyle type is an enumeration that defines the values `Left`, `Top`, `Right`, `Bottom`, `Fill`, and `None`. Only one value can be used at a time. For example, a control can't be docked to both the left and right edges of its container. Setting the Dock property to `DockStyle.Fill` causes the control to expand to fill the space available in its container. If the control is the only docked control in the container, it expands to fill the container. If there are other docked controls in the container, the control expands to fill the space not occupied by the other docked controls. For example, in Figure 5-9, the Dock property of textBox1 is set to `DockStyle.Left`, and the Dock property of textBox2 is set to `DockStyle.Fill`.

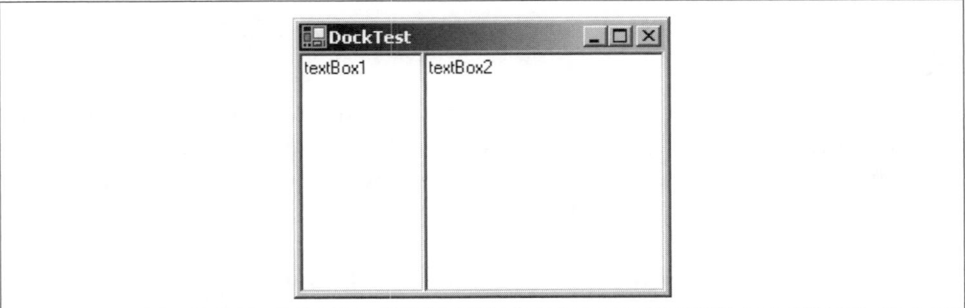

Figure 5-9. A left-docked control and a fill-docked control

Controlling dock order

Controls have an intrinsic order within their container. This is known as their *z-order* (pronounced "zee order"). The z-order of each control is unique within a given container. When two controls overlap in the same container, the control with the higher z-order eclipses the control with the lower z-order.

Docking behavior is affected by z-order. When two or more controls are docked to the same side of a form, they are docked side by side. For example, the two text-box controls shown in Figure 5-10 are both docked left.

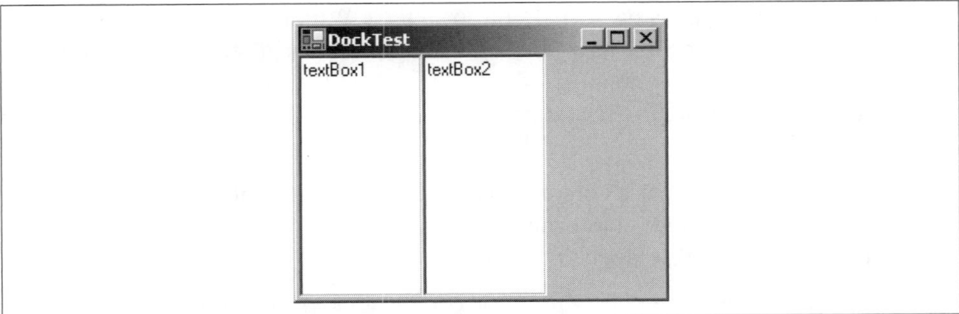

Figure 5-10. Docking two controls to the same side of a form

In such a situation, the relative position of each docked control is determined by its z-order. The control with the lowest z-order is positioned closest to the edge of the form. The control with the next higher z-order is placed next to that, and so on. In Figure 5-10, textBox1 has the lower z-order, and textBox2 has the higher z-order.

So how is z-order determined? In code, z-order is determined by the order in which controls are added to their container's Controls collection. The first control added through the collection's Add method has the highest z-order; the last control added has the lowest z-order. For example, to produce the display shown in Figure 5-10, textBox2 must be added to the Controls collection first, as shown here:

```
Me.Controls.Add(Me.textBox2)
Me.Controls.Add(Me.textBox1)
```

This results in textBox1 having the lower z-order and therefore getting docked directly to the edge of the form.

If the Controls collection's AddRange method is used to add an array of controls to a container, the first control in the array has the highest z-order and the last control in the array has the lowest z-order. For example, textBox1 and textBox2 in Figure 5-10 could have been added to their container using this code:

```
' Assumes Imports System.Windows.Forms
Me.Controls.AddRange(New Control( ) {Me.textBox2, Me.textBox1})
```

After controls have been added to their container's Controls collection, you can change their z-order by calling the Control class's SendToBack or BringToFront methods. The SendToBack method gives the control the lowest z-order within its container (causing it to dock closest to the edge of the form). The BringToFront method gives the control the highest z-order within its container (causing it to dock furthest from the edge of the form). For example, the following code forces the controls to dock as shown in Figure 5-10, regardless of the order in which they were added to the form's Controls collection:

```
Me.textBox2.BringToFront( )
```

The order in which the controls are instantiated in code and the order in which their respective Dock properties are set do not affect the controls' z-orders.

When you design forms using Visual Studio .NET's Windows Forms Designer, the controls added most recently have the highest z-orders and therefore dock furthest from the edges of their containers. The z-orders of the controls can be changed within the designer by right-clicking on a control and choosing "Bring to Front" or "Send to Back."

When one of the controls in a container is fill-docked, that control should be last in the dock order (i.e., it should have the highest z-order), so that it uses only the space that is not used by the other docked controls.

Dock order also comes into play when controls are docked to adjacent sides of a container, as shown in Figure 5-11.

The control with the lowest z-order is docked first. In Figure 5-11, textBox1 has the lowest z-order and so is docked fully to the left side of the form. textBox2 is then docked to what remains of the top of the form. If the z-order is reversed, the appearance is changed, as shown in Figure 5-12.

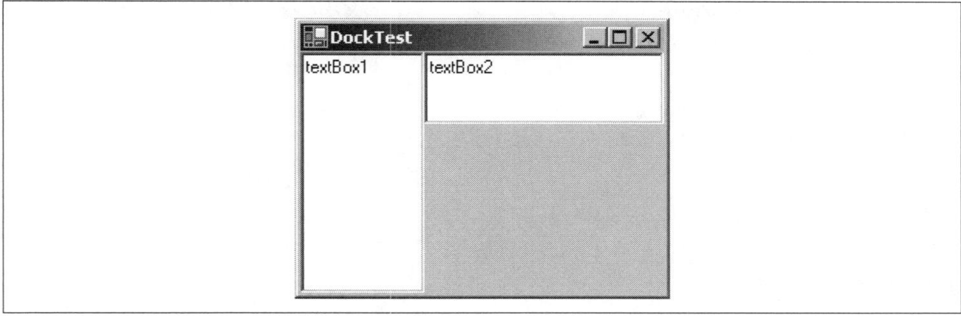

Figure 5-11. Docking two controls to adjacent sides of a form

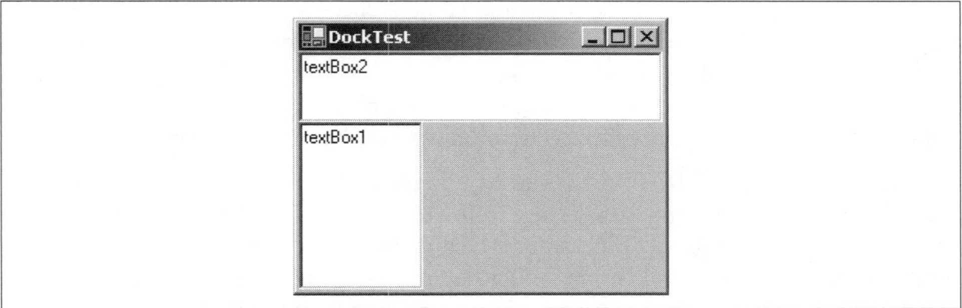

Figure 5-12. Reversing the dock order

In Figure 5-12, textBox2 has the lowest z-order and so is docked first, taking up the full length of the side to which it is docked (the top). Then textBox1 is docked to what remains of the left side of the form. This behavior can be exploited to provide complex docking arrangements, such as the one shown in Figure 5-13.

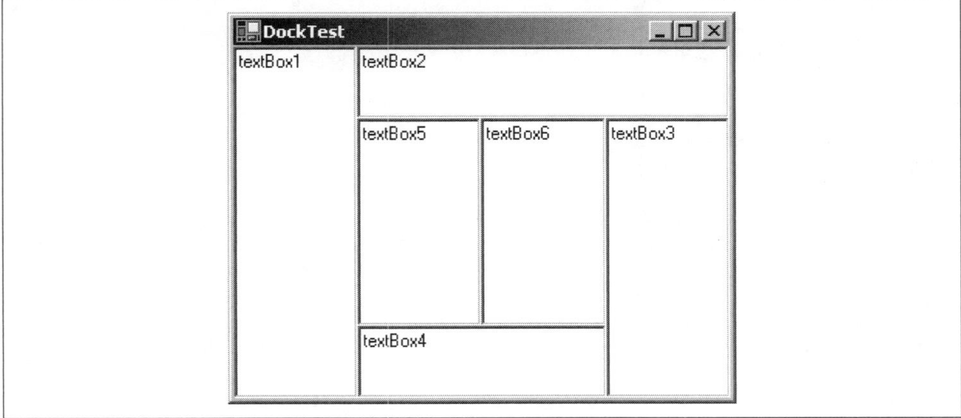

Figure 5-13. Complex docking arrangements are easily created

The text boxes in Figure 5-13 are in ascending z-order (textBox1 is lowest; textBox6 is highest). The Dock properties of the controls are set like this:

```
textBox1.Dock = DockStyle.Left
textBox2.Dock = DockStyle.Top
textBox3.Dock = DockStyle.Right
textBox4.Dock = DockStyle.Bottom
textBox5.Dock = DockStyle.Left
textBox6.Dock = DockStyle.Fill
```

The Splitter control

By default, the internal edges of docked controls aren't draggable. To make the edge of a given docked control draggable, add a Splitter control to the form. The Splitter control must appear in the dock order immediately after the control whose edge is to be draggable, so the Splitter control's z-order must be just above that control's z-order. Further, the Splitter control must be docked to the same edge of the form as the control whose edge is to be draggable. The Splitter control provides a vertical splitter if docked left or right and a horizontal splitter if docked top or bottom.

Consider again Figure 5-9. To make the edge between the two text-box controls draggable, a Splitter control must be added to the form (call it splitter1), and the z-order must be textBox2 (highest), then splitter1, and then textBox1 (lowest). This can be accomplished in the Visual Studio .NET Windows Forms Designer by adding the controls to the form in dock order (textBox1, splitter1, textBox2). As previously mentioned, if the controls have already been added to the form, their z-order can be rearranged by right-clicking the controls one-by-one in dock order and choosing "Bring To Front". The z-order can also be controlled in code, as previously discussed.

It is possible to automate the task of Splitter creation. The subroutine in Example 5-1 takes as a parameter a reference to a docked control and instantiates a Splitter control that makes the given control's inside edge draggable.

Example 5-1. Dynamically creating a Splitter control

```
Shared Sub AddSplitter(ByVal ctl As Control)

   ' Create a Splitter control.
   Dim split As New Splitter( )

   ' Get the Controls collection of the given control's container.
   Dim controls As System.Windows.Forms.Control.ControlCollection _
      = ctl.Parent.Controls

   ' Add the Splitter to the same container as the given control.
   controls.Add(split)

   ' Move the Splitter control to be immediately prior to the given
   ' control in the Controls collection. This causes the Splitter
   ' control's z-order to be just above the given control's z-order,
   ' which in turn means that the Splitter control will be docked
```

Example 5-1. Dynamically creating a Splitter control (continued)

```
    ' immediately following the given control.
    controls.SetChildIndex(split, controls.GetChildIndex(ctl))

    ' Dock the Splitter control to the same edge as the given control.
    split.Dock = ctl.Dock

End Sub
```

Common Dialog Boxes

There are several classes that implement common dialog boxes, such as color selection and print setup. These classes all derive from the CommonDialog class and, therefore, all inherit the ShowDialog method. The syntax of the ShowDialog method is:

```
Public Function ShowDialog( ) As System.Windows.Forms.DialogResult
```

Calling the ShowDialog method causes the dialog box to be displayed modally, meaning that other windows in the application can't receive input focus until the dialog box is dismissed. The call is asynchronous, meaning that code following the call to the ShowDialog method isn't executed until the dialog box is dismissed.

The return value of the ShowDialog method is of type DialogResult (defined in the System.Windows.Forms namespace). DialogResult is an enumeration that defines several values that a dialog box could return. The common dialog boxes, however, return only `OK` or `Cancel`, indicating whether the user selected the OK or Cancel button, respectively.

In Visual Studio .NET's Windows Forms Designer, common dialog boxes are added to forms in much the same way that controls and nonvisual components are. Just select the desired dialog box from the Windows Forms tab of the Toolbox. As with nonvisual components, a representation of the dialog box appears within a separate pane rather than directly on the form that is being designed. The properties of the component can then be set in Visual Studio .NET's Properties window. The Windows Forms Designer creates code that declares and instantiates the dialog box, but you must add code to show the dialog box and use the values found in its properties.

Alternatively, common dialog-box components can be instantiated and initialized directly in code, bypassing the Windows Forms Designer. For example, this method instantiates and shows a ColorDialog component:

```
' Assumes Imports System.Windows.Forms
Public Class SomeClass
   Public Sub SomeMethod( )
      Dim clrDlg As New ColorDialog( )
      If clrDlg.ShowDialog = DialogResult.OK Then
         ' Do something with the value found in clrDlg.Color.
      End If
   End Sub
End Class
```

The remainder of this section briefly describes each of the common dialog-box components.

ColorDialog

The ColorDialog component displays a dialog box that allows the user to choose a color. After the user clicks OK, the chosen color is available in the ColorDialog object's Color property. The Color property can also be set prior to showing the dialog box. This causes the dialog box to initially display the given color. Figure 5-14 shows an example of the ColorDialog dialog box.

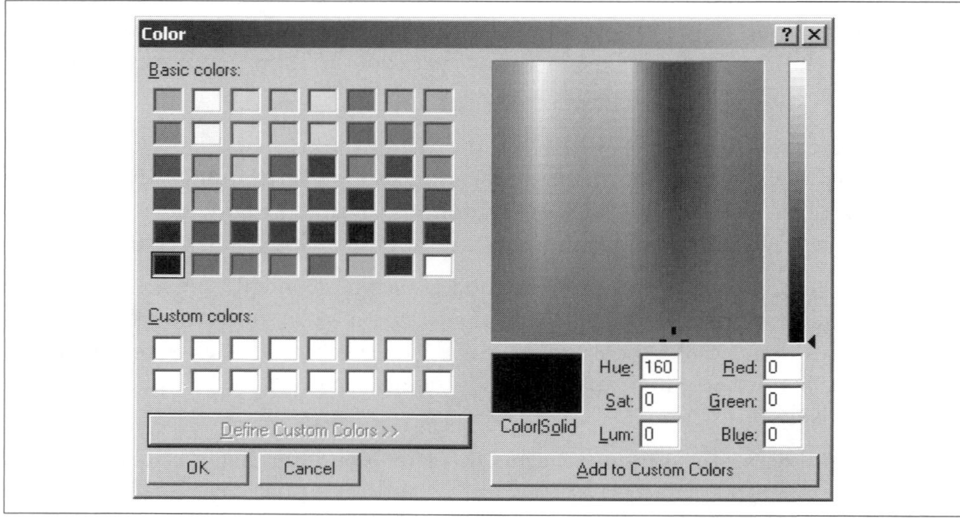

Figure 5-14. The ColorDialog dialog box

FontDialog

The FontDialog component displays a dialog box that allows the user to choose a font. After the user clicks OK, the chosen font is available in the FontDialog object's Font property. The Font property can also be set prior to showing the dialog box. This causes the dialog box to initially display the given font. Figure 5-15 shows an example of the FontDialog dialog box.

OpenFileDialog

The OpenFileDialog component displays a dialog box that allows the user to choose a file to open. After the user clicks OK, the name of the file (including the path) is available in the OpenFileDialog object's FileName property. The FileName property can be set prior to showing the dialog box. This causes the dialog box to initially display the given filename. Figure 5-16 shows an example of the OpenFileDialog dialog box.

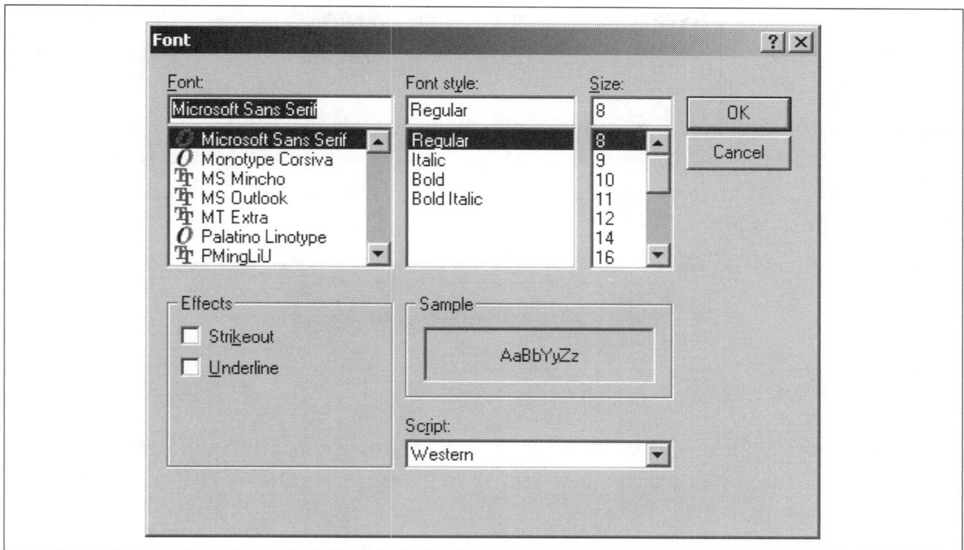

Figure 5-15. The FontDialog dialog box

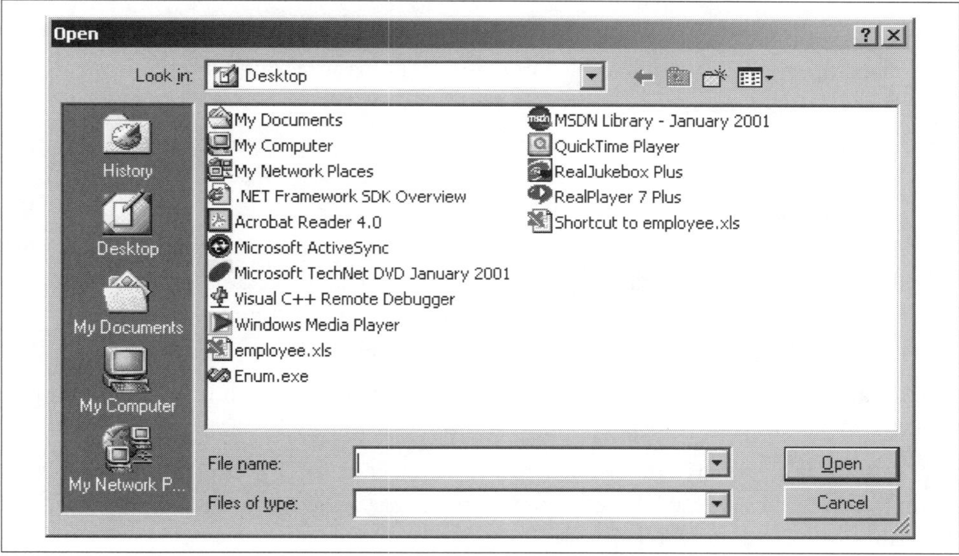

Figure 5-16. The OpenFileDialog dialog box

In most cases, your applications should set the InitialDirectory, Filter, and FilterIndex properties prior to calling ShowDialog. This is not necessary for proper functioning of the dialog box, but it will give your application a more professional look and feel.

The InitialDirectory property determines which directory is shown when the dialog box first appears. The default is an empty string, which causes the dialog box to display the user's My Documents directory.

The Filter property holds a String value that controls the choices in the "Files of type" drop-down list. The purpose of this drop-down list is to let the user limit the files shown in the dialog box based on filename extension. A typical example is shown in Figure 5-17.

Figure 5-17. A typical "Files of type" drop-down list

Even though the "Files of type" list can include many items and each item can represent many filename extensions, a single String property represents the whole thing. Here's how it works:

- Each item in the drop-down list is represented by a substring having two parts separated by the vertical bar character (|). The first part is the description that appears in the drop-down list (e.g., `"All Files (*.*)"`). The second part is the corresponding filter (e.g., `"*.*"`). Taking them together and adding the vertical bar character, the first item in the list in Figure 5-17 is represented by the substring:

  ```
  "All Files (*.*)|*.*"
  ```

- If a given item has multiple filters, the filters are separated by semicolons (;). The second item in the list in Figure 5-17 is therefore represented by:

  ```
  "Executable Files (*.exe; *.dll)|*.exe;*.dll"
  ```

- The value to assign to the Filter property is the concatenation of all the substrings thus attained, again separated by the vertical bar character. Therefore, the Filter property value that produced the drop-down list in Figure 5-17 is:

  ```
  "All Files (*.*)|*.*|Executable Files (*.exe; *.dll)|*.exe;*.dll"
  ```

The default value of the Filter property is an empty string, which results in an empty "Files of type" drop-down list.

The FilterIndex property determines which filter is in force when the dialog box is initially shown. This is a 1-based index that refers to the Filter string. For example, referring again to Figure 5-17, if the FilterIndex property is set to `1`, the "All Files" item will be selected when the dialog box is shown. If the FilterIndex is set to `2`, the "Executable Files" item will be shown. The default value is `1`.

PageSetupDialog

The PageSetupDialog component displays a dialog box that allows the user to choose page settings for a document. Certain properties in the PageSetupDialog object must be set prior to showing the dialog box. After the user clicks OK, new settings can be read from the object. See "Printing" in Chapter 4 for details. Figure 5-18 shows an example of the PageSetupDialog dialog box.

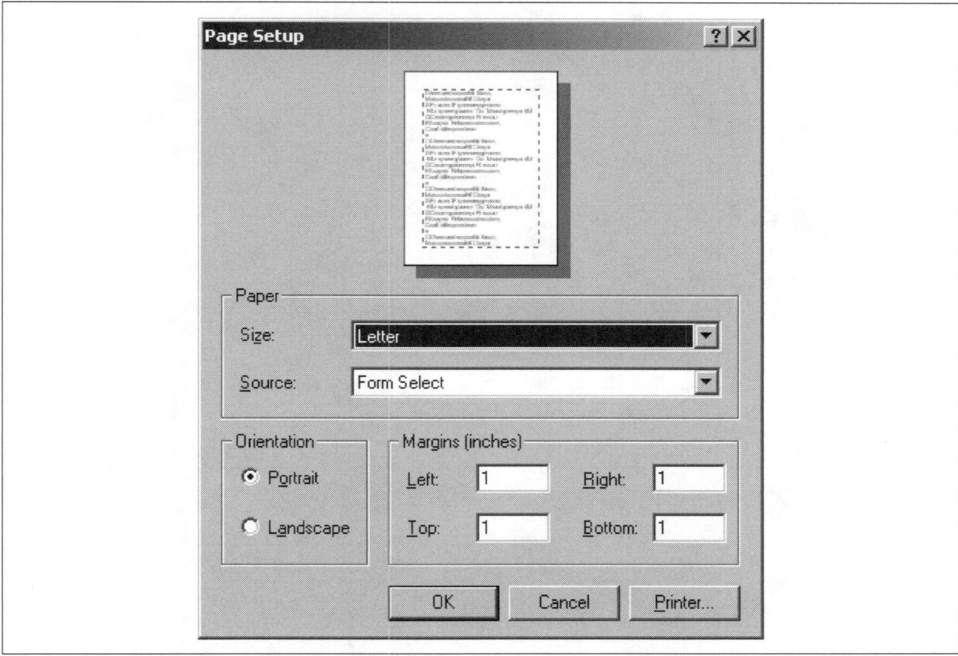

Figure 5-18. The PageSetupDialog dialog box

PrintDialog

The PrintDialog component displays a dialog box that allows the user to choose printer settings for a document. Certain properties in the PrintDialog object must be set prior to showing the dialog box. After the user clicks OK, new settings can be read from the object. See "Printing" in Chapter 4 for details. Figure 5-19 shows an example of the PrintDialog dialog box.

PrintPreviewDialog

The PrintPreviewDialog component displays a dialog box that allows the user to view a document before printing it. Prior to showing the dialog box, the Print-PreviewDialog object must be loaded with information about the document to be printed. See "Printing" in Chapter 4 for details. The dialog box itself displays a preview of the printed version of the document, allowing the user to navigate through it. Figure 5-20 shows an example of the PrintPreviewDialog dialog box, although this example doesn't have a document loaded.

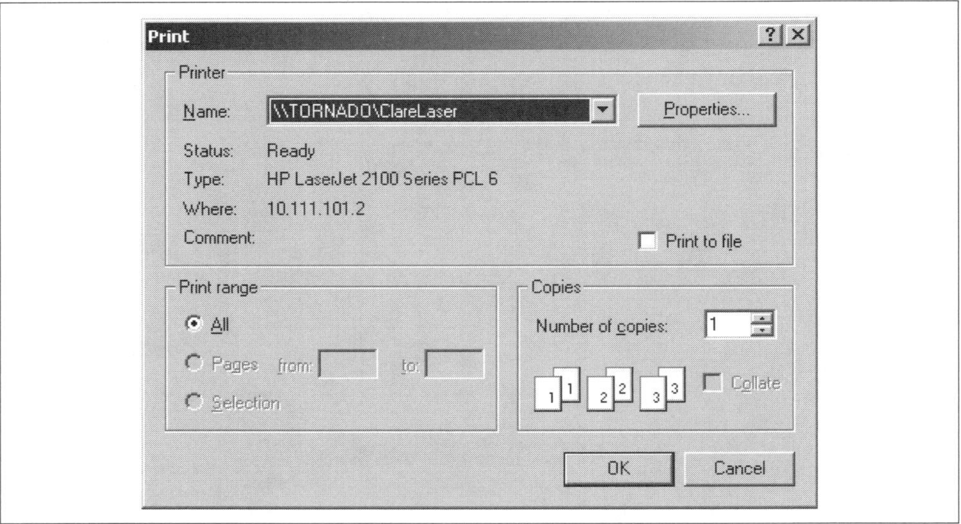

Figure 5-19. The PrintDialog dialog box

Figure 5-20. The PrintPreviewDialog dialog box

SaveFileDialog

The SaveFileDialog component displays a dialog box that allows the user to specify a filename to be used for saving. After the user clicks OK, the name of the file (including the path) is available in the SaveFileDialog object's FileName property (which can be set prior to showing the dialog box). This causes the dialog box to initially display the given filename. Figure 5-21 shows an example of the SaveFileDialog dialog box.

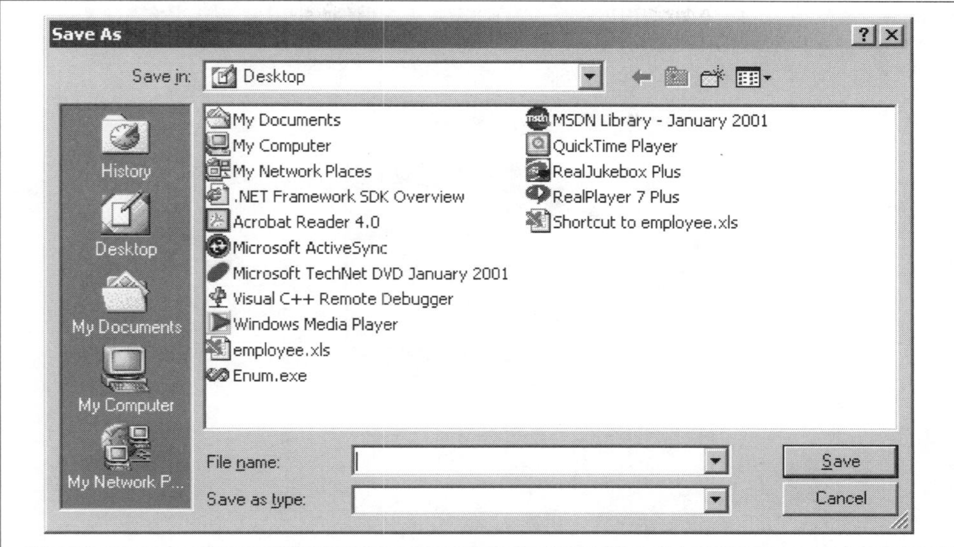

Figure 5-21. The SaveFileDialog dialog box

As with the OpenFileDialog component, most applications should set the InitialDirectory, Filter, and FilterIndex properties prior to calling ShowDialog. Their usage with the SaveFileDialog component is precisely the same as with OpenFileDialog.

Menus

The Windows Forms library provides three components for creating and managing menus:

- The MainMenu class manages the display of a menu across the top of a form.
- The ContextMenu class manages the display of a context menu (also known as a pop-up menu).
- The MenuItem class represents a specific menu item within a main menu or context menu.

Menus can be created either in the Visual Studio .NET Windows Forms Designer or programmatically.

Adding Menus in the Visual Studio .NET Windows Forms Designer

Visual Studio .NET includes an in-place WYSIWYG menu editor that is a dramatic improvement over the menu editor in Visual Basic 6. To create an application menu in the Windows Forms Designer, add a MainMenu component to the form. This causes a representation of the component to appear in the lower pane of the form's design view. When the component is selected, Visual Studio .NET adds a WYSIWYG editor to the top of the form, as shown in Figure 5-22.

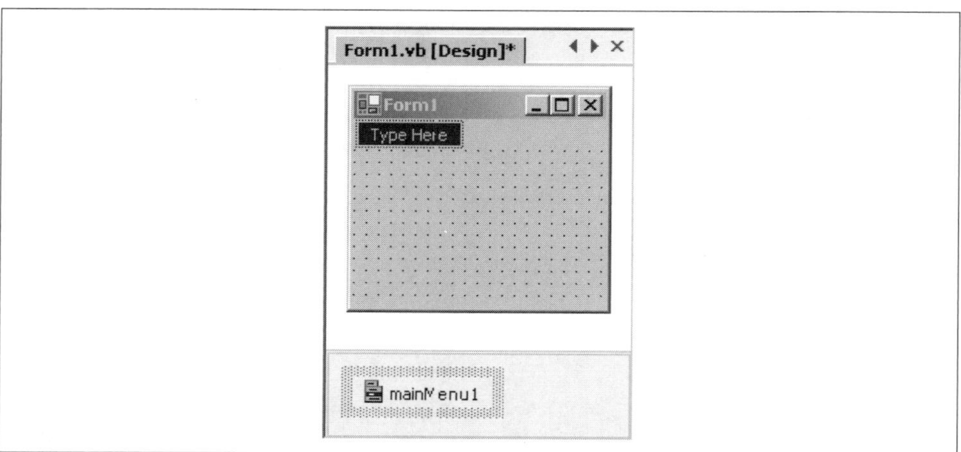

Figure 5-22. In-place editing of a main menu

To create a menu item, type a value into the "Type Here" box. The menu editor automatically adds "Type Here" boxes to the right and beneath the box in which you are typing. As was the case in previous Windows development environments, typing an ampersand (&) within the menu name causes the character following the ampersand to be an accelerator key. Typing a single hyphen (-) within a "Type Here" box creates a menu-separator bar. Figure 5-23 shows a menu containing several items.

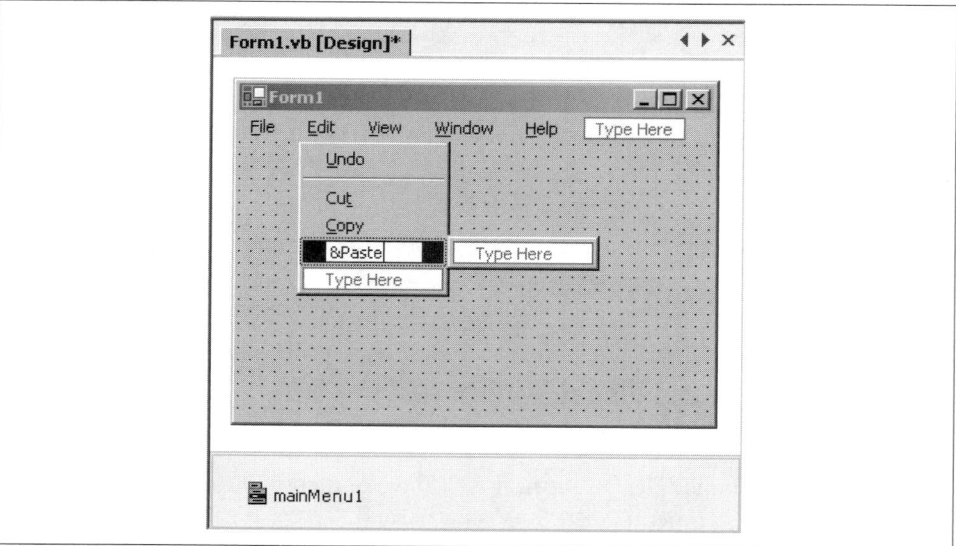

Figure 5-23. A menu containing several items

After a menu item has been added, its properties can be set in the Properties window. The Properties window of the Edit→Paste item shown in Figure 5-23 is shown in Figure 5-24.

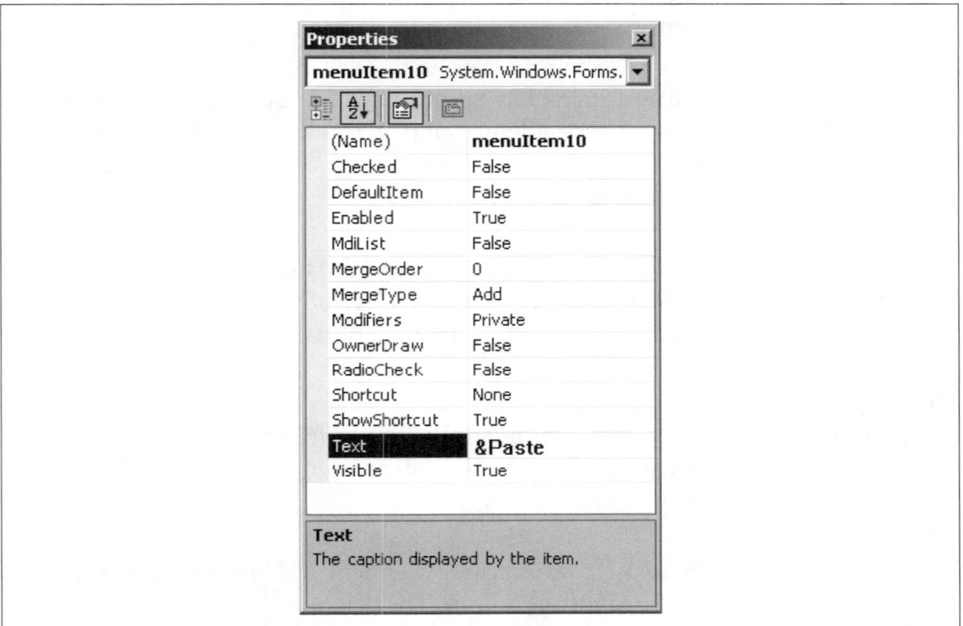

Figure 5-24. The Properties window display for the Edit → Paste menu item shown in Figure 5-23

The properties shown in Figure 5-24 are:

Checked
: Indicates whether a checkmark appears next to the menu item. The type is Boolean. The default is `False`.

DefaultItem
: Indicates whether the menu item is the default item in its menu or submenu. Default menu items are displayed in bold. The type is Boolean. The default is `False`.

Enabled
: Indicates whether the menu item is enabled. If this is `False`, the menu item is grayed and can't be selected. The type is Boolean. The default is `True`.

MdiList
: In MDI applications, indicates whether the menu item should have subitems for each of the open MDI child forms. This property should be set to `True` for the Windows menu item. The type is Boolean. The default is `False`.

MergeOrder

In applications where two menus might be merged (such as an MDI application where a child form menu might be merged with its parent form menu), sorts the merged menu items based on this property. The type is Integer. The default is `0`. See "MDI Applications" in Chapter 4 for more information.

MergeType

Indicates how two menu items having the same MergeOrder value should be merged. The value is of type MenuMerge (defined in the System.Windows.Forms namespace). The default is `MenuMerge.Add`. See "MDI Applications" in Chapter 4 for more information.

Modifiers

Specifies the declaration modifiers that are placed on the menu-item field declaration within the generated code. This is not actually a property of the MenuItem class. Rather, it becomes part of the field declaration in source code. The default is `Private`.

OwnerDraw

Indicates whether the menu item requires custom drawing. If you set this property to `True`, you must handle the menu item's DrawItem event. The type is Boolean. The default is `False`.

RadioCheck

If the Checked property is `True`, indicates whether to display the checkmark as a radio button instead. The type is Boolean. The default is `False`.

Shortcut

Specifies the shortcut key combination that invokes this menu item. The value is of type Shortcut (defined in the System.Windows.Forms namespace). The Shortcut enumeration defines a unique value for each potential shortcut key combination. The values of the Shortcut enumeration are shown in Table 5-1. The default is `Shortcut.None`.

Table 5-1. Values defined by the System.Windows.Forms.Shortcut enumeration

None	Ins	Del	F1
F2	F3	F4	F5
F6	F7	F8	F9
F10	F11	F12	ShiftIns
ShiftDel	ShiftF1	ShiftF2	ShiftF3
ShiftF4	ShiftF5	ShiftF6	ShiftF7
ShiftF8	ShiftF9	ShiftF10	ShiftF11
ShiftF12	CtrlIns	CtrlDel	CtrlA
CtrlB	CtrlC	CtrlD	CtrlE
CtrlF	CtrlG	CtrlH	CtrlI
CtrlJ	CtrlK	CtrlL	CtrlM

Table 5-1. Values defined by the System.Windows.Forms.Shortcut enumeration (continued)

CtrlN	CtrlO	CtrlP	CtrlQ
CtrlR	CtrlS	CtrlT	CtrlU
CtrlV	CtrlW	CtrlX	CtrlY
CtrlZ	CtrlF1	CtrlF2	CtrlF3
CtrlF4	CtrlF5	CtrlF6	CtrlF7
CtrlF8	CtrlF9	CtrlF10	CtrlF11
CtrlF12	CtrlShiftA	CtrlShiftB	CtrlShiftC
CtrlShiftD	CtrlShiftE	CtrlShiftF	CtrlShiftG
CtrlShiftH	CtrlShiftI	CtrlShiftJ	CtrlShiftK
CtrlShiftL	CtrlShiftM	CtrlShiftN	CtrlShiftO
CtrlShiftP	CtrlShiftQ	CtrlShiftR	CtrlShiftS
CtrlShiftT	CtrlShiftU	CtrlShiftV	CtrlShiftW
CtrlShiftX	CtrlShiftY	CtrlShiftZ	CtrlShiftF1
CtrlShiftF2	CtrlShiftF3	CtrlShiftF4	CtrlShiftF5
CtrlShiftF6	CtrlShiftF7	CtrlShiftF8	CtrlShiftF9
CtrlShiftF10	CtrlShiftF11	CtrlShiftF12	AltBksp
AltF1	AltF2	AltF3	AltF4
AltF5	AltF6	AltF7	AltF8
AltF9	AltF10	AltF11	AltF12

ShowShortcut

If a shortcut key combination is defined for the menu item, indicates whether the key combination should be shown on the menu. The type is Boolean. The default is `True`.

Text

Represents the text shown on the menu item. The type is String. The default is an empty string.

Visible

Indicates whether the menu item should be visible. The type is Boolean. The default is `True`.

The Windows Forms Designer creates code that declares a field for the MainMenu object, as well as fields for the MenuItem objects that represent each menu item in the menu. The designer also creates code that instantiates the objects at runtime and sets their properties according to the values set in the IDE's Properties window. In addition, the top-level MenuItem objects are added to the MenuItems collection of the MainMenu object, and the lower-level MenuItem objects are added to the Menu-Items collection of the menu of which they are submenus. Finally, the MainMenu object is assigned to the form's Menu property.

To create a context menu in the Windows Forms Designer, add a ContextMenu component to the form. This causes a representation of the component to appear in the lower pane of the form's design view. When the component is selected, Visual Studio .NET adds a WYSIWYG editor to the top of the form. Clicking on the editor drops down a "Type Here" box, as shown in Figure 5-25.

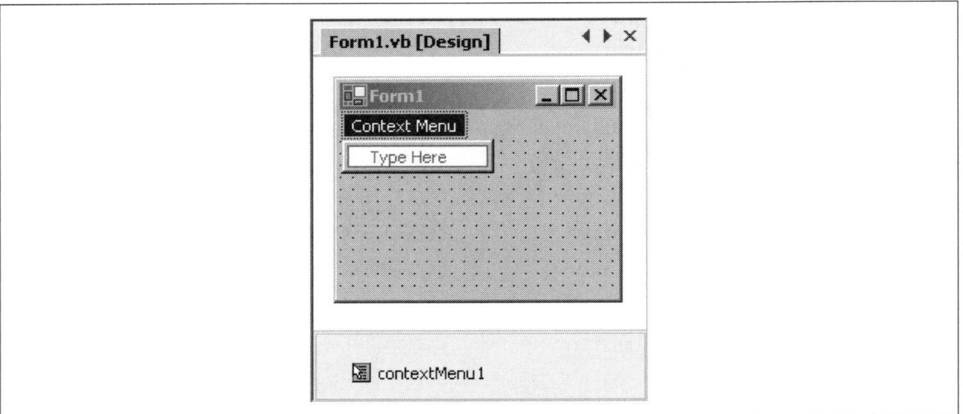

Figure 5-25. In-place editing of a context menu

Adding menu items and setting their properties work the same with context menus as with main menus. For a context menu to be displayed, it must be associated with some control on the form or with the form itself. When the user right-clicks on that control or form, the context menu is displayed. To make this association, perform these steps:

1. In the Windows Forms Designer, right-click the control or form that is to be associated with the context menu, and choose Properties.
2. In the Properties window, find the ContextMenu property, and click the arrow of the drop-down list associated with it.
3. The drop-down list displays the ContextMenu objects that are defined on the current form. Choose the desired one.

The same effect can be achieved in code by assigning the ContextMenu object to the ContextMenu property of a control or form, like this:

```
' Somewhere within the definition of a Form class.
Me.Button1.ContextMenu = Me.ContextMenu1
```

Programmatically Creating Menus

Main menus and context menus can be instantiated and populated directly in code. Example 5-2 shows how to create a simple main menu having File and Edit items, with the File item having an Exit item. Compile it from the command line with this command:

```
vbc filename.vb /r:System.dll,System.Drawing.dll,System.Windows.Forms.dll /t:winexe
```

The code in Example 5-2 is similar to the code that would be created by the Windows Forms Designer if its visual menu editor were used to create this menu. The essential steps are:

1. Declare a MainMenu object to represent the menu.
2. Declare a MenuItem object for each menu item.
3. Instantiate the MainMenu object and all the MenuItem objects.
4. Set the properties of the MenuItem objects (such as the Text property) as desired.
5. Add the top-level MenuItem objects to the MenuItems collection of the MainMenu object, then add the lower-level MenuItem objects to the MenuItems collection of the MenuItem object under which they should appear.

Example 5-2. Creating a main menu in code

```
Imports System.Drawing
Imports System.Windows.Forms

Module modMain
   <System.STAThreadAttribute( )> Public Sub Main( )
      System.Threading.Thread.CurrentThread.ApartmentState = _
         System.Threading.ApartmentState.STA
      System.Windows.Forms.Application.Run(New Form1( ))
   End Sub
End Module

Public Class Form1
   Inherits Form

   ' Declare the main menu component.
   Private myMenu As MainMenu

   ' Declare the menu items that will be in the menu. Use the
   ' WithEvents keyword so that event handlers can be added later.
   Private WithEvents mnuFile As MenuItem
   Private WithEvents mnuFileExit As MenuItem
   Private WithEvents mnuEdit As MenuItem

   Public Sub New( )

      ' Instantiate the menu objects.
      myMenu = New MainMenu( )
      mnuFile = New MenuItem( )
      mnuFileExit = New MenuItem( )
      mnuEdit = New MenuItem( )
```

Example 5-2. Creating a main menu in code (continued)

```
        ' Set the properties of the menu items.
        mnuFile.Text = "&File"
        mnuFileExit.Text = "E&xit"
        mnuEdit.Text = "&Edit"

        ' Connect the menu items to each other and to the main menu.
        mnuFile.MenuItems.Add(mnuFileExit)
        myMenu.MenuItems.Add(mnuFile)
        myMenu.MenuItems.Add(mnuEdit)

        ' Connect the main menu to the form.
        Me.Menu = myMenu

    End Sub

End Class
```

Handling Menu Events

User interaction with a menu causes menu events to be fired. The most common menu event is the Click event of the MenuItem class, which fires when a user clicks a menu item. Here is an example of a Click event handler (this code could be added to the Form1 class of Example 5-2):

```
Private Sub mnuFileExit_Click( _
   ByVal sender As Object, _
   ByVal e As EventArgs _
) Handles mnuFileExit.Click
   Me.Close( )
End Sub
```

The events of the MenuItem class are:

Click
: Fired when the menu item is chosen either by clicking it with the mouse or by pressing a shortcut key combination defined for the menu item. The syntax of the Click event is:

```
Public Event Click As System.EventHandler
```

This is equivalent to:

```
Public Event Click(ByVal sender As Object, ByVal e As System.EventArgs)
```

Disposed
: Fired when the MenuItem object's Dispose method is called. The syntax of the Disposed event is:

```
Public Event Disposed As System.EventHandler
```

This is equivalent to:

```
Public Event Disposed(ByVal sender As Object, ByVal e As System.EventArgs)
```

The event is inherited from the Component class.

DrawItem

Fired when the menu item needs to be drawn, when the MenuItem object's OwnerDraw property is True. The syntax of the DrawItem event is:

```
Public Event DrawItem As System.Windows.Forms.DrawItemEventHandler
```

This is equivalent to:

```
Public Event DrawItem( _
   ByVal sender As Object, _
   ByVal e As System.Windows.Forms.DrawItemEventArgs _
)
```

The *e* parameter, of type DrawItemEventArgs, provides additional information that is needed for drawing the menu item. The properties of the DrawItemEventArgs class are:

BackColor

The background color that should be used when drawing the item. The type is Color (defined in the System.Drawing namespace).

Bounds

The bounding rectangle of the menu item. The type is Rectangle (defined in the System.Drawing namespace).

Font

The font that should be used when drawing the item. The type is Font (defined in the System.Drawing namespace).

ForeColor

The foreground color that should be used when drawing the item. The type is Color (defined in the System.Drawing namespace).

Graphics

The graphics surface on which to draw the item. The type is Graphics (defined in the System.Drawing namespace).

Index

The index of the menu item within its parent menu. The type is Integer.

State

The state of the menu item. The type is DrawItemState (defined in the System.Windows.Forms namespace). DrawItemState is an enumeration that defines the values `None`, `Selected`, `Grayed`, `Disabled`, `Checked`, `Focus`, `Default`, `HotLight`, `Inactive`, `NoAccelerator`, `NoFocusRect`, and `ComboBoxEdit`.

MeasureItem

Fired prior to firing the DrawItem event when the MenuItem object's OwnerDraw property is True. The MeasureItem event allows the client to specify the size of the item to be drawn. The syntax of the MeasureItem event is:

```
Public Event MeasureItem As System.Windows.Forms.MeasureItemEventHandler
```

This is equivalent to:

```
Public Event MeasureItem( _
```

```
        ByVal sender As Object, _
        ByVal e As System.Windows.Forms.MeasureItemEventArgs _
    )
```

The *e* parameter, of type MeasureItemEventArgs, provides additional information needed by the event handler and provides fields that the event handler can set to communicate the item size to the MenuItem object. The properties of the MeasureItemEventArgs are:

Graphics
: The graphics device upon which the menu item will be drawn. This is needed so the client can determine the scale of the device upon which the menu item will be rendered. The type is Graphics (defined in the System. Drawing namespace).

Index
: The index of the menu item within its parent menu. The type is Integer.

ItemHeight
: The height of the menu item. The type is Integer.

ItemWidth
: The width of the menu item. The type is Integer.

Popup
: Fired when the submenu is about to be displayed, when a menu item has subitems associated with it. This provides the client with an opportunity to set the menu states (checked, enabled, etc.) of the submenu items to match the current program state. The syntax of the Popup event is:

```
Public Event Popup As System.EventHandler
```

This is equivalent to:

```
Public Event Popup(ByVal sender As Object, ByVal e As System.EventArgs)
```

Select
: Fired when the user places the mouse over the menu item or when the user highlights the menu item by navigating to it with the keyboard arrow keys. The syntax of the Select event is:

```
Public Event Select As System.EventHandler
```

This is equivalent to:

```
Public Event Select(ByVal sender As Object, ByVal e As System.EventArgs)
```

The ContextMenu class also exposes a Popup event, which is fired just before the context menu is displayed. The syntax of the Popup event is:

```
Public Event Popup As System.EventHandler
```

This is equivalent to:

```
Public Event Popup(ByVal sender As Object, ByVal e As System.EventArgs)
```

Cloning Menus

Sometimes menu items and their submenus need to appear on more than one menu. A common example is an application that has context menus containing some of the same functionality as the application's main menu. However, MenuItem objects don't work correctly if they are assigned to more than one menu. To provide an easy solution for developers who need to duplicate functionality on multiple menus, the MenuItem class provides the CloneMenu method. This method returns a new MenuItem object whose properties are set the same as those of the MenuItem object on which the CloneMenu method is called. If the original MenuItem object has submenus, the submenu MenuItem objects are cloned as well.

Example 5-3 shows the complete code for a program that has both a main menu and a context menu. It can be compiled from the command line with this command:

```
vbc filename.vb /r:System.dll,System.Drawing.dll,System.Windows.Forms.dll /t:winexe
```

The code in Example 5-3 sets up a menu item labeled Format that has four options beneath it: Font, ForeColor, BackColor, and Reset. After this menu structure is set up, it is added to the MainMenu object, which is then attached to the form, as shown here:

```
MainMenu1.MenuItems.Add(mnuFormat)
Menu = MainMenu1
```

An identical menu structure is then created and assigned to the ContextMenu object, which is then attached to the Label1 control, as shown here:

```
ContextMenu1.MenuItems.Add(mnuFormat.CloneMenu( ))
Label1.ContextMenu = ContextMenu1
```

The CloneMenu method even detects the event handlers that are defined for the MenuItems being cloned and automatically registers those handlers with the corresponding events on the newly created MenuItem objects. This means that the event handlers shown in Example 5-3 handle the events both from the main menu and from the context menu. Figure 5-26 shows the running application with the context menu displayed (the Label control was right-clicked).

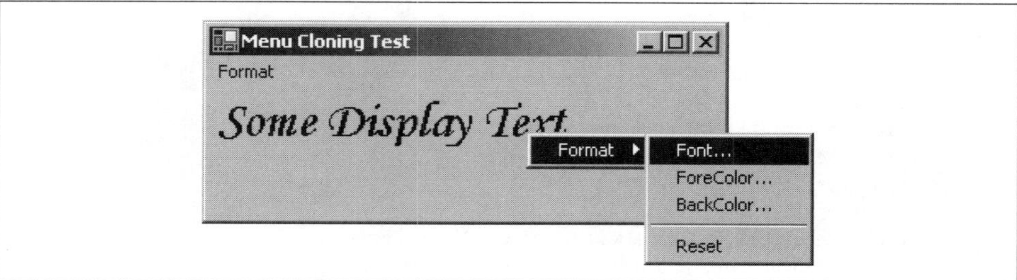

Figure 5-26. The display produced by Example 5-3

Example 5-3. Cloning menus

```
Imports System
Imports System.Drawing
Imports System.Windows.Forms

Module modMain
   <STAThreadAttribute( )> Public Sub Main( )
      System.Threading.Thread.CurrentThread.ApartmentState = _
         System.Threading.ApartmentState.STA
      Application.Run(New Form1( ))
   End Sub
End Module

Public Class Form1
   Inherits Form

   ' This member references the label used for displaying text.
   Private WithEvents Label1 As New Label( )

   ' These members store original font and color properties of the
   ' Label1 control.
   Private origFont As Font
   Private origForeColor As Color
   Private origBackColor As Color

   ' These members hold the MainMenu and ContextMenu objects.
   Private WithEvents MainMenu1 As New MainMenu( )
   Private WithEvents ContextMenu1 As New ContextMenu( )

   ' These members hold the MenuItem objects.
   Private WithEvents mnuFormat As New MenuItem( )
   Private WithEvents mnuFormatFont As New MenuItem( )
   Private WithEvents mnuFormatForeColor As New MenuItem( )
   Private WithEvents mnuFormatBackColor As New MenuItem( )
   Private mnuSeparator As New MenuItem( )
   Private WithEvents mnuFormatReset As New MenuItem( )

   Public Sub New( )
      MyBase.New( )

      ' Set up the Format menu.

      mnuFormat.Text = "F&ormat"
      mnuFormatFont.Text = "&Font..."
      mnuFormatForeColor.Text = "F&oreColor..."
      mnuFormatBackColor.Text = "&BackColor..."
      mnuSeparator.Text = "-"
      mnuFormatReset.Text = "&Reset"
      mnuFormat.MenuItems.AddRange(New MenuItem( ) {mnuFormatFont, _
         mnuFormatForeColor, mnuFormatBackColor, mnuSeparator, _
         mnuFormatReset})

      ' Attach the Format menu to the main menu and attach the main
```

Example 5-3. Cloning menus (continued)

```
      ' menu to the form.

      MainMenu1.MenuItems.Add(mnuFormat)
      Menu = MainMenu1

      ' Clone the Format menu, attach the clone to the context menu, and
      ' attach the context menu to the Label control.

      ContextMenu1.MenuItems.Add(mnuFormat.CloneMenu( ))
      Label1.ContextMenu = ContextMenu1

      ' Set up non-menu-related properties of the form and the label.
      AutoScaleBaseSize = New Size(5, 13)
      ClientSize = New Size(312, 81)
      Controls.Add(Label1)
      Menu = MainMenu1
      Name = "Form1"
      Text = "Menu Cloning Test"
      Label1.Text = "Some Display Text"
      Label1.AutoSize = True

      ' Save the original font and color properties of the Label1 control.
      origFont = Label1.Font
      origForeColor = Label1.ForeColor
      origBackColor = Label1.BackColor

   End Sub

   ' Font Click event handler
   Private Sub mnuFormatFont_Click( _
      ByVal sender As Object, _
      ByVal e As EventArgs _
   ) Handles mnuFormatFont.Click
      Dim dlg As New FontDialog( )
      dlg.Font = Label1.Font
      If dlg.ShowDialog = DialogResult.OK Then
         Label1.Font = dlg.Font
      End If
      dlg.Dispose( )
   End Sub

   ' ForeColor Click event handler
   Private Sub mnuFormatForeColor_Click( _
      ByVal sender As Object, _
      ByVal e As EventArgs _
   ) Handles mnuFormatForeColor.Click
      Dim dlg As New ColorDialog( )
      dlg.Color = Label1.ForeColor
      If dlg.ShowDialog = DialogResult.OK Then
         Label1.ForeColor = dlg.Color
      End If
      dlg.Dispose( )
```

Example 5-3. Cloning menus (continued)

```
    End Sub

    ' BackColor Click event handler
    Private Sub mnuFormatBackColor_Click( _
       ByVal sender As Object, _
       ByVal e As EventArgs _
    ) Handles mnuFormatBackColor.Click
       Dim dlg As New ColorDialog( )
       dlg.Color = Label1.BackColor
       If dlg.ShowDialog = DialogResult.OK Then
          Label1.BackColor = dlg.Color
       End If
       dlg.Dispose( )
    End Sub

    ' Resent Click event handler
    Private Sub mnuFormatReset_Click( _
       ByVal sender As Object, _
       ByVal e As EventArgs _
    ) Handles mnuFormatReset.Click
       Label1.Font = origFont
       Label1.ForeColor = origForeColor
       Label1.BackColor = origBackColor
    End Sub

End Class
```

Creating a Control

A control is a component with a visual representation. The Windows Forms class library provides the base functionality for controls through the Control class (defined in the System.Windows.Forms namespace). All controls derive directly or indirectly from the Control class. In addition, Windows Forms provides a class called UserControl for the purpose of making it easy to write custom control classes. The derivation of the UserControl class is shown in Figure 5-27.

Building Controls from Other Controls

The easiest way to create a new control is to aggregate and modify the functionality of one or more existing controls. To do this in Visual Studio .NET's Windows Forms Designer, perform the following steps:

1. Choose Project→Add User Control from the main menu.
2. Type the name of the *.vb* file that will hold the code for the control, and click OK. The designer displays a blank user control in design mode, as shown in Figure 5-28.

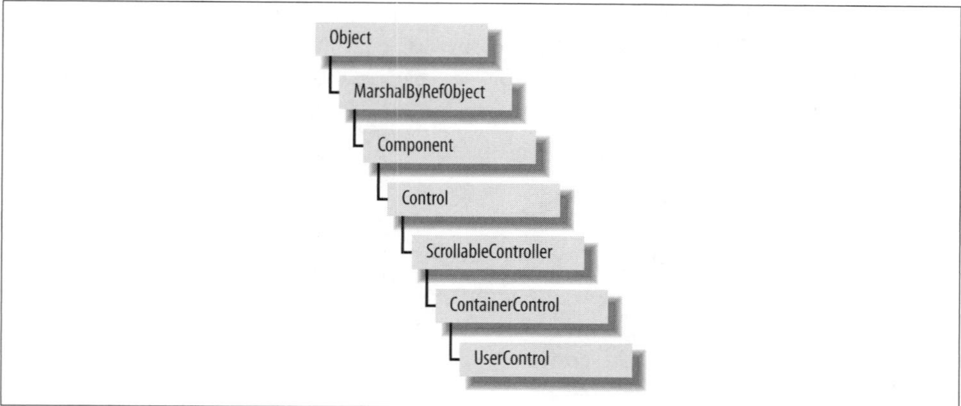

Figure 5-27. The derivation hierarchy of the UserControl class

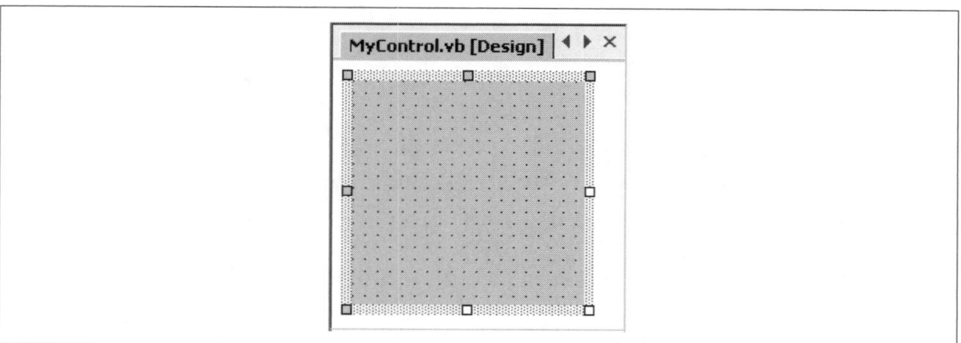

Figure 5-28. A blank user control in Visual Studio .NET's Windows Forms Designer

3. Add controls from the Toolbox window just as you would when laying out a form. Controls that are made part of another control are called *constituent controls*. Figure 5-29 shows a user control that has two constituent controls: a Label and a TextBox.

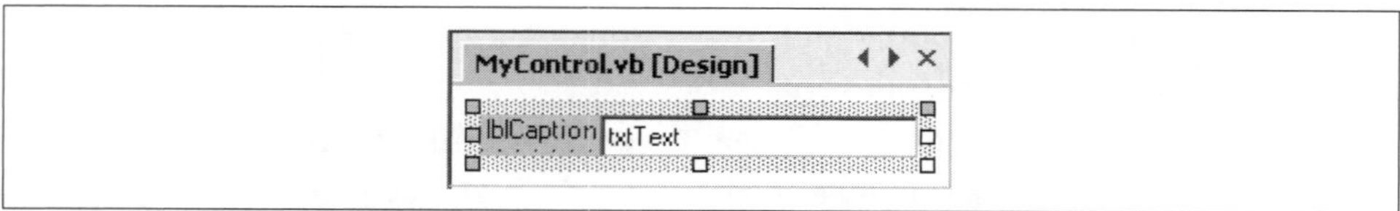

Figure 5-29. A user control with two constituent controls

The user control shown in Figure 5-29 is a good start on a captioned text-box control—a text box that carries around its own caption. These additional steps would also be helpful:

a. Set the Label control's AutoSize property to `True` so the label expands to the size needed for displaying its text.

b. Dock the Label control to the left side of the user control. This allows the TextBox control to be docked to the Label control. The benefit of docking the TextBox control to the Label control is that the TextBox control will move whenever the Label control resizes itself.

c. Dock the TextBox control to fill the remainder of the space.

4. Add any appropriate properties to the user control. This could involve overriding properties inherited from base classes or creating new properties. For the captioned text-box user control, do the following:

   a. Override the Text property. The purpose of this property is to allow the client environment to set and read the text displayed in the constituent TextBox control. Here is the code:

   ```
   Public Overrides Property Text( ) As String
   Get
      Return txtText.Text
   End Get
   Set(ByVal Value As String)
      txtText.Text = Value
   End Set
   End Property
   ```

   As can be seen from the code, the user control's Text property is simply mapped to the TextBox control's Text property.

   b. Create a new property for setting the caption text. Here is the code:

   ```
   Public Property Caption( ) As String
   Get
      Return lblCaption( ).Text
   End Get
   Set(ByVal Value As String)
      lblCaption( ).Text = Value
   End Set
   End Property
   ```

   In this case, the Caption property is mapped to the Label control's Text property.

5. Add any appropriate events to the user control. This could involve invoking base-class events or creating and invoking new events. For the captioned text-box user control, do the following:

   a. Add a handler for the constituent TextBox control's TextChanged property. Within the handler, invoke the base class's TextChanged event. Here is the code:

   ```
   Private Sub txtText_TextChanged( _
      ByVal sender As Object, _
      ByVal e As EventArgs _
   ) Handles txtText.TextChanged
      Me.OnTextChanged(e)
   End Sub
   ```

Notice that this code calls the OnTextChanged method, which is declared in the Control class. The purpose of this method is to fire the TextChanged event, which is also declared in the Control class (Visual Basic .NET doesn't provide a way to fire a base-class event directly.) There are On*EventName* methods for each of the events defined in the Control class.

The OnTextChanged method is overridable. If you override it in your derived class, be sure that your overriding method calls MyBase.OnTextChanged. If you don't, the TextChanged event won't be fired.

b. Declare a new event to notify the client when the user control's Caption property is changed. Name the event CaptionChanged. Add a handler for the Label control's TextChanged event and raise the CaptionChanged event from there. Here's the code:

```
Event CaptionChanged As EventHandler

Private Sub lblCaption_TextChanged( _
   ByVal sender As Object, _
   ByVal e As EventArgs _
) Handles lblCaption.TextChanged
   RaiseEvent CaptionChanged(Me, EventArgs.Empty)
End Sub
```

Note the arguments to the CaptionChanged event. The value `Me` is passed as the sender of the event, and `EventArgs.Empty` is passed as the event arguments. The Empty field of the EventArgs class returns a new, empty EventArgs object.

6. Add any appropriate attributes to the syntax elements of the class. For example, the Caption property will benefit from having a Category attribute and a Description attribute, as shown in bold here:

```
<Category("Appearance"), _
Description("The text appearing next to the textbox.")> _
Public Property _
   Caption( ) As String
Get
   Return lblCaption( ).Text
End Get
Set(ByVal Value As String)
   lblCaption( ).Text = Value
End Set
End Property
```

These attributes are compiled into the code and are picked up by the Visual Studio .NET IDE. The `Category` attribute determines in which category the property will appear in the Properties window. The `Description` attribute determines the help text that will be displayed in the Properties window when the user clicks on that property. See "Component Attributes" in Chapter 4 for a list of attributes defined in the System.ComponentModel namespace.

This is all very similar to creating forms. As with forms, custom controls can be defined directly in code. Example 5-4 shows a complete class definition for the captioned text-box control, created without the aid of the Windows Forms Designer. It can be compiled from the command line with this command:

```
vbc filename.vb /r:System.dll,System.Drawing.dll,System.Windows.Forms.dll /t:library
```

(Note the `/t:library` switch for creating a *.dll* rather than an *.exe* file.)

Example 5-4. A custom Control class

```
Imports System
Imports System.ComponentModel
Imports System.Drawing
Imports System.Windows.Forms

Public Class MyControl
   Inherits UserControl

   Private WithEvents lblCaption As Label
   Private WithEvents txtText As TextBox

   Event CaptionChanged As EventHandler

   Public Sub New( )
      MyBase.New( )

      ' Instantiate a Label object and set its properties.
      lblCaption = New Label( )
      With lblCaption
         .AutoSize = True
         .Dock = DockStyle.Left
         .Size = New Size(53, 13)
         .TabIndex = 0
         .Text = "lblCaption"
      End With

      ' Instantiate a TextBox object and set its properties.
      txtText = New TextBox( )
      With txtText
         .Dock = DockStyle.Fill
         .Location = New Point(53, 0)
         .Size = New Size(142, 20)
         .TabIndex = 1
         .Text = "txtText"
      End With

      ' Add the label and text box to the form's Controls collection.
      Me.Controls.AddRange(New Control( ) {txtText, lblCaption})

      ' Set the size of the form.
      Me.Size = New Size(195, 19)

   End Sub
```

Example 5-4. A custom Control class (continued)

```
    ' Override the Control class's Text property. Map it to the
    ' constituent TextBox control's Text property.
    <Category("Appearance"), _
    Description("The text contained in the textbox.")> _
    Public Overrides Property Text( ) As String
    Get
       Return txtText.Text
    End Get
    Set(ByVal Value As String)
       txtText.Text = Value
    End Set
    End Property

    ' Add a Caption property. Map it to the constituent Label
    ' control's Text property.
    <Category("Appearance"), _
    Description("The text appearing next to the textbox.")> _
    Public Property _
       Caption( ) As String
    Get
       Return lblCaption.Text
    End Get
    Set(ByVal Value As String)
       lblCaption.Text = Value
    End Set
    End Property

    ' When the constituent TextBox control's TextChanged event is
    ' received, fire the user control's TextChanged event.
    Private Sub txtText_TextChanged( _
       ByVal sender As Object, _
       ByVal e As EventArgs _
    ) Handles txtText.TextChanged
       Me.OnTextChanged(e)
    End Sub

    ' When the constituent Label control's TextChanged event is
    ' received, fire the user control's CaptionChanged event.
    Private Sub lblCaption_TextChanged( _
       ByVal sender As Object, _
       ByVal e As EventArgs _
    ) Handles lblCaption.TextChanged
       RaiseEvent CaptionChanged(Me, EventArgs.Empty)
    End Sub

End Class
```

After compiling the code in Example 5-4, either the custom control can be added to the Visual Studio .NET toolbox and added to forms just like other controls, or it can be referenced and instantiated from an application compiled at the command line.

To add the custom control to the Visual Studio .NET toolbox:

1. Deploy the custom control's *.dll* file into the client application's *bin* directory. (The *bin* directory is a directory created by Visual Studio .NET when the client application is created.)
2. From the Visual Studio .NET menu, select Tools→Customize Toolbox. The Customize Toolbox dialog box appears, as shown in Figure 5-30.

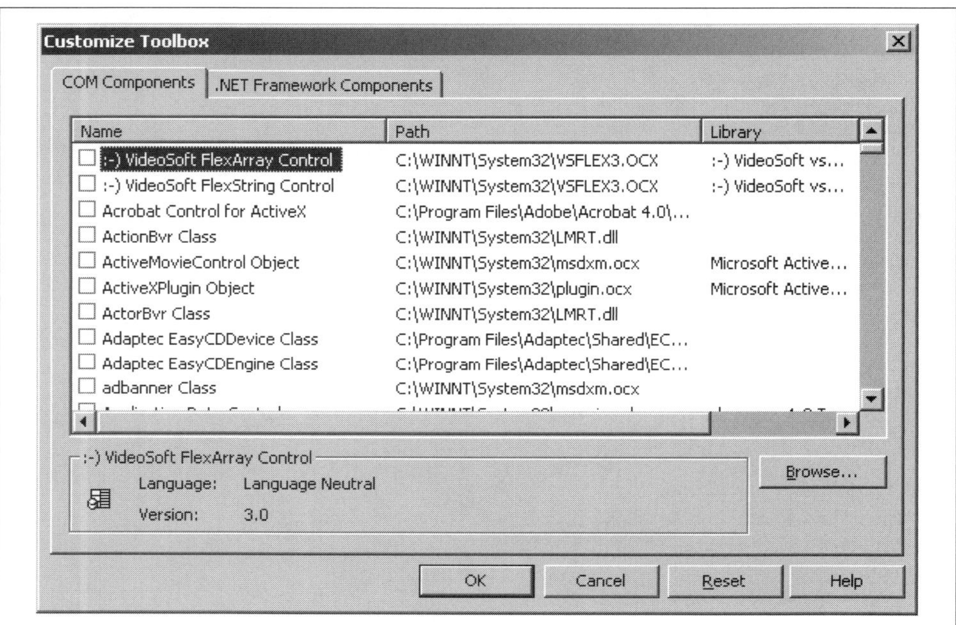

Figure 5-30. The Customize Toolbox dialog box

3. Click the .NET Framework Components tab, then click the Browse button.
4. Browse for and select the *.dll* file compiled from the code in Example 5-4.
5. The controls in the *.dll* file are added to the Customize Toolbox dialog box, as shown in Figure 5-31. (In this case there is only one control in the *.dll* file—the MyControl control.)
6. Ensure that a checkmark appears next to the control name, and click OK.

The control should now appear on the General tab of the Toolbox window, as shown in Figure 5-32.

After you add the custom control to the Toolbox, the control can be added to a form just like any other control.

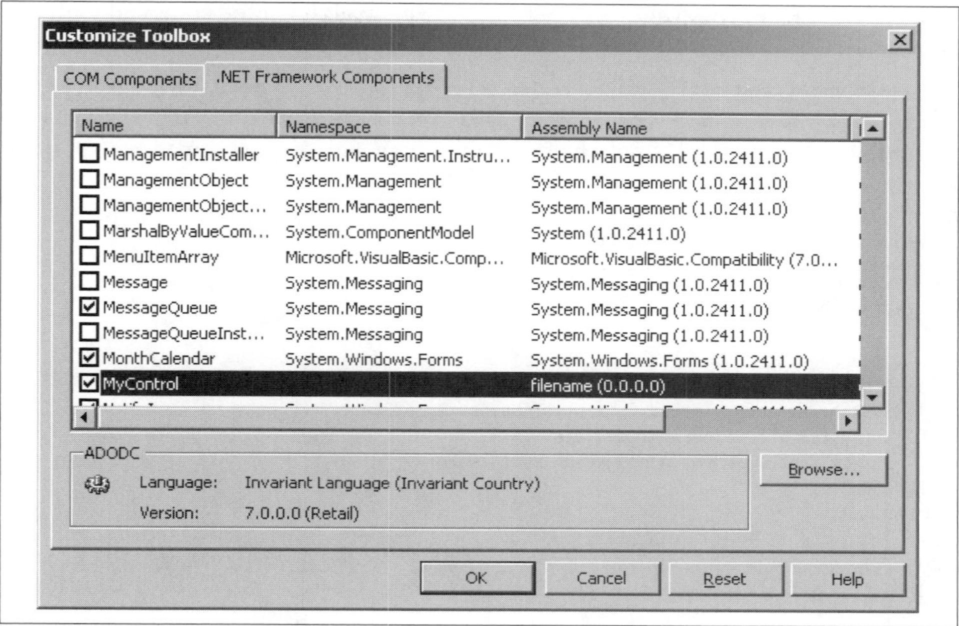

Figure 5-31. Adding a control to the Customize Toolbox dialog box

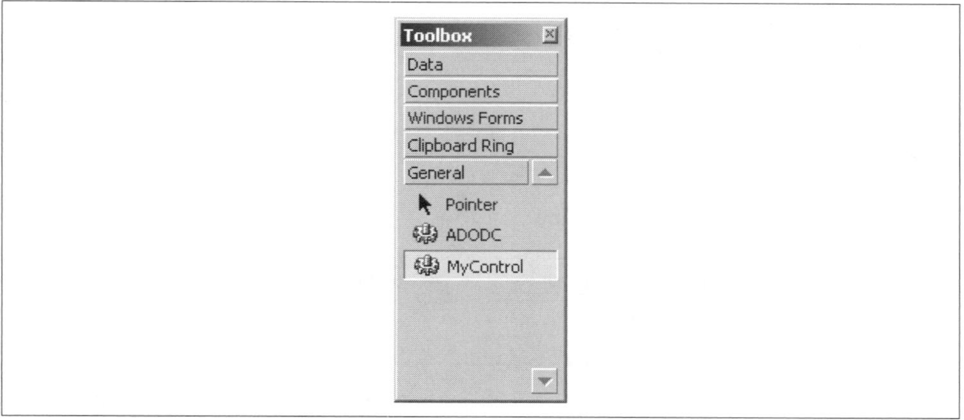

Figure 5-32. The Toolbox window, showing the custom control from Example 5-4

To use the custom control from a non–Visual Studio .NET application, these steps are required:

1. Deploy the custom control's *.dll* file into the same directory as the client *.vb* file.
2. Declare, instantiate, and use the control in client application code, in the same way that has been done throughout this chapter for standard controls.
3. Reference the control's assembly in the compilation command.

The code in Example 5-5 shows how to use the control. It can be compiled with this command:

```
vbc MyApp.vb /r:System.dll,System.Drawing.dll,System.Windows.Forms.dll,MyControl.dll /t:
winexe
```

(Note that the command should be typed on a single line. It is wrapped here only for printing in the book.)

Example 5-5. Using a custom control

```
Imports System.Drawing
Imports System.Windows.Forms

Module modMain
   <System.STAThreadAttribute( )> Public Sub Main( )
      System.Threading.Thread.CurrentThread.ApartmentState = _
         System.Threading.ApartmentState.STA
      System.Windows.Forms.Application.Run(New Form1( ))
   End Sub
End Module

Public Class Form1
   Inherits System.Windows.Forms.Form

   Private ctrl As New MyControl( )

   Public Sub New( )
      ctrl.Caption = "This is the caption."
      ctrl.Text = "This is the text."
      Controls.Add(ctrl)
   End Sub

End Class
```

The resulting display is shown in Figure 5-33.

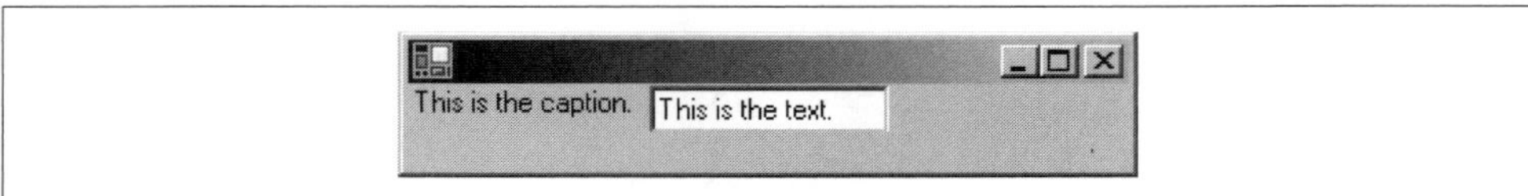

Figure 5-33. Using a custom control

Building Controls That Draw Themselves

Adding constituent controls to a user control is just one way to make a custom control. Another way is to draw the user interface of the control directly onto the control's surface. Example 5-6 shows the definition of a control that draws its own (albeit simple) user interface. Figure 5-34 shows the control after it has been placed on a form in design mode in the Windows Forms Designer.

Example 5-6. A control that renders itself

```
Public Class MyControl
   Inherits UserControl

   Protected Overrides Sub OnPaint(ByVal e As PaintEventArgs)
      e.Graphics.FillEllipse(New SolidBrush(Me.ForeColor), _
         Me.ClientRectangle)
   End Sub

   Public Sub New( )
      Me.ResizeRedraw = True
   End Sub

End Class
```

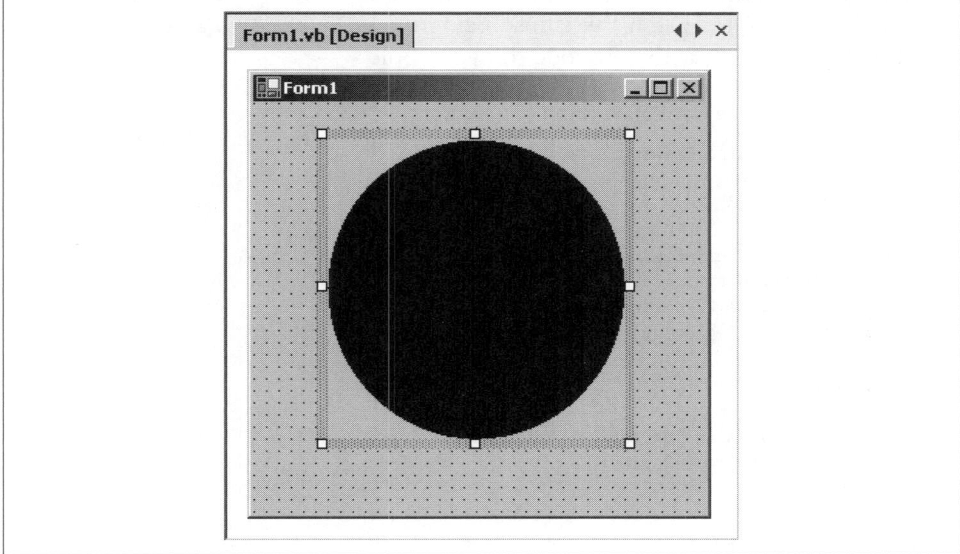

Figure 5-34. The MyControl control as it appears on a form in the Windows Forms Designer

The control in this example overrides the OnPaint method declared in the Control class. Windows invokes the OnPaint method whenever the control needs repainting. The PaintEventArgs object passed to the OnPaint method provides information useful within the OnPaint method. The PaintEventArgs type was discussed in detail in Chapter 4 under "2-D Graphics Programming with GDI+." The OnPaint method in Example 5-6 draws an ellipse sized to fill the client area of the control.

Setting the control's ResizeRedraw property to `True` causes the OnPaint method to be called whenever the control is resized. Because the appearance of the control in Example 5-6 depends on the size of the control, the control's constructor sets the ResizeRedraw property to `True`. When ResizeRedraw is `False` (the default), resizing the control does not cause the OnPaint method to be called.

Although the code in Example 5-6 was built by hand, the OnPaint method can also be added (by hand) to the code built by the Windows Forms Designer. In addition, the techniques of using constituent controls and drawing directly on the user control can both be used within the same user control.

Building Nonrectangular Controls

User controls are rectangular by default, but controls having other shapes can be made by setting the control's Region property. The Region property accepts a value of type Region (defined in the System.Drawing namespace). Objects of type Region define complex areas and are commonly used for window clipping. Consider again Example 5-6 and Figure 5-34. Notice in Figure 5-34 that the grid dots on the form do not show through the background of the control. Example 5-7 shows how to clip the area of the control to match the ellipse being drawn in the OnPaint method. It is based on Example 5-6, with new code shown in bold.

Example 5-7. Clipping the area of a control

```
' Assumes Imports System.Drawing.Drawing2D
Public Class MyControl
   Inherits UserControl

   Private Function CreateRegion( ) As Region
      Dim gp As New GraphicsPath( )
      gp.AddEllipse(Me.ClientRectangle)
      Dim rgn As New Region(gp)
      Return rgn
   End Function

   Protected Overrides Sub OnResize(ByVal e As EventArgs)
      Me.Region = Me.CreateRegion( )
   End Sub

   Protected Overrides Sub OnPaint(ByVal e As PaintEventArgs)
      e.Graphics.FillEllipse(New SolidBrush(Me.ForeColor), _
         Me.ClientRectangle)
   End Sub

   Public Sub New( )
      Me.ResizeRedraw = True
   End Sub

End Class
```

The CreateRegion method in Example 5-7 creates a region in the shape of an ellipse sized to fill the client area of the control. To create nonrectangular regions, you must instantiate a GraphicsPath object, use the drawing methods of the GraphicsPath class to define a complex shape within the GraphicsPath object, and then instantiate a Region object, initializing it from the GraphicsPath object. Example 5-7 calls the

GraphicsPath class's AddEllipse method to create an ellipse within the GraphicsPath object. Additional methods could be called to add more shapes (including line-drawn shapes) to the GraphicsPath object. The OnResize method in Example 5-7 ensures that the control's Region property is reset every time the control is resized. Figure 5-35 shows the control after it has been placed on a form in design mode in the Windows Forms Designer. Note that the grid dots now show through the corners of the control. This clipped area is no longer considered part of the control. If the user clicks on this area, the click passes through to the object underneath the control (in this case, the form).

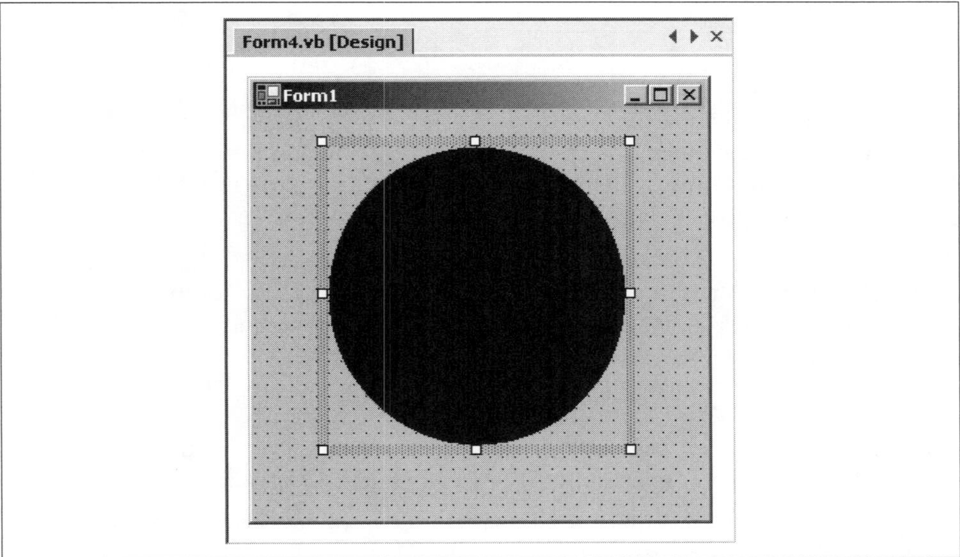

Figure 5-35. A control with its Region property set to clip everything outside of the ellipse

Summary

The Windows Forms architecture is broad and deep. This chapter has presented everything you need to know to get started developing GUI desktop applications, but there is more power waiting for you after you assimilate what's here. Once you master the material in this chapter, you can write complex GUI applications. You'll also be able to tackle and understand additional types and functionality documented in the online .NET reference material.

CHAPTER 6

ASP.NET and Web Forms: Developing Browser-Based Applications

ASP.NET is a technology for developing dynamic web pages. It has evolved from Microsoft's ASP technology, so experience with ASP transfers fairly well to ASP.NET. While I don't assume in this chapter that you have such experience, I do assume that you have at least a passing familiarity with HTML.

ASP.NET works with Microsoft's Internet Information Services (IIS) to dynamically create HTML content so it can be sent to a web browser. This technology supports all browsers, because ASP.NET runs entirely on the server and sends only HTML (and, optionally, client-side JavaScript) to the browser.

With ASP.NET, web browsing works like this:

1. A user enters a web page address into a browser (or links to the address from another web page). For example, *http://www.gotdotnet.com/default.aspx*.
2. The browser sends a request to the server (in this case, *www.gotdotnet.com*), asking for the given web page (in this case, *default.aspx*).
3. The server receives the request and attempts to fulfill it. How the server fills the request depends on the type of page requested, as indicated by the filename extension. Files with an *.html* or *.htm* extension are assumed to contain plain HTML text and are sent to the browser as is. Files with an *.aspx* extension are assumed to contain ASP.NET application code and are therefore *compiled* and *executed*. Executing the ASP.NET code usually results in generating HTML content and sending it to the browser. Note the following:
    - The browser is unaware that the content is dynamically generated. From the browser's perspective, the response could be from a static HTML file.
    - The *.aspx* file is compiled only once. The first time a browser requests the file, the ASP.NET framework compiles the file and stores the executable code on the server. Subsequent requests for the same page call directly into the executable code.

The term *Web Forms* refers to a set of classes in the .NET Framework that provides support for building web applications. With the Visual Studio .NET IDE's built-in awareness of Web Forms, building web pages now has (nearly) the same drag-and-drop simplicity as building form-based desktop applications.

In the ASP.NET framework, *.aspx* files can contain standard HTML tags (which are sent as is to the browser), Web Forms tags (which represent Web Forms classes and are interpreted by the ASP.NET runtime, rather than being sent to the browser), and code written in one of the .NET languages.

ASP.NET pages are compiled. Even if an *.aspx* file contains only HTML, it is still compiled. This is quite interestingly done. During the compilation process, ASP.NET reads the *.aspx* file and creates a class capable of outputting the HTML found in the file. If the *.aspx* file contains any embedded Visual Basic .NET (or other .NET language) code, this code is compiled into the class. For example, if the *.aspx* file contains an embedded subroutine declaration, the subroutine becomes a method of the compiled class. At runtime, the compiled class is asked to generate its HTML, which is then sent to the browser.

The compiled class that represents an ASP.NET web page is a .NET class. As such, it must inherit from some other class. By default, classes created by ASP.NET inherit from the Page class (defined in the System.Web.UI namespace). This means the generated classes have all the capabilities that are built into the Page class. These capabilities are described later in this chapter, in the "Handling Page Events" section.

If desired, ASP.NET pages can specify a class from which to inherit, as long as the specified class itself ultimately inherits from the Page class. This is the foundation for separating a page's code from its HTML. Code is placed in a class that inherits from the Page class. The web page then specifies a directive indicating that its compiled class should derive from the custom class, rather than directly from the Page class. This technique is referred to as *code behind*. The *.vb* file that contains the base-class definition is referred to as the *code-behind file*. The class from which the web page class inherits is called the *code-behind class*. These concepts are explained more fully throughout this chapter.

Creating a Web Form

The easiest way to design a web form is to use the Web Forms Designer in Visual Studio .NET. The developer uses visual tools to lay out the form, and the designer translates the layout into a web page and its associated Visual Basic .NET source code. Web page files (*.aspx*) and their associated Visual Basic .NET source-code files (*.vb*) are editable as plain text, if desired. If you don't have Visual Studio .NET, you can write the web pages and source code by hand using a text editor. The following two sections demonstrate both methods.

Creating a Form Using Visual Studio .NET

To create a web-based application in Visual Studio .NET:

1. Select File→New→Project. The New Project dialog box appears, as shown in Figure 6-1.

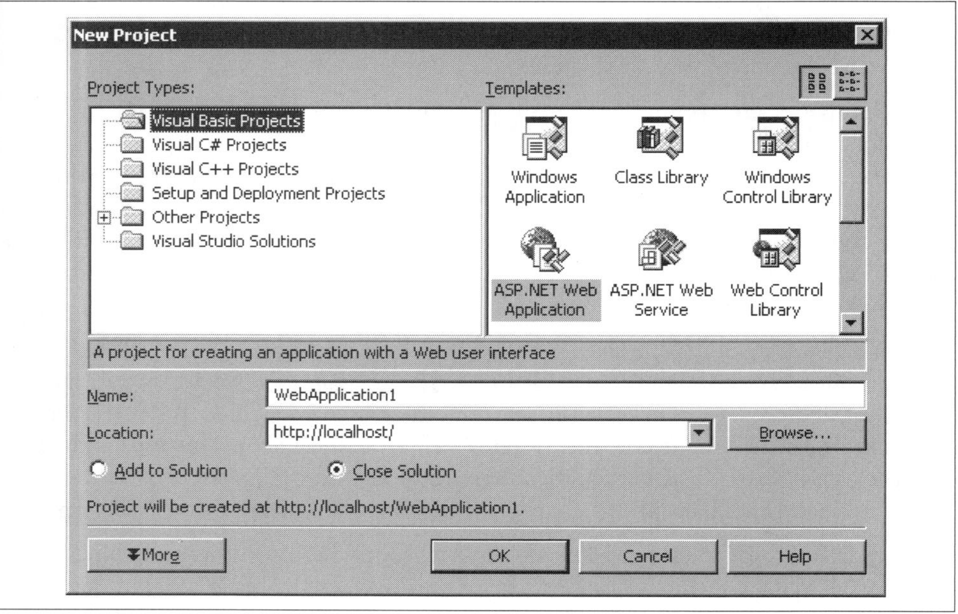

Figure 6-1. The New Project dialog box

2. Select "Visual Basic Projects" in the Project Types pane on the left side of the dialog box.
3. Select "ASP.NET Web Application" in the Templates pane on the right side of the dialog box.
4. Enter a name in the Name text box. This name is used as the name of a new folder, in which Visual Studio .NET places the project.
5. Enter a location in the Location text box (for example, *http://localhost/* or *http://localhost/MyProjects/*. The physical location of this folder is determined by settings in IIS, as configured in Internet Services Manager.

   The values entered for Location and Name determine the full path to the project. For example, if the Location is *http://localhost/MyProjects/* and the name is *SomeProject*, the full virtual path to the files in the project is *http://localhost/MyProjects/SomeProject/*. Furthermore, if the *MyProjects* virtual folder maps to the physical folder *C:\Documents and Settings\daveg\My Documents\My Code*, the full physical path to the files in the project is *C:\Documents and Settings\daveg\My Documents\My Code\SomeProject*.

If the Location is given simply as *http://localhost/* (i.e., as the hostname with no virtual folder name), the physical path is determined by IIS's settings for the host's default web site (again, as configured in Internet Services Manager). By default, this is *C:\Inetpub\wwwroot*. For example, if the Name is *SomeProject* and the Location is *http://localhost/*, the full physical path to the files in the project is *C:\Inetpub\wwwroot\SomeProject*.

6. Click OK. Visual Studio .NET creates a project with a web form in it and displays the form in the designer, as shown in Figure 6-2.

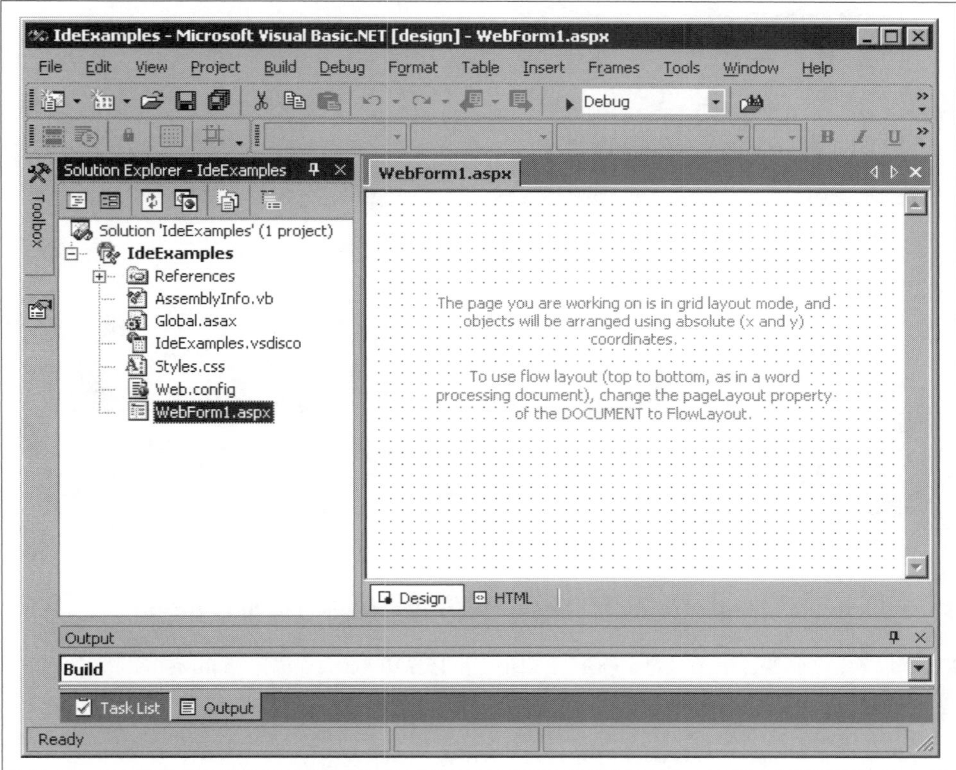

Figure 6-2. The Web Forms Designer in design view

There are three ways to view and work with a web form. The first is in design mode, which is the mode shown in Figure 6-2. In design mode, controls can be added to the form from the Toolbox and positioned as desired. This is similar to designing a form in a GUI desktop application. See later in this section for examples of adding controls to a form.

The second way to work with a web form is by directly editing its HTML. To view a form's HTML, click the HTML tag in the Web Forms Designer. The resulting display is shown in Figure 6-3.

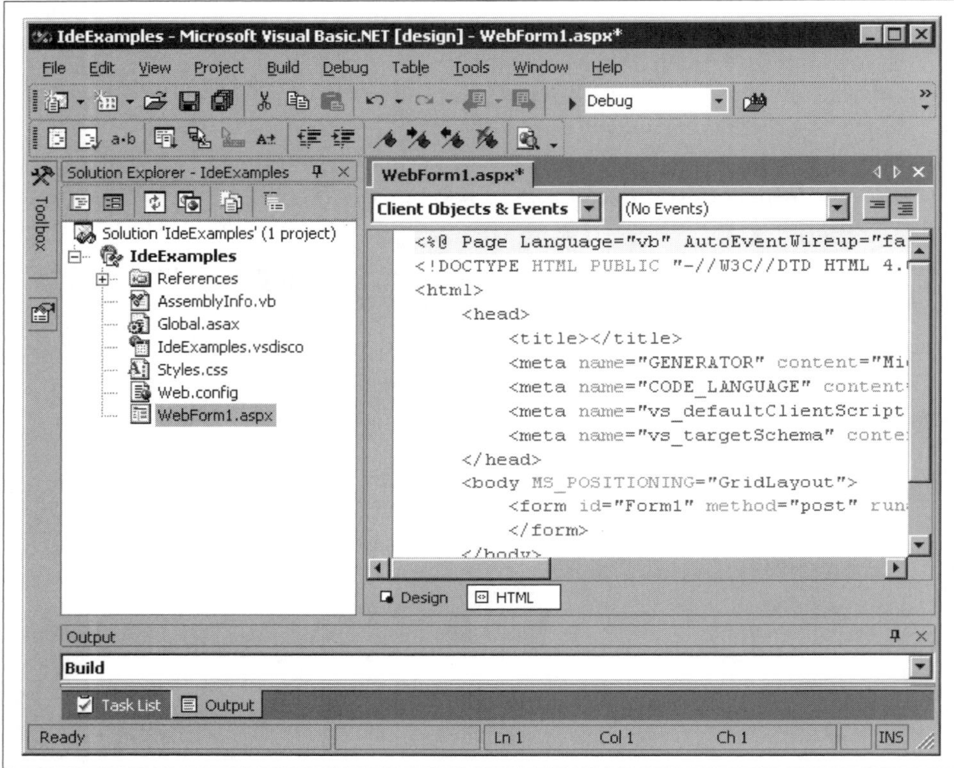

Figure 6-3. The Web Forms Designer in HTML view

The boilerplate HTML produced for a blank web form is shown in Example 6-1.

Example 6-1. The Web Forms Designer's boilerplate HTML for a blank web form

```
<%@ Page Language="vb" AutoEventWireup="false"
   Codebehind="WebForm1.aspx.vb" Inherits="IdeExamples.WebForm1"%>
<!DOCTYPE HTML PUBLIC "-//W3C//DTD HTML 4.0 Transitional//EN">
<html>
   <head>
      <title></title>
      <meta name="GENERATOR" content="Microsoft Visual Studio .NET 7.0">
      <meta name="CODE_LANGUAGE" content="Visual Basic 7.0">
      <meta name="vs_defaultClientScript" content="JavaScript">
      <meta name="vs_targetSchema"
         content="http://schemas.microsoft.com/intellisense/ie5">
```

Example 6-1. The Web Forms Designer's boilerplate HTML for a blank web form (continued)

```
   </head>
   <body MS_POSITIONING="GridLayout">
      <form id="Form1" method="post" runat="server">
      </form>
   </body>
</html>
```

The code in Example 6-1 has the following qualities:

- The Page directive at the beginning of the file provides information about how ASP.NET should process the page. Directives are described in detail later in this chapter, in the "Using Directives to Modify Web Page Compilation" section. The Page directive shown in Example 6-1 specifies the following settings:

  `Language="vb"`
  : Specifies which language compiler to use when compiling embedded code in this file. Example 6-1 doesn't have any embedded code, but the developer could add code later.

  `AutoEventWireup="false"`
  : Determines how events generated by server-side controls are handled. It is explained later in this chapter, under "AutoEventWireup" in the "Handling Page Events" section.

  `Codebehind="WebForm1.aspx.vb"`
  : Specifies the name of the code-behind file.

  `Inherits="IdeExamples.WebForm1"`
  : Specifies the name of the class from which this page should inherit. This must be the name of a class defined in the given code-behind file. In this example, the class name is WebForm1 in a namespace called IdeExamples.

- The `<meta>` tags contain information that is meaningful to the Web Forms Designer. Their presence is not necessary for the correct operation of the page.
- The `<body>` tag contains a Microsoft-specific attribute called `MS_POSITIONING`. This attribute is used by the Web Forms Designer and by the ASP.NET compiler to determine how to format the HTML generated by the compiled page. The attribute itself is not actually sent to the browser.
- The `<form>` tag is central to Web Forms. Web Forms uses the capabilities of the HTML `<form>` tag's post mechanism to implement interaction with the user. This will be discussed in more detail throughout this chapter. Note in Example 6-1 that the `<form>` tag has the `runat="server"` attribute. This means that this tag is not sent as is to the browser. Rather, the ASP.NET compiler processes this tag and its contents to determine the best way to render the form that it represents.

The third way to work with a web form is by editing the code in the form's code-behind page. To see the code created by the designer, right-click on the form, then select View Code. Doing this for the blank form shown in Figure 6-2 reveals the code shown here:

```
Public Class WebForm1
   Inherits System.Web.UI.Page

 Web Form Designer Generated Code

   Private Sub Page_Load(ByVal sender As System.Object, _
      ByVal e As System.EventArgs) Handles MyBase.Load
      'Put user code to initialize the page here.
   End Sub

End Class
```

This shows the definition of a class, WebForm1, that inherits from the Page class. The designer also creates a lot of boilerplate code that should not be modified by the developer. By default, it hides this code from view. To see the code, click on the "+" symbol that appears to the left of the line that says, "Web Form Designer Generated Code." Doing so reveals the code shown in Example 6-2. (Some of the lines in Example 6-2 have been wrapped for printing in this book.)

Example 6-2. The Web Forms Designer–generated code for a blank form

```
Public Class WebForm1
   Inherits System.Web.UI.Page

#Region " Web Form Designer Generated Code "

   'This call is required by the Web Form Designer.
   <System.Diagnostics.DebuggerStepThrough( )> _
   Private Sub InitializeComponent( )

   End Sub

   Private Sub Page_Init(ByVal sender As System.Object, _
      ByVal e As System.EventArgs) Handles MyBase.Init
      'CODEGEN: This method call is required by the Web Form Designer
      'Do not modify it using the code editor.
      InitializeComponent( )
   End Sub

#End Region

   Private Sub Page_Load(ByVal sender As System.Object, _
      ByVal e As System.EventArgs) Handles MyBase.Load
      'Put user code to initialize the page here
   End Sub

End Class
```

The Web Forms Designer autogenerates the code for three class members:

InitializeComponent method
: The code in this method should not be modified or added to by the developer in any way. The Web Forms Designer automatically updates it as needed.

Page_Init method
: This is an event handler that handles the base class's Init event. The Init event is inherited from the Control class (defined in System.Web.UI) and is raised when the Page object is created. This is the first event that is fired when the object is created. Code that initializes the object instance should be placed in this method. References to the page's controls are not yet available when the Init event is raised.

Page_Load method
: This is an event handler that handles the base class's Load event. The Load event is inherited from the Control class (defined in System.Web.UI) and is raised after the Page object has been initialized. References to the page's controls are available at this time.

The next steps in designing the form are to name the *.aspx* file and set some properties on the form, such as the title of the web page. To change the name of the form's file, right-click on the filename in the Solution Explorer window and select Rename. If you're following along with this example, enter *HelloBrowser.aspx* as the name of the file. This also automatically changes the name of the code-behind file to *HelloBrowser.aspx.vb*.

Changing the name of the file doesn't change the name of the code-behind class. To change the name of this class, right-click the form, select View Code, then change the class name in the class declaration from WebForm1 to HelloBrowser. To keep the code-behind file in sync with the *.aspx* file, you must also make a corresponding change to the `Inherits` attribute of the *.aspx* file's `Page` directive, as shown here:

```
<%@ Page Language="vb" AutoEventWireup="false"
   Codebehind="HelloBrowser.aspx.vb" Inherits="IdeExamples.HelloBrowser"%>
```

To change the web page's title, right-click the form in the designer and choose Properties. Scroll down the Properties window to find the Title property, then enter a new value, "Programming Visual Basic .NET". This is shown in Figure 6-4.

Next, you can add controls to the web form from the Visual Studio .NET toolbox. To display the toolbox, select View→Toolbox from the Visual Studio .NET main menu. For this example, double-click on the Label control in the toolbox to add a Label control on the form. Use the Properties window to change the label's Text property to "Hello, Browser!". Set the Name member of the Font property to "Arial" and the Size member to "X-Large".

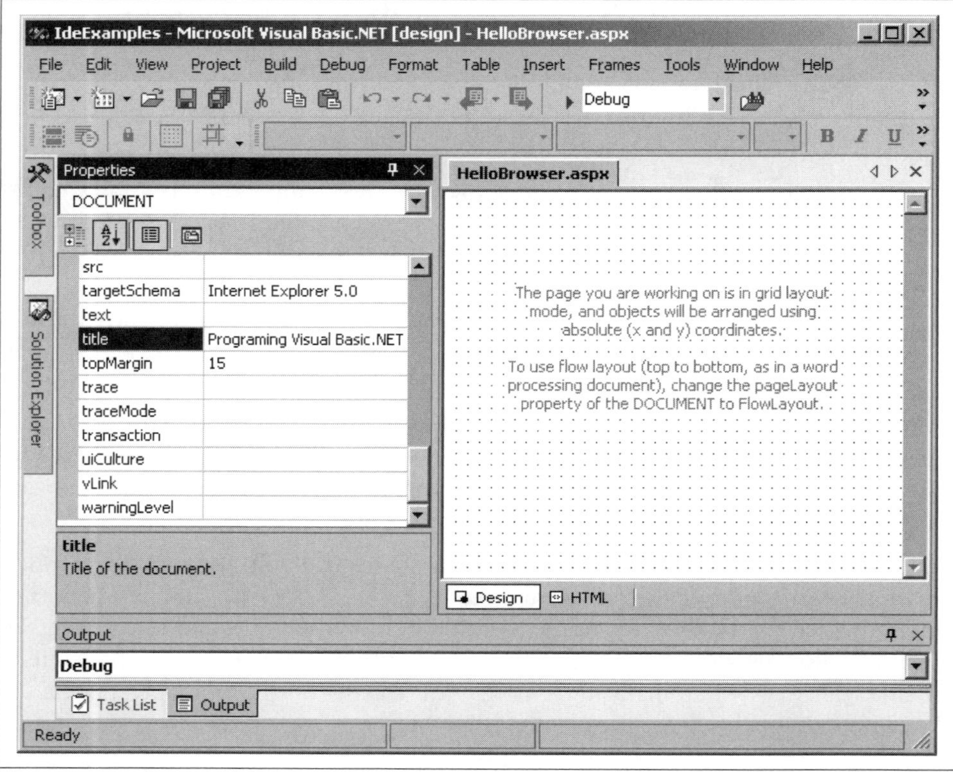

Figure 6-4. Changing the title of a web page

Next, double-click on the Button control in the toolbox to add a button control to the form. Use the Properties window to change the button's ID property to "btn-Black" and its Text property to "Black".

Add two more buttons, setting their ID properties to "btnBlue" and "btnGreen" and their Text properties to "Blue" and "Green", respectively.

Finally, position the controls as desired. The resulting form should look something like the one shown in Figure 6-5.

Press the F5 key to build and run the program. The result should look something like Figure 6-6.

The HTML generated by the designer is shown in Example 6-3.

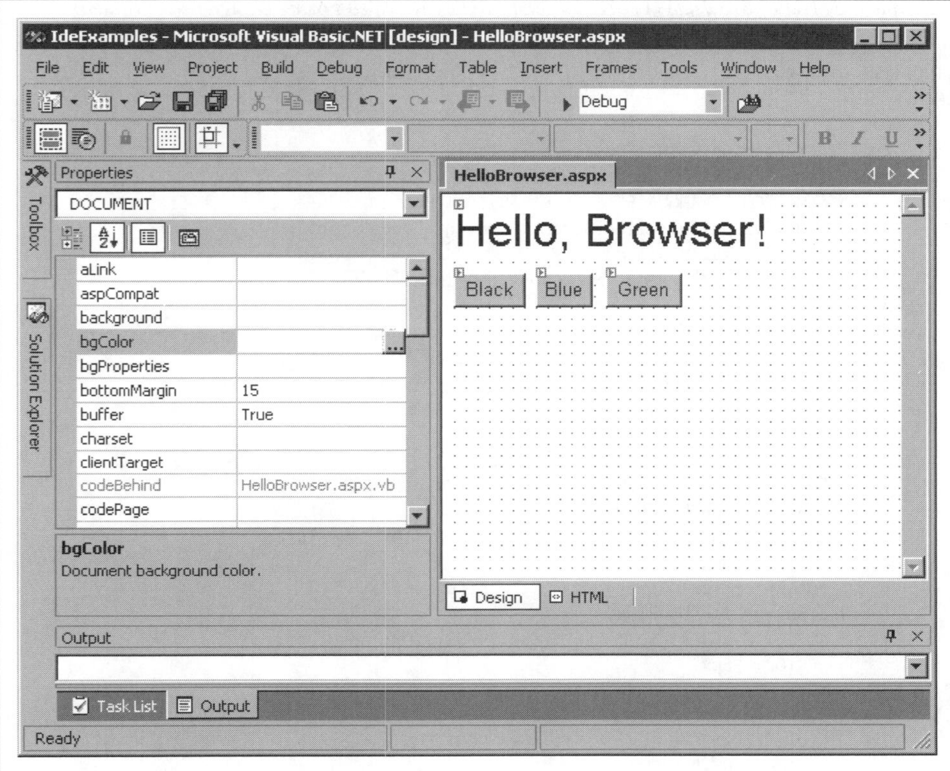

Figure 6-5. A web form with controls

Figure 6-6. Hello, Browser!, as created by the Web Forms Designer

Example 6-3. Hello, Browser! HTML, as generated by the Web Forms Designer

```
<%@ Page Language="vb" AutoEventWireup="false"
   Codebehind="HelloBrowser.aspx.vb"
```

Example 6-3. Hello, Browser! HTML, as generated by the Web Forms Designer (continued)

```
   Inherits="IdeExamples.HelloBrowser"%>
<!DOCTYPE HTML PUBLIC "-//W3C//DTD HTML 4.0 Transitional//EN">
<HTML>
  <HEAD>
      <title>Programing Visual Basic .NET</title>
      <meta name="GENERATOR" content="Microsoft Visual Studio .NET 7.0">
      <meta name="CODE_LANGUAGE" content="Visual Basic 7.0">
      <meta name="vs_defaultClientScript" content="JavaScript">
      <meta name="vs_targetSchema"
         content="http://schemas.microsoft.com/intellisense/ie5">
  </HEAD>
   <body MS_POSITIONING="GridLayout">
      <form id="Form1" method="post" runat="server">
         <asp:Label id="Label1"
            style="Z-INDEX: 101; LEFT: 8px; POSITION: absolute;
               TOP: 8px"
            runat="server" Font-Size="X-Large"
            Font-Names="Arial">Hello, Browser!</asp:Label>
         <asp:Button id="btnGreen"
            style="Z-INDEX: 104; LEFT: 112px; POSITION: absolute;
               TOP: 56px"
            runat="server" Text="Green"></asp:Button>
         <asp:Button id="btnBlue"
            style="Z-INDEX: 103; LEFT: 64px; POSITION: absolute;
               TOP: 56px"
            runat="server" Text="Blue"></asp:Button>
         <asp:Button id="btnBlack"
            style="Z-INDEX: 102; LEFT: 8px; POSITION: absolute;
               TOP: 56px"
            runat="server" Text="Black"></asp:Button>
      </form>
   </body>
</HTML>
```

The Visual Basic .NET code-behind code is shown in Example 6-4.

Example 6-4. Hello, Browser! code-behind code, generated by the Web Forms Designer

```
Public Class HelloBrowser
   Inherits System.Web.UI.Page
   Protected WithEvents btnBlack As System.Web.UI.WebControls.Button
   Protected WithEvents btnBlue As System.Web.UI.WebControls.Button
   Protected WithEvents btnGreen As System.Web.UI.WebControls.Button
   Protected WithEvents Label1 As System.Web.UI.WebControls.Label

#Region " Web Form Designer Generated Code "

   'This call is required by the Web Form Designer.
   <System.Diagnostics.DebuggerStepThrough( )> _
      Private Sub InitializeComponent( )

   End Sub
```

Example 6-4. Hello, Browser! code-behind code, generated by the Web Forms Designer (continued)

```
   Private Sub Page_Init(ByVal sender As System.Object, _
      ByVal e As System.EventArgs) Handles MyBase.Init
      'CODEGEN: This method call is required by the Web Form Designer
      'Do not modify it using the code editor.
      InitializeComponent( )
   End Sub

#End Region

   Private Sub Page_Load(ByVal sender As System.Object, _
      ByVal e As System.EventArgs) Handles MyBase.Load
      'Put user code to initialize the page here
   End Sub

End Class
```

The HTML that is sent to the browser is shown in Example 6-5.

Example 6-5. The HTML sent to the browser from the Hello, Browser! application

```
<!DOCTYPE HTML PUBLIC "-//W3C//DTD HTML 4.0 Transitional//EN">
<HTML>
  <HEAD>
      <title>Programing Visual Basic .NET</title>
      <meta name="GENERATOR" content="Microsoft Visual Studio .NET 7.0">
      <meta name="CODE_LANGUAGE" content="Visual Basic 7.0">
      <meta name="vs_defaultClientScript" content="JavaScript">
      <meta name="vs_targetSchema"
         content="http://schemas.microsoft.com/intellisense/ie5">
  </HEAD>
   <body MS_POSITIONING="GridLayout">
      <form name="Form1" method="post" action="HelloBrowser.aspx"
         id="Form1">
         <input type="hidden" name="__VIEWSTATE"
            value="dDwtMTcONzM4OTU5Ozs+" />
         <span id="Label1"
            style="font-family:Arial;font-size:X-Large; Z-INDEX: 101;
               LEFT: 8px; POSITION: absolute; TOP: 8px">
            Hello, Browser!</span>
         <input type="submit" name="btnGreen" value="Green" id="btnGreen"
            style="Z-INDEX: 104; LEFT: 112px; POSITION: absolute;
               TOP: 56px" />
         <input type="submit" name="btnBlue" value="Blue" id="btnBlue"
            style="Z-INDEX: 103; LEFT: 64px; POSITION: absolute;
               TOP: 56px" />
         <input type="submit" name="btnBlack" value="Black" id="btnBlack"
            style="Z-INDEX: 102; LEFT: 8px; POSITION: absolute;
               TOP: 56px" />
      </form>
   </body>
</HTML>
```

When the four controls were added to the form in the Web Forms Designer, the designer added four tags to the form's HTML: one for the label and three for the three buttons. Consider first the tag for the Label control:

```
<asp:Label id="Label1"
   style="Z-INDEX: 101; LEFT: 8px; POSITION: absolute; TOP: 8px"
   runat="server" Font-Size="X-Large"
   Font-Names="Arial">Hello, Browser!</asp:Label>
```

This is an `<asp:Label>` tag, which clearly isn't a standard HTML tag. Rather, it is recognized and acted on by the ASP.NET runtime. When the ASP.NET runtime sees this tag, the runtime instantiates an object of type Label (defined in the System.Web.UI.WebControls namespace) on the web server. The runtime initializes this control according to the attribute values of the `<asp:Label>` tag. The runtime then sets the control's Text property with the text found between the `<asp:Label>` tag and its closing tag, `</asp:Label>`. The Label object is responsible for outputting standard HTML that renders the value of the object. In this case, that HTML can be seen in Example 6-5. The portion of Example 6-5 related to the Label control is reproduced here:

```
<span id="Label1"
   style="font-family:Arial;font-size:X-Large; Z-INDEX: 101;
      LEFT: 8px; POSITION: absolute; TOP: 8px">
   Hello, Browser!</span>
```

As you can see, the Label control rendered itself as simple text (`Hello, Browser!`), surrounded by a `<span>` tag. The purpose of the `<span>` tag is to apply `id` and `style` attributes to the text.

Similarly, consider the first Button control added to the web form. The Web Forms Designer generated this HTML representation of the control:

```
<asp:Button id="btnGreen"
   style="Z-INDEX: 104; LEFT: 112px; POSITION: absolute; TOP: 56px"
   runat="server" Text="Green"></asp:Button>
```

The `<asp:Button>` tag represents the Button control. When the runtime sees this tag, it instantiates an object of type Button (defined in the System.Web.UI.WebControls namespace) on the server. This object is then responsible for outputting standard HTML that renders the value (and in this case, functionality) of the object. The HTML sent to the browser for this button is:

```
<input type="submit" name="btnGreen" value="Green" id="btnGreen"
   style="Z-INDEX: 104; LEFT: 112px; POSITION: absolute; TOP: 56px" />
```

Note that the Button control rendered itself as an `<input>` tag with `type="submit"`. This displays a button in the browser window. The other attributes of the tag specify its name, text, and style.

Label and Button controls are examples of server controls. The full set of server controls is listed later in this chapter, in the section "More About Server Controls."

Adding event handlers

The *Hello, Browser!* application built thus far has three buttons, but the application doesn't yet do anything in response to button clicks. To add a Click event handler to the existing code in Visual Studio .NET, follow these steps:

1. Switch to the code-view window for the web form.
2. At the top of the source-code window are two side-by-side drop-down lists. Select the desired control, btnBlack, in the lefthand list, then select the desired event, btnBlack_Click, in the righthand list. The Web Forms Designer adds an event handler to the code (see Figure 6-7).

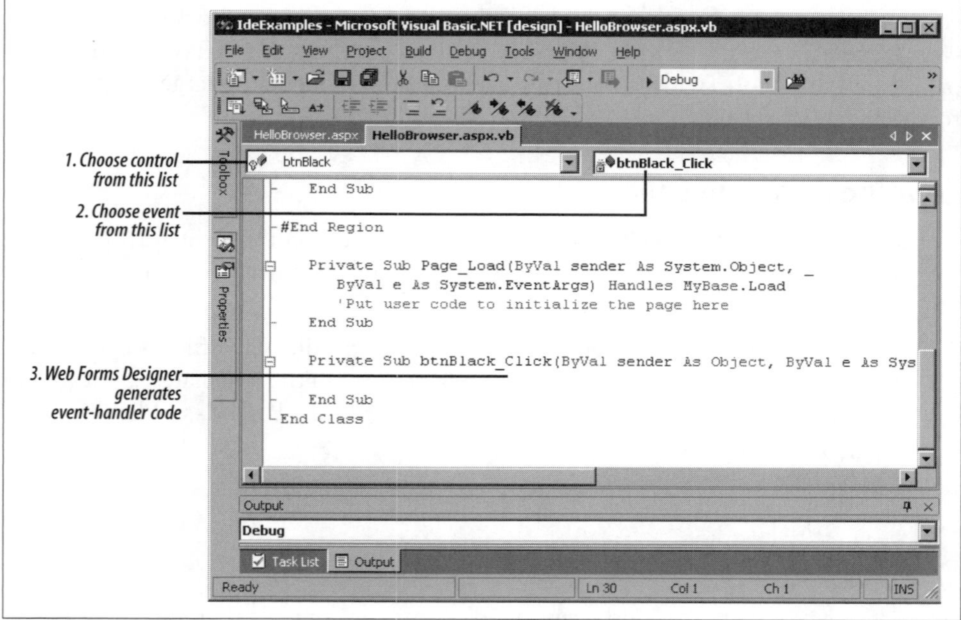

Figure 6-7. Choosing a control and event for which to add a handler

3. Add code to the event handler. For this exercise, have the event handler set the color of the Label control to black:

```
Private Sub btnBlack_Click( _
   ByVal sender As Object, _
   ByVal e As System.EventArgs _
) Handles btnBlack.Click
   Label1.ForeColor = System.Drawing.Color.Black
End Sub
```

4. Similarly, add event handlers for the btnBlue and btnGreen Button controls. The finished event handlers should look like this:

```
Private Sub btnBlue_Click( _
   ByVal sender As System.Object, _
```

```
        ByVal e As System.EventArgs _
    ) Handles btnBlue.Click
        Label1.ForeColor = System.Drawing.Color.Blue
    End Sub

    Private Sub btnGreen_Click( _
        ByVal sender As System.Object, _
        ByVal e As System.EventArgs _
    ) Handles btnGreen.Click
        Label1.ForeColor = System.Drawing.Color.Green
    End Sub
```

The web form created here allows the user to change the color of the words, "Hello, Browser!" by clicking on one of the form's three buttons. This was done by dragging controls onto the form and creating event handlers. At runtime, the ASP.NET framework generates the standard HTML that implements the given behavior. The developer now can work with a familiar event-driven model and largely ignore the requirements of HTML.

Creating a Form in Code

Although Visual Studio .NET's Web Forms Designer is convenient for developing web forms, it is not required. To create a web form without the assistance of Visual Studio .NET, follow these steps:

1. Create a *.vb* file that will serve as the code-behind file. This file can be named anything because the name itself will be referenced in the associated *.aspx* file. In the code-behind file, place a class that inherits from the Page class, like this:

```
Imports System.Web.UI

Public Class HelloBrowser
   Inherits Page

End Class
```

2. Add member variables and event handlers for the controls that are to appear on the form. For example:

```
Imports System.Web.UI
Imports System.Web.UI.WebControls

Public Class HelloBrowser
   Inherits Page

   Protected WithEvents Label1 As Label
   Protected WithEvents btnBlack As Button
   Protected WithEvents btnBlue As Button
   Protected WithEvents btnGreen As Button

   Protected Sub btnBlack_Click( _
      ByVal sender As Object, _
      ByVal e As System.EventArgs _
```

```
    ) Handles btnBlack.Click
       Label1.ForeColor = System.Drawing.Color.Black
    End Sub

    Protected Sub btnBlue_Click( _
       ByVal sender As System.Object, _
       ByVal e As System.EventArgs _
    ) Handles btnBlue.Click
       Label1.ForeColor = System.Drawing.Color.Blue
    End Sub

    Protected Sub btnGreen_Click( _
       ByVal sender As System.Object, _
       ByVal e As System.EventArgs _
    ) Handles btnGreen.Click
       Label1.ForeColor = System.Drawing.Color.Green
    End Sub

End Class
```

3. Create an *.aspx* file to serve as the application's main page. Reference the code-behind class using the Src and Inherits attributes of the Page directive, and include <asp:...> tags for the controls that are to appear on the form. For example:

```
<%@ Page Language="vb" AutoEventWireup="false"
   Src="HelloBrowser.vb" Inherits="HelloBrowser"%>
<html>
   <head>
      <title>Programing Visual Basic .NET</title>
   </head>
   <body>
      <form id="Form1" method="post" runat="server">
         <asp:Label id="Label1" runat="server" Font-Size="X-Large"
            Font-Names="Arial" Text="Hello, Browser!" /><br>
         <asp:Button id="btnGreen" runat="server" Text="Green" />
         <asp:Button id="btnBlue" runat="server" Text="Blue" />
         <asp:Button id="btnBlack" runat="server" Text="Black" />
      </form>
   </body>
</html>
```

   Here, the code-behind *.vb* file is referenced using the Src attribute; in the Visual Studio .NET code shown earlier, the code-behind file was referenced in the CodeBehind attribute. This is an important distinction. The CodeBehind attribute is used only by Visual Studio .NET; it's ignored by the ASP.NET compiler.

   Be sure that the value of the id attribute of each <asp:...> tag matches the name of the associated member variable in the code-behind class. This name is how the ASP.NET framework matches up each member variable with the corresponding server control.

To run this application, enter the two code fragments and save them into two files, named *HelloBrowser.vb* and *HelloBrowser.aspx*, respectively. The files must be located in an IIS virtual directory on a machine with the .NET Framework installed. After you save the files, point a web browser to *HelloBrowser.aspx*. The ASP.NET runtime automatically compiles and runs the application, delivering the output to the browser.

Setting control properties using attributes

The properties of server control objects can be initialized by specifying values for attributes within the `<asp:...>` tags. For example, the button created by the following tag has its Text property set to "Green":

```
<asp:Button id="btnGreen" runat="server" Text="Green" />
```

This assignment could instead have been handled elsewhere in code—either in a `<script>` block or in a code-behind class. In general, any writable property can be set using an attribute of the same name.

Adding event handlers

Define event handlers directly in the code-behind class for any events you wish to handle. For example:

```
Private Sub btnBlack_Click( _
   ByVal sender As Object, _
   ByVal e As System.EventArgs _
) Handles btnBlack.Click
   Label1.ForeColor = System.Drawing.Color.Black
End Sub

Private Sub btnBlue_Click( _
   ByVal sender As System.Object, _
   ByVal e As System.EventArgs _
) Handles btnBlue.Click
   Label1.ForeColor = System.Drawing.Color.Blue
End Sub

Private Sub btnGreen_Click( _
   ByVal sender As System.Object, _
   ByVal e As System.EventArgs _
) Handles btnGreen.Click
   Label1.ForeColor = System.Drawing.Color.Green
End Sub
```

Handling Page Events

The base Page class may at times raise events. These events can be handled by the derived Page class (the code-behind class) or by code embedded in the web page. Although it's possible to define an event-handler subroutine, the preferred response to events raised by the Page class is to override the protected methods provided by the Page class. For example, the following method could be placed in the code-behind class, providing a way to respond to the loading of the page:

```
Protected Overrides Sub OnLoad(e As EventArgs)
   MyBase.OnLoad(e)
   ' ...
End Sub
```

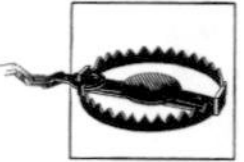

When overriding an On*Event*-style method, ensure that the overriding method calls the base-class implementation, in addition to its own processing. The job of the base-class implementation is to raise the corresponding event. If the base-class implementation is not called, the event won't be raised.

Following is the list of events a Page object might raise. The Page class itself doesn't define these events: it inherits them from its parent classes. This list of events includes a brief description of each event, the class in which the event is defined, and the syntax for overriding the protected method that corresponds to the event.

AbortTransaction (inherited from System.Web.UI.TemplateControl)
: Raised when a COM+ transaction in which the page is participating is aborted. Its syntax is:

```
Protected Overrides Sub OnAbortTransaction(ByVal e As EventArgs)
```

CommitTransaction (inherited from System.Web.UI.TemplateControl)
: Raised when a COM+ transaction in which the page is participating is committed. Its syntax is:

```
Protected Overrides Sub OnCommitTransaction(ByVal e As EventArgs)
```

DataBinding (inherited from System.Web.UI.Control)
: Raised when the page binds to a data source. Its syntax is:

```
Protected Overrides Sub OnDataBinding(ByVal e As EventArgs)
```

Disposed (inherited from System.Web.UI.Control)
: Raised after the Page object's Dispose method has finished its processing. The Dispose method is called by the ASP.NET framework after the page has been rendered and the object is no longer needed. There is no corresponding OnDisposed method. To add a handler for this event in a derived class, use the following code:

```
Private Sub Page_Disposed( _
   ByVal sender As Object, _
   ByVal e As EventArgs _
) Handles MyBase.Disposed
   ' ...
End Sub
```

Error (inherited from System.Web.UI.TemplateControl)
: Raised when an unhandled exception is thrown. This provides a last-chance opportunity to gracefully deal with unexpected errors (perhaps by displaying a

friendly "We're sorry, but our web application has barfed" message. Its syntax is:

```
Protected Overrides Sub OnError(ByVal e As EventArgs)
```

Init (inherited from System.Web.UI.Control)
Raised when the Page object has been created, but before the view state has been loaded. Its syntax is:

```
Protected Overrides Sub OnInit(ByVal e As EventArgs)
```

Load (inherited from System.Web.UI.Control)
Raised when the Page object has finished loading. Its syntax is:

```
Protected Overrides Sub OnLoad(ByVal e As EventArgs)
```

PreRender (inherited from System.Web.UI.Control)
Raised immediately prior to the page rendering itself. Its syntax is:

```
Protected Overrides Sub OnPreRender(ByVal e As EventArgs)
```

Unload (inherited from System.Web.UI.Control)
Raised after the page has been rendered but before the Page object's Dispose method is called. Its syntax is:

```
Protected Overrides Sub OnUnload(ByVal e As EventArgs)
```

The last four events are raised on each page request, in the order shown. The three events that are raised prior to page rendering (Init, Load, and PreRender) are raised at different points during the creation of the page:

- The Init event is raised after the Page object has been created but before it has loaded values into its constituent controls or processed any postback data.
- The Load event is raised after constituent controls have been loaded with their values. However, postback processing is not guaranteed to be finished.
- The PreRender event is raised after all loading and postback processing is finished and the page is about to be rendered into HTML.

AutoEventWireup

If the developer of a web page or code-behind class chooses to handle base-class events explicitly, the event-handler methods must be associated with the events that they are to handle. In Visual Basic .NET this is generally done with a `Handles` clause in the method definition, as described in Chapter 2 and shown by example here:

```
Protected Sub Page_Load( _
   ByVal sender As Object, _
   ByVal e As EventArgs _
) Handles MyBase.Load
   ' ...
End Sub
```

In addition to this syntax, ASP.NET provides an alternative way to hook up page event handlers to their associated events. If all of the following conditions are met, the ASP.NET framework automatically hooks up the page events with the correct handler methods:

- The `AutoEventWireup` attribute of the `@ Page` directive is set to `"true"` (which it is by default). This means that the `AutoEventWireup` attribute's value is `true` if the attribute is omitted from the `@ Page` directive, as well as if the `@ Page` directive itself is omitted.
- The handler-method name is of the form Page_*EventName*.
- The handler-method signature matches the signature of the corresponding event.

For example, if these conditions are met, the following code is automatically hooked up to the page's Load event:

```
Protected Sub Page_Load( _
   ByVal sender As Object, _
   ByVal e As EventArgs _
)
   ' ...
End Sub
```

The handler method can appear in either the page or the code-behind class (if any).

To disallow autowiring of events, specify `"false"` for the `AutoEventWireup` attribute, like this (other attributes omitted for brevity):

```
<%@ Page AutoEventWireup="false" %>
```

There is no clear advantage to either setting. Event autowiring may feel more familiar to developers who have used Visual Basic 6, where appropriately named methods automatically handled the corresponding events. On the other hand, some developers may feel more comfortable forcing event-handler methods to explicitly declare the events they are handling. In addition, the explicit declaration frees the developer from having to name the method according to the Page_*EventName* pattern.

More About Server Controls

ASP.NET provides two sets of server controls: *web controls* and *HTML controls*. Web controls (defined in the System.Web.UI.WebControls namespace) are similar to controls found in standard desktop applications. They shield the developer as much as possible from representing the controls in HTML. In other words, web controls are as similar as possible to desktop-application controls, leaving it up to each control to worry about how it will represent itself in HTML. This lets the developer design a UI without worrying much about the limitations of HTML. The controls presented thus far are web controls.

In contrast, HTML controls (defined in the System.Web.UI.HtmlControls namespace) are a thin wrapper over HTML client controls defined in the HTML standard. HTML server controls let the developer omit specific HTML client controls, while retaining the programmatic capabilities that server controls provide. Web page developers are likely to use HTML server controls only when they want to generate and manipulate specific HTML client controls with server-side technology. Microsoft makes no statement about which set of server controls is "better" to use. They present both, leaving it to the developer to decide which controls fit better into a given application.

Web Controls

The web controls can be created using HTML syntax as well as programmatically. When you create a control using HTML syntax, the control's tag name consists of the prefix `asp:` followed by the name of the control. For example, the following statement creates a CheckBox web control:

```
<asp:checkbox id="chkMail" text="Be placed on our mailing list? "
              autopostback="false" checked="true" runat="Server" />
```

Instances of web controls declared using HTML syntax have a number of common attributes that are worth noting. The `ID` attribute defines the name of the instance of the web control and should be used in all statements that create web controls. It corresponds to the control class's ID property, which defines the name by which the control is referenced programmatically. A second is `AutoPostBack`, an optional attribute common to many controls, which determines whether the state of the control is posted back to the server whenever it is clicked. By default, its value is `False`. It corresponds directly to the control class's AutoPostBack property. Finally, the `RunAt` attribute is required when creating a web control; without it, the downstream browser will attempt to interpret the HTML tag and will simply fail to render the control.

Each web control also has a class definition in the System.Web.UI.WebControls namespace of the .NET Framework Class Library. By using its `ID` attribute or ID property, you can reference in code a web control created using HTML syntax. For example, the following statement unchecks the CheckBox control we defined in the previous code fragment:

```
chkMail.Checked = False
```

Web controls can also be created programmatically, as the following code fragment, which creates a CheckBox control identical to the one defined earlier using HTML syntax, shows:

```
Dim chkMail As New CheckBox
chkMail.Text= "Be placed on our mailing list? "
chkMail.Checked = True
chkMail.AutoPostBack = False
```

Note that, except for `RunAt`, the attributes available for a control using HTML syntax correspond directly to a property of the control class both in name and in data type.

The following sections document the web controls available in the .NET Framework.

The Button control

The Button server control represents a command button and can be used as a Submit button (its default behavior) or any other type of command button on a form. The Submit button has the following HTML syntax:

```
<asp:Button id="ButtonName"
     Text="label"
     OnClick="OnClickMethod"
     runat="server"/>
```

When used as a command button for some other purpose, the Button control has the following HTML syntax:

```
<asp:Button id="ButtonName"
     Text="label"
     CommandName="command"
     CommandArgument="commandArgument"
     OnCommand="OnCommandMethod"
     runat="server"/>
```

The `OnClick` attribute defines the event handler that is executed when the button is clicked. The `Text` attribute determines the caption displayed on the button face. If used as a Submit button, the `CommandName` and `CommandArgument` attributes are not used; otherwise, at a minimum, the `CommandName` attribute, which indicates the command the button is to carry out, should be present. The optional `CommandArguments` attribute provides any arguments needed to execute the command. The `Text`, `CommandName`, and `CommandArgument` attributes all correspond to identically named properties of the System.Web.UI.WebControls.Button class.

When the Submit button is clicked, the event handler defined by the `OnClick` attribute is executed. The signature of the event is:

```
Sub OnClickMethod(sender As Object, e As EventArgs)
```

For any other command button, the Command event corresponds to the Submit button's Click event, and the event handler defined by the `OnCommand` attribute is executed. The event handler must have the following signature:

```
Sub OnCommandMethod(sender As Object, e As CommandEventArgs)
```

The CommandEventArgs object has two properties: CommandName, which corresponds to the `CommandName` attribute and represents the name of the command; and CommandArgument, which corresponds to the `CommandArgument` attribute and represents an argument supplied to the command. These property values can be used to identify which button was clicked in the event that a single event handler is used for more than one Button control.

The CheckBox control

The CheckBox control represents a checkbox that can have a value of `True` or `False` (or `On` or `Off`). It has the following HTML syntax:

```
<asp:CheckBox id="CheckBoxName"
     AutoPostBack="True|False"
     Text="CheckBoxCaption"
     TextAlign="Right|Left"
     Checked="True|False"
     OnCheckedChanged="OnCheckedChangedMethod"
     runat="server"/>
```

The `Checked` attribute determines whether the checkbox is initially checked. It corresponds to the CheckBox class's Checked property, which is a Boolean. The `Text` attribute defines the caption that appears to either the left (the default) or the right of the checkbox itself, depending on the value of the `TextAlign` attribute. The Text property of the CheckBox class similarly contains the checkbox's caption, while its alignment is determined by the CheckBox class's TextAlign property. The value of the TextAlign property is either of the two members of the TextAlign enumeration: `TextAlign.Left`, which positions the text to the left of the checkbox (the default); and `TextAlign.Right`, which positions the text to the right of the checkbox.

The `OnCheckedChanged` attribute defines an event handler that will be executed whenever the Checked property of the checkbox is changed. The event handler designated by the `OnCheckedChanged` attribute must have the following signature:

```
Sub OnCheckedChangeMethod(sender As Object, e As EventArgs)
```

The DropDownList control

The DropDownList control allows the user to make a single selection from a drop-down listbox. The DropDownList control has the following HTML syntax:

```
<asp:DropDownList id="DropDownListName" runat="server"
     DataSource="<% databindingexpression %>"
     DataTextField="DataSourceField"
     DataValueField="DataSourceField"
     AutoPostBack="True|False"
     OnSelectedIndexChanged="OnSelectedIndexChangedMethod">

   <asp:ListItem value="value" selected="True|False">
     Text
   </asp:ListItem>

</asp:DropDownList>
```

Rather than supplying the data either using HTML or programmatically, you can populate the listbox from a data source. The `DataSource` attribute defines the data source to which the listbox is bound, the `DataTextField` attribute defines the field that will determine which items are displayed in the listbox, and the `DataValueField` attribute defines the field whose rows will provide the value of each list item. Each of these attributes corresponds directly to a property of the System.Web.UI.WebControls.DropDownList class, which also allows you to dynamically populate a drop-down listbox at runtime.

In addition, the DropDownList class has a two major properties that don't correspond to attributes of the `DropDownList` tag. The SelectedIndex property returns the index of the selected item. The SelectedItem property returns the selected ListItem object in the drop-down list. Since the DropDownList object allows the user to select only a single item, these properties in most cases allow you to skip directly working with individual ListItem objects.

If the DropDownList is not bound to a data source, the `ListItem` tag is used to define each item in the list. *`Text`* determines the item's text that's displayed in the listbox. The `value` attribute determines the item's value. The `Selected` attribute determines whether or not the item is initially selected when the listbox is displayed.

Finally, the `OnSelectedIndexChanged` attribute defines an event handler that will be executed whenever a new item is selected in the drop-down listbox. The event handler designated by the `OnSelectedIndexChanged` attribute must have the following signature:

```
Sub OnSelectedIndexChangedMethod(sender As Object, e As EventArgs)
```

Programmatically, the items in the drop-down listbox consist of ListItem objects. These can be accessed through the ListBox class' Items property, which returns a ListItemCollection object consisting of all the ListItem objects in the listbox. You can add items to the end of the listbox by calling the ListItemCollection object's Add method, which has the following syntax:

```
ListItemCollection.Add(item)
```

where *`item`* is either a String or a ListItem object. To add an item to a particular place in the drop-down listbox, you can call the Insert method, which has the following syntax:

```
ListItemCollection.Insert(index, item)
```

where *`index`* is the zero-based position in the listbox at which the item is to be added and *`item`* is a String or a ListItem object to be added to the listbox. You can also remove items from the ListItemCollection by calling its Remove and RemoveAt methods. The syntax of the Remove method is:

```
ListItemCollection.Remove(item)
```

where *`item`* is a String or a ListItem object representing the item to be removed. The syntax of the RemoveAt method is:

```
ListItemCollection.RemoveAt(index)
```

where *`index`* is the position of the item to be removed from the listbox. The number of items in the drop-down listbox is provided by the ListItemCollection object's Count property.

Three properties of the individual ListItem objects also make it possible to work with the items in the list. The Text property contains the text of the ListItem object as it's displayed in the listbox. The Value property contains the value associated with the

ListItem object. Finally, the Selected property returns a Boolean indicating whether the item is selected.

The Image control

The Image control displays an image on a web page. Its HTML syntax is:

```
<asp:Image id="ImageName" runat="server"
     ImageUrl="string"
     AlternateText="string"
     ImageAlign="NotSet|AbsBottom|AbsMiddle|BaseLine|
                 Bottom|Left|Middle|Right|TextTop|Top"/>
```

The `ImageUrl` attribute contains the URL at which the image is found. The `AlternateText` attribute defines the text to be displayed in the event that the browser either does not support or is configured to not display images. The `ImageAlign` attribute determines the alignment of the image in relation to other elements on the page. All three attributes correspond to identically named properties of the Image class. The value of the ImageAlign property is a member of the ImageAlign enumeration and can be one of the following:

`ImageAlign.AbsBottom`
: The image's bottom edge is aligned with the bottom edge of the largest element on the same line.

`ImageAlign.AbsMiddle`
: The middle of the image is aligned with the middle of the largest element on the same line.

`ImageAlign.Baseline`
: The image's bottom edge is aligned with the bottom edge of the first line of text.

`ImageAlign.Bottom`
: The image's bottom edge is aligned with the bottom edge of the first line of text.

`ImageAlign.Left`
: The image is aligned on the left edge of the web page, with text wrapping on the right.

`ImageAlign.Middle`
: The middle of the image is aligned with the bottom edge of the first line of text.

`ImageAlign.NotSet`
: The image's alignment is not defined.

`ImageAlign.Right`
: The image is aligned on the right edge of the web page, with text wrapping on the left.

`ImageAlign.TextTop`
: The image's top edge is aligned with the top edge of the highest text on the line.

`ImageAlign.Top`
: The image's top edge is aligned with the top edge of the highest element on the same line.

The Label control

The Label control typically displays static text. Perhaps the simplest of controls, it has the following HTML syntax:

```
<asp:Label id="Label1"
     Text="label"
     runat="server"/>
```

The text displayed by the label is represented by the `Text` attribute. It directly corresponds to the identically named property of the System.Web.UI.WebControls.Label control.

The ListBox control

The ListBox control presents the user with a list of items and allows the user to select either a single item or multiple items. The ListBox control has the following HTML syntax:

```
<asp:ListBox id="ListboxName"
     DataSource="<% databindingexpression %>"
     DataTextField="DataSourceField"
     DataValueField="DataSourceField"
     AutoPostBack="True|False"
     Rows="rowcount"
     SelectionMode="Single|Multiple"
     OnSelectedIndexChanged="OnSelectedIndexChangedMethod"
     runat="server">

   <asp:ListItem value="value" selected="True|False">
     Text
   </asp:ListItem>

</asp:ListBox>
```

The `SelectionMode` attribute determines whether the user can select only a single item (the default) or multiple items. The `Rows` attribute determines the number of rows displayed in the listbox.

Rather than supplying the data either using HTML or programmatically, you can populate the list box from a data source. The `DataSource` attribute defines the data source to which the listbox is bound, the `DataTextField` attribute defines the field that will determine which items are displayed in the listbox, and the `DataValueField` attribute defines the field whose rows will provide the value of each list item.

Each of these attributes (`SelectionMode`, `Rows`, `DataSource`, `DataTextField`, `DataValueField`) directly corresponds to a property of the System.Web.UI.WebControls.

ListBox class. The value of the SelectionMode property must be a member of the ListSelectionMode enumeration; its two possible values are `ListSelectionMode.Single` and `ListSelectionMode.Multiple`. The Rows property is an Integer that determines how many rows the listbox displays.

In addition, the ListBox class has a two major properties that don't correspond to attributes of the `ListBox` tag. The SelectedIndex property returns the lowest index of a selected item. The SelectedItem property returns the first selected ListItem object in the listbox. For single-selection listboxes, these properties return the index of the selected item and the selected item itself, respectively. For multi-selection listboxes, you have to iterate the ListItemCollection collection to determine which items are selected.

If the listbox is not bound to a data source, the `ListItem` tag is used to define each item in the list. *`Text`* determines the item's text that's displayed in the listbox. The `value` attribute determines the item's value. The `Selected` attribute determines whether or not the item is initially selected when the listbox is displayed.

Finally, the `OnSelectedIndexChanged` attribute defines an event handler that will be executed whenever a new item is selected in the listbox. The event handler designated by the `OnSelectedIndexChanged` attribute must have the following signature:

```
Sub OnSelectedIndexChangedMethod(sender As Object, e As EventArgs)
```

Programmatically, the items in the listbox consist of ListItem objects. These can be accessed through the ListBox class' Items property, which returns a ListItemCollection object consisting of all the ListItem objects in the listbox. You can add items to the end of the listbox by calling the ListItemCollection object's Add method, which has the following syntax:

```
ListItemCollection.Add(item)
```

where *`item`* is either a String or a ListItem object. To add an item to a particular place in the listbox, you can call the Insert method, which has the following syntax:

```
ListItemCollection.Insert(index, item)
```

where *`index`* is the zero-based position in the listbox at which the item is to be added and *`item`* is a String or a ListItem object to be added to the listbox. You can also remove items from the ListItemCollection by calling its Remove and RemoveAt methods. The syntax of the Remove method is:

```
ListItemCollection.Remove(item)
```

where *`item`* is a String or a ListItem object representing the item to be removed. The syntax of the RemoveAt method is:

```
ListItemCollection.RemoveAt(index)
```

where *`index`* is the position of the item to be removed from the listbox. The number of items in the listbox is provided by the ListItemCollection object's Count property.

Three properties of the individual ListItem objects also make it possible to work with the items in the list. The Text property contains the text of the ListItem object as it's displayed in the listbox. The Value property contains the value associated with the ListItem object. Finally, the Selected property returns a Boolean indicating whether the item is selected. In the case of multi-selection listboxes, you can determine whether an item is selected by iterating the members of the ListItemCollection object and examining the Selected property of each, as the following code fragment shows:

```
Dim oList As ListItem
For Each oList In oListBox.Items
   If oList.Selected Then
      ' Do something
   End If
Next
```

The RadioButton control

The RadioButton control corresponds to a single button in a group of buttons used to indicate mutually exclusive choices. It has the following HTML syntax:

```
<asp:RadioButton id="RadioButtonName"
     AutoPostBack="True|False"
     Checked="True|False"
     GroupName="GroupName"
     Text="label"
     TextAlign="Right|Left"
     OnCheckedChanged="OnCheckedChangedMethod"
     runat="server"/>
```

As in the CheckBox control, the `Checked` attribute determines whether the control is checked. Only one control in the group designated by `GroupName` can be set to `True`. The default value of the `Checked` attribute is `False`. However, since it is possible for the `Checked` attributes of all radio buttons in a group to be `False`, it is important to initially set the `Checked` attribute of one member of the group to `True`. The `GroupName` attribute provides a common name by which all radio buttons in the group can be identified. The `Text` attribute defines the caption that appears either to the left (the default) or to the right of the radio button, depending on the setting of the `TextAlign` attribute.

Each of these attributes of the RadioButton control directly corresponds to an identically named property of the System.Web.UI.WebControls.RadioButton class. The value of the TextAlign property is either of the two members of the TextAlign enumeration: `TextAlign.Left`, which positions the text to the left of the checkbox (the default); and `TextAlign.Right`, which positions the text to the right of the checkbox. The Checked property is a Boolean that can be programmatically set and can also change as a result of user interaction. Note that the user changing the Checked property of another radio button in the group from `False` to `True` automatically changes the value of the Checked property of any checked radio button from `True` to `False`.

Finally, the OnCheckedChanged attribute defines an event handler that will be executed whenever the Checked property of the radio button is changed. The event handler designated by the OnCheckedChanged attribute must have the following signature:

```
Sub OnCheckedChangedMethod(sender As Object, e As EventArgs)
```

The Table control

The Table control corresponds to a table consisting of multiple rows, each having one or more columns. A table need not be symmetrical—that is, it need not have the same number of columns in each row. The Table control has the following HTML syntax:

```
<asp:Table id="TableName"
     BackImageUrl="url"
     CellSpacing="cellspacing"
     CellPadding="cellpadding"
     GridLines="None|Horizontal|Vertical|Both"
     HorizontalAlign="Center|Justify|Left|NotSet|Right"
     runat="server">

   <asp:TableRow>

      <asp:TableCell>
         Cell text
      </asp:TableCell>

   </asp:TableRow>

</asp:Table>
```

The TableRow tag defines a new table row, while the TableCell tag defines a new cell within a particular row. The contents of the individual cell are defined by *Cell text*. The HorizontalAlign attribute determines the horizontal alignment of the table on the page. The GridLines attribute determines the appearance of grid lines in the table. The CellSpacing attribute determines the number of pixels that separate individual cells of the table, while the CellPadding attribute determines the number of pixels between the cell's border and its contents. The BackImageURL attribute contains the URL of an image to be used as the background for the table.

Each of these attributes corresponds to an identically named property of the Table class. The CellPadding and CellSpacing properties are of type Integer. The value of the HorizontalAlign property is one of the following members of the HorizontalAlign enumeration: Center, Justify, Left, NotSet, and Right. The value of the GridLines property is one of the following members of the GridLines enumeration: Both, Horizontal, None, and Vertical.

You programmatically manipulate a table by manipulating its rows and its individual cells. The table rows are accessible through the Table object's Rows property, which returns a TableRowCollection object containing TableRow objects that represent the rows of the table. The TableRowCollection collection allows you to add rows to the end of the table by calling its Add method, which has the following syntax:

```
TableRowCollection.Add(row)
```

where *row* is a TableRow object that represents a row of the table. To add a row to a particular place in the table, you can call the Insert method, which has the following syntax:

```
TableRowCollection.Insert(index, row)
```

where *index* is the zero-based position in the table at which the row is to be added and *row* is a RowTable object representing the row to be added to the table. You can also remove rows from the table by calling the TableRowCollection object's Remove and RemoveAt methods. The syntax of the Remove method is:

```
TableRowCollection.Remove(row)
```

where *row* is a TableRow object representing the row to be deleted. The syntax of the RemoveAt method is:

```
TableRowCollection.RemoveAt(index)
```

where *index* is the position of the row to be removed from the table. The number of items in the table is provided by the TableRowCollection object's Count property. Individual TableRow objects representing individual rows of the table can be retrieved using the Item property, whose syntax is:

```
TableRowCollection.Item(index)
```

where *index* is the zero-based ordinal position of the row whose TableRow object you wish to retrieve.

Once you've retrieved a reference to an individual table row, you can use its Cells property to retrieve a reference to a TableCellCollection object, which contains a collection of TableCell objects representing the individual cells of the row. Like the TableRowCollection class, the TableCellCollection class has members to add and remove individual cells as well as to determine how many cells are in the collection. Its syntax for adding and removing cells is identical to that of the TableRowCollection class, except that TableCell objects are used instead of TableRow objects. Finally, to retrieve an individual cell, you use the TableCellCollection object's Item method, which has the following syntax:

```
TableCellCollection.Item(index)
```

where *index* is the zero-based ordinal position of the cell in the row. The property returns a TableCell object representing the cell.

Finally, the TableCell class has a number of properties that control the content and appearance of the cell. The Text property determines the cell's content. The Boolean Wrap property determines whether the contents of the cell wrap in the cell; its default value is True. The RowSpan and ColumnSpan properties are Integer values that indicate how many table rows and how many table columns the cell spans. The HorizontalAlign property, whose value is a member of the HorizontalAlign enumeration discussed earlier in this section, determines the horizontal alignment of the cell's contents. The VerticalAlign property determines the vertical alignment of the cell's contents. Its value must be a member of the VerticalAlign enumeration, which has the following members: Bottom, Middle, NotSet, and Top.

The TextBox control

The TextBox control corresponds to a single- or multi-line text box for displaying information and getting textual input from the user. It has the following HTML syntax:

```
<asp:TextBox id="TextBoxName"
     AutoPostBack="True|False"
     Columns="characters"
     MaxLength="characters"
     Rows="rows"
     Text="text"
     TextMode="Single|Multiline|Password"
     Wrap="True|False"
     OnTextChanged="OnTextChangedMethod"
     runat="server"/>
```

The Text attribute defines the actual text to be stored in the text box when the control is rendered. The Columns attribute determines the number of characters that the text box displays, while the MaxLength attribute determines the total number of characters that can be input into the text box. The TextMode attribute determines whether the TextBox control has one line (the default), multiple lines, or a single line into which the user is to enter a password. For a multi-line text box, the Rows attribute determines how many rows the text box displays, and the Wrap attribute determines whether text wraps onto the next line. By default, Wrap is False; input will appear on a single line until the user enters a carriage return.

Each of these attributes directly corresponds to an identically named property of the System.Web.UI.WebControls.TextBox class. The MaxLength, Columns, and Rows properties are all of type Integer and all have a default value of 0. In the case of the MaxLength property, this means that there is no limit to the number of characters that can be input to the text box. For the Columns and Rows properties, it means that as many columns or (in the case of multi-line text boxes) rows as possible will be displayed based on the size of the text box. The value of the TextMode property must be a member of the TextBoxMode enumeration; possible values are TextBoxMode.SingleLine (the default), TextBoxMode.MultiLine, and TextBoxMode.Password. The Text property, of course, is the most important property of the control. Its value includes any carriage return and linefeed characters (the vbCrLf character) entered by the user if the TextMode property is set to TextBoxMode.MultiLine. In addition, if the TextMode property is set to `TextBoxMode.Password`, asterisks are displayed whenever the user enters a character; however, the actual string input by the user is stored as is in the Text property.

Finally, the `OnTextChanged` attribute defines an event handler that will be executed whenever the Text property of the text box is changed. The event handler designated by the `OnTextChanged` attribute must have the following signature:

```
Sub OnTextChangedMethod(sender As Object, e As EventArgs)
```

Other web controls

The remaining controls defined in the System.Web.UI.WebControls namespace are:

AdRotator
: Displays an advertisement. The AdRotator control can be set to display a different ad each time the page is viewed.

Calendar
: Displays a one-month calendar on the web page and allows the user to select a date.

CheckBoxList
: Displays a group of checkboxes on the web page.

CompareValidator
: Validates the value entered into a control by comparing it to the value in another control or to a constant value. See "Adding Validation" later in this chapter for more information.

CustomValidator
: Validates the value entered into a control by running custom validation code. See "Adding Validation" later in this chapter for more information.

DataGrid
: Displays the values from a data source in a table format on the web page. See Chapter 8 for more information.

DataGridItem
: Represents a row in the DataGrid control.

DataList
: Displays the values from a data source in a list-control format on the web page.

DataListItem
: Represents an item in the DataList control.

HyperLink
: Displays a link to another web page. The link can be text or an image.

ImageButton
: Displays an image on the web page. This control differs from the Image control in that it generates a server-side event when the image is clicked.

LinkButton
: Displays a link to another web page. The LinkButton control has the same appearance as the HyperLink control, but it has the same behavior as the Button control.

Literal
: Displays static text on the web page.

Panel
: Contains other controls on the web page.

RadioButtonList
: Displays a list of radio buttons on the web page.

RangeValidator
: Validates the value entered into a control by comparing it to a given range of values. See "Adding Validation" later in this chapter for more information.

RegularExpressionValidator
: Validates the value entered into a control by matching it against a given regular expression. See "Adding Validation" for more information.

RequiredFieldValidator
: Validates a value entered into a control by ensuring that the value is different from the control's original value. See "Adding Validation" for more information.

TableHeaderCell
: Represents a header cell in a Table control.

ValidationSummary
: Displays a summary of validation errors on the web page. See "Adding Validation" for more information.

HTML Controls

The controls defined in the System.Web.UI.HtmlControls namespace are:

HtmlAnchor
: Wraps the HTML `<a>` tag.

HtmlButton
: Wraps the HTML `<button>` tag.

HtmlForm
: Wraps the HTML `<form>` tag.

HtmlGenericControl
: Represents any HTML tag (such as `<body>`) that isn't wrapped by a specific HTML server control.

HtmlImage
: Wraps the HTML `<img>` tag.

HtmlInputButton
: Wraps the HTML `<input type="button">`, `<input type="submit">`, and `<input type="reset">` tags.

HtmlInputCheckBox
: Wraps the HTML `<input type="checkbox">` tag.

HtmlInputFile
: Wraps the HTML `<input type="file">` tag.

HtmlInputHidden
: Wraps the HTML `<input type="hidden">` tag.

HtmlInputImage
: Wraps the HTML `<input type="image">` tag.

HtmlInputRadioButton
: Wraps the HTML `<input type="radio">` tag.

HtmlInputText
: Wraps the HTML `<input type="text">` and `<input type="password">` tags.

HtmlSelect
: Wraps the HTML `<select>` tag.

HtmlTable
: Wraps the HTML `<table>` tag.

HtmlTableCell
: Wraps the HTML `<td>` and `<th>` tags.

HtmlTableRow
: Wraps the HTML `<tr>` tag.

HtmlTextArea
: Wraps the HTML `<textarea>` tag.

Handling Control Events

Controls on a web form are represented in the code-behind class as fields—one field for each control. For example, when the Visual Studio .NET Web Forms Designer is used to add a text box to a form, the following declaration is added to the code-behind class:

```
Protected WithEvents TextBox1 As System.Web.UI.WebControls.TextBox
```

This declaration doesn't instantiate the control; it only defines a field that can hold a reference to a control of type TextBox. In addition, the designer adds this tag to the web page:

```
<asp:TextBox id="TextBox1"
   style="Z-INDEX: 105; LEFT: 8px; POSITION: absolute;
   TOP: 8px" runat="server">
</asp:TextBox>
```

The <asp:TextBox> tag signifies that ASP.NET should instantiate a TextBox control when a browser requests this page. The `id="TextBox1"` attribute names the control TextBox1. This name is what associates the control with the TextBox1 field in the code-behind class.

If code behind is not being used, it is not necessary to declare a member variable to hold a reference to the control. The ASP.NET framework will implicitly do this when the web page is compiled.

As discussed in Chapter 2, when a field declaration includes the `WithEvents` keyword, the containing class can handle events raised by the referenced object. To do so, the containing class defines a handler method with a signature matching the event signature. The handler method includes a `Handles` clause to link the method to the desired event on the object. For example, here is the definition of a handler method for the TextChanged event of TextBox1:

```
Private Sub TextBox1_TextChanged( _
   ByVal sender As System.Object, _
   ByVal e As System.EventArgs _
) Handles TextBox1.TextChanged
   ' ...
End Sub
```

The event-handler method can be given any name, but it is a common convention to use a name of the form *FieldName_EventName*.

Also by convention, event signatures for controls conform to the signature shown, with the exception of the *e* parameter being some other type derived from the EventArgs type. The *sender* parameter passed to the handler method holds a reference to the object that fired the event, and the *e* parameter holds a reference to an object that provides any extra information needed for the event. Events that pass a generic EventArgs argument have no event information to pass. Events that pass an argument of a type derived from EventArgs pass additional information within the fields of the passed object.

You can determine the correct signature for handling a specific event by referring to the control's documentation or by using Visual Studio .NET's built-in object browser. In addition, the Visual Studio .NET Web Forms Designer can automatically generate a handler-method declaration for any event exposed by any control on a given form.

Programmatically Instantiating Controls

It's easy to dynamically instantiate server controls at runtime. A convenient place to do this is in an override of the OnPreRender method of the Page class. Recall that the OnPreRender method is called after the page and its controls have been instantiated and initialized but prior to any rendering. Controls created here and added to the Page object's Controls collection will be rendered on the page. The code is simple:

```
Private WithEvents ctl As TextBox

Protected Overrides Sub OnPreRender(ByVal e As EventArgs)

   ' Instantiate a TextBox control and set some of its properties.
   ctl = New TextBox( )
   ctl.ID = "TextBox1"
   ctl.Text = "This is my text box."

   ' Add the control to the page.
   Me.Controls.Add(ctl)

   ' Let the base class raise the PreRender event.
   MyBase.OnPreRender(e)

End Sub
```

This code can be placed either in a code-behind class or directly within a `<script>` block in the *.aspx* page.

The Controls property of the Page class is of type ControlCollection. The Add method of the ControlCollection class adds the given control to the end of the collection. Visually, the newly added control appears as the last element in the rendered page. To add the control at a specific location in the collection, use the ControlCollection class's AddAt method. The AddAt method syntax looks like this:

```
Public Overridable Sub AddAt( _
   ByVal index As Integer, _
   ByVal child As System.Web.UI.Control)
```

The parameters of the AddAt method are:

index
: Specifies the position in the collection at which to insert the new control. This number is zero-based.

child
: Specifies the control to add to the collection.

The AddAt method is even more convenient when used with the ControlCollection class's IndexOf method. The IndexOf method returns the integer index within the collection of a given control. For example, assuming that a web page has a control named Label2 and that the variable `ctl` contains a reference to a newly created control, the following line adds the new control to the page, rendering it immediately prior to the Label2 control:

```
Me.Controls.AddAt(Me.Controls.IndexOf(Label2), ctl)
```

Adding Validation

Validating user input is a common requirement of any application that relies on the user to provide data. The ASP.NET framework provides tools to make input validation easy. ASP.NET supports validation by providing server controls that handle the validation process. Each server control placed on a form is responsible for validating the value in some other control on the form. The validation process occurs both on the client (if the browser is capable) and on the server, or just on the server (if the browser can't handle it). Validation occurs on the server, even if it occurs on the client, to prohibit a hostile client from submitting invalid data.

The server controls that relate to validation are:

CompareValidator
: Compares the value in a control with either a constant value or the value in another control. The developer chooses the comparison to be performed (equal, less than, greater than, etc.). The validation succeeds if the comparison is `True`.

CustomValidator
: Allows the application to perform validation logic that isn't provided by the standard comparison controls.

RangeValidator
: Compares the value in a control to a given range. The validation succeeds if the value is within the range.

RegularExpressionValidator
: Compares the value in a control to a given regular expression. The validation succeeds if the value is matched by the regular expression.

RequiredFieldValidator
: Checks that a value has been entered into a control. The validation succeeds if the value is nonempty.

ValidationSummary
: Provides an on-screen summary of the validation errors that have occurred on the page.

These controls are defined in the System.Web.UI.WebControls namespace.

The first step in using validation controls is to build a web page in the usual way. Example 6-6 shows the code for a simple data-input web page. Validation controls have not yet been added to this page—that will be done next. Figure 6-8 shows the resulting display.

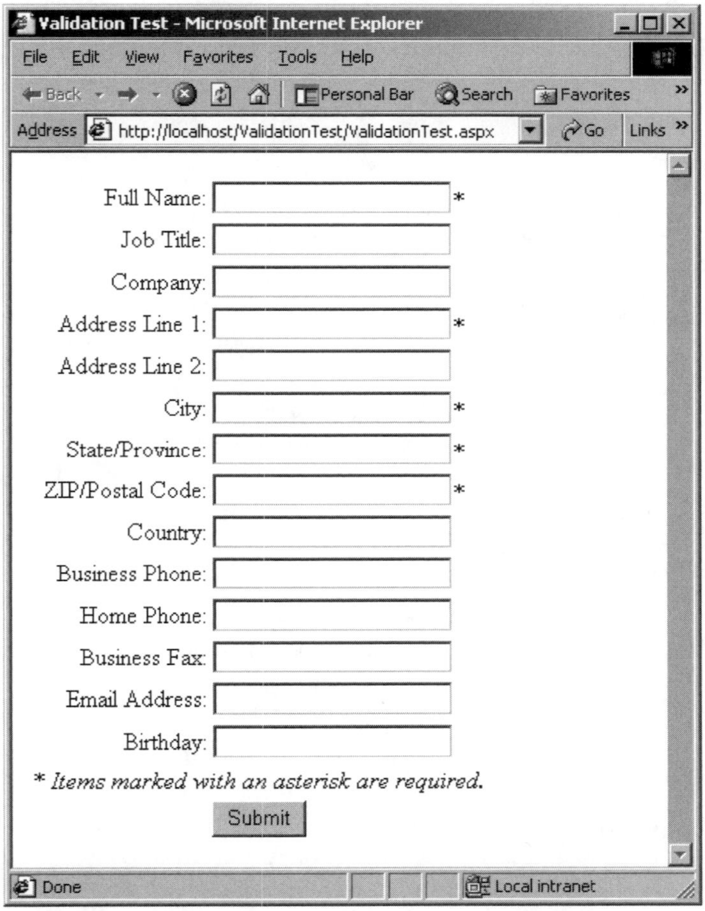

Figure 6-8. The output from Example 6-6

Example 6-6. A simple data-input web form

```
<%@ Page Explicit="True" Strict="True" %>

<html>

   <head>
      <title>Validation Test</title>
   </head>

   <body>
      <form action="ValidationTest.aspx" method="post" runat="server">
         <table>
            <tr>
               <td align="right">Full Name:</td>
```

Example 6-6. A simple data-input web form (continued)

```
            <td><asp:TextBox id="txtFullName" runat="server" />*</td>
         </tr>
         <tr>
            <td align="right">Job Title:</td>
            <td><asp:TextBox id="txtJobTitle" runat="server" /></td
         </tr>
         <tr>
            <td align="right">Company:</td>
            <td><asp:TextBox id="txtCompany" runat="server" /></td>
         </tr>
         <tr>
            <td align="right">Address Line 1:</td>
            <td><asp:TextBox id="txtAddressLine1" runat="server" />*</td>
         </tr>
         <tr>
            <td align="right">Address Line 2:</td>
            <td><asp:TextBox id="txtAddressLine2" runat="server" /></td>
         </tr>
         <tr>
            <td align="right">City:</td>
            <td><asp:TextBox id="txtCity" runat="server" />*</td>
         </tr>
         <tr>
            <td align="right">State/Province:</td>
            <td><asp:TextBox id="txtStateProvince" runat="server" />*</td>
         </tr>
         <tr>
            <td align="right">ZIP/Postal Code:</td>
            <td><asp:TextBox id="txtPostalCode" runat="server" />*</td>
         </tr>
         <tr>
            <td align="right">Country:</td>
            <td><asp:TextBox id="txtCountry" runat="server" /></td>
         </tr>
         <tr>
            <td align="right">Business Phone:</td>
            <td><asp:TextBox id="txtBusinessPhone" runat="server" /></td>
         </tr>
         <tr>
            <td align="right">Home Phone:</td>
            <td><asp:TextBox id="txtHomePhone" runat="server" /></td>
         </tr>
         <tr>
            <td align="right">Business Fax:</td>
            <td><asp:TextBox id="txtBusinessFax" runat="server" /></td>
         </tr>
         <tr>
            <td align="right">Email Address:</td>
            <td><asp:TextBox id="txtEmailAddress" runat="server" /></td>
         </tr>
         <tr>
            <td align="right">Birthday:</td>
```

Example 6-6. A simple data-input web form (continued)

```
            <td><asp:TextBox id="txtBirthday" runat="server" /></td>
         </tr>
         <tr>
            <td colspan="2">
               * <i>Items marked with an asterisk are required.</i>
            </td>
         </tr>
         <tr>
            <td colspan="2" align="center">
               <asp:Button id="btnSubmit" text="Submit" runat="server" />
            </td>
         </tr>
      </table>
   </form>
</body>

</html>
```

Validation controls can be added either manually in code or graphically by using the Web Forms Designer in Visual Studio .NET. This section shows how to add the controls in code. All the information in this section is also applicable when using Visual Studio .NET.

The following validations will be added for the code in Example 6-6:

- Full Name, Address Line 1, City, State/Province, and ZIP/Postal Code will be required fields.
- If Email Address is filled in, it will be checked for correct format.
- If Birthday is entered, it will be checked to ensure that the date entered is no later than the current system date on the web server.

The modified code is shown in Example 6-7. Code that differs from Example 6-6 is shown in bold.

Example 6-7. A simple data-input web form with validation controls

```
<%@ Page Explicit="True" Strict="True" %>

<script language="vb" runat="server">

   Private Sub Page_Load(ByVal sender As Object, ByVal e As EventArgs)
      cmpBirthday.ValueToCompare = DateTime.Today.ToString("yyyy-MM-dd")
   End Sub

</script>

<html>

   <head>
      <title>Validation Test 2</title>
```

Example 6-7. A simple data-input web form with validation controls (continued)

```
</head>

<body>
   <form action="ValidationTest2.aspx" method="post" runat="server">
      <table>
         <tr>
            <td align="right">Full Name:</td>
            <td><asp:TextBox id="txtFullName" runat="server" />*</td>
            <td>
               <asp:RequiredFieldValidator id="recFldFullName"
                  ControlToValidate="txtFullName"
                  ErrorMessage="Full Name is required."
                  runat="server" />
            </td>
         </tr>
         <tr>
            <td align="right">Job Title:</td>
            <td><asp:TextBox id="txtJobTitle" runat="server" /></td
         </tr>
         <tr>
            <td align="right">Company:</td>
            <td><asp:TextBox id="txtCompany" runat="server" /></td>
         </tr>
         <tr>
            <td align="right">Address Line 1:</td>
            <td><asp:TextBox id="txtAddressLine1" runat="server" />*</td>
            <td>
               <asp:RequiredFieldValidator id="recFldAddressLine1"
                  ControlToValidate="txtAddressLine1"
                  ErrorMessage="Address Line 1 is required."
                  runat="server" />
            </td>
         </tr>
         <tr>
            <td align="right">Address Line 2:</td>
            <td><asp:TextBox id="txtAddressLine2" runat="server" /></td>
         </tr>
         <tr>
            <td align="right">City:</td>
            <td><asp:TextBox id="txtCity" runat="server" />*</td>
            <td>
               <asp:RequiredFieldValidator id="recFldCity"
                  ControlToValidate="txtCity"
                  ErrorMessage="City is required."
                  runat="server" />
            </td>
         </tr>
         <tr>
            <td align="right">State/Province:</td>
            <td><asp:TextBox id="txtStateProvince" runat="server" />*</td>
            <td>
```

Example 6-7. A simple data-input web form with validation controls (continued)

```
            <asp:RequiredFieldValidator id="recFldStateProvince"
               ControlToValidate="txtStateProvince"
               ErrorMessage="State/Province is required."
               runat="server" />
         </td>
      </tr>
      <tr>
         <td align="right">ZIP/Postal Code:</td>
         <td><asp:TextBox id="txtPostalCode" runat="server" />*</td>
         <td>
            <asp:RequiredFieldValidator id="recFldPostalCode"
               ControlToValidate="txtPostalCode"
               ErrorMessage="ZIP/Postal Code is required."
               runat="server" />
         </td>
      </tr>
      <tr>
         <td align="right">Country:</td>
         <td><asp:TextBox id="txtCountry" runat="server" /></td>
      </tr>
      <tr>
         <td align="right">Business Phone:</td>
         <td><asp:TextBox id="txtBusinessPhone" runat="server" /></td>
      </tr>
      <tr>
         <td align="right">Home Phone:</td>
         <td><asp:TextBox id="txtHomePhone" runat="server" /></td>
      </tr>
      <tr>
         <td align="right">Business Fax:</td>
         <td><asp:TextBox id="txtBusinessFax" runat="server" /></td>
      </tr>
      <tr>
         <td align="right">Email Address:</td>
         <td><asp:TextBox id="txtEmailAddress" runat="server" /></td>
         <td>
            <asp:RegularExpressionValidator id="regExEmailAddress"
               ControlToValidate="txtEmailAddress"
               ErrorMessage="Email format must be name@company.com."
               ValidationExpression=
                  "^[\w-]+@[\w-]+\.(com|net|org|edu|mil)$"
               runat="server" />
         </td>
      </tr>
      <tr>
         <td align="right">Birthday:</td>
         <td><asp:TextBox id="txtBirthday" runat="server" /></td>
         <td>
            <asp:CompareValidator id="cmpBirthday"
               ControlToValidate="txtBirthday"
               Type="Date"
```

Example 6-7. A simple data-input web form with validation controls (continued)

```
                        Operator="LessThanEqual"
                        ErrorMessage="Birthday must not be later than today."
                        runat="server" />
                  </td>
               </tr>
               <tr>
                  <td colspan="2">
                     * <i>Items marked with an asterisk are required.</i>
                  </td>
               </tr>
               <tr>
                  <td colspan="2" align="center">
                     <asp:Button id="btnSubmit" text="Submit" runat="server" />
                  </td>
               </tr>
            </table>
         </form>
      </body>

</html>
```

When the web page from Example 6-7 is displayed in a browser, it appears identical to Figure 6-8. What's different in this version is that if any of the required fields are empty, if the Email Address field is not in the correct format, or if the Birthday field contains a date in the future, appropriate messages are shown when the user clicks the Submit button. Figure 6-9 shows the resulting display. Note that on a computer screen, the error messages are shown in red by default.

Note the following in Example 6-7:

- To make the given fields required, RequiredFieldValidator controls were added, one per field.
- To prohibit invalid entries in the Email Address field, a RegularExpressionValidator control was added.*
- To prohibit future dates from the Birthday field, a CompareValidator control was added. Note that the value to which to compare (the current date) can't be specified within the `<asp:CompareValidator>` tag, so this was coded into the Page_Load method near the top of the example.

* The regular expression used here is a simple one taken from the Microsoft documentation. It matches only the simplest email addresses of the form *user@company.com* and should not be used in production systems. It turns out that matching Internet email addresses in the general case is not a trivial endeavor. See the book *Mastering Regular Expressions* by Jeffrey E. F. Friedl (O'Reilly) for a description of the problem and its solution.

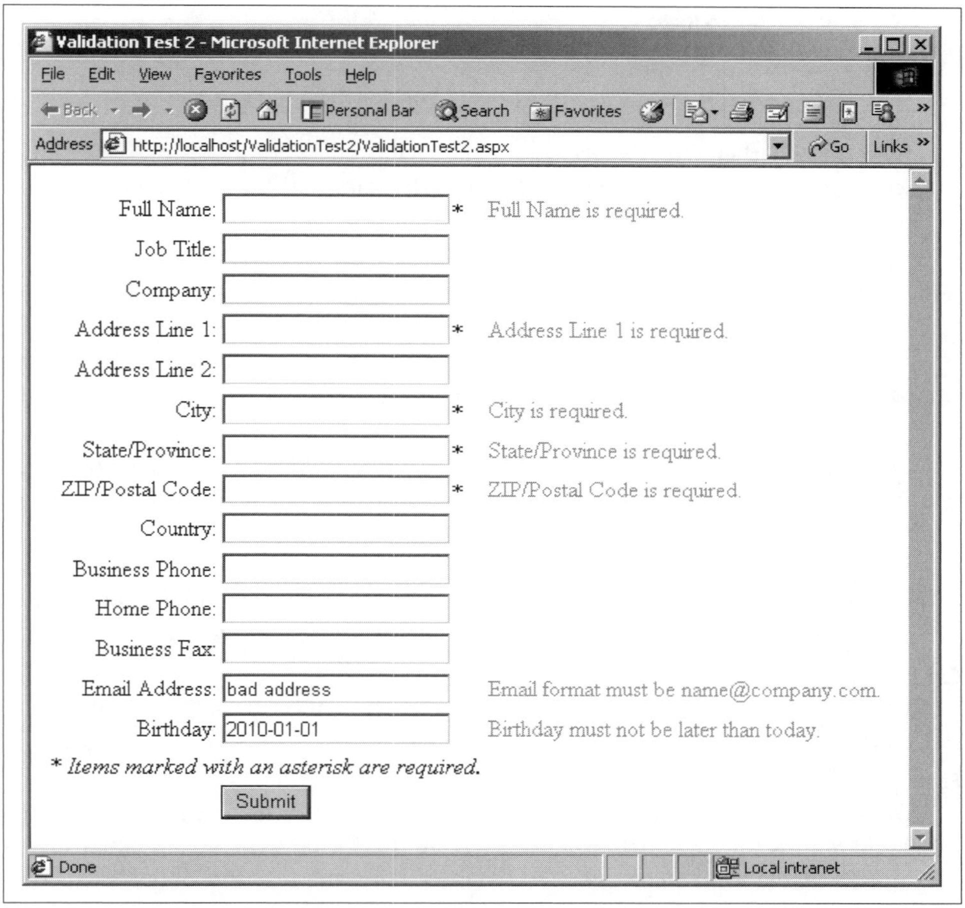

Figure 6-9. *The output from Example 6-7 when fields are missing or invalid*

The RequiredFieldValidator control is the only validation control that checks for a missing entry. The other validation controls perform their validations only if data has been entered into the corresponding fields. If no data has been entered, the validation succeeds. If it is necessary to enforce the entry of a field, a RequiredFieldValidator control must be used in addition to any other validation controls associated with the field.

More About Validation-Control Tag Attributes

In addition to the attributes supported by all web controls, the validation controls recognize the following attributes within their respective tags:

`ControlToValidate`
: Represents the name of the control to validate, as given by the control's ID property.

`Display`
: Specifies whether visual space for the error message should be reserved on the web page, even if the message isn't currently being displayed. The possible values are:

    `"Dynamic"`
    : Space for the error message is added to the page if validation fails.

    `"Static"`
    : Space for the error message is added to the page, regardless of whether the message is actually displayed. This is the default.

    `"None"`
    : The error message is never displayed, even if validation fails. This setting is used when the error message is displayed only in a validation summary control.

`EnableClientSideScript`
: Specifies whether to enable client-side validation (if supported by the browser). The default is `"True"`.

`ErrorMessage`
: Provides the message displayed to the user if validation fails. The default is an empty string.

`ForeColor`
: Defines the color in which the error message is displayed. The default is `"Red"`. Valid values for this attribute are given by the Color structure (defined in the System.Drawing namespace). See Chapter 4 for information about the Color structure.

The CompareValidator control recognizes these additional attributes:

`ControlToCompare`
: The name of the control that contains the value to compare. If this attribute is specified, the `ValueToCompare` attribute should not be specified.

`Operator`
: The comparison to be performed. The possible values are:

    `"DataTypeCheck"`
    : Validation succeeds if the value in the control to validate can convert to the type specified by the `Type` attribute.

    `"Equal"`
    : Validation succeeds if the value in the control to validate is equal to the comparison value.

"GreaterThan"
: Validation succeeds if the value in the control to validate is greater than the comparison value.

"GreaterThanEqual"
: Validation succeeds if the value in the control to validate is greater than or equal to the comparison value.

"LessThan"
: Validation succeeds if the value in the control to validate is less than the comparison value.

"LessThanEqual"
: Validation succeeds if the value in the control to validate is less than or equal to the comparison value.

"NotEqual"
: Validation succeeds if the value in the control to validate is not equal to the comparison value.

`Type`
: The data type of the values being compared. The values are converted to this type before the comparison is made. The possible values are `"Currency"`, `"Date"`, `"Double"`, `"Integer"`, and `"String"`.

`ValueToCompare`
: The value to use for comparison. If this attribute is specified, the `ControlToCompare` attribute should not be specified.

The CustomValidator control recognizes this additional attribute:

`ClientValidationFunction`
: The name of the client-side script function to call to perform client-side validation.

Server-side custom validation is performed by responding to the CustomValidator control's ServerValidate event. See "Performing Custom Validation" later in this chapter for details.

The RangeValidator control recognizes these additional attributes:

`MaximumValue`
: The maximum value of the range. The default is an empty string.

`MinimumValue`
: The minimum value of the range. The default is an empty string.

`Type`
: The data type of the value being validated. The value being validated, as well as the maximum and minimum values, are all converted to this type before the comparisons are made. The possible values are `"Currency"`, `"Date"`, `"Double"`, `"Integer"`, and `"String"`. The default is `"String"`.

The RegularExpressionValidator control recognizes this additional attribute:

`ValidationExpression`
: The regular expression against which to validate.

The RequiredFieldValidator control recognizes this additional attribute:

`InitialValue`
: The value considered a "blank" value. The default is an empty string. Validation fails if and only if the value in the control to be validated matches the value given in the `InitialValue` attribute.

Using Validation-Control Properties

The names of the attributes listed in the previous section are also the names of the corresponding properties of the control classes. These properties can be read or set in code, if desired. For example, after a value is specified for the `ErrorMessage` attribute, that value can be read in code by reading the ErrorMessage property of the control. Similarly, attributes need not be used at all. Instead, values can be directly written to the corresponding properties in code.

In addition to the properties that match the attributes in the previous section, the validator controls all have the following properties:

Enabled
: This Boolean property specifies whether the validation control is enabled. When this property is set to `False`, the control does not attempt to perform validation. The default is `True`.

IsValid
: This Boolean property indicates whether the value in the associated control passes validation.

PropertiesValid
: This read-only Boolean property indicates whether the value specified by the ControlToValidate property is a valid control on the page.

RenderUplevel
: This read-only Boolean property indicates whether the browser supports up-level rendering.

Providing a Summary View of Validation Failures

In addition to placing each error message next to the field that is in error, there is another option. Using the ValidationSummary control, you can display a summary of a web page's validation errors either on the page, in a message box (if the browser is enabled for client-side JavaScript), or both. For example, you could add the following fragment to the code in Example 6-7 (new code is shown in bold; the surrounding lines are shown for context):

```
<body>
   <form action="ValidationTest2.aspx" method="post" runat="server">
      <asp:ValidationSummary
         HeaderText="Some information is missing or mis-typed. Please
            make corrections for the following items, then click the
            Submit button again. Thank you!"
         runat="server" />
      <table>
         <tr>
```

The ValidationSummary control automatically detects validation controls that are on the same page. If validation fails, the ValidationSummary control displays the ErrorMessage properties from all validation controls that reported failure. This displays in addition to the display of each individual validation control. In practice, it is unlikely that both displays are desired, so the `Display` attribute of each validation control can be set to `"None"` to suppress individual display, like this:

```
<asp:RequiredFieldValidator id="recFldFullName"
    ControlToValidate="txtFullName"
   ErrorMessage="Full Name is required."
   Display="None"
   runat="server" />
```

Figure 6-10 shows how these changes affect the web page when validation fails.

The attributes recognized by the ValidationSummary control are:

`DisplayMode`
: Specifies the format in which the error messages are displayed. The possible values are:

  `"BulletList"`
  : Displays the error messages in a bulleted list. This is the default.

  `"List"`
  : Displays the error messages in a list without bullets.

  `"SingleParagraph"`
  : Displays the error messages in paragraph form.

`EnableClientScript`
: Specifies whether to enable a client-side script (if supported by the browser). The default is `"True"`.

`ForeColor`
: Defines the color in which the summary is displayed. The default is `"Red"`. Valid values for this attribute are given by the Color structure (defined in the System.Drawing namespace). See Chapter 4 for information about the Color structure.

`HeaderText`
: Displays a message above the summarized items. The default is an empty string.

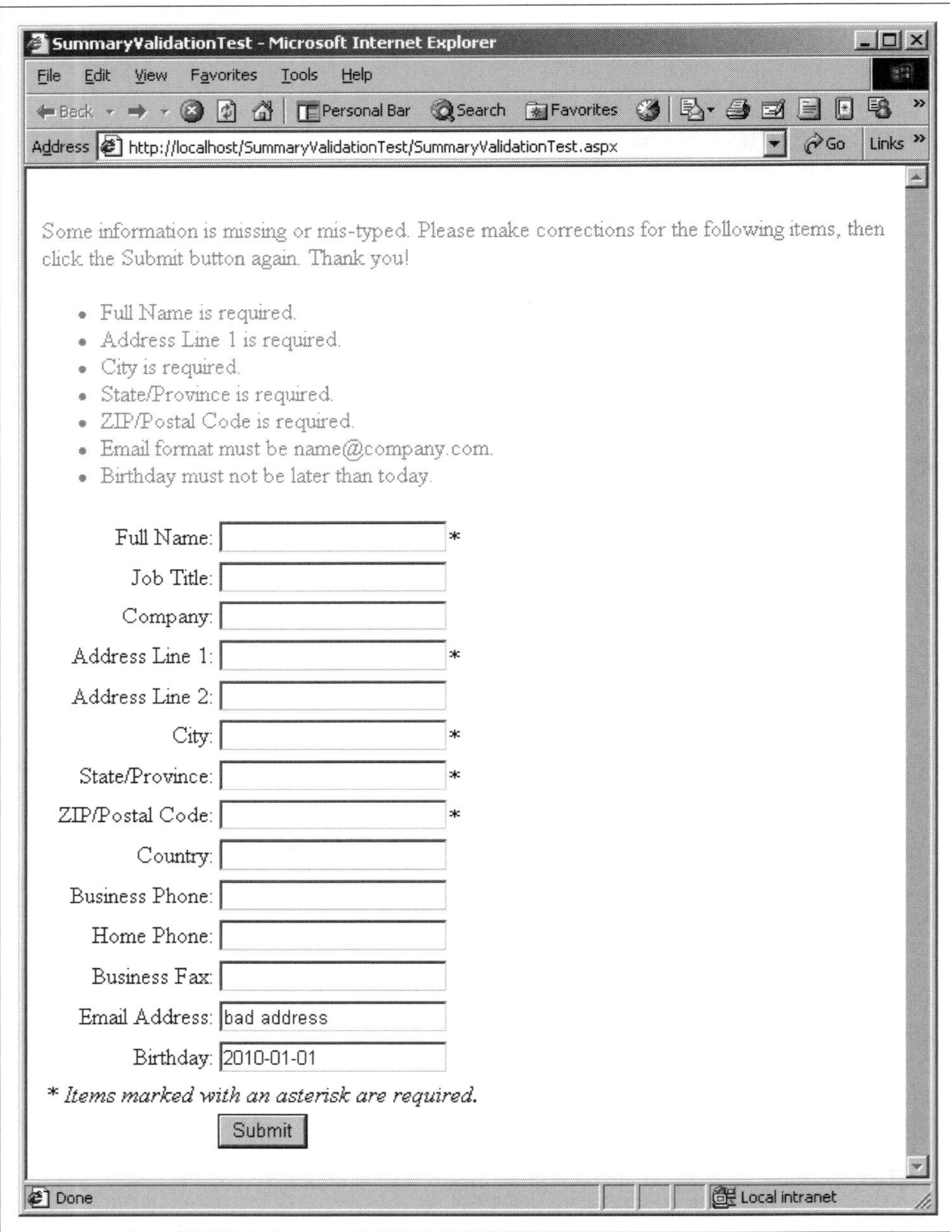

Figure 6-10. Using the ValidationSummary control

`ShowMessageBox`
: Indicates whether to show the summary in a message box using a client-side script. If this attribute is set to "True" and the browser supports JavaScript, the

summary is shown in a message box (see Figure 6-11). If set to `"False"`, no message box is shown. The default is `"False"`.

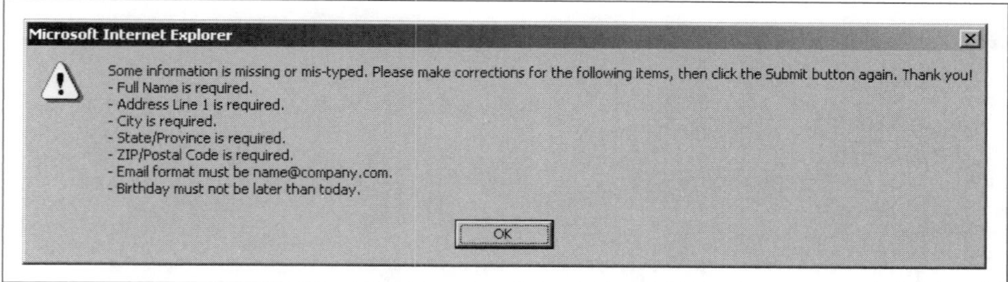

Figure 6-11. Showing the validation summary in a message box

`ShowSummary`
: Indicates whether to show the summary on the web page. If this attribute is set to `"True"`, the summary is shown on the web page. If set to `"False"`, the summary is not shown on the web page. The default is `"True"`.

Note that the `ShowMessageBox` and `ShowSummary` attributes are independent of each other. If both are set to `"True"`, the summary is shown in both ways.

These attributes all correspond to like-named properties of the ValidationSummary class and can be read and modified in code.

Performing Custom Validation

For situations in which the standard validation controls aren't sufficient, ASP.NET provides the CustomValidator control. This control allows the developer to specify custom functions—on both the client and the server—that validate the contents of the associated control. The client-side validation function must be a JavaScript or VBScript code block that is part of the web page. The server-side validation function is a method defined in the web page class.

Example 6-8 shows code using a CustomValidator control. The code generates a page with a single text box in which the user is expected to type a mathematical expression. The validation that occurs on the value simply ensures that there are an equal number of left and right parentheses. Figure 6-12 shows the display before validation occurs. Figure 6-13 shows the display when validation fails.

Example 6-8. Using the CustomValidator control

```
<%@ Page Explicit="True" Strict="True" %>

<script language="VB" runat="server">

   Private Sub cstExpression_ServerValidate( _
      ByVal sender As Object, _
```

Example 6-8. Using the CustomValidator control (continued)

```
      ByVal e As ServerValidateEventArgs _
   )
      e.IsValid = _
         (CountSubString(e.Value, "(") = CountSubString(e.Value, ")"))
   End Sub

   Private Function CountSubString( _
      ByVal strSearchThis As String, _
      ByVal strSearchFor As String _
   ) As Integer
      Dim count As Integer = 0
      Dim pos As Integer = strSearchThis.IndexOf(strSearchFor)
      Do While pos <> -1
         count += 1
         pos = strSearchThis.IndexOf(strSearchFor, _
            pos + strSearchFor.Length)
      Loop
      Return count
   End Function

</script>

<script language="JavaScript">

   function countSubString(searchThis, searchFor) {
      var count = 0;
      var pos = searchThis.indexOf(searchFor);
      while pos != -1 {
         count++;
         pos = searchThis.indexOf(searchFor, pos + searchFor.length);
      }
      return count;
   }

   function cstExpression_ClientValidate(sender, e) {
      e.IsValid =
         (countSubString(e.Value, "(") == countSubString(e.Value, ")"))
   }

</script>

<html>

   <head>
      <title>CustomValidator Test</title>
   </head>

   <body>
      <form action="CustomValidatorTest.aspx" method="post" runat="server">
         <table>
            <tr>
               <td align="right">Enter an expression:</td>
```

Example 6-8. Using the CustomValidator control (continued)

```
            <td><asp:TextBox id="txtExpression" runat="server" /></td>
         </tr>
         <tr>
            <td colspan="2">
               <asp:CustomValidator id="cstExpression"
                  ControlToValidate="txtExpression"
                  OnServerValidate="cstExpression_ServerValidate"
                  ClientValidateFunction="cstExpression_ClientValidate"
                  ErrorMessage="The number of left parentheses in
                     the expression must be the same as the number
                     of right parentheses."
                  runat="server" />
            </td>
         </tr>
         <tr>
            <td colspan="2" align="center">
               <asp:Button id="btnSubmit" text="Submit"
                  runat="server" />
            </td>
         </tr>
      </table>
   </form>
</body>

</html>
```

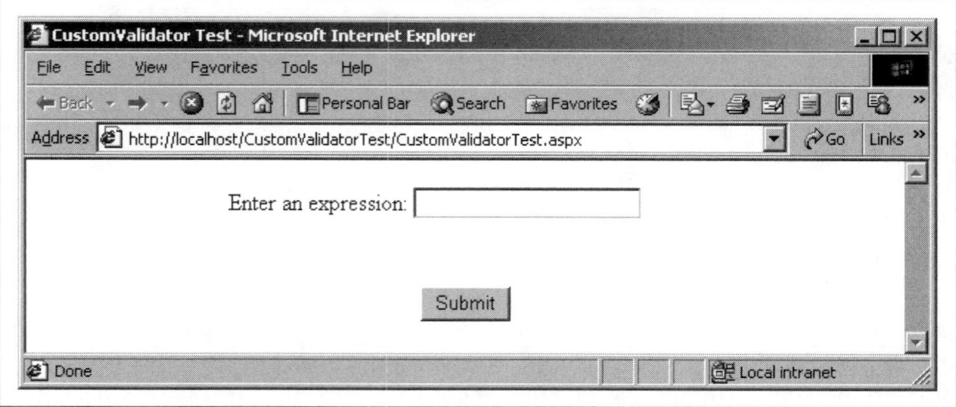

Figure 6-12. The display from Example 6-8 before validation occurs

The code in Example 6-8 is straightforward. First, a server-side method called cstExpression_ServerValidate is added to the page to handle server-side validation. This method is actually an event handler with a signature that's appropriate for the CustomValidator control's ServerValidate event. Setting the `OnServerValidate` attribute of the `<asp:CustomValidator>` tag wires the handler method to the event. Second, a client-side function, *cstExpression_ClientValidate*, is added to the page to

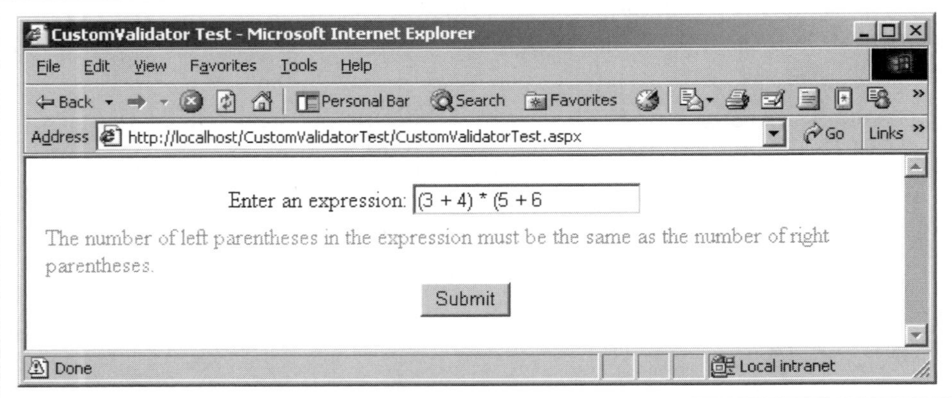

Figure 6-13. The display from Example 6-8 when validation fails

handle client-side validation. This function is called by the client-side validation code when it is time for the txtExpression field to be validated. Setting the `ClientValidateFunction` attribute of the `<asp:CustomValidator>` tag wires up this function.

Using Directives to Modify Web Page Compilation

You can modify web page compilation by including *directives*. Directives are keywords that are recognized and acted on by the ASP.NET page compiler. They affect a page's compilation, rather than its presentation. Directives are delimited by the characters `<%@` and `%>` and can appear at any location in the source file (although Microsoft says that "standard practice" is to place them at the top of the file). For example, the following `<%@ Page %>` directive was shown in Example 6-1, earlier in this chapter:

```
<%@ Page Language="vb" AutoEventWireup="false"
   CodeBehind="WebForm1.aspx.vb" Inherits="IdeExamples.WebForm1"%>
```

Directives are similar in form to HTML tags. There is the directive itself, followed by one or more attributes that specify various settings associated with the directive. A directive without attributes has no effect. Directives are different from HTML tags in that the delimiters are different and in that directives have no closing tags.

ASP.NET defines the following directives and associated attributes:

`@ Assembly`
: Provides a way to reference assemblies defined elsewhere. This directive's attributes are:

`Name`

Specifies the name of an assembly in the global assembly cache. For example:

```
<%@ Assembly Name="System.Windows.Forms" %>
```

`SRC`

Specifies the path of a Visual Basic .NET source file to be compiled and referenced. The path is relative to the web application's virtual folder. For example:

```
<%@ Assembly SRC="SomeClass.vb" %>
```

Either the `Name` or the `SRC` attribute can be specified, but not both. If multiple assemblies are to be referenced, the `@ Assembly` directive should appear multiple times, like this:

```
<%@ Assembly Name="System.Windows.Forms" %>
<%@ Assembly Name="System.Drawing" %>
```

Note the following when using the `@ Assembly` directive:

- Assemblies located in the application's */bin* folder are automatically referenced—there is no need to use the `@ Assembly` directive.
- The `@ Assembly` directive can't reference compiled assemblies that aren't in the global assembly cache.
- Source files referenced with the `SRC` attribute must be located somewhere underneath the web application's virtual folder.

`@ Control`

Modifies compilation of a user control. (User controls are discussed in the "User Controls" section later in this chapter.) This directive's attributes are:

`AutoEventWireup`

Indicates whether the control's events are *autowired* to appropriate handlers found within the Control class. Allowed values are `"true"` and `"false"`. The default is `"true"`. This is identical to the same concept found in Page classes. See "AutoEventWireup" in the "Handling Page Events" section earlier in this chapter.

`ClassName`

Specifies a class name for the compiled control. This can be any name that is valid for a Visual Basic .NET class. By default, the name is constructed from the filename of the user control. If the filename is "*filename*.ascx", then the `ClassName` value is "*filename*_ascx".

`CodeBehind`

Is used by Visual Studio .NET projects instead of the `Src` attribute to specify a code-behind file.

`CompilerOptions`
: Specifies arbitrary arguments to be passed to the Visual Basic .NET compiler. The format of these arguments is the same as for the Visual Basic .NET command-line compiler. The default is the empty string. (Command-line compiler options are not documented in this book.)

`Debug`
: Specifies whether to compile the control in debug mode. Allowed values are `"true"` and `"false"`. The default is `"false"`. Compiling in debug mode enables features such as rich error messages (suitable for developers) and setting breakpoints.

`Description`
: Is a place for the developer to describe the control. Neither ASP.NET nor Visual Studio .NET uses it in any way.

`EnableViewState`
: Specifies whether view state will be maintained across page requests. Allowed values are `"true"` and `"false"`. The default is `"true"`. See "Maintaining State" later in this chapter for more information.

`Explicit`
: Specifies whether the control will be compiled with `Option Explicit` turned on. Allowed values are `"true"` and `"false"`. The default is `"true"`. See Chapter 2 for a discussion of this compiler option.

`Inherits`
: Specifies a class from which the compiled control class will inherit. The value can be the name of any accessible class that inherits from the UserControl class (defined in the System.Web.UI namespace). If this attribute is not specified, the compiled control class inherits directly from the UserControl class.

`Language`
: Specifies the programming language in which embedded code is written. This can be different from the language in which the control's code-behind class is written.

`Src`
: Specifies a file containing the source for the control's code-behind class, if any. By default, user controls don't have a code-behind class.

`Strict`
: Specifies whether the control will be compiled with `Option Strict` turned on. Allowed values are `"true"` and `"false"`. The default is `"false"`. See Chapter 2 for a discussion of this compiler option.

`WarningLevel`
: Specifies the warning level at which the compiler aborts compilation of the control. Allowed values are `"0"`, `"1"`,`"2"`, `"3"`, and`"4"`.

`@ Implements`
: Specifies the name of an interface that is implemented by the web page. This directive serves the same function as the `Implements` statement in Visual Basic .NET. The `@ Implements` directive has one attribute:

  `Interface`
  : Designates the implemented interface. Only one interface can appear in each `@ Implements` directive. To specify more than one interface, provide multiple `@ Implements` directives.

  Recall that *.aspx* files are compiled into classes. This is why a web page can implement an interface. The actual implementation must be provided just as it would be in a Visual Basic .NET class definition. In this case, however, the implementation appears as Visual Basic .NET code within a `<script>` block in the *.aspx* file.

`@ Import`
: Imports a namespace into the page, allowing classes to be referred to by their short names rather than by their fully qualified names. This directive serves the same function as the `Imports` keyword in Visual Basic .NET. The `@ Import` directive has one attribute:

  `Namespace`
  : Designates the namespace to import. Only one namespace can appear in each `@ Import` directive. To import more than one namespace, provide multiple `@ Import` directives.

  Only namespaces that exist within *referenced assemblies* can be included in the `@ Import` directive. In Visual Studio .NET projects, referenced assemblies appear beneath the References item in the Solution Explorer window. You can add assembly references to the project by right-clicking on the References item, selecting Add Reference, and then choosing or browsing to the desired assembly in the Add Reference dialog box. In projects that are created without the aid of Visual Studio .NET, assemblies are referenced in one of three ways. Assemblies that are in the global assembly cache (GAC) can be referenced by using the `@ Assembly` directive. Assemblies that are not in the GAC can be referenced by placing them in a *bin* directory within the application's root directory. Finally, at the command line, the DLL in which an assembly resides can be referenced using the `/reference` (or `/r`) switch.

  See also the `@ Reference` directive later in this list.

`@ OutputCache`
: Specifies output cache settings. Aside from the attributes listed here, caching is not discussed in this book.

  `Duration`
  : The number of seconds to cache the page or user control. There is no default—this attribute must be specified if the `@ OutputCache` directive is used.

`Location`
: The location of the output cache. Allowed values are "Any" (allows the framework to choose where to place the cache), "Client" (the cache is placed on the browser client), "Downstream" (the cache is placed on a server that is downstream from the server processing the request), "None" (output is not cached), and "Server" (the cache is placed on the server processing the request).

The remaining attributes, `VaryByCustom`, `VaryByHeader`, `VaryByParam`, and `VaryByControl`, are beyond the scope of this book.

`@ Page`
: Modifies compilation of a web page. This directive's attributes are:

`AspCompat`
: Indicates whether to run this page on a single-threaded apartment (STA) thread. Allowed values are "true" and "false". The default is "false". Running the page on an STA thread lets it call components that require an STA thread, such as components written in Visual Basic 6.

In spite of its name, this attribute doesn't enable embedding classic ASP in an ASP.NET (*.aspx*) source file.

`AutoEventWireup`
: Indicates whether the page's events are autowired to appropriate handlers found within the Page class. Allowed values are "true" and "false". The default is "true". See "AutoEventWireup" in the "Handling Page Events" section earlier in this chapter.

`Buffer`
: Indicates whether to enable response buffering for the page. Allowed values are "true" and "false". The default is "true". When response buffering is enabled, the entire response is generated before any of it is sent to the browser. If response buffering is disabled, data is sent to the browser as it is generated.

`ClassName`
: Specifies a class name for the compiled page. This can be any name that is valid for a Visual Basic .NET class. By default, the name is constructed from the filename of the web page. If the filename is "*filename*.aspx", the `ClassName` value is "*filename*_aspx".

`ClientTarget`
: Overrides the ASP.NET framework's automatic detection of browser capabilities. Set this attribute to "Uplevel" or "Downlevel" to force ASP.NET to forego browser detection and just assume the corresponding capabilities. Alternatively, set this attribute to the value given by the browser setting within the `<browserCaps>` section of a web application's *.config* file to cause ASP.NET to assume the capabilities defined within that section. The default

is an empty string. This attribute corresponds to the ClientTarget property of the Page class.

`CodeBehind`
: Used by Visual Studio .NET projects instead of the `Src` attribute to specify a code-behind file.

`CodePage`
: Specifies the code page (that is, the character set) to use in rendering the web page. The value can be any valid code page. The default is the default code page for the web server.

`CompilerOptions`
: Specifies arbitrary arguments to be passed to the Visual Basic .NET compiler. The format of these arguments is the same as for the Visual Basic .NET command-line compiler. The default is the empty string. (Command-line compiler options are not documented in this book.)

`ContentType`
: Specifies the type of data to be rendered by the page. The value can be any valid content type as defined by the Multipurpose Internet Mail Extensions (MIME) specification. The default is `"text/html"`.

`Culture`
: Specifies the culture to be used by the page. The culture specifies language and formatting conventions used in rendering content. The value can be any standard culture name, as given in Appendix C. The default is determined by the configuration of the web server.

`Debug`
: Specifies whether to compile the page in debug mode. Allowed values are `"true"` and `"false"`. The default is `"false"`. Compiling in debug mode enables features such as rich error messages (suitable for developers) and setting breakpoints.

`Description`
: Provides a place for the developer to describe the page. Neither ASP.NET nor Visual Studio .NET uses it in any way.

`EnableSessionState`
: Specifies the availability of session state for the page. Allowed values are `"true"` (indicating that session state is to be enabled), `"false"` (indicating that session state is not to be enabled), and `"ReadOnly"` (indicating that session state is enabled, but read-only). The default is `"true"`. See "Maintaining State" later in this chapter for more information.

`EnableViewState`
: Specifies whether view state will be maintained across page requests. Allowed values are `"true"` and `"false"`. The default is `"true"`. See "Maintaining State" later in this chapter for more information.

`EnableViewStateMac`
: Specifies whether to use increased security to verify that the user has not tampered with the view state received in a postback. Allowed values are `"true"` and `"false"`. The default is `"false"`.

`ErrorPage`
: Specifies the URL of a web page to which the user should be redirected if an unhandled exception occurs during the processing of the page request.

  Note that this redirection occurs only if custom errors are enabled. This is controlled by the `<customErrors>` section in the application's *web.config* file or in the machine's *machine.config* file. By default, the *machine.config* file contains this entry:

```
<customErrors
   mode="RemoteOnly" />
```

This means that if an unhandled exception occurs, redirection to the page specified by the `ErrorPage` attribute occurs only if the browser is not running on the web server. This is a good default configuration, since a developer testing on a web server probably would like to see the IIS-generated exception page rather than a customer-friendly error page. See Chapter 3 for more information about configuration files.

`Explicit`
: Specifies whether the page will be compiled with `Option Explicit` turned on. Allowed values are `"true"` and `"false"`. The default is `"true"`. See Chapter 2 for a discussion of this compiler option.

`Inherits`
: Specifies a class from which the compiled page class will inherit. The value can be the name of any accessible class that inherits from the Page class (defined in the System.Web.UI namespace). If this attribute is not specified, the compiled page class inherits directly from the Page class.

`Language`
: Specifies the programming language in which embedded code is written. This can be different from the language in which the page's code-behind class is written.

`LCID`
: Specifies the locale to be used by this page (LCID stands for *locale identifier*). The LCID is a four-byte unsigned integer that identifies the culture used when rendering the page. Specifying a value for LCID is an alternative to specifying a value for the `Culture` attribute. See Appendix C for a list of cultures and corresponding LCIDs.

`ResponseEncoding`
: Specifies the character-encoding format to use for the web page. The default is `"UTF-8"`.

`Src`

Specifies the name of a file containing the source for the page's code-behind class, if any. By default, web pages don't have a code-behind class.

`Strict`

Specifies whether the page will be compiled with `Option Strict` turned on. Allowed values are `"true"` and `"false"`. The default is `"false"`. See Chapter 2 for a discussion of this compiler option.

`Trace`

Specifies whether to enable tracing. Allowed values are `"true"` and `"false"`. The default is `"false"`.

`TraceMode`

When tracing is enabled, specifies how trace messages will be sorted. Allowed values are `"SortByCategory"` and `"SortByTime"`. The default is `"SortByTime"`.

`Transaction`

Specifies whether and how the page participates in transactions. Allowed values are `"NotSupported"`, `"Supported"`, `"Required"`, and `"RequiresNew"`. The default is `"NotSupported"`. Transaction processing is not discussed in this book.

`WarningLevel`

Specifies the warning level at which the compiler aborts compilation of the page. Allowed values are `"0"`, `"1"`,`"2"`, `"3"`, and`"4"`.

`@ Reference`

Provides a way to reference the data type for a control or page, which will be dynamically loaded from the current page using the Page class's LoadControl method. This directive's attributes are:

`Page`

The name of an *.aspx* file that defines a web page to be dynamically referenced from the current page.

`Control`

The name of an *.ascx* file that defines a web control to be dynamically referenced from the current page.

Only one attribute (either `Page` or `Control`) is allowed in a single `@ Reference` directive. To specify multiple pages or controls, specify multiple `@ Reference` directives on separate lines.

The `@ Reference` directive is useful if the page has code similar to this:

```
<script language="VB" runat="server">
   Protected Overrides Sub OnLoad(ByVal e As EventArgs)
      Dim ctl As Control
      ctl = LoadControl("SomeControl.ascx")
      Controls.Add(ctl)
```

```
    End Sub
</script>
```

This code loads a control from an *.ascx* file and adds it to the current page's collection of controls. This works just fine, but if this code needs to access properties and methods of the loaded control without resorting to late binding, it's in trouble. It has no way to convert the Control reference in `ctl` to the appropriate data type. This is where the `@ Reference` directive comes in. Referencing the *.ascx* file in an `@ Reference` directive makes the data type available to the source code on the rest of the page. Here's how it would look:

```
<%@ Reference Control="SomeControl.ascx" %>
<script language="VB" runat="server">
    Protected Overrides Sub OnLoad(ByVal e As EventArgs)
        Dim ctl As SomeControl
        ctl = CType(LoadControl("SomeControl.ascx"), SomeControl)
        ctl.SomeProperty = "SomeValue"
        Controls.Add(ctl)
    End Sub
</script>
```

`ctl` is now strongly typed, and the type SomeControl is available to the application code.

`@ Register`

Allows user controls and custom server controls to be added to a web page. It has two forms. The first form allows all the controls in an entire namespace to be referenced. It looks like this:

```
<%@ Register
    TagPrefix="tagprefix_name"
    Namespace="namespace_name"
    Assembly="assembly_name"
%>
```

When this format is used, you can use any of the controls within the referenced namespace on the web page by including a tag of this form:

```
<tagprefix_name:class_name runat="server" />
```

The second form of the `@ Register` directive registers a single control that resides in a source file. It looks like this:

```
<%@ Register
    TagPrefix="tagprefix_name"
    TagName="tagname"
    Src="path"
%>
```

When this format is used, you can use the specific control found in the source file on the web page by including a tag of this form:

```
<tagprefix_name:tagname runat="server" />
```

In either form, you can set properties of the control object by specifying the properties as attributes of the tag, like this:

```
<tagprefix_name:tagname MyPropertyName="some value" runat="server" />
```

See "Designing Custom Controls" later in this chapter for additional examples.

The attributes of the `@ Register` directive are:

`TagPrefix`
: A name that represents the namespace being referenced

`TagName`
: A name that represents the class being referenced

`Namespace`
: The namespace to reference

`Src`
: The source file containing the control

ASP.NET Objects: Interacting with the Framework

The ASP.NET framework exposes functionality to web applications through a number of so-called *intrinsic* objects. These objects are available through the Server, Application, Session, Cache, Request, and Response properties of the Page object. This section gives an overview of these objects.

The Server Object

The Server object is an instance of the HttpServerUtility class (defined in the System.Web namespace). This object provides information and services related to the web server. The HttpServerUtility class has two properties:

MachineName
: Gets the name of the machine on which the application is running. The type is String.

ScriptTimeout
: Gets or sets the web-request timeout in seconds. The type is Integer. The default is 90 seconds.

Some of the commonly used methods are:

ClearError
: Clears the last exception that occurred (see also GetLastError in this list). The syntax is:

```
Public Sub ClearError( )
```

Execute
: Executes a request to another page. After the other page is processed, processing of the current page continues. The Execute method has two overloads. The first is:

```
Public Overloads Sub Execute(ByVal path As String)
```

The *path* parameter specifies the path of the web page file to be executed. With this form of the Execute method, the output of the web page is intermingled with the output of the calling page.

The second overload is:

```
Public Overloads Sub Execute(ByVal path As String, _
   ByVal writer As System.IO.TextWriter)
```

Again, the *path* parameter specifies the path of the web page file to be executed. The *writer* parameter specifies an object of type TextWriter (defined in the System.IO namespace) that is to receive the output from the executed web page. (The TextWriter class is not documented in this book.)

GetLastError

Gets the last exception that was thrown (see also ClearError in this list). The syntax is:

```
Public Function GetLastError( ) As System.Exception
```

HtmlEncode and HtmlDecode

Encode and decode strings, respectively, that might contain HTML characters. Each method has two overrides: one that returns the encoded or decoded string as a String and one that writes the encoded or decoded string into an object of type TextWriter (defined in the System.IO namespace). (The TextWriter class is not documented in this book.) The syntax for these methods is:

```
Public Overloads Function HtmlEncode(ByVal s As String) As String
```

The *s* parameter is the string to encode. The return value of the function is the encoded string.

```
Public Overloads Sub HtmlEncode(ByVal s As String, _
   ByVal output As System.IO.TextWriter)
```

The *s* parameter is the string to encode. The encoded string is written to the TextWriter object passed in the *output* parameter.

```
Public Overloads Function HtmlDecode(ByVal s As String) As String
```

The *s* parameter is the string to decode. The return value of the function is the decoded string.

```
Public Overloads Sub HtmlDecode(ByVal s As String, _
   ByVal output As System.IO.TextWriter)
```

The *s* parameter is the string to decode. The decoded string is written to the TextWriter object passed in the *output* parameter.

MapPath

Returns the physical path that corresponds to the given virtual path. The syntax is:

```
Public Function MapPath(ByVal path As String) As String
```

Transfer

Stops execution of the current page and begins execution of the specified page. This method differs from the Redirect method of the Response object. The Redirect method directs the browser to request a new page, whereas the Transfer method simply starts executing a new page. The Transfer method has two overrides. The first is:

```
Public Overloads Sub Transfer(ByVal path As String)
```

The *path* parameter specifies the virtual path of the new page. The second override is:

```
Public Overloads Sub Transfer(ByVal path As String, _
   ByVal preserveForm As Boolean)
```

UrlEncode and UrlDecode

Encode and decode strings, respectively, so that they can be used within URLs. Each method has two overrides: one that returns the encoded or decoded string as a String and one that writes the encoded or decoded string into an object of type TextWriter (defined in the System.IO namespace). (The TextWriter class is not documented in this book.) The syntax for these methods is:

```
Public Overloads Function UrlEncode(ByVal s As String) As String
```

The *s* parameter is the string to encode. The return value of the function is the encoded string.

```
Public Overloads Sub UrlEncode(ByVal s As String, _
   ByVal output As System.IO.TextWriter)
```

The *s* parameter is the string to encode. The encoded string is written to the TextWriter object passed in the *output* parameter.

```
Public Overloads Function UrlDecode(ByVal s As String) As String
```

The *s* parameter is the string to decode. The return value of the function is the decoded string.

```
Public Overloads Sub UrlDecode(ByVal s As String, _
   ByVal output As System.IO.TextWriter)
```

The *s* parameter is the string to decode. The decoded string is written to the TextWriter object passed in the *output* parameter.

The Application Object

The Application object is an instance of the HttpApplicationState class (defined in the System.Web namespace). This object holds application state to be used by all web requests in an application. See "Maintaining State" later in this chapter for more information.

The Session Object

The Session object is an instance of the HttpSessionState class (defined in the System.Web.SessionState namespace). This object holds application state that is specific to the current web request's session. See "Maintaining State" later in this chapter for more information.

The Cache Object

The Cache object is an instance of the Cache class (defined in the System.Web.Caching namespace). This object caches dynamically created objects on the server, thereby improving average performance for the web site's users. Caching is not discussed further in this book.

The Request Object

The Request object is an instance of the HttpRequest class (defined in the System.Web namespace). This object provides information and services related to the current web request. These are the commonly used properties of the HttpRequest class:

ApplicationPath
: The virtual path of the root folder of the application. This is a read-only property. The type is String.

Browser
: Information about the capabilities of the client browser. This is a read-only property. The type is HttpBrowserCapabilities (defined in the System.Web namespace). The properties of the HttpBrowserCapabilities type are listed later in this chapter under "Discovering Browser Capabilities."

Cookies
: The collection of client-side cookies sent by the browser. This is a read-only property. The type is HttpCookieCollection (defined in the System.Web namespace). See the discussion of cookies later in this chapter under "Maintaining State."

FilePath
: The virtual path of the current request. The type is String.

IsAuthenticated
: An indication of whether the user has been authenticated. The type is Boolean.

IsSecureConnection
: An indication of whether the current request is over a secure (HTTPS) connection.

The Response Object

The Response object is an instance of the HttpResponse class (defined in the System.Web namespace). This object provides information and services related to the response that results from the current web request. These are the commonly used properties of the Response object:

BufferOutput
: An indication of whether output will be buffered while being generated. The type is Boolean. When this property is `False`, output is sent to the client as it is generated. When it is `True` (its default value), output is buffered until it has been completely generated, then it is sent to the client. If a particular page request requires a lot of processing, but portions of the page become available throughout that processing, it is beneficial to set this property to `False` so that the client gets at least some output as soon as possible. On the other hand, the benefit to setting this property to `True` is that the output can be stopped or changed, or the page can be redirected, in the middle of page processing without sending spurious output to the client.

Cache
: The caching policy of a web page. The type is HttpCachePolicy (defined in the System.Web namespace). Caching is not discussed in this book.

Charset
: The character set used in the output stream. The type is String. The default is `"utf-8"`.

ContentEncoding
: The character encoding used in the output stream. The type is Encoding (defined in the System.Text namespace). The default is an instance of the UTF8Encoding class (defined in the System.Text namespace).

ContentType
: The MIME content type of the output stream. The type is String. The default is `"text/html"`.

Cookies
: A collection of HttpCookie objects representing cookies to be transmitted to the client browser. The type is HttpCookieCollection (defined in the System.Web namespace). See the discussion of cookies later in this chapter under "Maintaining State."

Expires
: The number of minutes for which the client browser should cache the web page output. The type is Integer. The default is `0`.

ExpiresAbsolute
: The date and time until which the client browser should cache the web page output. The type is Date. The default is `DateTime.MinValue`.

Status
: The HTTP status text to be returned to the client browser. The type is String. The default is `"200 OK"`.

StatusCode
: The HTTP status code to be returned to the client browser. The type is Integer. The default is `200`.

StatusDescription
: The HTTP status description to be returned to the client browser. The type is String. The default is "OK".

These are some commonly used methods of the HttpResponse class:

Redirect
: Sends a redirect message to the client browser. Client browsers respond by requesting the web page specified in the redirect message. The syntax is:

```
Public Sub Redirect(ByVal url As String)
```

The *url* parameter specifies the address of the new page to be requested.

Write
: Writes a value directly to the output stream. This method is useful within script blocks that are embedded on the web page. There are versions of this method that write a single character, an array of characters, an object, and a string. The syntax for the version that writes a string is:

```
Public Overloads Sub Write(ByVal s As String)
```

Discovering Browser Capabilities

One of ASP.NET's strengths is that it accommodates differences in client browsers without requiring any special effort from the application developer. However, it is often desirable for a web application to discover the capabilities of the browser making a given request. For this purpose, ASP.NET makes browser information available to the web application. ASP.NET's Request object (available through the Page object's Request property) has a Browser property that returns an object of type HttpBrowserCapabilities. The properties of this object are:

ActiveXControls
: Indicates whether the client browser supports ActiveX controls. The type is Boolean.

AOL
: Indicates whether the client browser is an America Online browser. The type is Boolean.

BackgroundSounds
: Indicates whether the client browser supports background sounds. The type is Boolean.

Beta
: Indicates whether the client browser is a beta release. The type is Boolean.

Browser
: Indicates the browser string (e.g., "IE") received in the User-Agent header of the HTTP request. The type is String.

CDF
: Indicates whether the browser supports Channel Definition Format for webcasting. The type is Boolean.

ClrVersion
: Indicates the version of the .NET CLR installed on the client (if any). The type is Version (defined in the System namespace).

Cookies
: Indicates whether the client browser supports cookies. The type is Boolean.

Crawler
: Indicates whether the client browser is a web crawler (an automated program used by online search engines to discover web content). The type is Boolean.

EcmaScriptVersion
: Indicates the version of ECMA Script that the client browser supports. The type is Version (defined in the System namespace).

Frames
: Indicates whether the client browser supports Frames. The type is Boolean.

JavaApplets
: Indicates whether the client browser supports Java applets. The type is Boolean.

JavaScript
: Indicates whether the client browser supports JavaScript. The type is Boolean.

MajorVersion
: Indicates the major version number of the client browser. The type is Integer.

MinorVersion
: Indicates the minor version number of the client browser. The type is Double. For example, if the version of the client browser is 8.15, the value of the MinorVersion property is `0.15`.

MSDomVersion
: Indicates the version of the Microsoft XML document object model that the client browser supports. The type is Version (defined in the System namespace).

Platform
: Indicates the platform on which the client browser is running. The type is String. For example, for a browser running on Windows 2000 Professional, the Platform property returns `"WinNT"`.

Tables
: Indicates whether the client browser supports HTML tables. The type is Boolean.

Type
: Indicates the name and major version number of the client browser (e.g., `"IE6"`). The type is String.

VBScript
Indicates whether the client browser supports VBScript. The type is Boolean.

Version
Indicates the full version number of the client browser (e.g., `"8.15"`). The type is String.

W3CDomVersion
Indicates the version of the W3C XML document object model that the client browser supports. The type is Version (defined in the System namespace).

Win16
Indicates whether the client browser is running on a 16-bit Windows operating system. The type is Boolean.

Win32
Indicates whether the client browser is running on a 32-bit Windows operating system. The type is Boolean.

Maintaining State

The process of serving web pages is inherently stateless. By default, each request to a web server is isolated from every other request that a user might make. This is a fine model for serving static web pages, but it's not very useful for full-featured applications. To be useful, applications must keep track of state. This section describes the different options that web developers have for storing state.

The Session Object

When a user browses to a web page served by IIS, IIS considers it the start of a *session* for that user. A session is an abstract concept that refers to the period of time within which a particular user is interacting with a web application. Although it's easy to determine when a session starts, it's not so easy to know when that session ends. This is because of the inherent disconnectedness of web browsing. After any given web request is serviced, IIS doesn't really know whether the user will issue more requests (browse to more pages). For this reason, IIS establishes a session time-out period. If no new requests are received from a user after a given amount of time, IIS considers that session to have ended.

A session corresponds to a single use of a web application by a single user. To assist the web application in maintaining state for the duration of a session, ASP.NET provides an intrinsic object called the Session object. When a session begins, ASP.NET instantiates a Session object. During processing of web requests, the application can store information into the Session object in name/value pairs. Later requests received during the same session can read the information stored in the Session object. The Session object is of type HttpSessionState (defined in the System.Web.SessionState namespace) and is available through the Page class's Session property. Here is an example of saving information into a session object:

```
Session("FirstName") = txtFirstName.Text
```

For example, this code could be run in response to the user clicking a Submit button on a form. The code assumes that the page has a text box named txtFirstName, in which the user has presumably typed a name. The value thus saved is available (until the session ends) to all subsequent web requests by the same user. For example, a subsequent page could use this value to personalize a message, like this:

```
Response.Write("Hello, " & Session("FirstName") & ", welcome to ASP.NET!")
```

The commonly used properties of the HttpSessionState class are:

Count
: The number of items stored in the Session object. The type is Integer.

IsNewSession
: An indication of whether the current request created the session. The type is Boolean.

Keys
: A collection of all *keys* used in the Session object. A key is the name of the data being stored in the Session object, as opposed to the value of that data. For example, in the following line of code, the key is `"FirstName"`:

```
Session("FirstName") = txtFirstName.Text
```

The following code fragment loops through all the keys in the Session object:

```
Dim str As String
For Each str In Session.Keys
   ' ...
Next
```

The type of the Keys property is KeysCollection (defined within the Name-ObjectCollectionBase class in the System.Collections.Specialized namespace).

StaticObjects
: A collection of objects declared with the `<object scope="Session">` tag in the application's *global.asax* file. The type is HttpStaticObjectsCollection (defined in the System.Web namespace). See "Application-Level Code and global.asax," later in this chapter.

Timeout
: The session timeout, in minutes. If a new request isn't received in this amount of time, the session ends. The type is Integer. The default is `20`.

Some commonly used methods of the HttpSessionState class are:

Abandon
: Ends the current session. The syntax is:

```
Public Sub Abandon()
```

Clear

Clears all values from the Session object. The syntax is:

```
Public Sub Clear( )
```

Remove

Clears a single item from the Session object. The syntax is:

```
Public Sub Remove(ByVal name As String)
```

The Application Object

Some state should be maintained at the application level rather than at the session level, meaning that the state information is available to all sessions in the application. This is what the Application object is for. It is used just like the Session object, except that values stored in the Application object are visible to all sessions in the application. The Application object is instantiated when the first session begins, and it ends when no more sessions exist.

Be careful when writing new values to the Application object. Because a single Application object is shared by all concurrent sessions (which may be running on separate threads in IIS), threading-concurrency issues come into play. For example, consider an application in which each session stores its user's name into an array that is stored in the Application object. The application might use this information to display a summary screen of all users currently active in the application. Simplistic code to accomplish this task might look like this:

```
' Wrong!
Dim names As ArrayList = Application("Names")
If names Is Nothing Then
   names = New ArrayList( )
   Application("Names") = names
End If
names.Add(txtName.Text)
```

Again, this code might be executed in response to a button-click event in which the user submits some information collected on a form. It assumes that there is a text box named txtName on the form. The information thus collected can be used by any session in the application. Note that all sessions in the application add their data to the same array list. A simple page to view this information might look like this:

```
<%@ Page AutoEventWireup="false" Language="VB" Debug="true" %>

<script runat="server">

   Protected Overrides Sub OnLoad(e As EventArgs)
      lstNames.DataSource = Application("Names")
      lstNames.DataBind( )
   End Sub

</script>

<html>
```

```
    <body>
        Currently active users:<br>
        <asp:ListBox id="lstNames" runat="server" />
    </body>
</html>
```

Here the code is loading a ListBox control with the contents of the array list saved in the Application object. (Data binding is explained in Chapter 8.)

There's nothing conceptually wrong with this approach, but the code that saves the information needs a little more attention. The problem is that two separate requests in the same application, but in different sessions, could attempt to modify the array list at the same time. The array list is not thread-safe, so problems could ensue, possibly resulting in lost data or application exceptions. To resolve this issue, wrap the code that sets the values in calls to the Application object's Lock and UnLock methods, like this:

```
Application.Lock( )
Dim names As ArrayList = Application("Names")
If names Is Nothing Then
   names = New ArrayList( )
   Application("Names") = names
End If
names.Add(txtName.Text)
names = Nothing
Application.UnLock
```

During the time after the Lock method has been called but before the UnLock method has been called, if code on another thread calls the Lock method, that thread will block (temporarily cease to run) until the code on the first thread calls the UnLock method. This ensures that two threads aren't accessing the array list at the same time. The downside to this is that performance is hurt if multiple threads are blocked waiting for access to the same application data. This makes it imperative to call UnLock as soon as possible and not to forget to call it.

The Application object is an instance of the HttpApplicationState class (defined in the System.Web namespace). Commonly used properties of the HttpApplicationState class are:

AllKeys

An array of all keys used in the Application object. A key is the name of the data being stored in the Application object, as opposed to the value of that data. For example, in the following line of code, the session key is `"Names"`:

```
Application("Names") = names
```

The following code fragment loops through all the keys in the Application object:

```
For Each str In Application.AllKeys
   ' ...
Next
```

The type of the AllKeys property is String Array.

Count
The number of items stored in the Application object. The type is Integer.

StaticObjects
A collection of objects declared with the `<object scope="Application">` tag in the application's *global.asax* file. The type is HttpStaticObjectsCollection (defined in the System.Web namespace). See "Application-Level Code and global.asax" later in this chapter.

The commonly used methods of the HttpApplicationState class are:

Clear
Clears all values from the Application object. The syntax is:

```
Public Sub Clear( )
```

Lock
As explained earlier, prohibits code in other sessions from writing to the Application object until UnLock is called. The syntax is:

```
Public Sub Lock( )
```

Remove
Clears a single item from the Application object. The syntax is:

```
Public Sub Remove(ByVal name As String)
```

UnLock
Unlocks the Application object after a call to Lock. The syntax is:

```
Public Sub UnLock( )
```

Cookies

Another way to save information between web page requests is to save it on the client in a *cookie*. A cookie is a name/value pair that the browser saves on behalf of the application. Cookies are keyed to the domain of the application that created them. When the browser requests a page, it automatically transmits the cookies that belong to that domain as part of the page request. The application can then read the values of the cookies and take appropriate action. Cookies are an industry standard and should work with any browser. However, be aware that users can turn off cookies in their browser settings, so an application that relies on cookies may not be accessible to all users.

Cookies generally are used in two ways. One is to save some sort of identifying information about the user, so that when the user returns to a given site, the application knows who the user is. The other way is to save some sort of information indicating the application's state between web page requests within a single session. This allows the application to recover its state on each page request. Although any information can be saved in a cookie, the best practice is to use some sort of key to look up the actual information on the server side. This practice minimizes traffic to and from the client, helps to ensure that potentially sensitive information is not stored on the client, and helps to ensure that the client can't spoof the server by substituting incorrect information in the cookies.

Cookies are created by adding items to the Cookies collection of the ASP.NET Response object (available through the Response property of the Page class). For example:

```
Dim cookie As New HttpCookie("MyCookieName", "MyCookieValue")
Response.Cookies.Add(cookie)
```

That's all it takes. The ASP.NET framework copies the information into the HTTP response to the client browser. The browser then stores the information on the client computer in a way that is determined by the type of browser being used.

The constructor of the HttpCookie class has two versions. The one shown earlier takes two strings: the first is the name of the cookie, and the second is its value. The other version of the HttpCookie class constructor takes a single parameter: a string that is the name of the cookie. The value of the cookie is then set by assigning a value to the HttpCookie object's Value or Values property (discussed in the following list). The properties of the HttpCookie class are:

Domain
: Represents the domain associated with the cookie. The default value is the domain of the web page request being serviced. If the web server is *//localhost*, the default value of this property is `Nothing`. The type is String.

Expires
: Represents the date and time at which the cookie expires. The default is `DateTime.MinValue`, which results in a cookie that doesn't expire. The type is Date.

HasKeys
: Indicates whether the cookie has *subkeys*. Subkeys permit a cookie to have more than one value. See also the Values property. The default is `False`. The type is Boolean.

Item
: Provides a way to access the values of subkeys for cookies with subkeys. The Item property is an indexed property that takes the subkey name as the index and returns its value. This property is provided for syntactic similarity with classic ASP. New code should instead use the Values collection to access the values of subkeys.

Name
: Represents the name of the cookie, as given in the HttpCookie class constructor. The type is String.

Path
: Represents the path associated with the cookie. The default is `"/"`. The type is String.

Secure
: Indicates whether the cookie should be transmitted only over a secure (HTTPS) connection. The default is `False`. The type is Boolean.

Value
: Represents the value of the cookie. The default is an empty string. The type is String.

Values
: If the cookie has subkeys, the Values property is an instance of NameValuesCollection (defined in the System.Collections.Specialized namespace). This collection holds the subkey name/value pairs.

On subsequent requests, the cookies are available for reading from the Cookies collection of the ASP.NET Request object (available through the Request property of the Page class). For example:

```
Dim cookie As HttpCookie = Request.Cookies("MyCookie")
Label1.Text = cookie.Value
```

Application-Level Code and global.asax

All of the code shown so far has been written at the page level, appearing either in an *.aspx* file or in a code-behind file that implements a Page-derived class. However, there needs to be a way to handle events and manipulate properties at the application level as well, without regard to any particular page. For this purpose there is the *global.asax* file. *global.asax* is a file that optionally can appear in a web application's root directory. If it is present, it can contain code and settings that are automatically processed by the ASP.NET framework at the appropriate times.

Session and Application Startup and Shutdown

Some applications may need to run certain code whenever a new session is started or is about to end, or when the application as a whole is first started or is about to end. This is done by placing code in the application's *global.asax* file, as shown in Example 6-9.

Example 6-9. Responding to session and application start and end in a global.asax file

```
<script language="vb" runat="server">

   Public Sub Session_OnStart( )
      ' ...
   End Sub

   Public Sub Session_OnEnd( )
      ' ...
   End Sub
```

Example 6-9. Responding to session and application start and end in a global.asax file (continued)

```
   Public Sub Application_OnStart( )
      ' ...
   End Sub

   Public Sub Application_OnEnd( )
      ' ...
   End Sub

</script>
```

Notice that code is placed in `<script>` blocks.

The code in Example 6-9 defines four subroutines:

Session_OnStart
: Called by the ASP.NET framework when a session starts

Session_OnEnd
: Called by the ASP.NET framework when a session ends

Application_OnStart
: Called by the ASP.NET framework when an application starts (that is, when the application's first session starts)

Application_OnEnd
: Called by the ASP.NET framework when an application ends (that is, when the application's last remaining session ends)

These four subroutines aren't event handlers—they are simply subroutines that are automatically executed when present. They are typically used to set up and dispose of information needed at the session or application level. For example, an online shopping application could use the Application_OnStart subroutine to read popular product information from a database and cache it in the Application object, thereby improving performance for users of the application.

global.asax Compiles to a Class

The first time an application is accessed, its *global.asax* file is compiled into a class that inherits from the HttpApplication class (defined in the System.Web namespace). The subroutines declared in *global.asax* become methods of the compiled class. Although the members of the HttpApplication class are not discussed further in this book, be aware that, if desired, those members can be accessed by code in *global.asax*. In addition, events exposed by the HttpApplication class can be handled by adding event handlers to *global.asax*. Each event handler must have the right signature, as defined by that event's documentation and a `Handles MyBase.`*`EventName`* clause to register the handler with the event. Again, the events exposed by the HttpApplication class aren't discussed further in this book. However, in case you would like to pursue it on your own, Example 6-10 shows how such an event handler can be declared in *global.asax*.

Example 6-10. Handling an HttpApplication class event in global.asax

```
<script language="vb" runat="server">

   ' ...

   ' Handle the base class's BeginRequest event. The name of the
   ' event handler is not important, but the signature and the
   ' Handles clause are.
   Private Sub HttpApplication_BeginRequest( _
      ByVal sender As Object, _
      ByVal e As EventArgs _
   ) Handles MyBase.BeginRequest
      ' ...
   End Sub

</script>
```

Adding Global Objects

An application often needs to instantiate an object and make it available to all pages within a session or within the entire application. One way to do this is by instantiating the object in the Session_OnStart or Application_OnStart methods and saving the object reference in the ASP.NET Session or Application object, respectively. Pages can then read the object reference from the Session or Application object and use it as needed.

A slightly more convenient way to achieve a similar result is to place an `<object>` element in the *global.asax* file. The `<object>` element indicates that an instance of the given class should be created and made available to all pages in the session or application (depending on the attributes specified). ASP.NET makes the object available to all pages in the application by adding a property to every page in the application. The property is named identically to the `ID` attribute of the `<object>` element. For example, here is an `<object>` element that creates a Hashtable object that is available application-wide:

```
<object
   id="myHashtable"
   runat="server"
   scope="Application"
   class="System.Collections.Hashtable" />
```

This declaration specifies the following:

- An instance of the Hashtable class (defined in the System.Collection namespace) will be created (`class="System.Collections.Hashtable"`).
- This single instance of the Hashtable class will be shared by all pages in the application (`scope="Application"`). If there is to be a separate instance for each session, specify `scope="Session"`.

- A property named myHashtable will be added to every page in the application to permit web page code easy access to the object (`id="myHashtable"`).

Code to access the object instance from a web page would look like this:

```
<%@ Page Language="vb" %>

<script runat="server">
   Protected Overrides Sub OnLoad(ByVal e As EventArgs)
      ' Do something with the object created in global.asax.
      myHashtable.Add("SomeKey", "SomeValue")
   End Sub
</script>

' ...
```

The property that is automatically compiled into the page (in this case, the myHashtable property) is compiled into the class that is compiled from the *.aspx* file. It is not compiled into the page's code-behind class (if there is one). This means that the property is available to code that is embedded in the *.aspx* file, but not to code in the code-behind class.

All objects created as a result of `<object>` elements appearing in *global.asax* are added to the StaticObjects collection of either the Session object or the Application object (depending on the value specified for the `scope` attribute of the `<object>` element). For example, the myHashtable object could be accessed in this way:

```
<%@ Page Language="vb" %>

<script runat="server">
   Protected Overrides Sub OnLoad(ByVal e As EventArgs)
      ' Do something with the object created in global.asax.
      Dim ht As Hashtable
      ht = CType(Application.StaticObjects("myHashTable"), Hashtable)
      ht.Add("foo", "bar")
   End Sub
</script>

' ...
```

This has the advantage of also working from the code-behind class, or from any code that has access to the ASP.NET Application (or Session) object.

Web-Application Security

Many web applications have portions that should be viewed or used only by certain users. In such applications, users must somehow identify themselves to the application so that the application can then determine what the users may access. In security terminology, the process of identifying the user is known as *authentication*. After authentication occurs, the system must determine whether the given user is permitted to access the requested resource. This is called *authorization*. The part of the application to be protected is known as a *protected resource*.

Authentication

Authentication is the process by which a web application reliably discovers the identity of an application user. The purpose of discovering the user's identity is to determine whether the user is authorized to access a given resource. Depending on the application, the accuracy of this process may be critical. An online-banking application, for example, must be quite sure that the user who claims to be you really is you before it allows the user to transfer all of your money to a bank in Bora-Bora. There are different ways that this can be done, depending on the type of application being written and on the level of protection required.

ASP.NET supports several authentication mechanisms:

Forms authentication
: Allows the developer to design a login form that is presented to the user when she attempts to access a protected resource. If the user successfully logs in, the browser is directed back to the resource that she was attempting to access. This is a good general-purpose solution for most Internet applications.

Windows authentication
: Allows IIS and the Windows operating system to authenticate the user. Windows authentication can include any one or more of the following authentication types: Basic, Digest, or Integrated Windows.

Passport authentication
: Allows ASP.NET applications to use Microsoft's Passport service to authenticate users. Doing so requires paying a fee and signing up with the service. This method of authentication is not discussed further in this book.

All of the authentication mechanisms (except for Integrated Windows authentication) can be compromised to varying degrees by a hostile person using a network "sniffer" to eavesdrop on network traffic. Therefore, these mechanisms should always be combined with the use of Secure Sockets Layer (SSL) or another type of message encryption. SSL is a web standard that is not specifically related to .NET, and it is not covered in this book.

Using a secure connection, such as SSL, is especially important when using Forms or Basic authentication, as these mechanisms send sensitive information over the network in clear text. Digest authentication doesn't send passwords in clear text, but it is still sensitive to various attacks when not used in conjunction with other security techniques.

In the following sections, we'll examine each of these methods of authentication in greater detail.

Forms authentication

With Forms authentication, requests for protected resources by users who have not yet been authenticated are redirected to a login page. The application developer creates the login page, so the page can have any appearance and perform any logic that is appropriate to the application. Usually, the login page has fields for the user to enter a username and password, as well as logic to check the username and password against a list. After the login page is satisfied, the user is redirected to the original resource. Example 6-11 shows how a login page might be coded.

Example 6-11. A login page

```
<%@ Page Language="vb" AutoEventWireup="False" Explicit="True" Strict="True" %>
<%@ Import Namespace="System.Web.Security" %>

<script runat="server">

   Private Sub signIn_Click(ByVal sender As Object, e As EventArgs)
      If ((username.Text = "SomeUsername") And _
         (password.Text = "SomePassword")) Then
         FormsAuthentication.RedirectFromLoginPage(username.Text, _
            Not autoSignOut.Checked)
      Else
         msg.Text = "Your sign-in information appears to be incorrect." _
            & " Please try again."
      End If
   End Sub

</script>

<html>

   <body>

      <form runat="server">

         </p>Please sign in.</p>

         <p>
            Username:
            <asp:TextBox ID="username" runat="server" /><br>
            Password:
            <asp:TextBox ID="password" TextMode="Password"
               runat="server" /><br>
            <asp:CheckBox ID="autoSignOut"
               Text="Sign me out automatically when I close my browser."
               runat="server" />
         </p>

         <p>
            <asp:Button ID="signIn" Text="Sign In" OnClick="signIn_Click"
               runat="server" />
         </p>
```

Example 6-11. A login page (continued)

```
         <p>
            <asp:Label ID="msg" ForeColor="red" runat="server" />
         </p>

      </form>

   </body>

</html>
```

This is a simple form that asks for a username and password and provides a Sign In button for submitting the information. When the button is clicked, the signIn_Click method is run. At this point, the code must determine whether a valid username and password have been entered. For this demonstration, the code simply checks whether the username SomeUsername and the password SomePassword were entered. A real-world production application would probably look up the username and password in a database. The Forms authentication mechanism doesn't know or care how the user is authenticated and, in fact, doesn't even care if it's done with a username/password scheme.

It's up to the login form to decide what to do if the user doesn't enter correct information. In Example 6-11, the login form simply displays a message and encourages the user to try again. A real-world application might limit the number of tries, might offer to create a new login ID, or might offer to email the user's password to him. Again, it is up to the application designer to decide what is best for the given application.

If the login form determines that the user has entered correct information, it calls the RedirectFromLoginPage method of the FormsAuthentication class (defined in the System.Web.Security namespace). Calling this method redirects the user to the protected resource that was originally requested. The RedirectFromLoginPage method has a couple of overloads. The syntax of the overload used in Example 6-11 is:

```
Public Overloads Shared Sub RedirectFromLoginPage( _
   ByVal userName As String, _
   ByVal createPersistentCookie As Boolean)
```

The parameters are:

userName
: This is a name by which the user is identified by the rest of the application. If the login form collects the username from the user (as Example 6-11 does), that username can be used here. If the login form uses some other information to identify the user, the application designer should determine what username value makes the most sense to use.

createPersistentCookie

As part of the Forms authentication mechanism, a cookie is created and sent to the client computer. The *createPersistentCookie* parameter determines whether that cookie persists across invocations of the browser. If this parameter is set to False, closing the browser window results in the cookie being lost. If the user opens another browser window and attempts to access a protected resource, he will be redirected again to the login page. If the *createPersistentCookie* parameter is set to True, the user can close the browser and open a new one without being required to reauthenticate.

After the login page is developed, an entry must be made in the web application's *web.config* file to indicate that Forms authentication will be used for authentication. Modify the <authentication> element in the application's *web.config* file. This element is a subelement of the <system.web> element, which in turn is a subelement of the <configuration> element. Example 6-12 shows how it should look.

Example 6-12. Setting Forms authentication

```
<?xml version="1.0" encoding="utf-8" ?>
<configuration>
  <system.web>
    <authentication mode="Forms">
      <forms loginUrl="SignIn.aspx" name="myWebApplication" />
    </authentication>
    <authorization>
       <deny users="?" />
    </authorization>
  </system.web>
</configuration>
```

The mode attribute of the <authentication> element controls the kind of authentication to be performed. For Forms authentication, set this to "Forms". When using Forms authentication, the <forms> element must also be present. The loginUrl attribute of this element gives the relative URL of the login page. The name attribute gives the name to use for the cookie that is transmitted to the browser. The default value of the name attribute is ".ASPXAUTH". The <forms> element also allows a path attribute. This attribute specifies the URL path for which the cookie is valid. The default value of the path attribute is "/".

In IIS, the web site should be configured to allow anonymous access. This keeps IIS from attempting to authenticate the user and allows the ASP.NET runtime to handle the authentication. Note also the <authorization> element in Example 6-12:

```
<authorization>
   <deny users="?" />
</authorization>
```

Authentication won't occur unless the user attempts to access a protected resource. If all resources on the site allow anonymous access, there is no reason to attempt to authenticate the user. This simple <authorization> element denies access to all anonymous users, thereby triggering the authentication process. The <authorization> element is further explained later in this section.

Example 6-13 shows a sample web page that might be protected by Forms authentication. There is nothing special about the page—the implementation of Forms authentication is handled by ASP.NET and the developer-supplied login page. However, the page in Example 6-13 shows the name of the authenticated user, demonstrating that authentication has indeed occurred. Figure 6-14 shows the login page from Example 6-11 as it appears in a browser, and Figure 6-15 shows the page from Example 6-13.

Example 6-13. A sample web page that expects authentication

```
<%@ Page Language="vb" AutoEventWireup="False" Explicit="True" Strict="True" %>

<script runat="server">

   Protected Overrides Sub OnLoad(ByVal e As EventArgs)
      MyBase.OnLoad(e)
      msg.Text = "Hello, " & Me.User.Identity.Name & "!"
   End Sub

   Private Sub signOut_Click(ByVal sender As Object, ByVal e As EventArgs)
      FormsAuthentication.SignOut( )
      Response.Redirect("SignIn.aspx")
   End Sub

</script>

<html>
   <head>
      <title>Authentication Test</title>
   </head>

   <body>
      <form runat="server">
         <h1>Authentication Test</h1>
         <p>
            <asp:Label ID="msg" runat="server" />
         </p>
         <p>
            <asp:Button ID="signOut" Text="Sign Out"
               OnClick="signOut_Click" runat="server" />
         </p>
      </form>
   </body>

</html>
```

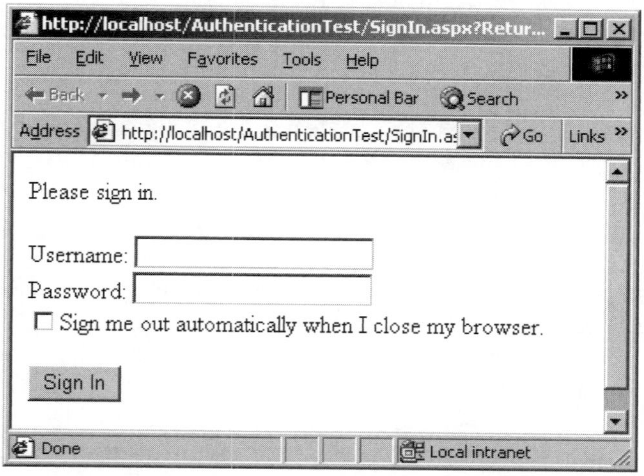

Figure 6-14. The browser display produced by Example 6-11

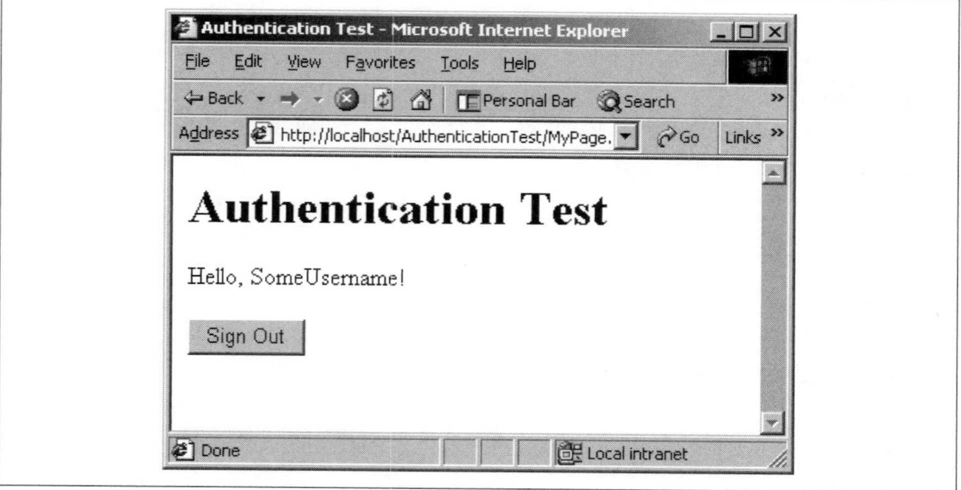

Figure 6-15. The browser display produced by Example 6-13, after authentication has occurred

Windows authentication

With Windows authentication, the ASP.NET runtime lets IIS and the Windows operating system handle user authentication. Three kinds of authentication come under this category: Integrated Windows authentication, Digest authentication, and Basic authentication. To use one of these authentication methods, the web site in IIS must be set to disallow anonymous access, and one or more of these three authentication mechanisms must be enabled. If more than one is enabled, the most secure browser-supported method will be used in any given session.

Integrated Windows authentication. This is the most secure of the three methods of Windows authentication, but it works only when the browser is Internet Explorer (IE) and only when the user is logged into a Windows system on a domain accessible and trusted by the web server. When the user attempts to access protected resources, the server requests the user's identity from the client. The client uses the operating system's built-in network-authentication mechanisms to communicate the user's identity reliably and securely to the server. This all happens automatically—no intervention from the user is needed. This is a good option for corporate intranets.

Digest authentication. This is an industry-standard mechanism that should work with non-IE browsers. When the user tries to access a protected resource, the server asks the client for the user's identity. The browser pops up a dialog box asking for a username and password. The username and a hash of the password are sent to the server, which then tries to verify that the username and password identify a valid login account. Although this mechanism doesn't send the password in clear text, it is not considered to be a strong security mechanism. Someone eavesdropping on the client/server communication can use the gathered information to attack the system in various ways.

Basic authentication. This is another industry-standard mechanism. It works the same as Digest authentication, except that passwords are sent in clear text over the network.

In the web application's *web.config* file, the `<authentication>` element is used to indicate that Windows authentication should be used. Example 6-14 shows how.

Example 6-14. Setting Windows authentication

```
<?xml version="1.0" encoding="utf-8" ?>
<configuration>
  <system.web>
    <authentication mode="Windows" />
    <authorization>
       <deny users="?" />
    </authorization>
  </system.web>
</configuration>
```

Understanding authentication

Choosing an authentication mechanism is something that must be done at the site level. Therefore, only the *web.config* file in the application's root directory should have an `<authentication>` element.

Setting an authentication mechanism does not in itself protect resources. The authentication mechanism simply determines how a user's identity will be determined if that user attempts to access protected resources. If no resources are protected, the authentication mechanism won't be activated. Determining whether resources are protected is what authorization is all about.

Authorization

Authorization involves determining whether the authenticated user is authorized to view a given web page or to execute some given code. As with authentication, page-access authorization can be handled either by ASP.NET or by the Windows operating system. Code-access authorization is handled by checks that the application developer writes into the application.

ASP.NET authorization

Access to web pages and other files is controlled by the <authorization> element in the application's *web.config* file. The settings affect all files in the virtual directory that contains the *web.config* file and all of its virtual subdirectories, unless it is overridden by a setting in a *web.config* file in a virtual subdirectory. Therefore, if web pages or other files are to have different accessibility rules, they must appear in different directories and there must be different *web.config* files in each directory.

In this section's examples, the <authentication> element isn't shown. It is assumed that the appropriate <authentication> element appears in the root directory's *web.config* file, as discussed in the previous section.

An example <authorization> element is shown here:

```
<?xml version="1.0" encoding="utf-8" ?>
<configuration>
   <system.web>
      <authorization>
         <allow users="*" />
      </authorization>
   </system.web>
</configuration>
```

This <authorization> element indicates that all users (including anonymous users) are permitted to access all resources. This setting applies to resources in the same directory in which the *web.config* file appears, plus resources in all the subdirectories of that directory (except for any subdirectory that contains its own *web.config* file with overriding entries).

Authorization to resources is specified with <allow> and <deny> elements, which appear within the <authorization> element. Attributes of the elements specify who is being allowed or denied access. The value of the users attribute is one or more usernames, separated by commas. For example, these are all valid <allow> elements:

```
<allow users="*" />
<allow users="SomeUsername, SomeOtherUsername" />
```

```
<allow users="SOME-DOMAIN\SomeUser" />
<allow users="?" />
```

Note the following:

- `"*"` signifies all users (including anonymous users). If this is the only setting that appears, authentication won't occur. The system already knows that access will be granted, so it won't take the trouble to determine who the user is.
- `"?"` specifically signifies anonymous users.
- If Windows authentication is used, the username should include the domain name, like this: `"DOMAIN-NAME\username"`.
- If Forms authentication is used, the username should match the name that was supplied to the first argument of the RedirectFromLoginPage method of the FormsAuthentication class (defined in the System.Web.Security namespace). This method was discussed in the previous section.

Users can be explicitly denied access if they are named in a `<deny>` element. The usage is the same as the `<allow>` element.

When multiple `<allow>` and `<deny>` elements appear in a configuration file, they are examined by ASP.NET in the order in which they appear. As soon as ASP.NET finds an element that can be applied to the current user, the examination halts, and access is either allowed or denied, depending on the element that was found. Consider this *web.config* file:

```
<?xml version="1.0" encoding="utf-8" ?>
<configuration>
   <system.web>
      <authorization>
         <allow users="*" />
         <deny users="daveg" />
      </authorization>
   </system.web>
</configuration>
```

Although the author of this configuration file probably intended that user daveg be denied access, ASP.NET doesn't see it that way. The first entry in the `<authorization>` section grants access to all users, including daveg, so the second entry isn't even seen. To achieve the desired effect, reverse the entries:

```
<?xml version="1.0" encoding="utf-8" ?>
<configuration>
   <system.web>
      <authorization>
         <deny users="daveg" />
         <allow users="*" />
      </authorization>
   </system.web>
</configuration>
```

In this case, when daveg attempts to access resources in a directory protected by this configuration file, ASP.NET will note that the first entry can be applied to daveg and will apply it. The second entry isn't seen. When other users attempt to access the same resources, ASP.NET notes that the first entry can't be applied to them and continues looking. The second entry then allows access to all other users.

The following <authorization> section allows access to authenticated users, regardless of who they are. Anonymous users are denied access.

```
<?xml version="1.0" encoding="utf-8" ?>
<configuration>
   <system.web>
      <authorization>
         <deny users="?" />
         <allow users="*" />
      </authorization>
   </system.web>
</configuration>
```

When nested directories each contain their own *web.config* files, the <authorization> element in the current directory's *web.config* file is examined first. If no entries explicitly grant or deny access to the current user, the *web.config* file in the parent directory is examined, and so on, up to the computer's *machine.config* file. As soon as an entry is found that explicitly allows or denies access, this examination stops. By default, the *machine.config* file's <authorization> section contains the entry:

```
<allow users="*" />
```

Thus, if there is no explicit <deny> entry at a lower level, all users are granted access.

In addition to specifying authorization based on username, it is also possible to specify authorization based on role membership. Thus, a business application could define certain roles, such as "Customer Service Rep," "Accounting Specialist," "Auditor," etc., and specifty authorization for the roles rather than for individual users. Users can then be assigned to and removed from these roles as necessary.

The way a user is made a member of a role depends on the type of authentication being used. If Windows authentication is used, role membership is determined by membership in Windows groups. In other words, the Windows groups to which the user belongs are what ASP.NET considers as the user's roles. If Forms authentication is used, the application must specify the roles to which the user belongs. The easiest way to do this is for Microsoft to put an additional parameter in the RedirectFromLoginPage method that allows the code on the login page to specify a string array containing role names. They don't do this, however, so we have to find another way. This requires that we understand a little more about what happens during authentication.

As you know, whenever a page that requires authorization is requested, it triggers the authentication process to determine who the user is. The first time this happens, the user is redirected to the login page, which collects the user's credentials and stores an authorization cookie on the user's browser. Subsequent page requests find the cookie and use it to reauthenticate the user to the application. Note that authentication occurs during every page access but that the Forms authentication mechanism handles subsequent authentication requests without further input from the user.

There is an event that gets triggered during each authentication request. This can be handled by placing a method called Application_AuthenticateRequest in the application's *global.asax* file. It is in this event handler that roles can be specified for the authenticated user. Example 6-15 shows the code.

Example 6-15. Specifying user roles using Forms authentication

```
Public Sub Application_AuthenticateRequest( _
   ByVal sender As Object, _
   ByVal e As EventArgs _
)

   ' Do this only after the user has authenticated.
   If Not (Context.User Is Nothing) Then
      If Context.User.Identity.IsAuthenticated Then

         ' Get the username.
         Dim username As String = Context.User.Identity.Name

         ' Get the user's roles. In a real application this line
         ' should be replaced with a lookup based on the username.
         ' In addition, performance can be improved by caching the
         ' roles in session state or in a browser cookie.
         Dim roles( ) As String = {"Administrator", "User"}

         ' Create a new principal from the username and the roles.
         Dim ident As _
            New System.Security.Principal.GenericIdentity(username)
         Dim prin As _
            New System.Security.Principal.GenericPrincipal(ident, roles)

         ' Associate the new security principal with the request.
         Context.User = prin

      End If
   End If

End Sub
```

Example 6-15 examines the User property of the request context to determine whether the user has authenticated to the system. If so, a new security principal is created based on the username and desired roles. This security principal is then attached to the request context. Having done so, the user can be allowed or denied access to pages based on role membership.

To control access based on role membership, use the roles attribute of the <allow> and <deny> elements. Usage is similar to the usage of the users attribute, except that role names are given instead of usernames. For example, if the pages in a certain directory should be limited to members of the Accounting Specialist role, a *web.config* file should be placed in that directory and should have the following entries in its <authorization> section:

```
<?xml version="1.0" encoding="utf-8" ?>
<configuration>
   <system.web>
      <authorization>
         <allow roles="Accounting Specialist" />
         <deny users="*" />
      </authorization>
   </system.web>
</configuration>
```

When specifying Windows group names as role names, include the entity that defines the group. For example, for groups defined in a domain:

```
"DOMAIN-NAME\GroupName"
```

For groups defined on the web server machine:

```
"MACHINE\GroupName"
```

Windows NTFS authorization

This method of authorization works only in conjunction with Windows authentication. Because users are authenticated against Windows user accounts, access to resources can be allowed or denied by using built-in Windows security. Use the Windows administration tools to allow or deny access for specific users or groups to specific files within the web application. Because this is purely a Windows administration task and is not specifically related to .NET, it won't be discussed further here.

Code-access authorization

Code written on a web page or in a code-behind file can discover the username and role membership of the current user and use this information to modify program behavior. For example, application menu options could be disabled or removed if the user is not a member of a certain role.

The current user's information is available through the Page object's User property. This property is of type IPrincipal (defined in the System.Security.Principal namespace). The IPrincipal type has a property called Identity, which provides information about the user's identity. The type of the Identity property is IIdentity (defined in the System.Security.Principal namespace). The IIdentity type has three properties:

AuthenticationType
: A string that identifies the type of authentication that was used. Some common values are:

  `"Forms"`
  : Forms authentication

  `"NTLM"`
  : Integrated Windows authentication

  `"Digest"`
  : Digest authentication

  `"Basic"`
  : Basic authentication

IsAuthenticated
: A Boolean value indicating whether the user has been authenticated.

Name
: A string containing the username.

A web page can take action based on a username, using the following code:

```
If Me.User.Identity.Name = "SOME-DOMAIN\daveg" Then
   ' Do something.
Else
   ' Do something else.
End If
```

Role membership is tested by using the IsInRole method of the IPrincipal type. For example:

```
If Me.User.IsInRole("SOME-DOMAIN\Employees") Then
   ' Do something.
Else
   ' Do something else.
End If
```

Accessing Network Resources

After a user authenticates to the web application, it may be appropriate for the web application to access network resources on behalf of the user. For example, a web application might give a company's employees access to their corporate email accounts while away from the office. To do this, the web application must log into the company's email server and retrieve information belonging to the person using the application. Normally, such access to private information is blocked by the Windows security mechanism because the web-server process does not have appropriate rights to access resources owned by the user. There are two ways to resolve this issue. One is to give the necessary rights to the process under which the web server is running; the other is for the web server to *impersonate* the authenticated user. Each is discussed here in turn.

IUSR_ComputerName

When IIS is installed on a computer, the installation process creates a username on that computer called "IUSR_*ComputerName*", where *ComputerName* is the name of the computer on which IIS is installed. This is the default username under which web requests are run. IIS can be configured to use any user account for this purpose, including domain user accounts. If you're writing a web application that accesses network resources but doesn't depend on the identity of the web user for rights to those resources, set up a domain username that has rights to the resources and configure IIS to use that username. See the IIS documentation for information on how to configure this username.

Impersonation

Applications that need to access resources using the rights of the currently authenticated web user must use impersonation. *Impersonation* is a Windows security term that refers to a thread's ability to assume a different security identity for a period of time. In ASP.NET, it allows an application to assume the identity of the web user so that the application can access resources on behalf of the user. Impersonation happens automatically when using Windows authentication (as described earlier in this chapter). The application is written simply to access the desired resources, and the Windows security mechanism ensures that the access succeeds or fails depending on the end user's access rights.

If the application is using Forms authentication, impersonation must be explicitly coded. Unfortunately, the .NET Framework doesn't provide a mechanism to do this. If an application that uses Forms authentication needs to impersonate a user, it must call directly into the Windows API. The general steps are:

1. Call the Windows *LogonUser* function to authenticate a given user.
2. Instantiate a WindowsIdentity object (defined in the System.Security.Principal namespace) to represent the authenticated user.
3. Call the WindowsIdentity object's Impersonate method to impersonate the user.
4. Access the protected resource.
5. Undo the impersonation.

Example 6-16 gives the complete code for this process.

Example 6-16. Impersonating a Windows user from code

```
' Values used by the LogonUser function's logonType parameter
Public Enum LogonType
   LOGON32_LOGON_INTERACTIVE = 2
   LOGON32_LOGON_NETWORK = 3
   LOGON32_LOGON_BATCH = 4
   LOGON32_LOGON_SERVICE = 5
   LOGON32_LOGON_UNLOCK = 7
   LOGON32_LOGON_NETWORK_CLEARTEXT = 8
```

Example 6-16. Impersonating a Windows user from code (continued)

```
   LOGON32_LOGON_NEW_CREDENTIALS = 9
End Enum

' Values used by the LogonUser function's logonProvider parameter
Public Enum LogonProvider
   LOGON32_PROVIDER_DEFAULT = 0
   LOGON32_PROVIDER_WINNT35 = 1
   LOGON32_PROVIDER_WINNT40 = 2
   LOGON32_PROVIDER_WINNT50 = 3
End Enum

Declare Function LogonUser Lib "advapi32.dll" Alias "LogonUserA" ( _
   ByVal username As String, _
   ByVal domain As String, _
   ByVal password As String, _
   ByVal logonType As LogonType, _
   ByVal logonProvider As LogonProvider, _
   ByRef token As IntPtr _
) As Integer

Private Sub DoSomethingUseful( )

   ' Logon credentials
   Dim username As String = "username"
   Dim domain As String = "DOMAIN"
   Dim password As String = "password"

   ' A handle to the user who will be impersonated
   Dim token As IntPtr

   ' Log the user into Windows.
   Dim bLogonSuccessful As Boolean = Convert.ToBoolean( _
      LogonUser( _
         username, domain, password, _
         LogonType.LOGON32_LOGON_NETWORK, _
         LogonProvider.LOGON32_PROVIDER_DEFAULT, token))
   If Not bLogonSuccessful Then
      ' Throw an exception.
   End If

   ' Create a WindowsIdentity object that represents the logged-in user.
   Dim ident As New System.Security.Principal.WindowsIdentity(token)

   ' Impersonate the user.
   Dim ctx As System.Security.Principal.WindowsImpersonationContext = _
      ident.Impersonate( )

   '
   ' Access the protected resource here.
   ' ...
   '
```

Example 6-16. Impersonating a Windows user from code (continued)

```
    ' Stop impersonating the user.
    ctx.Undo( )

End Sub
```

The *LogonUser* function is not part of the .NET Framework—it is part of the underlying Windows API. To access it, one must use the `Declare` statement or use the .NET Framework's P/Invoke capability. In Example 6-16, the `Declare` statement is used to give the code access to the *LogonUser* function.

The *LogonUser* function takes six parameters. The first three, *`username`*, *`domain`*, and *`password`*, provide the logon credentials of the user who will be authenticated. The next two parameters, *`logonType`* and *`logonProvider`*, provide further control of the logon process. (A discussion of these two parameters is beyond the scope of this book.) Search for "LogonUser" in the Microsoft Developer Network (MSDN) online documentation (*http://msdn.microsoft.com/library/*) for details about the values that can be provided. The final parameter, *`token`*, is a `ByRef` parameter that receives a handle to the logged-in user (if the function is successful). The return value is an Integer that indicates whether the function was successful. A return value of `0` indicates failure; anything other than `0` indicates success. In Example 6-16, this value is converted to a Boolean using the Convert class (defined in the System namespace).

After the user is logged in, the *`token`* value is passed to the constructor of the WindowsIdentity class (defined in the System.Security.Principal namespace). This creates a WindowsIdentity object that represents the authenticated user. This object has an Impersonate method, which is called to start the impersonation. An object of type WindowsImpersonationContext (defined in the System.Security.Principal namespace) is returned from the Impersonate method. This object is used later to undo the impersonation. After the Impersonate method is called, the code can safely access protected resources. When finished, the Undo method of the WindowsImpersonationContext object is called to stop impersonation.

Designing Custom Controls

ASP.NET provides the ability to define two kinds of custom controls: *user controls* and *server controls*. The purpose of both is the same: to encapsulate visual and programmatic behaviors for use on web pages. (For example, a control can be used to encapsulate a navigation bar that appears on every page in a site.) Their differences lie in how they are created and in their capabilities. User controls are created in much the same way as standard ASP.NET pages and can include HTML, embedded code, and code-behind files. This allows web developers to quickly and easily create controls using techniques with which they are already familiar. In contrast, server controls are created entirely in code and provide much more sophisticated control over rendering, postback processing, and event generation. This means that custom server controls can do everything that built-in ASP.NET server controls can do. Even so, user controls are usually the right choice because they are so simply created. Server controls are not needed unless user controls are not sufficient for a given purpose. This section shows how to create both kinds of controls.

User Controls

The easiest way to create a new control is to aggregate and modify the functionality of one or more existing controls. This is done by creating a user-control file (*.ascx*) and then referencing it from a web page file (*.aspx*). Example 6-17 shows a simple user-control file.

Example 6-17. A user control for implementing a menu

```
<%@ Control Language="VB" %>

<script Language="VB" runat="Server">


   Public Property SearchText( ) As String
   Get
      Return txtSearchFor.Text
   End Get
   Set
      txtSearchFor.Text = Value
   End Set
   End Property

   Public Event StartSearch(ByVal sender As Object, ByVal e As EventArgs)

   Private Sub btnStartSearch_Click( _
      ByVal sender As Object, _
      ByVal e As EventArgs _
   )
      RaiseEvent StartSearch(Me, EventArgs.Empty)
   End Sub

</script>

<asp:Label id="lblSearch" runat="Server" Text="Search" /><br>
<asp:TextBox id="txtSearchFor" runat="server" Text="" />
<asp:Button id="btnStartSearch" runat="server" Text="Go" OnClick="btnStartSearch_Click" />
<br>
<asp:HyperLink id="AdvancedSearchLink" runat="server" Text="Advanced"
   NavigateUrl="http://advanced_search.aspx" Target="_top" />
```

Note these characteristics of user controls:

- They are defined by *.ascx* files.
- They contain HTML and script, just as standard ASP.NET web pages do.

- They have an @ Control directive instead of an @ Page directive.
- They do not have <html>, <head>, <body>, or <form> tags.

Example 6-18 shows a web page file that references the user control from Example 6-17. (It is assumed that the text in Example 6-18 has been saved into a file named *search.ascx*).

Example 6-18. Referencing a user control from a web page

```
<%@ Page Language="VB" Explicit="True" Strict="True"%>
<%@ Register TagPrefix="dg" TagName="search" Src="search.ascx" %>

<script runat="server">

   Private Sub search1_StartSearch(ByVal sender As Object, e As EventArgs)
      lblMsg.Text = "You entered: " & search1.SearchText
   End Sub

</script>

<html>

   <head>
      <title>User Control Test</title>
   </head>

   <body>
      <form action="index.aspx" method="post" runat="server">
         <table border="1">
            <tr>
               <td valign="top">
                  <h1>Welcome to my web site!</h1>
                  <p>Please use the search box at the right to
                     search for items on this site.
                  </p>
               </td>
               <td valign="top"><dg:search id="search1" runat="server"
                  OnStartSearch="search1_StartSearch" /></td>
            </tr>
            <tr>
               <td><asp:Label id="lblMsg" runat="server" /></td>
            </tr>
         </table>
      </form>
   </body>

</html>
```

The web page must have an @ Register directive to provide a reference to the user-control source file. When referencing user controls, three attributes are relevant: Src, TagPrefix, and TagName. The Src attribute identifies the location of the *.ascx* file that defines the user control. The TagPrefix and TagName attributes together determine how the user-control class is referred to in the body of the web page. Look again at the @ Register directive shown in Example 6-18:

```
<%@ Register TagPrefix="dg" TagName="search" Src="search.ascx" %>
```

Later in Example 6-18, an instance of the user-control class is created within a table cell (shown again here, but without the table-cell definition, to avoid clutter):

```
<dg:search id="search1" runat="server"
  OnStartSearch="search1_StartSearch" />
```

This is the same syntax that's used when instantiating a server control. The runat attribute is required and must always be set to "server". The id attribute allows you to programmatically refer to this instance of the control within code. Lastly, attributes having the form On*EventName* are special. Such attributes instruct the compiler to associate an event with a handler defined in the web page class. In Example 6-18, the StartSearch event defined by the user control is associated with the search_StartSearch method, which just sets the Text property of a label to show that the event was received.

Figure 6-16 shows the resulting browser display, and Example 6-19 shows the HTML that is sent to the browser.

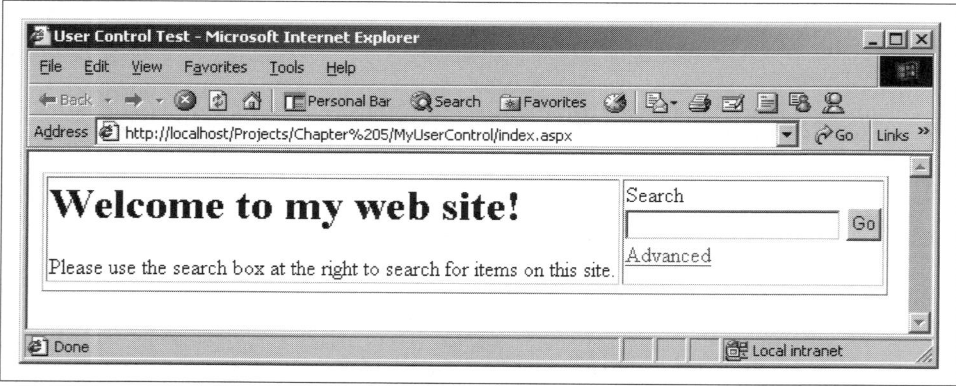

Figure 6-16. Output from Example 6-18

Example 6-19. HTML generated by ASP.NET when executing Example 6-18

```
<html>

  <head>
    <title>User Control Test</title>
  </head>

  <body>
    <form name="ctrl0" method="post" action="index.aspx" id="ctrl0">
      <input type="hidden" name="__VIEWSTATE"
        value="dDwxNzk2NDQ0MTYzOzs+" />
```

Example 6-19. HTML generated by ASP.NET when executing Example 6-18 (continued)

```
         <table border="1">
            <tr>
               <td valign="top">
                  <h1>Welcome to my web site!</h1>
                  <p>Please use the search box at the right to
                     search for items on this site.
                  </p>
               </td>
               <td valign="top">
                  <span id="search1_lblSearch">Search</span><br>
                  <input name="search1:txtSearchFor" type="text"
                     value="Enter a search string here."
                     id="search1_txtSearchFor" />
                  <input type="submit" name="search1:btnStartSearch"
                     value="Go" id="search1_btnStartSearch" /><br>
                  <a id="search1_AdvancedSearchLink"
                     href="http://advanced_search.aspx" target="_top">
                     Advanced
                  </a>
               </td>
            </tr>
            <tr>
               <td><span id="lblMsg"></span></td>
            </tr>
         </table>
      </form>
   </body>

</html>
```

User controls can use code behind. The technique is the same as with web pages.

Server Controls

ASP.NET provides the ability to develop custom server controls (also known as *web controls*). A server control is a class that inherits from the WebControl class (in the System.Web.UI.WebControls namespace) and overrides the Render method. This section describes how to create a server control in the Visual Studio .NET IDE, as well as manually.

Creating a custom server control using Visual Studio .NET

To create a custom server control in Visual Studio .NET:

1. Select File→New→Project. The New Project dialog box appears, as previously shown in Figure 6-1.
2. Select "Visual Basic Projects" in the Project Types pane on the left side of the dialog box.

3. Select "Web Control Library" in the Templates pane on the right side of the dialog box.
4. Enter a name in the Name text box.
5. Enter a location in the Location text box.
6. Click OK. Visual Studio .NET creates a project with some boilerplate code that implements a server control. The code generated by Visual Studio .NET is shown in Example 6-20.

Example 6-20. Code generated by Visual Studio .NET for a new web-control project

```
Imports System.ComponentModel
Imports System.Web.UI

<DefaultProperty("Text"), _
ToolboxData("<{0}:WebCustomControl1 runat=server></{0}:WebCustomControl1>")> _
Public Class WebCustomControl1
   Inherits System.Web.UI.WebControls.WebControl

   Dim _text As String

   <Bindable(True), Category("Appearance"), DefaultValue("")> _
   Property [Text]( ) As String
      Get
         Return _text
      End Get

      Set(ByVal Value As String)
         _text = Value
      End Set
   End Property

   Protected Overrides Sub Render( _
      ByVal output As System.Web.UI.HtmlTextWriter _
   )
      output.Write([Text])
   End Sub

End Class
```

Note the following about the code in Example 6-20:

- It defines a class that inherits from the WebControl class (defined in the System.Web.UI.WebControls namespace).
- The class has two custom attributes associated with it: `DefaultProperty` (defined in the System.ComponentModel namespace) and `ToolboxData` (defined in the System.Web.UI namespace). These attributes are not required, but they provide useful information to the Visual Studio .NET Web Forms Designer when the control is referenced in a web-form project.

- The class has a property called Text. This is not a requirement for web controls; it is just a design pattern used by Visual Studio .NET.
- The Text property has three custom attributes: `Bindable`, `Category`, and `DefaultValue` (all defined in the System.ComponentModel namespace). Again, these custom attributes are not required, but they provide information to the Visual Studio .NET Web Forms Designer when the control is referenced in a web-form project.
- The class defines an override for the Render method (originally declared in the WebControl class). The ASP.NET framework calls this method to ask the control to render itself into HTML. It is up to the control developer (you) to render output that appropriately represents the control. The boilerplate code simply outputs the value of the Text property.

Creating a custom server control in code

To create a custom server control without the benefit of Visual Studio .NET, derive a class from the WebControl class and override the Render method. For good measure, add the `ToolboxData` custom attribute to the class, as exemplified by the Visual Studio .NET–generated code in Example 6-20. An example is shown in Example 6-21.

Example 6-21. A web control designed without Visual Studio .NET

```
Imports System.ComponentModel
Imports System.Web.UI

Namespace OReilly.VBNET

<ToolboxData("<{0}:HelloWebControl runat=server></{0}:HelloWebControl>")> _
Public Class HelloWebControl
   Inherits System.Web.UI.WebControls.WebControl

   Protected Overrides Sub Render( _
      ByVal output As System.Web.UI.HtmlTextWriter _
   )
      output.Write("<i>hello, world</i>")
   End Sub

End Class

End Namespace
```

The control in Example 6-21 renders the hard-coded string `"<i>hello, world</i>"` within the page on which it is placed. (Placing custom controls on web forms is described shortly.)

To compile the code in Example 6-21, save it to a file named *HelloWebControl.vb*, and execute the following command from the command line:

```
vbc.exe HelloWebControl.vb /r:System.dll,System.Web.dll /t:library
```

This creates the file *HelloWebControl.dll*, which can then be referenced from a web project, as explained next.

Using a custom server control in Visual Studio .NET

To add a custom server control to the Visual Studio .NET Toolbox, perform the following steps:

1. Right-click on the Toolbox in Visual Studio .NET and select Customize Toolbox. The Customize Toolbox dialog box appears, as shown in Figure 6-17. (If the Toolbox isn't visible, select View→Toolbox from the Visual Studio .NET main menu.)

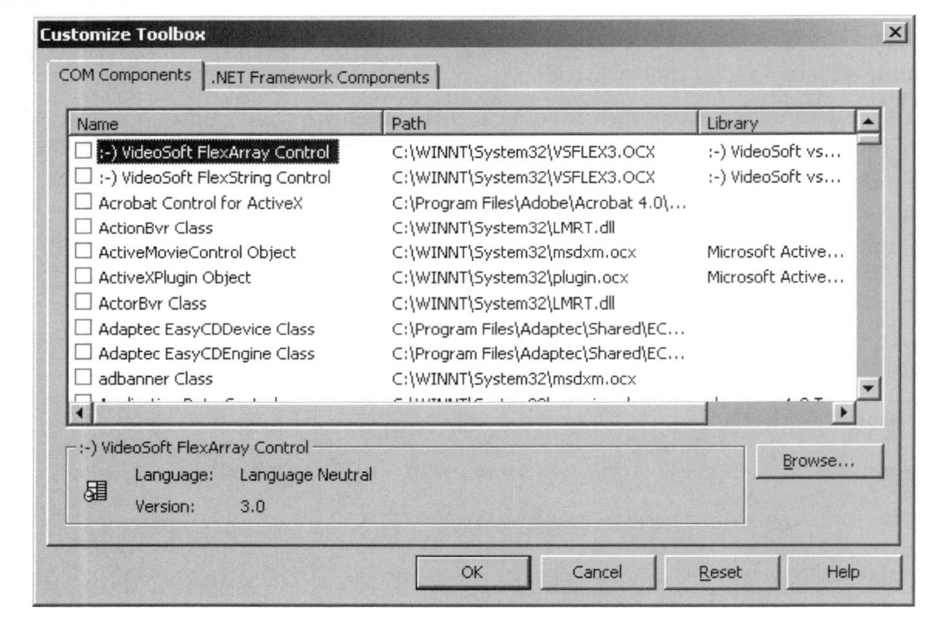

Figure 6-17. The Customize Toolbox dialog box

2. Click on the .NET Framework Components tab.
3. Click on the Browse button, browse to your custom server control's compiled *.dll*, and click the Open button. The controls in the *.dll* are added to the list view, as shown in Figure 6-18. (In this case there is only one control in the *.dll*.) Note that the checkbox next to the control is not yet checked.
4. Click the checkbox next to the control, then click OK.

After the control has been added to the Toolbox, it can be dropped onto a web form and manipulated in the same way as the built-in server controls. Example 6-22 displays the HTML view of a new web page with an instance of the control from

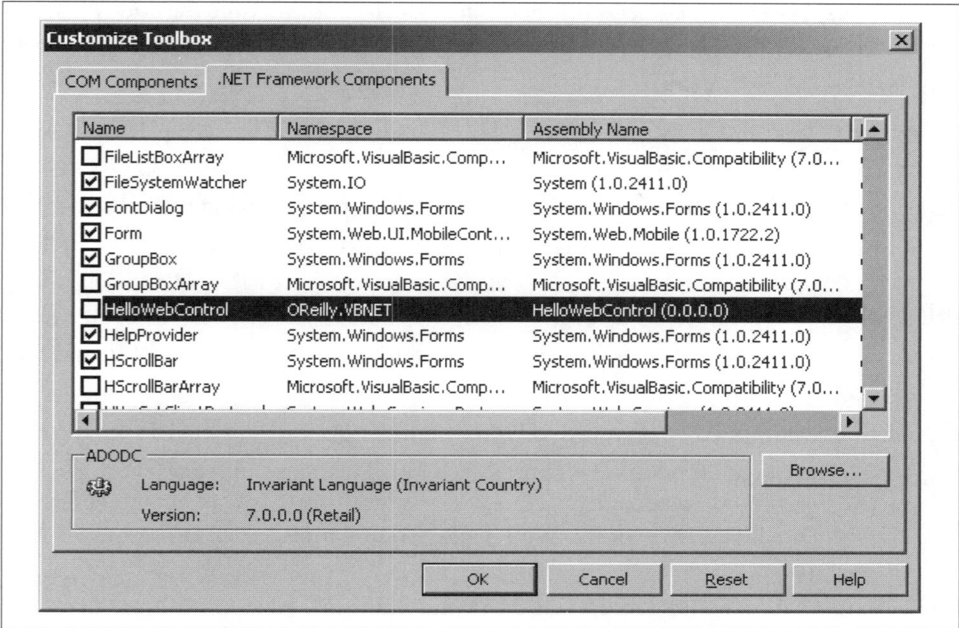

Figure 6-18. The control has been added to the Customize Toolbox dialog box

Example 6-21 placed on it. The lines related to the control are shown in bold, but the entire HTML view is shown for context.

Example 6-22. The HTML view generated by Visual Studio .NET when a custom control is added to a web form

```
<%@ Page Language="vb" AutoEventWireup="false"
   Codebehind="WebForm1.aspx.vb" Inherits="WebApplication1.WebForm1"%>
<%@ Register TagPrefix="cc1" Namespace="OReilly.VBNET"
   Assembly="HelloWebControl" %>
<!DOCTYPE HTML PUBLIC "-//W3C//DTD HTML 4.0 Transitional//EN">
<HTML>
   <HEAD>
      <title></title>
      <meta name="GENERATOR" content="Microsoft Visual Studio .NET 7.0">
      <meta name="CODE_LANGUAGE" content="Visual Basic 7.0">
      <meta name=vs_defaultClientScript content="JavaScript">
      <meta name=vs_targetSchema
         content="http://schemas.microsoft.com/intellisense/ie5">
   </HEAD>
   <body MS_POSITIONING="GridLayout">

      <form id="Form1" method="post" runat="server">
         <cc1:HelloWebControl id="HelloWebControl1"
            style="Z-INDEX: 101; LEFT: 8px; POSITION: absolute; TOP: 8px"
            runat="server"></cc1:HelloWebControl>
```

Example 6-22. The HTML view generated by Visual Studio .NET when a custom control is added to a web form (continued)

```
      </form>

   </body>
</HTML>
```

The code-behind file that goes with Example 6-22 has the following line added to it:

```
Protected WithEvents HelloWebControl1 As OReilly.VBNET.HelloWebControl
```

Using a custom server control manually

To use a custom server control in a project created without the benefit of Visual Studio .NET, perform the following:

1. Move the compiled web control *dll* into the web application's *bin* directory.
2. In the web page on which the control is to appear, place an `@ Register` directive to register the custom control. (The `@ Register` directive was explained in the "Using Directives to Modify Web Page Compilation" section earlier in this chapter.)
3. Use the custom control in the same way that built-in server controls are used.

Example 6-23 shows an *.aspx* page that uses the HelloWebControl control developed earlier in this section. Example 6-24 shows the HTML that is sent to the browser when this page is processed. Figure 6-19 shows the resulting display.

Example 6-23. Using a custom control

```
<%@ Page Language="vb" AutoEventWireup="false" %>
<%@ Register TagPrefix="OReilly" Namespace="OReilly.VBNET"
   Assembly="HelloWebControl" %>
<html>
   <body>
      <form id="Form1" method="post" runat="server">
         <OReilly:HelloWebControl id="HelloWebControl1" runat="server" />
      </form>
   </body>
</html>
```

Example 6-24. HTML generated from the page in Example 6-23

```
<html>
   <body>
      <form name="Form1" method="post" action="TestMyControl.aspx"
         id="Form1">
<input type="hidden" name="__VIEWSTATE" value="dDwyMDYOODMOMjA7Oz4=" />

         <i>hello, world</i>
      </form>
   </body>
</html>
```

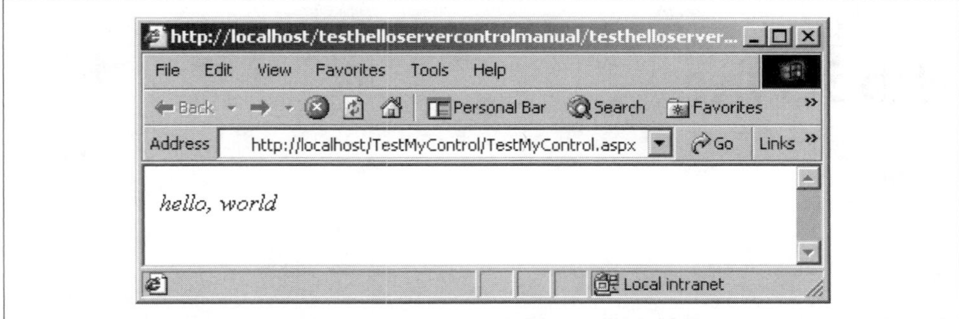

Figure 6-19. Display generated by the page in Example 6-23

Summary

ASP.NET is a brand-new framework for delivering web-based applications. It is similar in concept and usage to Microsoft's previous ASP technology, though it is far more powerful.

CHAPTER 7

Web Services

A web service is a function call over the Internet. Web services are to distributed-application development as components are to desktop-application development. With web services, a component-library developer can expose programmatic functionality over the Internet. The author of a client application can easily use that functionality, even though the client application may exist on a computer on the other side of the world. Furthermore, the client application doesn't have to be web-based. It can just as easily be a GUI-based application, as long as the computer it's running on is connected to the Internet.

Web services are not limited to Microsoft products. They are an industrywide movement, with industrywide standardization. Web services running on one vendor's platform can be used by clients running on entirely different and otherwise incompatible platforms, since they are built on HTTP, XML, and SOAP. These three specifications have extremely broad industry support and are available on virtually all major hardware and operating-system platforms.

HTTP (HyperText Transfer Protocol) is a protocol that was originally developed to allow users to navigate through *hypermedia*—documents and other media that link to still other documents and media. This protocol has become the basis for today's World Wide Web. HTTP has primarily been used to transport documents that are in the form of *HTML* (HyperText Markup Language), a plain-text document markup language.

Virtually every general-purpose computer in the world is connected to the Internet and has the capability to browse web pages. Said another way, virtually every computer in the world has the ability to transfer data using the HTTP protocol. Because of this, it makes sense to harness the power of HTTP for more than just requesting and delivering web pages. In addition to these tasks, HTTP is now used to transport XML and SOAP.

XML (eXtensible Markup Language) is a specification for encoding all kinds of data as plain-text documents. Unlike HTTP, XML doesn't define a transport mechanism. XML documents can be transmitted over HTTP, email, FTP, or any other transport mechanism.

SOAP (Simple Object Access Protocol) is a specification that defines how to encode function calls as XML documents.

A *web service* is nothing more than a web server that knows how to listen for and respond to SOAP messages carried over HTTP. How the web service is implemented is irrelevant to the client of the web service. The client simply knows that it can send SOAP messages to a web server located at a specific URL and receive SOAP responses.

ASP.NET makes it easy both to expose web services and to use them. In both cases, the ASP.NET runtime encapsulates the communication mechanism, including generating and receiving appropriate SOAP messages. The author of a web service merely writes a class that exposes the desired functionality. ASP.NET does the hard work of handling incoming SOAP messages and forwarding calls to the appropriate method of the class. When the method returns, ASP.NET wraps up the return value and sends it back to the client in a SOAP response.

To the .NET application developer using web services, a web service seems like just another type that exposes methods to call. Behind the scenes, ASP.NET translates each method call into a SOAP request to invoke the remote functionality.

Creating a Web Service

Example 7-1 shows the source code for a simple web service.

Example 7-1. A simple web service

```
<%@ WebService Language="VB" Class="HelloWebService" %>

Imports System.Web.Services

<WebService(Namespace:="http://yourcompany.com/")> _
Public Class HelloWebService
   Inherits WebService

   <WebMethod> Public Function SayHello(ByVal Name As String) As String
      Return "Hello, " & Name & ", welcome to web services!"
   End Function

End Class
```

To create and deploy this web service, perform these steps:

1. Create a virtual directory in IIS.
2. Enter the code from Example 7-1, and save it in the virtual directory in a file with an *.asmx* extension—for example, *HelloWebService.asmx*.

After you do so, clients can access the service. Later in this chapter, you'll see how to write a web-service client.

Note the following features of the code in Example 7-1:

- An `@ WebService` directive appears at the top of the file. This directive specifies the language in which the code is written and the name of the class that contains the implementation of the web service.
- The lines following the `@ WebService` directive are *not* enclosed in `<script>` tags.
- The System.Web.Services namespace is imported. This namespace contains the WebServiceAttribute, WebMethodAttribute, and WebService types used in this example.
- The implementation class inherits from the WebService class (defined in the System.Web.Services namespace). This is not strictly necessary and could have been omitted from Example 7-1. However, inheriting from the WebService class gives the implementation class access to ASP.NET intrinsic objects (Session, Application, etc., as described in Chapter 6).
- The SayHello method is marked with the `WebMethod` attribute. This is required for the web service to expose the method.

When a request for the *.asmx* file comes into the web server, ASP.NET compiles the code in the file and automatically generates the plumbing to expose the marked methods as web-service methods.

If desired, you can compile the implementation class separately instead of placing the source in the *.asmx* file. To do so, place the source code for the class only (not the `@ WebService` directive) in a *.vb* file, and compile it to a *.dll* using either the command-line compiler or Visual Studio .NET. Note that the compiler must reference *System.Web.Services.dll* (to gain access to the types in the System.Web.Services namespace) and *System.dll* (because the WebService class exposes methods inherited from the System.ComponentModel.Component class). Here's a sample command line:

```
vbc HelloWebService.vb /r:System.Web.Services.dll,System.dll /t:library
```

After compiling the class into a *.dll* file, copy the file into a directory named *bin* in the web application's virtual directory. Then edit the *.asmx* file so that it contains only the `@ WebService` directive, as shown in the first line of Example 7-1. When the ASP.NET framework processes the `@ WebService` directive in the *.asmx* file, it will look through all of the assemblies in the *bin* directory for one that contains the class named in the `Class` attribute of the `@ WebService` directive.

The WebService Attribute

The `WebService` attribute (that is, the WebServiceAttribute class, defined in the System.Web.Services namespace) provides a way to attach a name, namespace, and description to a web service. The properties that can be set for the WebService attribute are:

Description

A description of the web service. The default is an empty string.

Name

The name of the web service. The default is the name of the class implementing the web service.

Namespace

The namespace of the web service. To avoid name clashes between web services, they are given namespaces in URI format. A simple way to build a unique namespace for your company's web services is to base it on your company's URL (because URLs are valid URIs). For example:

```
http://yourcompany.com/webservices/
```

Although this looks like a URL, it isn't. It doesn't need to correspond to a site that can be reached on the Internet. It just needs to be a unique name that is under your company's control and has no chance of clashing with anyone else's namespace. The default for this property is `"http://tempuri.org/"`. The default is OK for testing web services, but should not be used for production web services.

Here's how the `WebService` attribute might look when you specify all three properties:

```
<WebService( _
   Description:="My first web service.", _
   Name:="FirstWebService", _
   Namespace:="http://yourcompany.com/")> _
Public Class HelloWebService
   Inherits WebService
   ' ...
End Class
```

Note that the `WebService` attribute is not required for a class to implement a web service. It only provides a way to specify the given properties of the web service.

The WebMethod Attribute

The `WebMethod` attribute (that is, the WebMethodAttribute class, defined in the System.Web.Services namespace) identifies a method as being a web method. When the ASP.NET framework finds this method in a class being used as a web service, it wires up the plumbing necessary to expose the method as part of the web service. The properties that can be set for the `WebMethod` attribute are:

BufferResponse

Specifies whether to buffer the response to the client while it is being built. The type is Boolean. The default is `True`.

CacheDuration

Specifies whether responses are cached and, if so, how long they are cached (in seconds). The type is Integer. A value of `0` (the default) specifies that responses aren't cached.

Description

Specifies a description of the web method. Tools can retrieve this description and display it to potential users. The type is String. The default is an empty string.

EnableSession

Specifies whether session state is enabled for the web service. The type is Boolean. The default is `False`.

MessageName

Specifies the name of the web-service method. The type is String. The default is the name of the method as it appears in the implementation class.

Web services don't support method overloading. If you're writing a class that will be used as the implementation of a web service, don't overload method names. If you're using an existing class that already has overloaded method names, use the WebMethod attribute's `MessageName` attribute to control the names presented to clients of the web service.

TransactionOption

Specifies how the web method participates in transactions. The type is TransactionOption (defined in the System.EnterpriseServices namespace). The default is `Disabled`.

Transactions can't propagate across web-service method invocations. Therefore, web methods can participate in transactions only as the root of a transaction. They can't enlist on a transaction that is in progress.

The WebService Class

To obtain access to the ASP.NET framework's environment objects, a web-service class can inherit from the WebService class (defined in the System.Web.Services namespace). Doing so causes the web-service class to inherit five properties:

Application

This is an object that can be used to hold application state. See Chapter 6 for more information.

Context

This is the *context* of the web-service request. This is an instance of the HttpContext class (defined in the System.Web namespace). This object contains references to various items of information concerning the current web-service request.

Server

This is an object that holds information about the web server. See Chapter 6 for more information.

Session

This is an object that can be used to hold session state. See Chapter 6 for more information.

User

If Windows authentication is used to authenticate the web-service client, the User property references an object containing information about the user. The type of this property is IPrincipal.

Testing a Web Service with a Browser

Web services deployed on ASP.NET can easily be tested with a web browser, because the ASP.NET framework itself includes the ability to generate browser screens based on the definition of the web service. For example, browsing to the *.asmx* file shown in Example 7-1 (using the URL *http://localhost/WebServices/HelloWebService.asmx*) produces the browser screen shown in Figure 7-1.

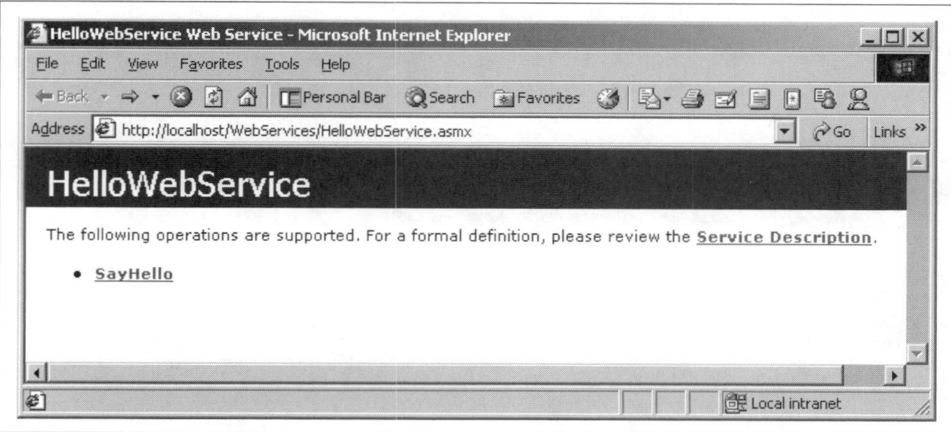

Figure 7-1. Browsing to a web service hosted in ASP.NET

To test a web service in a web browser, the *.asmx* file must be deployed in an IIS virtual directory. Using the browser to view the *.asmx* file directly from disk doesn't work.

The "HelloWebService" in large font in Figure 7-1 is the name of the web service exposed at the given URL. This is the name of the implementation class (or the value given by the *Name* parameter of the `WebService` attribute, if present). Underneath the main heading there are two additional links. The first, marked "Service Description", links to the WSDL description of the service. (Web-service descriptions and WSDL are explained in the next section.)

The second, at the bottom of the test window, is the list of web methods exposed by the web service. In the case of HelloWebService, there is only a single method, Say-

Hello. Clicking on the name of the method brings up a screen with information about that method and with a mechanism for testing it. The screen is shown in Figure 7-2.

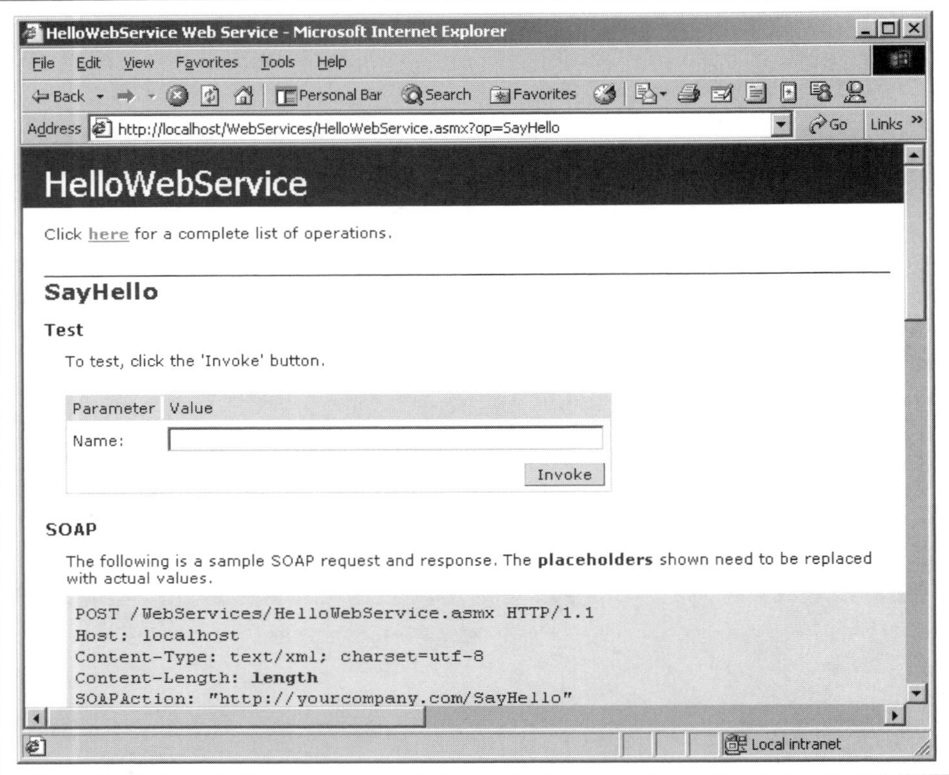

Figure 7-2. The test screen for the SayHello web method

Near the top of the test screen for the SayHello web method is a place to enter a value for the method's single parameter, *Name*, and a button that invokes the method. At the bottom of the screen is a list of sample invocations and responses for the web method, in the protocols that ASP.NET understands. ASP.NET web services can be invoked using the SOAP, HTTP GET, or HTTP POST protocols. When you're developing clients on the .NET platform, none of this matters to you—.NET does the work of wrapping invocations in the appropriate SOAP messages. However, when you're calling a web service from a platform that doesn't have native support for writing web-service clients, this information can be very helpful. Additionally, the HTTP GET and HTTP POST protocols may be simpler to implement on platforms that don't provide SOAP support. These protocols won't be discussed further, however, because this book is about developing on the .NET platform.

Clicking the Invoke button on the screen shown in Figure 7-2 invokes the web service using the HTTP GET protocol. The response is an XML document that encodes the result of the web-method invocation (see Figure 7-3). This is not a SOAP response. Rather, it is in the format used when responding to HTTP GET or HTTP POST invocations. It is sufficiently readable to see that the web method is performing as expected.

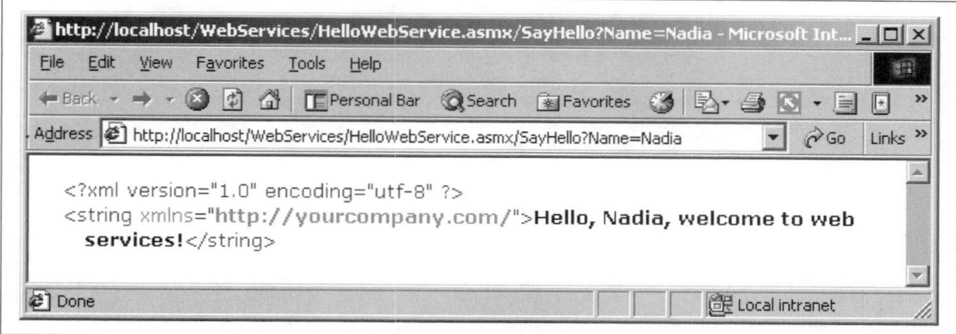

Figure 7-3. The result of clicking the Invoke button in Figure 7-2

Web-Service Descriptions

Web Service Description Language (WSDL) is a specification for encoding the definition of a web service as an XML document. This is analogous to providing type information for traditional COM software components. A web-service description identifies the name and URL of a web service, the web methods that are available from that service, the methods' parameter names and types, and the methods' return types.

ASP.NET automatically generates the WSDL documents for web services that it hosts. This document can be viewed by clicking the "Service Description" link in the service test page (refer back to Figure 7-1). A portion of this document for the HelloWebService service is shown in Figure 7-4.

As you can see in Figure 7-4, the WSDL document is intended more for tools that can read its contents than it is for humans. As shown in the next section, WSDL documents are used by client tools to generate code that knows how to talk to the given web service.

Consuming a Web Service

On the .NET platform, consuming a web service is as easy as creating one. This section contains the steps for creating a web-service client that can call the web service shown in Example 7-1.

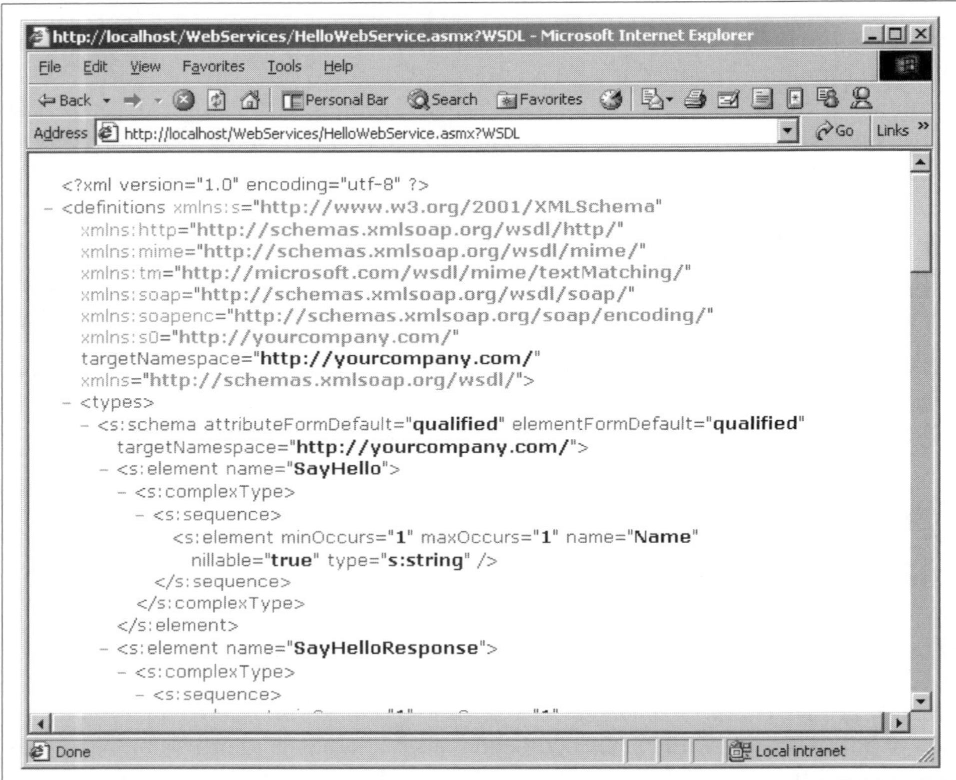
http://localhost/WebServices/HelloWebService.asmx?WSDL - Microsoft Internet Explorer
File Edit View Favorites Tools Help
Back Personal Bar Search Favorites
Address http://localhost/WebServices/HelloWebService.asmx?WSDL
Go Links
<?xml version="1.0" encoding="utf-8" ?>
- <definitions xmlns:s="http://www.w3.org/2001/XMLSchema"
xmlns:http="http://schemas.xmlsoap.org/wsdl/http/"
xmlns:mime="http://schemas.xmlsoap.org/wsdl/mime/"
xmlns:tm="http://microsoft.com/wsdl/mime/textMatching/"
xmlns:soap="http://schemas.xmlsoap.org/wsdl/soap/"
xmlns:soapenc="http://schemas.xmlsoap.org/soap/encoding/"
xmlns:s0="http://yourcompany.com/"
targetNamespace="http://yourcompany.com/"
xmlns="http://schemas.xmlsoap.org/wsdl/">
- <types>
- <s:schema attributeFormDefault="qualified" elementFormDefault="qualified"
targetNamespace="http://yourcompany.com/">
- <s:element name="SayHello">
- <s:complexType>
- <s:sequence>
<s:element minOccurs="1" maxOccurs="1" name="Name"
nillable="true" type="s:string" />
</s:sequence>
</s:complexType>
</s:element>
- <s:element name="SayHelloResponse">
- <s:complexType>
- <s:sequence>
Done
Local intranet

Figure 7-4. Viewing a WSDL document

Consuming a Web Service in Visual Studio .NET

To use a web service from a Visual Studio .NET project, right-click on the References node in the Solution Explorer window, and select Add Web Reference. This causes the Add Web Reference dialog box to appear.

In the Address field of the Add Web Reference dialog box, enter the URI of a web-service description document, and click the Add Reference button. When adding references to web services hosted by ASP.NET, the web-service description document is obtained by appending `?wsdl` to the path of the service itself. For example: *http://www.company.com/myWebService.asmx?wsdl* or *http://localhost/WebServices/HelloWebService.asmx?wsdl*.

Visual Studio .NET reads the web-service description document and builds a corresponding proxy class that knows how to access the described web service. The proxy class is local and exposes the same functionality as the web service. To call the web service from within the project, instantiate the proxy class and call its methods. For example, the following code instantiates the HelloWebService class and calls its SayHello method in response to a button click:

```
' Assumes that this code is part of a form having a button named
' btnOk_Click, a text box named txtName, and a text box named txtResult.
Private Sub btnOk_Click( _
   ByVal sender As System.Object, _
   ByVal e As System.EventArgs _
) Handles btnOk.Click

   If txtName.Text <> "" Then
      Dim sName As String = txtName.Text
      Dim oWS As New localhost.HelloWebService( )
      Dim sMsg As String = oWS.SayHello(sName)
      oWS.Dispose( )
      txtResult.Text = sMsg
   End If

End Sub
```

Note that the web-server machine name is used as the namespace for the web-service class. Thus, for a class called HelloWebService exposed by the same machine as the caller, the namespace is localhost, and the fully qualified name of the class is localhost.HelloWebService. For machine names containing dots, the order of the parts is reversed. Thus, if the HelloWebService service were exposed by a machine named webservices.somecompany.com, the HelloWebService class namespace would be com.somecompany.webservices, and the fully qualified class name of the class would be com.somecompany.webservices.HelloWebService.

Internally, the proxy class packages up method calls into SOAP wrappers and forwards them to the web service. This process is transparent to the client of the proxy class.

Consuming a Web Service in Notepad

To use a web service from a project that is not developed within the Visual Studio .NET IDE, use the command-line *wsdl.exe* tool to create a proxy class that wraps the web service. For example:

```
wsdl http://localhost/WebServices/HelloWebService.asmx?wsdl /language:vb
```

The *wsdl.exe* tool takes as an argument the URL of a web-service description document. As explained in the preceding discussion of Visual Studio .NET, when consuming services hosted by ASP.NET, the web-service description document is obtained by appending `?wsdl` to the path of the web service, as was done here.

The output of the *wsdl.exe* tool is a source-code file containing the definition of a proxy class that knows how to access the described web service. The *wsdl.exe* tool's `/language` switch controls whether the source is written in Visual Basic .NET or C#. The name of the class in the generated source code is equal to the name of the service, as given in the web-service description document. Example 7-2 shows the output of the *wsdl.exe* tool when run on the HelloWebService service from Example 7-1. (Note that several of the lines have been reformatted to make them fit in this book. Other than that, the code is unchanged.)

Example 7-2. Sample output of the wsdl.exe tool

```
'------------------------------------------------------------------------------
' <autogenerated>
'     This code was generated by a tool.
'     Runtime Version: 1.0.2914.16
'
'     Changes to this file may cause incorrect behavior and will be lost if
'     the code is regenerated.
' </autogenerated>
'------------------------------------------------------------------------------

Option Strict Off
Option Explicit On

Imports System
Imports System.Diagnostics
Imports System.Web.Services
Imports System.Web.Services.Protocols
Imports System.Xml.Serialization

'
'This source code was auto-generated by wsdl, Version=1.0.2914.16.
'


<System.Web.Services.WebServiceBindingAttribute( _
   Name:="HelloWebServiceSoap", _
   [Namespace]:="http://yourcompany.com/")> _
Public Class HelloWebService
   Inherits System.Web.Services.Protocols.SoapHttpClientProtocol

   <System.Diagnostics.DebuggerStepThroughAttribute( )> _
   Public Sub New( )
      MyBase.New
      Me.Url = "http://localhost/WebServices/HelloWebService.asmx"
   End Sub

   <System.Diagnostics.DebuggerStepThroughAttribute( ), _
   System.Web.Services.Protocols.SoapDocumentMethodAttribute( _
      "http://yourcompany.com/SayHello", _
      RequestNamespace:="http://yourcompany.com/", _
      ResponseNamespace:="http://yourcompany.com/", _
      Use:=System.Web.Services.Description.SoapBindingUse.Literal, _
      ParameterStyle:= _
         System.Web.Services.Protocols.SoapParameterStyle.Wrapped)> _
   Public Function SayHello(ByVal Name As String) As String
      Dim results( ) As Object = Me.Invoke("SayHello", New Object( ) {Name})
      Return CType(results(0),String)
   End Function
```

Example 7-2. Sample output of the wsdl.exe tool (continued)

```
   <System.Diagnostics.DebuggerStepThroughAttribute( )> _
   Public Function BeginSayHello( _
      ByVal Name As String, _
      ByVal callback As System.AsyncCallback, _
      ByVal asyncState As Object _
   ) As System.IAsyncResult
      Return Me.BeginInvoke("SayHello", New Object( ) {Name}, callback, _
         asyncState)
   End Function

   <System.Diagnostics.DebuggerStepThroughAttribute( )> _
   Public Function EndSayHello( _
      ByVal asyncResult As System.IAsyncResult _
   ) As String
      Dim results( ) As Object = Me.EndInvoke(asyncResult)
      Return CType(results(0),String)
   End Function
End Class
```

After creating the proxy class, write client code to make use of it. Using the proxy class is just like using any other .NET class. The proxy class hides method calls being forwarded over the Web. Example 7-3 shows code that uses the proxy class from Example 7-2.

Example 7-3. Client code for use with Example 7-2

```
Imports System

Public Module SomeApplication
   Public Sub Main( )
      Dim myService As New HelloWebService( )
      Console.WriteLine(myService.SayHello("Annemarie"))
   End Sub
End Module
```

Note that the client code simply instantiates the proxy class and calls its SayHello method.

Lastly, compile the proxy class and the client code together. Here's an example of compiling from the command line (note that this should be entered as a single command and is shown on two lines here only for printing in this book):

```
vbc SomeApplication.vb HelloWebService.vb /reference:System.Web.Services.dll,System.
Xml.dll,System.dll
```

The three assemblies referenced in this command are required by the proxy class.

Synchronous Versus Asynchronous Calls

Web-method calls are synchronous by default. That is, the caller waits while the call is sent over the network and while the result is calculated and sent back. When dealing with the Internet, this can be a lengthy process (a fraction of a second to several seconds). There are times when it would be useful for the client to go off and perform some other processing while waiting for the web method to complete. Fortunately, the autogenerated proxy class (created by either Visual Studio .NET or *wsdl.exe*) provides a way to do this. Example 7-4 shows client code that calls the SayHello web method asynchronously.

Example 7-4. Calling SayHello asynchronously

```
Private myService As New HelloWebService( )

Private Sub btnInvoke_Click( _
   ByVal sender As System.Object, _
   ByVal e As System.EventArgs _
) Handles btnInvoke.Click
   ' Assumes that there is a text box named txtName.
   myService.BeginSayHello(txtName.Text, AddressOf MySayHelloCallback, _
      Nothing)
End Sub

Private Sub MySayHelloCallback(ByVal ar As IAsyncResult)
   ' Assumes that there is a text box named txtResult.
   txtResult.Text = myService.EndSayHello(ar)
End Sub
```

For each web method, the web-service proxy class exposes two additional methods, named Begin*WebMethodName* and End*WebMethodName*, where *WebMethodName* is the name of the web method to be invoked. The purpose of the Begin*WebMethodName* method is to invoke the web method and immediately return. This allows client code to continue executing while the web service processes the request. When the response arrives from the web service, it is held until the client calls the End*WebMethodName* method. If the client calls the End*WebMethodName* method before the web method's response arrives, the client blocks until the response arrives. If the client calls the End*WebMethodName* method after the response arrives, the method immediately returns with the response value.

The parameters of the Begin*WebMethodName* method are exactly the same as the parameters of the web-method call itself, plus two additional parameters:

callback
: If the client would like to be notified when the web method's response has arrived, it can pass a delegate reference in this parameter. The type of this parameter is AsyncCallback, which is defined in the System namespace as:

```
Public Delegate Sub AsyncCallback(ByVal ar As IAsyncResult)
```

To pass a *callback* function to the Begin*WebMethodName* method, write a method having the appropriate signature and then use the `AddressOf` operator to create a delegate from that method, as shown in Example 7-4.

If the client does not want to be notified when the web method's response has arrived, it can pass `Nothing` in this parameter.

asyncState

If the client would like to provide some arbitrary additional information to the callback function, it can do so by assigning a value to the *asyncState* parameter. This parameter is of type Object, so any value can be passed. The value passed in this parameter is passed on to the callback function when the web-method call returns. If no additional information needs to be passed to the callback function, pass `Nothing` in this parameter.

The Begin*WebMethodName* method has no return value.

When the *callback* function is called, it receives a reference to an object that implements IAsyncResult (defined in the System namespace). The AsyncState property of this object holds the value passed in the *asyncState* parameter of the Begin*WebMethodName* method.

The first parameter of the End*WebMethodName* method is the IAsyncResult reference obtained in the *callback* function. Alternatively, the client can pass `Nothing` in this parameter if not using a *callback* function. The End*WebMethodName* method may have additional parameters, depending on whether the corresponding web method has any `ByRef` parameters. If there are any such parameters, they appear here in the signature of the End*WebMethodName* method. In addition, the return value of the End*WebMethodName* method is the return value of the web method.

Web-Service Discovery

Up to this point, we have assumed that the client of a web service knows where to find that web service's WSDL document. This may not always be the case. For example, consider a client application that runs on a portable device. Its purpose is to make a reservation on the user's behalf at the nearest hotel meeting the user's preset price and service guidelines. Before the client application can communicate with a hotel's reservation web service, the client must have a way to discover that the service is even there. This is the purpose of web-service directories.

Web-service directories provide a way for clients to find web services that perform a certain task or a certain kind of task. They are like the yellow pages in a telephone directory, in which businesses are listed according to the product or service they provide. Standards are just now being developed for web-service directories. One strong contender is called *Universal Description, Discovery, and Integration* (UDDI). Information about this standard and the implementations that currently exist can be found at *http://www.uddi.org*.

You may also have heard of *DISCO* files. (DISCO is short for discovery.) DISCO is a Microsoft-exclusive specification for encoding the addresses of multiple WSDL documents into a single XML document. DISCO doesn't have directory capabilities and so is falling into disuse as UDDI grows.

Limitations of Web Services

The ASP.NET framework makes it so easy to expose and consume web services that it's easy to forget about the communication layer between the client and server. Because web services are built on the SOAP protocol, their capabilities are limited to the capabilities of SOAP. The most important points to remember are:

No callback mechanism
: For a web service to call back to a client, the client has to handle incoming HTTP requests. Virtually no client systems are configured this way, so callbacks generally are not an option. If a callback system is absolutely required, it could be faked by writing methods in the client and server allowing the client component to periodically poll the server to determine if events have occurred.

No transactions across the Web
: The SOAP protocol currently does not provide any transaction support. A web-service method can begin a new transaction, and local resources will enlist on that transaction, but a web service can't enlist on an existing transaction.

Exceptions are returned as SOAP faults
: When there is some error in processing a web-method call, the web service responds with a SOAP fault. If the client of the web service is implemented on the .NET platform, the client receives a SoapException exception (defined in the System.Web.Services.Protocols namespace), even if both the client and server are using .NET. Put another way, even if both client and server are running on .NET, exceptions thrown on the server aren't raised as the same exception on the client.

Performance is an issue
: There is overhead associated with representing function calls as XML. This overhead is a necessary evil when communicating over the Internet across network firewalls. However, web services are not a good choice for cross-component communication when the components are running on the same machine or even on different machines on the same LAN. Web services provide no benefit in these scenarios.

Summary

Web services are a new, industry-standard mechanism for connecting software components across the Internet. This mechanism is based on HTTP, XML, and SOAP—all widely accepted standards. The .NET Framework provides support for developers of web services and web-service clients, making it just as easy to expose and consume web services as it is to write and use a simple class that exposes methods.

CHAPTER 8

ADO.NET: Developing Database Applications

Many software applications benefit from storing their data in database management systems. A database management system is a software component that performs the task of storing and retrieving large amounts of data. Examples of database management systems are Microsoft SQL Server and Oracle Corporation's Oracle.

Microsoft SQL Server and Microsoft Access both include a sample database called Northwind. The Northwind database is used in the examples throughout this chapter.

All examples in this chapter assume that the following declaration appears in the same file as the code:

```
Imports System.Data
```

Examples that use SQL Server also assume this declaration:

```
Imports System.Data.SqlClient
```

and examples that use Access assume this declaration:

```
Imports System.Data.OleDb
```

A Brief History of Universal Data Access

Database management systems provide APIs that allow application programmers to create and access databases. The set of APIs that each manufacturer's system supplies is unique to that manufacturer. Microsoft has long recognized that it is inefficient and error prone for an applications programmer to attempt to master and use all the APIs for the various available database management systems. What's more, if a new database management system is released, an existing application can't make use of it without being rewritten to understand the new APIs. What is needed is a common database API.

Microsoft's previous steps in this direction included Open Database Connectivity (ODBC), OLE DB, and ADO (not to be confused with ADO.NET). Microsoft has made improvements with each new technology.

With .NET, Microsoft has released a new mechanism for accessing data: ADO.NET. The name is a carryover from Microsoft's ADO (ActiveX Data Objects) technology, but it no longer stands for ActiveX Data Objects—it's just ADO.NET. To avoid confusion, I will refer to ADO.NET as ADO.NET and to ADO as *classic* ADO.

If you're familiar with classic ADO, be careful—ADO.NET is not a descendant, it's a new technology. In order to support the Internet evolution, ADO.NET is highly focused on disconnected data and on the ability for anything to be a source of data. While you will find many concepts in ADO.NET to be similar to concepts in classic ADO, it is not the same.

Managed Providers

When speaking of data access, it's useful to distinguish between providers of data and consumers of data. A *data provider* encapsulates data and provides access to it in a generic way. The data itself can be in any form or location. For example, the data may be in a typical database management system such as SQL Server, or it may be distributed around the world and accessed via web services. The data provider shields the data consumer from having to know how to reach the data. In ADO.NET, data providers are referred to as *managed providers*.

A *data consumer* is an application that uses the services of a data provider for the purposes of storing, retrieving, and manipulating data. A customer-service application that manipulates a customer database is a typical example of a data consumer. To consume data, the application must know how to access one or more data providers.

ADO.NET is comprised of many classes, but five take center stage:

Connection
: Represents a connection to a data source.

Command
: Represents a query or a command that is to be executed by a data source.

DataSet
: Represents data. The DataSet can be filled either from a data source (using a DataAdapter object) or dynamically.

DataAdapter
: Used for filling a DataSet from a data source.

DataReader
: Used for fast, efficient, forward-only reading of a data source.

With the exception of DataSet, these five names are not the actual classes used for accessing data sources. Each managed provider exposes classes specific to that provider. For example, the SQL Server managed provider exposes the SqlConnection, SqlCommand, SqlDataAdapter, and SqlDataReader classes. The DataSet class is used with all managed providers.

Any data-source vendor can write a managed provider to make that data source available to ADO.NET data consumers. Microsoft has supplied two managed providers in the .NET Framework: SQL Server and OLE DB.

The examples in this chapter are coded against the SQL Server managed provider, for two reasons. The first is that I believe that most programmers writing data access code in Visual Basic .NET will be doing so against a SQL Server database. Second, the information about the SQL Server managed provider is easily transferable to any other managed provider.

Connecting to a SQL Server Database

To read and write information to and from a SQL Server database, it is necessary first to establish a connection to the database. This is done with the SqlConnection object, found in the System.Data.SqlClient namespace. Here's an example:

```
' Open a database connection.
Dim strConnection As String = _
   "Data Source=localhost;Initial Catalog=Northwind;" _
   & "Integrated Security=True"
Dim cn As SqlConnection = New SqlConnection(strConnection)
cn.Open( )
```

This code fragment instantiates an object of type SqlConnection, passing its constructor a connection string. Calling the SqlConnection object's Open method opens the connection. A connection must be open for data to be read or written, or for commands to be executed. When you're finished accessing the database, use the Close method to close the connection:

```
' Close the database connection.
cn.Close( )
```

The connection string argument to the SqlConnection class's constructor provides information that allows the SqlConnection object to find the SQL Server database. The connection string shown in the earlier code fragment indicates that the database is located on the same machine that is running the code snippet (`Data Source=localhost`), that the database name is Northwind (`Initial Catalog=Northwind`), and that the user ID that should be used for logging in to SQL Server is the current Windows login account (`Integrated Security=True`). Table 8-1 shows the valid SQL Server connection string settings.

Table 8-1. SQL Server connection string settings

Setting	Default Value	Description
Addr		Synonym for Data Source.
Address		Synonym for Data Source.
Application Name		The name of the client application. If provided, SQL Server uses this name in its sysprocesses table to help identify the process serving this connection.
AttachDBFilename		Synonym for Initial File Name.
Connect Timeout	15	Synonym for Connection Timeout.
Connection Timeout	15	The number of seconds to wait for a login response from SQL Server. If no response is received during this period, an SqlException exception is thrown. This setting corresponds to the SqlConnection object's Connection-Timeout property.
Current Language		The language to use for this session with SQL Server. The value of this setting must match one of the entries in either the "name" column or the "alias" column of the "master.dbo.syslanguages" system table. If this setting is not specified, SQL Server uses either its system default language or a user-specific default language, depending on its configuration. The language setting affects the way dates are displayed and may affect the way SQL Server messages are displayed. Search for "SQL Server Language Support" in SQL Server Books Online for more information.
Data Source		The name or network address of the computer on which SQL Server is located. This setting corresponds to the SqlConnection object's DataSource property.
extended properties		Synonym for Initial File Name.
Initial Catalog		The name of the database to use within SQL Server. This setting corresponds to the SqlConnection object's Database property.
Initial File Name		The full pathname of the primary file of an attachable database. If this setting is specified, the Initial Catalog setting must also be specified. Search for "Attaching and Detaching Databases" in SQL Server Books Online for more information. AttachDBFilename and extended properties are synonyms for Initial File Name.
Integrated Security	'false'	Indicates whether to use NT security for authentication. A value of 'true' or 'sspi' (Security Support Provider Interface) indicates that NT security should be used. A value of 'false' indicates that SQL Server security should be used. Search for "How SQL Server Implements Security" in SQL Server Books Online for more information.

Table 8-1. SQL Server connection string settings (continued)

Setting	Default Value	Description
`Net`	'dbmssocn'	Synonym for `Network Library`.
`Network Address`		Synonym for `Data Source`.
`Network Library`	'dbmssocn'	The name of the *.dll* that manages network communications with SQL Server. The default value, 'dbmssocn', is appropriate for clients that communicate with SQL Server over TCP/IP. Search for "Communication Components" and "Net-Libraries and Network Protocols" in SQL Server Books Online for more information.
`Password`		The SQL Server login password for the user specified in the `User ID` setting.
`Persist Security Info`	'false'	Specifies whether SqlConnection object properties can return security-sensitive information while a connection is open. Before a connection is opened, its security-sensitive properties return whatever was placed in them. After a connection is opened, properties return security-sensitive information only if the `Persist Security Info` setting was specified as 'true'. For example, if `Persist Security Info` is 'false' and the connection has been opened, the value returned by the SqlConnection object's ConnectionString property does not show the `Password` setting, even if the `Password` setting was specified.
`Pwd`		Synonym for `Password`.
`Server`		Synonym for `Data Source`.
`Trusted_Connection`	'false'	Synonym for `Integrated Security`.
`User ID`		The SQL Server login account to use for authentication.
`Workstation ID`	the client computer name	The name of the computer that is connecting to SQL Server.

Connecting to an OLE DB Data Source

OLE DB is a specification for wrapping data sources in a COM-based API so that data sources can be accessed in a polymorphic way. The concept is the same as ADO.NET's concept of managed providers. OLE DB predates ADO.NET and will eventually be superseded by it. However, over the years, OLE DB providers have been written for many data sources, including Oracle, Microsoft Access, Microsoft Exchange, and others, whereas currently only one product—SQL Server—is natively supported by an ADO.NET managed provider. To provide immediate support in ADO.NET for a wide range of data sources, Microsoft has supplied an ADO.NET managed provider for OLE DB. That means that ADO.NET can work with any data source for which there is an OLE DB data provider. Furthermore, because there is an OLE DB provider that wraps ODBC (an even older data-access technology), ADO.NET can work with virtually all legacy data, regardless of the source.

SQL Server Authentication

Before a process can access data that is located in a SQL Server database, it must log in to SQL Server. The SqlConnection object communicates with SQL Server and performs this login based on information provided in the connection string. Logging in requires *authentication*. Authentication means proving to SQL Server that the process is acting on behalf of a user who is authorized to access SQL Server data. SQL Server recognizes two methods of authentication:

- SQL Server Authentication, which requires the process to supply a username and password that have been set up in SQL Server by an administrator. Beginning with SQL Server 2000, this method of authentication is no longer recommended (and is disabled by default).
- Integrated Windows Authentication, in which no username and password are provided. Instead, the Windows NT or Windows 2000 system on which the process is running communicates the user's Windows login name to SQL Server. The Windows user must be set up in SQL Server by an administrator in order for this to work.

To use SQL Server Authentication:

1. (SQL Server 2000 only) Enable SQL Server Authentication. In Enterprise Manager, right-click on the desired server, click Properties, and then click the Security tab. Select "SQL Server and Windows" and click OK.
2. The network administrator sets up a login account using Enterprise Manager, specifying that the account will use SQL Server Authentication and supplying a password. Programming books (including this one) typically assume the presence of a user named "sa" with an empty password, because this is the default system administrator account set up on every SQL Server installation (good administrators change the password, however).
3. The network administrator assigns rights to this login account as appropriate.
4. The data access code specifies the account and password in the connection string passed to the SqlConnection object. For example, the following connection string specifies the "sa" account with a blank password:

   ```
   "Data Source=SomeMachine; Initial Catalog=Northwind; User ID=sa; Password="
   ```

To use Integrated Windows Authentication:

1. The network administrator sets up the login account using Enterprise Manager, specifying that the account will use Windows Authentication and supplying the Windows user or group that is to be given access.
2. The network administrator assigns rights to this login account as appropriate.
3. The data access code indicates in the connection string that Integrated Windows Security should be used, as shown here:

   ```
   "Data Source= SomeMachine; Initial Catalog=Northwind; Integrated Security=True"
   ```

—continued—

When using Integrated Windows Authentication, it is necessary to know what Windows login account a process will run under and to set up appropriate rights for that login account in SQL Server Enterprise Manager. A program running on a local machine generally runs under the login account of the user that started the program. A component running in Microsoft Transaction Server (MTS) or COM+ runs under a login account specified in the MTS or COM+ Explorer. Code that is embedded in an ASP.NET web page runs under a login account specified in Internet Information Server (IIS). Consult the documentation for these products for information on specifying the login account under which components run. Consult the SQL Server Books Online for information on setting up SQL Server login accounts and on specifying account privileges.

Connecting to an OLE DB data source is similar to connecting to SQL Server, with a few differences: the OleDbConnection class (from the System.Data.OleDb namespace) is used instead of the SqlConnection class, and the connection string is slightly different. When using the OleDbConnection class, the connection string must specify the OLE DB provider that is to be used as well as additional information that tells the OLE DB provider where the actual data is. For example, the following code opens a connection to the Northwind sample database in Microsoft Access:

```
' Open a connection to the database.
Dim strConnection As String = _
   "Provider=Microsoft.Jet.OLEDB.4.0;Data Source=" _
   & "C:\Program Files\Microsoft Office\Office\Samples\Northwind.mdb"
Dim cn As OleDbConnection = New OleDbConnection(strConnection)
cn.Open( )
```

Similarly, this code opens a connection to an Oracle database:

```
' Open a connection to the database.
Dim strConnection As String = _
   "Provider=MSDAORA.1;User ID=MyID;Password=MyPassword;" _
   & "Data Source=MyDatabaseService.MyDomain.com"
Dim cn As OleDbConnection = New OleDbConnection(strConnection)
cn.Open( )
```

The values of each setting in the connection string, and even the set of settings that are allowed in the connection string, are dependent on the specific OLE DB provider being used. Refer to the documentation for the specific OLE DB provider for more information.

Table 8-2 shows the provider names for several of the most common OLE DB providers.

Table 8-2. Common OLE DB provider names

Data source	OLE DB provider name
Microsoft Access	`Microsoft.Jet.OLEDB.4.0`
Microsoft Indexing Service	`MSIDXS.1`
Microsoft SQL Server	`SQLOLEDB.1`
Oracle	`MSDAORA.1`

Reading Data into a DataSet

The DataSet class is ADO.NET's highly flexible, general-purpose mechanism for reading and updating data. Example 8-1 shows how to issue a SQL `SELECT` statement against the SQL Server Northwind sample database to retrieve and display the names of companies located in London. The resulting display is shown in Figure 8-1.

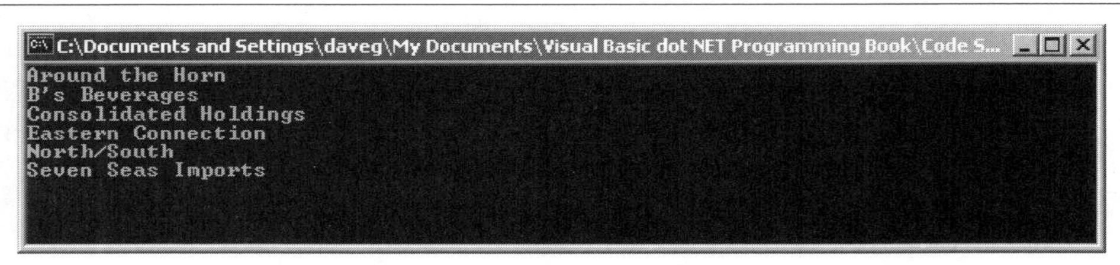

Figure 8-1. The output generated by the code in Example 8-1

Example 8-1. Retrieving data from SQL Server using a SQL SELECT statement

```
' Open a connection to the database.
Dim strConnection As String = _
   "Data Source=localhost; Initial Catalog=Northwind;" _
   & "Integrated Security=True"
Dim cn As SqlConnection = New SqlConnection(strConnection)
cn.Open( )

' Set up a data set command object.
Dim strSelect As String = "SELECT * FROM Customers WHERE City = 'London'"
Dim dscmd As New SqlDataAdapter(strSelect, cn)

' Load a data set.
Dim ds As New DataSet( )
dscmd.Fill(ds, "LondonCustomers")

' Close the connection.
cn.Close( )

' Do something with the data set.
Dim dt As DataTable = ds.Tables.Item("LondonCustomers")
Dim rowCustomer As DataRow
For Each rowCustomer In dt.Rows
```

Example 8-1. Retrieving data from SQL Server using a SQL SELECT statement (continued)

```
   Console.WriteLine(rowCustomer.Item("CompanyName"))
Next
```

The code in Example 8-1 performs the following steps to obtain data from the database:

1. Opens a connection to the database using a SqlConnection object.
2. Instantiates an object of type SqlDataAdapter in preparation for filling a DataSet object. In Example 8-1, a SQL `SELECT` command string and a Connection object are passed to the SqlDataAdapter object's constructor.
3. Instantiates an object of type DataSet and fills it by calling the SqlDataAdapter object's Fill method.

The DataSet Class

The DataSet class encapsulates a set of tables and the relations between those tables. Figure 8-2 shows a class model diagram containing the DataSet and related classes. The DataSet is always completely disconnected from any data source. In fact, the DataSet has no knowledge of the source of its tables and relations. They may be dynamically created using methods on the DataSet, or they may be loaded from a data source. In the case of the SQL Server managed provider, a DataSet can be loaded from a SQL Server database using an SqlDataAdapter object. This is what was done in Example 8-1.

After a DataSet is loaded, its data can be changed, added to, or deleted, all without affecting the data source. Indeed, a database connection does not need to be maintained during these updates. When ready, the updates can be written back to the database by establishing a new connection and calling the SqlDataAdapter object's Update method. Examples of writing updates to a database are shown later in this chapter.Navigating the DataSet

In this section you'll learn how to find specific data in a DataSet object, how to make changes to that data, and how to write those changes back to a database.

Finding Tables

The DataSet object's Tables property holds a TablesCollection object that contains the DataTable objects in the DataSet. The following code loops through all the tables in the DataSet and displays their names:

```
' Iterate through the tables in the DataSet ds.
Dim dt As DataTable
For Each dt In ds.Tables
   Console.WriteLine(dt.TableName)
Next
```

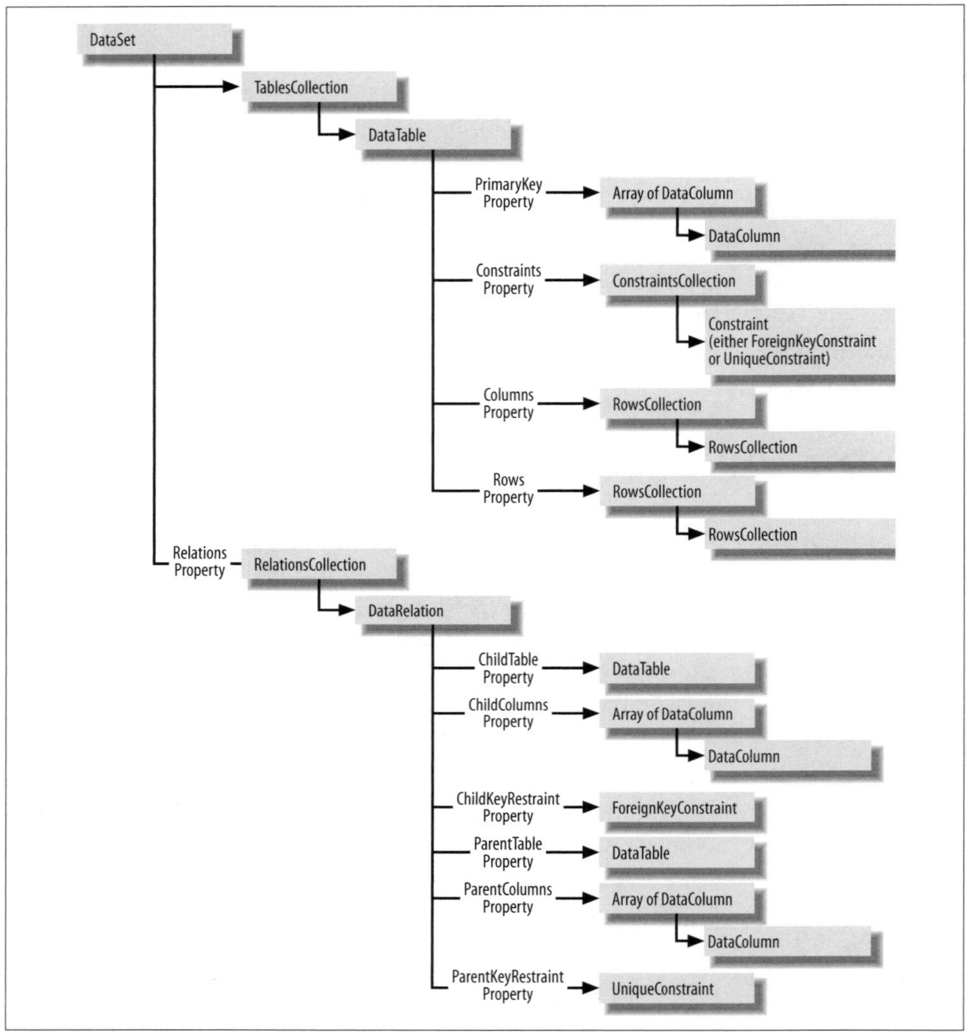

Figure 8-2. A class model diagram for the DataSet and related classes

This code does the same thing, using a numeric index on the TablesCollection object:

```
' Iterate through the tables in the DataSet ds.
Dim n As Integer
For n = 0 To ds.Tables.Count - 1
   Console.WriteLine(ds.Tables(n).TableName)
Next
```

The TablesCollection object can also be indexed by table name. For example, if the DataSet ds contains a table named "Categories", this code gets a reference to it:

```
Dim dt As DataTable = ds.Tables("Categories")
```

Finding Rows

The DataTable object's Rows property holds a DataRowCollection object that in turn holds the table's DataRow objects. Each DataRow object holds the data for that particular row. The following code loops through all the rows in the DataTable and displays the value of the first column (column 0) in the row:

```
' Iterate through the rows.
Dim row As DataRow
For Each row In dt.Rows
   Console.WriteLine(row(0))
Next
```

This code does the same thing, using a numeric index on the RowsCollection object:

```
' Iterate through the rows.
Dim n As Integer
For n = 0 To dt.Rows.Count - 1
   Console.WriteLine(dt.Rows(n)(0))
Next
```

To assist with locating specific rows within a table, the DataTable class provides a method called Select. The Select method returns an array containing all the rows in the table that match the given criteria. The syntax of the Select method is:

```
Public Overloads Function Select( _
   ByVal filterExpression As String, _
   ByVal sort As String, _
   ByVal recordStates As System.Data.DataViewRowState _
) As System.Data.DataRow( )
```

The parameters of the Select method are:

filterExpression
: This parameter gives the criteria for selecting rows. It is a string that is in the same format as the `WHERE` clause in an SQL statement.

sort
: This parameter specifies how the returned rows are to be sorted. It is a string that is in the same format as the `ORDER BY` clause in an SQL statement.

recordStates
: This parameter specifies the versions of the records that are to be retrieved. Record versions are discussed in the later section "Changing, Adding, and Deleting Rows." The value passed in this parameter must be one of the values given by the System.Data.DataViewRowState enumeration. Its values are:

  `CurrentRows`
  : Returns the current version of each row, regardless of whether it is unchanged, new, or modified.

  `Deleted`
  : Returns only rows that have been deleted.

`ModifiedCurrent`
: Returns only rows that have been modified. The values in the returned rows are the current values of the rows.

`ModifiedOriginal`
: Returns only rows that have been modified. The values in the returned rows are the original values of the rows.

`New`
: Returns only new rows.

`None`
: Returns no rows.

`OriginalRows`
: Returns only rows that were in the table prior to any modifications. The values in the returned rows are the original values.

`Unchanged`
: Returns only unchanged rows.

These values can be combined using the `And` operator to achieve combined results. For example, to retrieve both modified and new rows, pass this value:

```
DataViewRowState.ModifiedCurrent And DataViewRowState.New
```

The return value of the Select method is an array of DataRow objects.

The Select method is overloaded. It has a two-parameter version that is the same as the full version, except that it does not take a *recordStates* parameter:

```
Public Overloads Function Select( _
   ByVal filterExpression As String, _
   ByVal sort As String _
) As System.Data.DataRow( )
```

Calling this version of the Select method is the same as calling the full version with a *recordStates* value of `DataViewRowState.CurrentRows`.

Similarly, there is a one-parameter version that takes only a *filterExpression*:

```
Public Overloads Function Select( _
   ByVal filterExpression As String _
   ) As System.Data.DataRow( )
```

This is the same as calling the three-parameter version with *sort* equal to `""` (the empty string) and *recordStates* equal to `DataViewRowState.CurrentRows`.

Lastly, there is the parameterless version of Select:

```
Public Overloads Function Select( ) As System.Data.DataRow( )
```

This is the same as calling the three-parameter version with *filterExpression* and *sort* equal to `""` (the empty string) and *recordStates* equal to `DataViewRowState.CurrentRows`.

As an example of using the Select method, this line of code returns all rows whose Country column contains the value "Mexico":

```
Dim rows() As DataRow = dt.Select("Country = 'Mexico'")
```

Because the *sort* and *recordStates* parameters were not specified, they default to "" (the empty string) and DataViewRowState.CurrentRows, respectively.

The Select method versus the SQL SELECT statement

If an application is communicating with a database over a fast, persistent connection, it is more efficient to issue SQL SELECT statements that load the DataSet with only the desired records, rather than to load the DataSet with a large amount of data and then pare it down with the DataTable's Select method. The Select method is useful for distributed applications that might not have a fast connection to the database. Such an application might load a large amount of data from the database into a DataSet object, then use several calls to the DataTable's Select method to locally view and process the data in a variety of ways. This is more efficient in this case because the data is moved across the slow connection only once, rather than once for each query.

Finding Column Values

The DataRow class has an Item property that provides access to the value in each column of a row. For example, this code iterates through all the columns of a row, displaying the value from each column (assume that row holds a reference to a DataRow object):

```
' Iterate through the column values.
Dim n As Integer
For n = 0 To row.Table.Columns.Count - 1
   Console.WriteLine(row(n))
Next
```

Note the expression used to find the number of columns: row.Table.Columns.Count. The DataRow object's Table property holds a reference to the DataTable object of which the row is a part. As will be discussed shortly, the Table object's Columns property maintains a collection of column definitions for the table. The Count property of this collection gives the number of columns in the table and therefore in each row.

The DataRow object's Item property is overloaded to allow a specific column value to be accessed by column name. The following code assumes that the DataRow row contains a column named "Description". The code displays the value of this column in this row:

```
Console.WriteLine(row("Description"))
```

Finding Column Definitions

The DataTable object's Columns property holds a ColumnsCollection object that in turn holds the definitions for the columns in the table. The following code iterates through the columns in the table and displays their names:

```
' Iterate through the columns.
Dim column As DataColumn
For Each column In dt.Columns
   Console.WriteLine(column.ColumnName)
Next
```

This code does the same thing, using a numeric index on the ColumnsCollection object:

```
' Iterate through the columns.
Dim n As Integer
For n = 0 To dt.Columns.Count - 1
   Console.WriteLine(dt.Columns(n).ColumnName)
Next
```

The ColumnsCollection object can also be indexed by column name. For example, if DataTable dt contains a column named "Description", this code gets a reference to the associated DataColumn object:

```
Dim column As DataColumn = dt.Columns("Description")
```

Changing, Adding, and Deleting Rows

To change data in a DataSet, first navigate to a row of interest and then assign new values to one or more of its columns. For example, the following line of code assumes that row is a DataRow object that contains a column named "Description". The code sets the value of the column in this row to be "Milk and cheese":

```
row("Description") = "Milk and cheese"
```

Adding a new row to a table in a DataSet is a three-step process:

1. Use the DataTable class's NewRow method to create a new DataRow. The method takes no parameters.
2. Set the values of the columns in the row.
3. Add the new row to the table.

For example, assuming that dt is a DataTable object, and that the table has columns named "CategoryName" and "Description", this code adds a new row to the table:

```
' Add a row.
Dim row As DataRow = dt.NewRow( )
row("CategoryName") = "Software"
row("Description") = "Fine code and binaries"
dt.Rows.Add(row)
```

The DataRow object referenced by `row` in this code can be indexed by the names "CategoryName" and "Description" because the DataRow object was created by the DataTable object's NewRow method and so has the same schema as the table. Note that the NewRow method does not add the row to the table. Adding the new row to the table must be done explicitly by calling the DataRowCollection class's Add method through the DataTable class's Rows property.

Deleting a row from a table is a one-liner. Assuming that `row` is a reference to a DataRow, this line deletes the row from its table:

```
row.Delete( )
```

When changes are made to a row, the DataRow object keeps track of more than just the new column values. It also keeps track of the row's original column values and the fact that the row has been changed. The Item property of the DataRow object is overloaded to allow you to specify the desired version of the data that you wish to retrieve. The syntax of this overload is:

```
Public Overloads ReadOnly Property Item( _
   ByVal columnName As String, _
   ByVal version As System.Data.DataRowVersion _
) As Object
```

The parameters are:

`columnName`
: The name of the column whose value is to be retrieved.

`version`
: The version of the data to retrieve. This value must be a member of the System.Data.DataRowVersion enumeration. Its values are:

  `Current`
  : Retrieve the current (changed) version.

  `Default`
  : Retrieve the current version if the data has been changed, the original version if not.

  `Original`
  : Retrieve the original (unchanged) version.

  `Proposed`
  : Retrieve the proposed change. Proposed changes are changes that are made after a call to a DataRow object's BeginEdit method but before a call to its EndEdit or CancelEdit methods. For more information, see "Relations Between DataTables in a DataSet" later in this chapter.

For example, after making some changes in DataRow `row`, the following line displays the original version of the row's Description column:

```
Console.WriteLine(row("Description", DataRowVersion.Original))
```

The current value of the row would be displayed using any of the following lines:

```
Console.WriteLine(row("Description", DataRowVersion.Current))
Console.WriteLine(row("Description", DataRowVersion.Default))
Console.WriteLine(row("Description"))
```

Calling the DataSet object's AcceptChanges method commits outstanding changes. Calling the DataSet object's RejectChanges method rolls records back to their original versions.

The code shown in this section affects only the DataSet object, not the data source. To propagate these changes, additions, and deletions back to the data source, use the Update method of the SqlDataAdapter class, as described in the next section, "Writing Updates Back to the Data Source."

If there are relations defined between the DataTables in the DataSet, it may be necessary to call the DataRow object's BeginEdit method before making changes. For more information, see "Relations Between DataTables in a DataSet" later in this chapter.

Writing Updates Back to the Data Source

Because DataSets are always disconnected from their data sources, making changes in a DataSet never has any effect on the data source. To propagate changes, additions, and deletions back to a data source, call the SqlDataAdapter class's Update method, passing the DataSet and the name of the table that is to be updated. For example, the following call to Update writes changes from the DataTable named Categories back to the SQL Server table of the same name:

```
da.Update(ds, "Categories")
```

Before using the Update method, however, you should understand how an SqlDataAdapter object performs updates. To change, add, or delete records, an SqlDataAdapter object must send SQL `UPDATE`, `INSERT`, or `DELETE` statements, respectively, to SQL Server. The forms of these statements either can be inferred from the `SELECT` statement that was provided to the SqlDataAdapter object or can be explicitly provided to the SqlDataAdapter object.

Example 8-2 shows an example of allowing an SqlDataAdapter object to infer the SQL `UPDATE`, `INSERT`, and `DELETE` statements required for applying updates to a database.

Example 8-2. Allowing an SqlDataAdapter object to infer SQL UPDATE, INSERT, and DELETE statements from a SELECT statement

```
' Open a database connection.
Dim strConnection As String = _
   "Data Source=localhost;Initial Catalog=Northwind;" _
   & "Integrated Security=True"
Dim cn As SqlConnection = New SqlConnection(strConnection)
```

Example 8-2. Allowing an SqlDataAdapter object to infer SQL UPDATE, INSERT, and DELETE statements from a SELECT statement (continued)

```
cn.Open( )

' Create a data adapter object and set its SELECT command.
Dim strSelect As String = _
   "SELECT * FROM Categories"
Dim da As SqlDataAdapter = New SqlDataAdapter(strSelect, cn)

' Set the data adapter object's UPDATE, INSERT, and DELETE
' commands. Use the SqlCommandBuilder class's ability to auto-
' generate these commands from the SELECT command.
Dim autogen As New SqlCommandBuilder(da)

' Load a data set.
Dim ds As DataSet = New DataSet( )
da.Fill(ds, "Categories")

' Get a reference to the "Categories" DataTable.
Dim dt As DataTable = ds.Tables("Categories")

' Modify one of the records.
Dim row As DataRow = dt.Select("CategoryName = 'Dairy Products'")(0)
row("Description") = "Milk and stuff"

' Add a record.
row = dt.NewRow( )
row("CategoryName") = "Software"
row("Description") = "Fine code and binaries"
dt.Rows.Add(row)

' Delete a record.
row = dt.Select("CategoryName = 'MyCategory'")(0)
row.Delete( )

' Update the database.
da.Update(ds, "Categories")

' Close the database connection.
cn.Close( )
```

Note the following in Example 8-2:

1. A SqlDataAdapter object is constructed with an argument of `"SELECT * FROM Categories"`. This initializes the value of the SqlDataAdapter object's SelectCommand property.
2. A SqlCommandBuilder object is constructed with the SqlDataAdapter object passed as an argument to its constructor. This step hooks the SqlDataAdapter object to the SqlCommandBuilder object so that later, when the SqlDataAdapter object's Update method is called, the SqlDataAdapter object can obtain

SQL UPDATE, INSERT, and DELETE commands from the SqlCommandBuilder object.

3. The SqlDataAdapter object is used to fill a DataSet object. This results in the DataSet object containing a DataTable object, named "Categories", that contains all the rows from the Northwind database's Categories table.
4. One record each in the table is modified, added, or deleted.
5. The SqlDataAdapter object's Update method is called to propagate the changes back to the database.

Step 5 forces the SqlCommandBuilder object to generate SQL statements for performing the database update, insert, and delete operations.When the Update method is called, the SqlDataAdapter object notes that no values have been set for its UpdateCommand, InsertCommand, and DeleteCommand prperties, and therefore queries the SqlCommandBuilder object for these commands. If any of these properties had been set on the SqlDataAdapter object, those values would have been used instead.

The SqlCommandBuildObject can be examined to see what commands were created. To see the commands that are generated in Example 8-2, add the following lines anywhere after the declaration and assignment of the autogen variable:

```
Console.WriteLine("UpdateCommand: " & autogen.GetUpdateCommand.CommandText)
Console.WriteLine("InsertCommand: " & autogen.GetInsertCommand.CommandText)
Console.WriteLine("DeleteCommand: " & autogen.GetDeleteCommand.CommandText)
```

The auto-generated UPDATE command contains the following text (note that line breaks have been added for clarity in the book):

```
UPDATE Categories
SET CategoryName = @p1 , Description = @p2 , Picture = @p3
WHERE (
  (CategoryID = @p4)
  AND
  ((CategoryName IS NULL AND @p5 IS NULL) OR (CategoryName = @p6)) )
```

Similarly, the INSERT command is:

```
INSERT INTO Categories( CategoryName , Description , Picture )
VALUES ( @p1 , @p2 , @p3)
```

And the DELETE command is:

```
DELETE FROM  Categories
WHERE (
  (CategoryID = @p1)
  AND
  ((CategoryName IS NULL AND @p2 IS NULL) OR (CategoryName = @p3)) )
```

Note the use of formal parameters (@p0, @p1, etc.) in each of these statements. For each row that is to be changed, added, or deleted, the parameters are replaced with values from the row, and the resulting SQL statement is issued to the database. The choice of which value from the row to use for which parameter is controlled by the SqlCommand object's Parameters property. This property contains an SqlParameter-Collection object that in turn contains one SqlParameter object for each formal parameter. The SqlParameter object's ParameterName property matches the name of the formal parameter (including the "@"), the SourceColumn property contains the name of the column from which the value is to come, and the SourceVersion property specifies the version of the value that is to be used. Row versions were discussed in the previous section, "Changing, Adding, and Deleting Rows."

If desired, a DataSet object's UpdateCommand, InsertCommand, and DeleteCommand properties can be set directly. Example 8-3 sets the value of UpdateCommand and then performs an update using this command.

Example 8-3. Setting a DataSet object's UpdateCommand property

```
' Open a database connection.
Dim strConnection As String = _
   "Data Source=localhost;Initial Catalog=Northwind;" _
   & "Integrated Security=True"
Dim cn As SqlConnection = New SqlConnection(strConnection)
cn.Open( )

' Set up a data adapter object.
Dim da As SqlDataAdapter = New SqlDataAdapter("SELECT * FROM Categories", cn)

' Create an UPDATE command.
'
' This is the command text.
' Note the parameter names: @Description and @CategoryID.
Dim strUpdateCommand As String = _
   "UPDATE Categories" _
   & " SET Description = @Description" _
   & " WHERE CategoryID = @CategoryID"
'
' Create a SqlCommand object and assign it to the UpdateCommand property.
da.UpdateCommand = New SqlCommand(strUpdateCommand, cn)
'
' Set up parameters in the SqlCommand object.
Dim param As SqlParameter
'
' @CategoryID
param = da.UpdateCommand.Parameters.Add( _
   New SqlParameter("@CategoryID", SqlDbType.Int))
param.SourceColumn = "CategoryID"
param.SourceVersion = DataRowVersion.Original
'
' @Description
param = da.UpdateCommand.Parameters.Add( _
   New SqlParameter("@Description", SqlDbType.NChar, 16))
param.SourceColumn = "Description"
param.SourceVersion = DataRowVersion.Current
```

Example 8-3. Setting a DataSet object's UpdateCommand property (continued)

```
' Load a data set.
Dim ds As DataSet = New DataSet( )
da.Fill(ds, "Categories")

' Get the table.
Dim dt As DataTable = ds.Tables("Categories")

' Get a row.
Dim row As DataRow = dt.Select("CategoryName = 'Dairy Products'")(0)

' Change the value in the Description column.
row("Description") = "Milk and stuff"

' Perform the update.
da.Update(ds, "Categories")

' Close the database connection.
cn.Close( )
```

Relations Between DataTables in a DataSet

The DataSet class provides a mechanism for specifying relations between tables in a DataSet. The DataSet class's Relations property contains a RelationsCollection object, which maintains a collection of DataRelation objects. Each DataRelation object represents a parent/child relationship between two tables in the DataSet. For example, there is conceptually a parent/child relationship between a `Customers` table and an `Orders` table, because each order must belong to some customer. Modeling this relationship in the DataSet has these benefits:

- The DataSet can enforce relational integrity.
- The DataSet can propagate key updates and row deletions.
- Data-bound controls can provide a visual representation of the relation.

Example 8-4 loads a `Customers` table and an `Orders` table from the Northwind database and then creates a relation between them. The statement that actually creates the relation is shown in bold.

Example 8-4. Creating a DataRelation between DataTables in a DataSet

```
' Open a database connection.
Dim strConnection As String = _
   "Data Source=localhost;Initial Catalog=Northwind;" _
   & "Integrated Security=True"
Dim cn As SqlConnection = New SqlConnection(strConnection)
cn.Open( )

' Set up a data adapter object.
Dim strSql As String = "SELECT * FROM Customers" _
   & " WHERE City = 'Buenos Aires' AND Country = 'Argentina'"
```

Example 8-4. Creating a DataRelation between DataTables in a DataSet (continued)

```
Dim da As SqlDataAdapter = New SqlDataAdapter(strSql, cn)

' Load a data set.
Dim ds As DataSet = New DataSet( )
da.Fill(ds, "Customers")

' Set up a new data adapter object.
strSql = "SELECT Orders.*" _
   & " FROM Customers, Orders" _
   & " WHERE (Customers.CustomerID = Orders.CustomerID)" _
   & "    AND (Customers.City = 'Buenos Aires')" _
   & "    AND (Customers.Country = 'Argentina')"
da = New SqlDataAdapter(strSql, cn)

' Load the data set.
da.Fill(ds, "Orders")

' Close the database connection.
cn.Close( )

' Create a relation.
ds.Relations.Add("CustomerOrders", _
   ds.Tables("Customers").Columns("CustomerID"), _
   ds.Tables("Orders").Columns("CustomerID"))
```

As shown in Example 8-4, the DataRelationCollection object's Add method creates a new relation between two tables in the DataSet. The Add method is overloaded. The syntax used in Example 8-4 is:

```
Public Overloads Overridable Function Add( _
   ByVal name As String, _
   ByVal parentColumn As System.Data.DataColumn, _
   ByVal childColumn As System.Data.DataColumn _
) As System.Data.DataRelation
```

The parameters are:

name
: The name to give to the new relation. This name can be used later as an index to the RelationsCollection object.

parentColumn
: The DataColumn object representing the parent column.

childColumn
: The DataColumn object representing the child column.

The return value is the newly created DataRelation object. Example 8-4 ignores the return value.

The DataSet's XML Capabilities

The DataSet class has several methods for reading and writing data as XML, including:

GetXml
: Returns a string containing an XML representation of the data in the DataSet object.

GetXmlSchema
: Returns a string containing the XSD schema for the XML returned by the GetXml method.

WriteXml
: Writes the XML representation of the data in the DataSet object to a Stream object, a file, a TextWriter object, or an XmlWriter object. This XML can either include or omit the corresponding XSD schema.

WriteXmlSchema
: Writes the XSD schema for the DataSet to a Stream object, a file, a TextWriter object, or an XmlWriter object.

ReadXml
: Reads the XML written by the WriteXml method.

ReadXmlSchema
: Reads the XSD schema written by the WriteXmlSchema method.

Example 8-5 shows how to write a DataSet to a file as XML using the WriteXml method.

Example 8-5. Saving a DataSet to a file as XML

```
' Open a database connection.
Dim strConnection As String = _
   "Data Source=localhost;Initial Catalog=Northwind;" _
   & "Integrated Security=True"
Dim cn As SqlConnection = New SqlConnection(strConnection)
cn.Open( )

' Set up a data adapter object.
Dim strSql As String = "SELECT * FROM Customers" _
   & " WHERE CustomerID = 'GROSR'"
Dim da As SqlDataAdapter = New SqlDataAdapter(strSql, cn)

' Load a data set.
Dim ds As DataSet = New DataSet("MyDataSetName")
da.Fill(ds, "Customers")

' Set up a new data adapter object.
strSql = "SELECT Orders.*" _
   & " FROM Customers, Orders" _
   & " WHERE (Customers.CustomerID = Orders.CustomerID)" _
   & "    AND (Customers.CustomerID = 'GROSR')"
```

Example 8-5. Saving a DataSet to a file as XML (continued)

```
da = New SqlDataAdapter(strSql, cn)

' Load the data set.
da.Fill(ds, "Orders")

' Close the database connection.
cn.Close( )

' Create a relation.
ds.Relations.Add("CustomerOrders", _
   ds.Tables("Customers").Columns("CustomerID"), _
   ds.Tables("Orders").Columns("CustomerID"))

' Save as XML.
ds.WriteXml("c:\temp.xml")
```

The majority of the code in Example 8-5 simply loads the DataSet with data. Actually writing the XML is done with the DataSet's WriteXml method at the end of Example 8-5. The contents of the file thus created are shown in Example 8-6. Some lines in Example 8-6 have been wrapped for printing in this book.

Example 8-6. The file produced by the code in Example 8-5

```
<?xml version="1.0" standalone="yes"?>
<MyDataSetName>
  <Customers>
    <CustomerID>GROSR</CustomerID>
    <CompanyName>GROSELLA-Restaurante</CompanyName>
    <ContactName>Manuel Pereira</ContactName>
    <ContactTitle>Owner</ContactTitle>
    <Address>5th Ave. Los Palos Grandes</Address>
    <City>Caracas</City>
    <Region>DF</Region>
    <PostalCode>1081</PostalCode>
    <Country>Venezuela</Country>
    <Phone>(2) 283-2951</Phone>
    <Fax>(2) 283-3397</Fax>
  </Customers>
  <Orders>
    <OrderID>10268</OrderID>
    <CustomerID>GROSR</CustomerID>
    <EmployeeID>8</EmployeeID>
    <OrderDate>1996-07-30T00:00:00.0000000-05:00</OrderDate>
    <RequiredDate>1996-08-27T00:00:00.0000000-05:00</RequiredDate>
    <ShippedDate>1996-08-02T00:00:00.0000000-05:00</ShippedDate>
    <ShipVia>3</ShipVia>
    <Freight>66.29</Freight>
    <ShipName>GROSELLA-Restaurante</ShipName>
    <ShipAddress>5th Ave. Los Palos Grandes</ShipAddress>
    <ShipCity>Caracas</ShipCity>
    <ShipRegion>DF</ShipRegion>
    <ShipPostalCode>1081</ShipPostalCode>
```

Example 8-6. The file produced by the code in Example 8-5 (continued)

```
    <ShipCountry>Venezuela</ShipCountry>
  </Orders>
  <Orders>
    <OrderID>10785</OrderID>
    <CustomerID>GROSR</CustomerID>
    <EmployeeID>1</EmployeeID>
    <OrderDate>1997-12-18T00:00:00.0000000-06:00</OrderDate>
    <RequiredDate>1998-01-15T00:00:00.0000000-06:00</RequiredDate>
    <ShippedDate>1997-12-24T00:00:00.0000000-06:00</ShippedDate>
    <ShipVia>3</ShipVia>
    <Freight>1.51</Freight>
    <ShipName>GROSELLA-Restaurante</ShipName>
    <ShipAddress>5th Ave. Los Palos Grandes</ShipAddress>
    <ShipCity>Caracas</ShipCity>
    <ShipRegion>DF</ShipRegion>
    <ShipPostalCode>1081</ShipPostalCode>
    <ShipCountry>Venezuela</ShipCountry>
  </Orders>
</MyDataSetName>
```

The syntax of this overloaded version of the WriteXml function is:

```
Public Overloads Sub WriteXml(ByVal fileName As String)
```

The *fileName* parameter specifies the full path of a file into which to write the XML.

The XML document written by the DataSet class's WriteXml method can be read back into a DataSet object using the ReadXml method. Example 8-7 reads back the file written by the code in Example 8-5.

Example 8-7. Recreating a DataSet object from XML

```
Dim ds As New DataSet( )
ds.ReadXml("c:\temp.xml")
```

The XML created by the WriteXml method contains only data—no schema information. The ReadXml method is able to infer the schema from the data. To explicitly write the schema information, use the WriteXmlSchema method. To read the schema back in, use the ReadXmlSchema method.

The GetXml and GetXmlSchema methods work the same as the WriteXml and WriteXmlSchema methods, except that each returns its result as a string rather than writing it to a file.

Binding a DataSet to a Windows Forms DataGrid

DataSet and DataTable objects can be bound to Windows Forms DataGrid objects to provide an easy way to view data. This is done by calling a DataGrid object's Set-

DataBinding method, passing the object that is to be bound to the grid. The syntax of the SetDataBinding method is:

```
Public Sub SetDataBinding( _
   ByVal dataSource As Object, _
   ByVal dataMember As String _
)
```

The parameters are:

dataSource
: The source of the data to show in the grid. This can be any object that exposes the `System.Collections.IList` or `System.Data.IListSource` interfaces, which includes the DataTable and DataSet classes discussed in this chapter.

dataMember
: If the object passed in the *dataSource* parameter contains multiple tables, as a DataSet object does, the *dataMember* parameter identifies the table to display in the DataGrid. If a DataTable is passed in the *dataSource* parameter, the *dataMember* parameter should contain either `Nothing` or an empty string.

Example 8-8 shows how to bind a DataSource object to a DataGrid. The DataSource object contains a `Customers` table and an `Orders` table, and a relation between them. The call to the DataGrid object's SetDataBinding method specifies that the `Customers` table should be shown in the grid. Figure 8-3 shows the resulting DataGrid display.

Example 8-8. Creating a DataSet and binding it to a Windows Forms DataGrid

```
' Open a database connection.
Dim strConnection As String = _
   "Data Source=localhost;Initial Catalog=Northwind;" _
   & "Integrated Security=True"
Dim cn As SqlConnection = New SqlConnection(strConnection)
cn.Open( )

' Set up a data adapter object.
Dim strSql As String = _
   "SELECT CustomerID, CompanyName, ContactName, Phone FROM Customers" _
   & " WHERE City = 'Buenos Aires' AND Country = 'Argentina'"
Dim da As SqlDataAdapter = New SqlDataAdapter(strSql, cn)

' Load a data set.
Dim ds As DataSet = New DataSet( )
da.Fill(ds, "Customers")

' Set up a new data adapter object.
strSql = _
   "SELECT Orders.OrderID, Orders.CustomerID, Orders.OrderDate," _
   & " Orders.ShippedDate" _
   & " FROM Customers, Orders" _
   & " WHERE (Customers.CustomerID = Orders.CustomerID)" _
   & "    AND (Customers.City = 'Buenos Aires')" _
   & "    AND (Customers.Country = 'Argentina')"
```

Example 8-8. Creating a DataSet and binding it to a Windows Forms DataGrid (continued)

```
da = New SqlDataAdapter(strSql, cn)

' Load the data set.
da.Fill(ds, "Orders")

' Close the database connection.
cn.Close( )

' Create a relation.
ds.Relations.Add("CustomerOrders", _
   ds.Tables("Customers").Columns("CustomerID"), _
   ds.Tables("Orders").Columns("CustomerID"))

' Bind the data set to a grid.
' Assumes that grid contains a reference to a
' System.WinForms.DataGrid object.
grd.SetDataBinding(ds, "Customers")
```

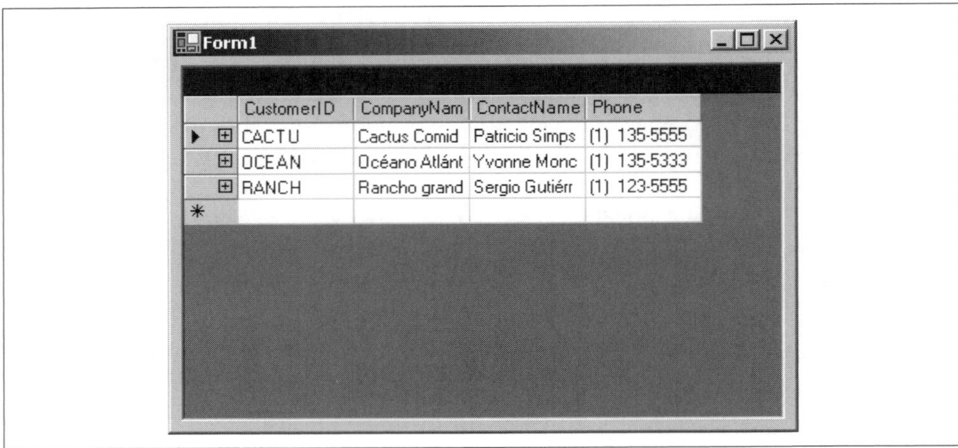

Figure 8-3. The display generated by the code in Example 8-8

Note in Figure 8-3 that each row in this DataGrid has a "+" icon. The reason is that the DataGrid object has detected the relation between the `Customers` table and the `Orders` table. Clicking on the "+" reveals all of the relations for which the `Customers` table is the parent. In this case, there is only one, as shown in Figure 8-4.

The name of the relation in the display is a link. Clicking on this link loads the grid with the child table in the relation, as shown in Figure 8-5.

While the child table is displayed, the corresponding row from the parent table is displayed in a header (shown in Figure 8-5). To return to the parent table, click the left-pointing triangle in the upper-right corner of the grid.

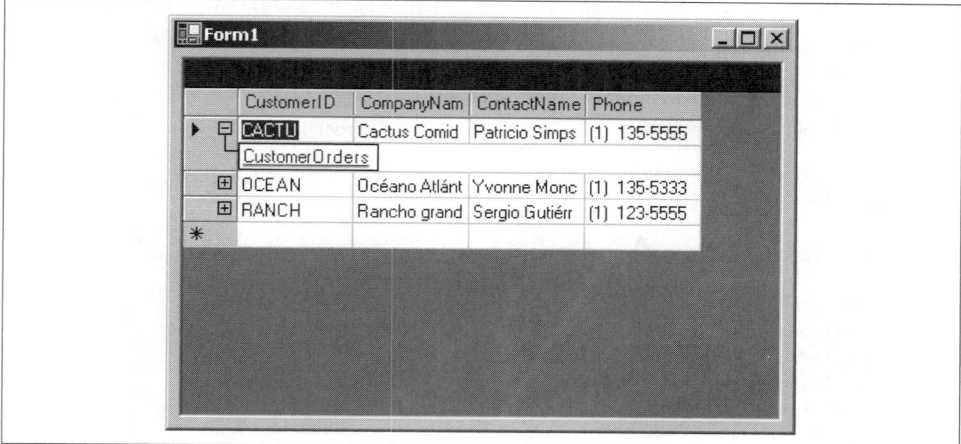

Figure 8-4. Clicking the "+" reveals relations

Form1

Customers: CustomerID: CACTU CompanyName: Cactus Comidas

OrderID	CustomerID	OrderDate	ShippedDate
10521	CACTU	29-Apr-1997	02-May-1997
10782	CACTU	17-Dec-1997	22-Dec-1997
10819	CACTU	07-Jan-1998	16-Jan-1998
10881	CACTU	11-Feb-1998	18-Feb-1998
10937	CACTU	10-Mar-1998	13-Mar-1998
11054	CACTU	28-Apr-1998	(null)

Figure 8-5. The Orders table

Binding a DataSet to a Web Forms DataGrid

Example 8-9 shows how to bind a DataTable object to a Web Forms DataGrid object. Figure 8-6 shows the resulting display in a web browser.

Example 8-9. Creating a DataTable and binding it to a Web Forms DataGrid

```
<%@ Page Explicit="True" Strict="True" %>

<script language="VB" runat="server">

   Protected Sub Page_Load(ByVal Sender As System.Object, _
      ByVal e As System.EventArgs)
```

Example 8-9. Creating a DataTable and binding it to a Web Forms DataGrid (continued)

```
      If Not IsPostback Then ' True the first time the browser hits the page.
         ' Bind the grid to the data.
         grdCustomers.DataSource = GetDataSource( )
         grdCustomers.DataBind( )
      End If

   End Sub ' Page_Load

   Protected Function GetDataSource( ) As System.Collections.ICollection

      ' Open a database connection.
      Dim strConnection As String = _
         "Data Source=localhost;Initial Catalog=Northwind;" _
         & "Integrated Security=True"
      Dim cn As New System.Data.SqlClient.SqlConnection(strConnection)
      cn.Open( )

      ' Set up a data adapter object.
      Dim strSql As String = _
         "SELECT CustomerID, CompanyName, ContactName, Phone" _
         & " FROM Customers" _
         & " WHERE City = 'Buenos Aires' AND Country = 'Argentina'"
      Dim da As New System.Data.SqlClient.SqlDataAdapter(strSql, cn)

      ' Load a data set.
      Dim ds As New System.Data.DataSet( )
      da.Fill(ds, "Customers")

      ' Close the database connection.
      cn.Close( )

      ' Wrap the Customers DataTable in a DataView object.
      Dim dv As New System.Data.DataView(ds.Tables("Customers"))

      Return dv

   End Function ' GetDataSource

</script>

<html>
   <body>

      <asp:DataGrid id=grdCustomers runat="server" ForeColor="Black">
         <AlternatingItemStyle BackColor="Gainsboro" />
         <FooterStyle ForeColor="White" BackColor="Silver" />
         <ItemStyle BackColor="White" />
         <HeaderStyle Font-Bold="True" ForeColor="White"
               BackColor="Navy" />
      </asp:DataGrid>

   </body>
</html>
```

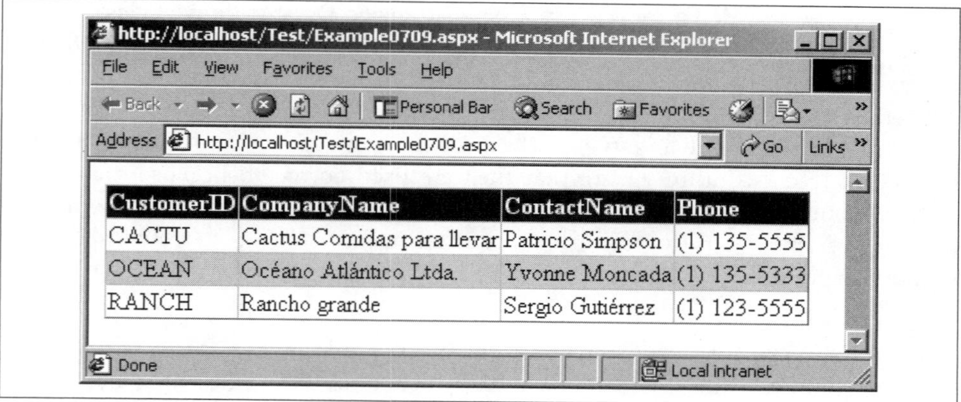

CustomerID	CompanyName	ContactName	Phone
CACTU	Cactus Comidas para llevar	Patricio Simpson	(1) 135-5555
OCEAN	Océano Atlántico Ltda.	Yvonne Moncada	(1) 135-5333
RANCH	Rancho grande	Sergio Gutiérrez	(1) 123-5555

Figure 8-6. The display generated by the code in Example 8-9

Note the following:

- Unlike the Windows Forms DataGrid class, the Web Forms DataGrid class has no SetDataBinding method. Instead, set the Web Forms DataGrid's DataSource property and then call the DataGrid's DataBind method.
- Unlike the Windows Forms DataGrid class, the Web Forms DataGrid class's DataSource property can't directly consume a DataTable or DataSet. Instead, the data must be wrapped in a DataView or DataSetView object. The properties and methods of the DataView and DataSetView classes provide additional control over how data is viewed in a bound DataGrid. DataView and DataSetView objects can be used by either Windows Forms or Web Forms DataGrids, but they are mandatory with Web Forms DataGrids.
- The DataGrid's DataSource property can consume any object that exposes the `System.Collections.ICollection` interface.

Typed DataSets

There is nothing syntactically wrong with this line of code:

```
Dim dt As System.Data.DataTable = ds.Tables("Custumers")
```

However, "Custumers" is misspelled. If it were the name of a variable, property, or method, it would cause a compile-time error (assuming the declaration were not similarly misspelled). However, because the compiler has no way of knowing that the DataSet `ds` will not hold a table called `Custumers`, this typographical error will go unnoticed until runtime. If this code path is not common, the error may go unnoticed for a long time, perhaps until after the software is delivered and running on thousands of client machines. It would be better to catch such errors at compile time.

Microsoft has provided a tool for creating customized DataSet-derived classes. Such classes expose additional properties based on the specific schema of the data that an object of this class is expected to hold. Data access is done through these additional properties rather than through the generic Item properties. Because the additional properties are declared and typed, the Visual Basic .NET compiler can perform compile-time checking to ensure that they are used correctly. Because the class is derived from the DataSet class, an object of this class can do everything that a regular DataSet object can do, and it can be used in any context in which a DataSet object is expected.

Consider again Example 8-1, shown earlier in this chapter. This fragment of code displays the names of the customers in the Northwind database that are located in London. Compare this to Example 8-10, which does the same thing but uses a DataSet-derived class that is specifically designed for this purpose.

Example 8-10. Using a typed DataSet

```
' Open a database connection.
Dim strConnection As String = _
   "Data Source=localhost;Initial Catalog=Northwind;" _
   & "Integrated Security=True"
Dim cn As SqlConnection = New SqlConnection(strConnection)
cn.Open( )

' Set up a data adapter object.
Dim strSelect As String = "SELECT * FROM Customers WHERE City = 'London'"
Dim da As New SqlDataAdapter(strSelect, cn)

' Load a data set.
Dim ds As New LondonCustomersDataSet( )
da.Fill(ds, "LondonCustomers")

' Close the database connection.
cn.Close( )

' Do something with the data set.
Dim i As Integer
For i = 0 To ds.LondonCustomers.Count - 1
   Console.WriteLine(ds.LondonCustomers(i).CompanyName)
Next
```

Note that in Example 8-10, `ds` is declared as type LondonCustomersDataSet, and this class has properties that relate specifically to the structure of the data that is to be loaded into the DataSet. However, before the code in Example 8-10 can be written, it is necessary to generate the LondonCustomersDataSet and related classes.

First, create an XML schema file that defines the desired schema of the DataSet. The easiest way to do this is to write code that loads a generic DataSet object with data having the right schema and then writes that schema using the DataSet class's

WriteXmlSchema method. Example 8-11 shows how this was done with the `LondonCustomers` DataSet.

Example 8-11. Using the WriteXmlSchema method to generate an XML schema

```
' This code is needed only once. Its purpose is to create
' an .xsd file that will be fed to the xsd.exe tool.

' Open a database connection.
Dim strConnection As String = _
   "Data Source=localhost;Initial Catalog=Northwind;" _
   & "Integrated Security=True"
Dim cn As SqlConnection = New SqlConnection(strConnection)
cn.Open( )

' Set up a data adapter object.
Dim strSelect As String = "SELECT * FROM Customers WHERE City = 'London'"
Dim da As New SqlDataAdapter(strSelect, cn)

' Load a data set.
Dim ds As New DataSet("LondonCustomersDataSet")
da.Fill(ds, "LondonCustomers")

' Close the database connection.
cn.Close( )

' Save as XSD.
ds.WriteXmlSchema("c:\LondonCustomersDataSet.xsd")
```

Next, run Microsoft's *XML Schema Definition Tool* (*xsd.exe*) against the XML schema file you just generated. Here is the command line used for the `LondonCustomers` DataSet:

```
xsd /d /l:VB LondonCustomersDataSet.xsd
```

The `/d` option indicates that a custom DataSet and related classes should be created. The `/l:VB` option specifies that the generated source code should be written in Visual Basic .NET (the tool is also able to generate C# source code). With this command line, the tool generates a file named *LondonCustomersDataSet.vb*, which contains the source code.

Finally, add the generated *.vb* file to a project and make use of its classes.

Reading Data Using a DataReader

As you have seen, the DataSet class provides a flexible way to read and write data in any data source. There are times, however, when such flexibility is not needed and when it might be better to optimize data-access speed as much as possible. For example, an application might store the text for all of its drop-down lists in a database table and read them out when the application is started. Clearly, all that is needed here is to read once through a result set as fast as possible. For needs such as this, ADO.NET has DataReader classes.

Unlike the DataSet class, DataReader classes are connected to their data sources. Consequently, there is no generic DataReader class. Rather, each managed provider exposes its own DataReader class, which implements the `System.Data.IDataReader` interface. The SQL Server managed provider exposes the SqlDataReader class (in the System.Data.SqlClient namespace). DataReader classes provide sequential, forward-only, read-only access to data. Because they are optimized for this task, they are faster than the DataSet class.

Example 8-12 shows how to read through a result set using an SqlDataReader object.

Example 8-12. Using a SqlDataReader object

```
' Open a database connection.
Dim strConnection As String = _
   "Data Source=localhost;Initial Catalog=Northwind;" _
   & "Integrated Security=True"
Dim cn As SqlConnection = New SqlConnection(strConnection)
cn.Open( )

' Set up a command object.
Dim strSql As String = "SELECT * FROM Customers" _
   & " WHERE Country = 'Germany'"
Dim cmd As New SqlCommand(strSql, cn)

' Set up a data reader.
Dim rdr As SqlDataReader
rdr = cmd.ExecuteReader( )

' Use the data.
Do While rdr.Read
   Console.WriteLine(rdr("CompanyName"))
Loop

' Close the database connection.
cn.Close( )
```

Opening a connection to the database is done the same as when using a DataSet object. However, with a DataReader object, the connection must remain open while the data is read. Instead of an SqlDataAdapter object, an SqlCommand object is used to hold the command that will be executed to select data from the database. The Sql-Command class's ExecuteReader method is called to execute the command and to return an SqlDataReader object. The SqlDataReader object is then used to read through the result set. Note the `Do While` loop in Example 8-12, repeated here:

```
Do While rdr.Read
   Console.WriteLine(rdr("CompanyName"))
Loop
```

Developers who are used to coding against classic ADO will note that this loop appears to lack a "move to the next row" statement. However, it is there. The SqlDataReader class's Read method performs the function of positioning the SqlDataReader object onto the next row to be read. In classic ADO, a RecordSet object was initially positioned on the first row of the result set. After reading each record, the RecordSet object's MoveNext method had to be called to position the RecordSet onto the next row in the result set. Forgetting to call MoveNext was a common cause of infinite loops. Microsoft removed this thorn as follows:

- The DataReader object is initially positioned just prior to the first row of the result set (and therefore has to be repositioned before reading any data).
- The Read method repositions the DataReader to the next row, returning `True` if the DataReader is positioned onto a valid row and `False` if the DataReader is positioned past the last row in the result set.

These changes result in tight, easy-to-write loops such as the one in Example 8-12.

The DataReader provides an Item property for reading column values from the current row. The Item property is overloaded to take either an integer that specifies the column number, which is zero-based, or a string that specifies the column name. The Item property is the default property of the SqlDataReader class, so it can be omitted. For example, this line:

```
Console.WriteLine(rdr("CompanyName"))
```

is equivalent to this line:

```
Console.WriteLine(rdr.Item("CompanyName"))
```

Executing Stored Procedures Through a SqlCommand Object

To execute a stored procedure, set an SqlCommand object's CommandText property to the name of the stored procedure to be executed, and set the CommandType property to the constant `CommandType.StoredProcedure` (defined in the System.Data namespace). Then call the ExecuteNonQuery method. Example 8-13 does just that.

Example 8-13. Executing a parameterless stored procedure

```
' Open a database connection.
Dim strConnection As String = _
   "Data Source=localhost;Initial Catalog=Northwind;" _
   & "Integrated Security=True"
Dim cn As SqlConnection = New SqlConnection(strConnection)
cn.Open( )

' Set up a command object. (Assumes that the database contains a
' stored procedure called "PurgeOutdatedOrders".)
Dim cmd As New SqlCommand("PurgeOutdatedOrders", cn)
```

Example 8-13. Executing a parameterless stored procedure (continued)

```
cmd.CommandType = CommandType.StoredProcedure

' Execute the command.
cmd.ExecuteNonQuery( )

' Close the database connection.
cn.Close( )
```

Example 8-13 assumes for the sake of demonstration that the database contains a stored procedure called "PurgeOutdatedOrders". If you would like to have a simple stored procedure that works with Example 8-13, use this one:

```
CREATE PROCEDURE PurgeOutdatedOrders AS
DELETE FROM Orders
WHERE OrderDate < '04-Jul-1990'
   AND ShippedDate IS NOT NULL
```

See your SQL Server documentation for information on how to create stored procedures.

Some stored procedures have parameters, and some have a return value. For these stored procedures, the SqlCommand class provides the Parameters property. The Parameters property contains a reference to an SqlParameterCollection object. To pass parameters to a stored procedure and/or to read the return value of a stored procedure, add SqlParameter objects to this collection.

Example 8-14 calls a stored procedure that takes a single argument.

Example 8-14. Executing a parameterized stored procedure

```
' Open a database connection.
Dim strConnection As String = _
   "Data Source=localhost;Initial Catalog=Northwind;" _
   & "Integrated Security=True"
Dim cn As SqlConnection = New SqlConnection(strConnection)
cn.Open( )

' Set up a command object. (Assumes that the database contains a
' stored procedure called "PurgeOutdatedOrders2".)
Dim cmd As New SqlCommand("PurgeOutdatedOrders2", cn)
cmd.CommandType = CommandType.StoredProcedure

' Set up the @BeforeDate parameter for the stored procedure.
Dim param As New SqlParameter("@BeforeDate", SqlDBType.DateTime)
param.Direction = ParameterDirection.Input
param.Value = #7/4/1990#
cmd.Parameters.Add(param)

' Execute the command.
```

Example 8-14. Executing a parameterized stored procedure (continued)

```
cmd.ExecuteNonQuery( )

' Close the database connection.
cn.Close( )
```

Example 8-14 assumes for the sake of demonstration that the database contains a stored procedure called "PurgeOutdatedOrders2". If you would like to have a simple stored procedure that works with Example 8-14, use this one:

```
CREATE PROCEDURE PurgeOutdatedOrders2
@BeforeDate datetime
AS
DELETE FROM Orders
WHERE OrderDate < @BeforeDate
   AND ShippedDate IS NOT NULL
```

See your SQL Server documentation for information on how to create stored procedures.

The steps taken in Example 8-14 are:

1. Open a connection to the database.
2. Instantiate an SqlCommand object using this constructor:

   ```
   Public Overloads Sub New( _
      ByVal cmdText As String, _
      ByVal connection As System.Data.SqlClient.SqlConnection _
   )
   ```

   The *cmdText* parameter specifies the name of the stored procedure, and the *connection* parameter specifies the database connection to use.
3. Set the SqlCommand object's CommandType property to `CommandType.StoredProcedure` to indicate that the *cmdText* parameter passed to the constructor is the name of a stored procedure.
4. Create an SqlParameter object to pass a value in the `PurgeOutdatedOrders2` stored procedure's *@BeforeDate* parameter. This is done as follows:
   a. Instantiate an SqlParameter object using this constructor:

      ```
      Public Overloads Sub New( _
         ByVal parameterName As String, _
         ByVal dbType As System.Data.SqlClient.SqlDbType _
      )
      ```

      The *parameterName* parameter specifies the name of the stored procedure parameter and should match the name as given in the stored procedure. The *dbType* parameter specifies the SQL Server data type of the parameter. This parameter can take any value from the SqlDbType enumeration.

   b. Set the SqlParameter object's Direction property to `ParameterDirection.Input`. This indicates that a value will be passed from the application to the stored procedure.

   c. Set the Value property of the SqlParameter object.

   d. Add the SqlParameter object to the SqlCommand object's Parameters collection by calling the SqlParameterCollection object's Add method.

5. Execute the stored procedure.

Note the SqlParameter class's Direction property. Setting this property to the appropriate value from the ParameterDirection enumeration (declared in the System.Data namespace), can make a SqlParameter object an input parameter, an output parameter, an in/out parameter, or the stored procedure's return value. The values in the ParameterDirection enumeration are:

`Input`
: The parameter provides a value to the stored procedure.

`InputOutput`
: The parameter provides a value to the stored procedure and receives a new value back from the stored procedure.

`Output`
: The parameter receives a value back from the stored procedure.

`ReturnValue`
: The parameter receives the stored procedure's return value.

Summary

In this chapter, you learned about Microsoft's data-access technology, ADO.NET. You learned how to connect to a database, how to read data with either a DataSet object or a DataReader object, how to navigate and change data in a DataSet, how to use the DataSet's XML capabilities, how to generate typed DataSets, and how to execute stored procedures using an SqlCommand object.

APPENDIX A
Custom Attributes Defined in the System Namespace

This appendix lists the custom attribute classes that exist in the System namespace. Custom attributes are explained in Chapter 2.

AttributeUsage

Valid on Class

Description

When defining an attribute class, the `AttributeUsage` attribute specifies the program elements upon which the newly defined attribute can be placed.

The AttributeUsageAttribute class constructor is:

```
Public Sub New(ByVal validOn As System.AttributeTargets)
```

The *`validOn`* parameter indicates the program elements to which the newly defined attribute can be applied. Permitted values are: `Assembly`, `Module`, `Class`, `Struct`, `Enum`, `Constructor`, `Method`, `Property`, `Field`, `Event`, `Interface`, `Parameter`, `Delegate`, `ReturnValue`, and `All`.

The properties of the AttributeUsageAttribute class are:

AllowMultiple
: Indicates whether the attribute can be used more than once on a single program element. The type is Boolean. The default is `False`.

Inherited
: Indicates whether the newly defined attribute is automatically inherited by derived classes and overridden members. The type is Boolean. The default is `False`.

ValidOn
: Indicates the program elements to which the newly defined attribute can be applied. The type is AttributeTargets (defined in the System namespace).

See Chapter 2 for information on defining custom attributes.

CLSCompliant

Valid on All

Description

Specifies whether the program element is CLS-compliant. The CLSCompliantAttribute class constructor is:

```
Public Sub New(ByVal isCompliant As Boolean)
```

The *isCompliant* parameter indicates whether the program element is CLS-compliant.

The CLSCompliantAttribute class has a single property:

IsCompliant
: Indicates whether the program element is CLS-compliant. The type is Boolean.

See Chapter 3 for information on the CLS and on what it means for a program element to be CLS-compliant.

ContextStatic

Valid on Field

Description

Specifies that the value of a static field is not shared between contexts (that is, each context has its own value). Contexts are not discussed in this book.

Flags

Valid on Enum

Description

Specifies that an enumerated type should be treated as a set of flags, which can be added together, rather than as strictly separate values. This attribute takes no arguments and has no properties. See Chapter 2 for information on declaring enumerated types.

LoaderOptimization

Valid on Method

Description

Specifies a loader optimization for an application. This attribute should be used only on an application's Main method.

The LoaderOptimizationAttribute class constructor is:

```
Public Sub New(ByVal value As System.LoaderOptimization)
```

The *value* parameter indicates the loader optimization that is to be performed. Permitted values are: `MultiDomain`, `MultiDomainHost`, `NotSpecified`, and `SingleDomain`.

The LoaderOptimizationAttribute class has a single property:

Value
: Indicates the loader optimization that is to be performed. The type is LoaderOptimization (defined in the System namespace).

Loader optimizations are not discussed in this book.

MTAThread

Valid on Method

Description

Specifies that the application is to use the *multithreaded apartment* model. This attribute should be used only on an application's Main method. The `MTAThread` attribute takes no arguments and has no properties. Threading models are not discussed in this book.

NonSerialized

Valid on Field

Description

When a type implements the `ISerializable` interface (defined in the System.Runtime.Serialization namespace) or has the `Serializable` attribute, all of its fields are serializable. To prohibit a particular field in a serializable type from being serializable, mark it with the `NonSerialized` attribute. This attribute takes no arguments and has no properties.

Obsolete

Valid on

Class, Struct, Enum, Constructor, Method, Property, Field, Event, Interface, and Delegate

Description

Indicates that the given program element is obsolete.

The ObsoleteAttribute class has three overloads. The first takes no parameters and merely marks a program element as obsolete. The second overload looks like this:

```
Public Overloads Sub New(ByVal message As String)
```

The *message* parameter gives a free-form text message, which can be shown to a programmer making use of the obsolete program element. The third overload looks like this:

```
Public Overloads Sub New(ByVal message As String, ByVal error As Boolean)
```

In addition to the *message* parameter, this overload has an *error* parameter, which indicates whether it is an error to use the given program element.

The properties of the ObsoleteAttribute class are:

IsError
: Indicates whether it is an error to use the program element. The type is Boolean. The default is `False`.

Message
: A free-form text message, which can be shown to a programmer making use of the obsolete program element.

ParamArray

Valid on Parameter

Description

Indicates that a parameter actually stands for a variable number of parameters. This attribute need never be used by Visual Basic .NET programs because Visual Basic .NET has a `ParamArray` keyword. It's interesting to note that the `ParamArray` keyword is compiled into the `ParamArray` attribute. This attribute takes no arguments and has no properties. See Chapter 2 for information about the `ParamArray` keyword.

Serializable

Valid on Class, Struct, Enum, and Delegate

Description

Indicates that a type is serializable. This attribute takes no arguments and has no properties.

STAThread

Valid on Method

Description

Specifies that the application is to use the *single-threaded apartment* model. This attribute should be used only on an application's Main method. The `STAThread` attribute takes no arguments and has no properties. Threading models are not discussed in this book.

ThreadStatic

Valid on Field

Description

Specifies that the value of a static field is not shared across threads (that is, each thread in the application has its own value). This attribute takes no arguments and has no properties.

APPENDIX B

Exceptions Defined in the System Namespace

This appendix lists the exception classes that exist in the System namespace. Exceptions are explained in Chapter 2.

AppDomainUnloadedException
: Occurs upon an attempt to access an unloaded application domain.

ApplicationException
: Represents the base class from which to derive application-defined exceptions.

ArgumentException
: Represents the base class for ArgumentNullException, ArgumentOutOfRangeException, and DuplicateWaitObjectException.

ArgumentNullException
: Occurs when a value of `Nothing` is passed to a method that requires a valid object reference.

ArgumentOutOfRangeException
: Occurs when a value passed to a method is outside the range that the method expects.

ArithmeticException
: Represents the base class for DivideByZeroException, NotFiniteNumberException, and OverflowException.

ArrayTypeMismatchException
: Occurs upon an attempt to store a value of the wrong type in an array.

BadImageFormatException
: Occurs upon an attempt to run an executable file that is in the wrong format.

CannotUnloadAppDomainException
: Occurs when an attempt to unload an application domain fails.

ContextMarshalException
: Occurs when an attempt to marshal an object across a context boundary fails.

DivideByZeroException
: Occurs when the divisor in an integer division is 0. Floating point division by 0 doesn't throw an exception.

DllNotFoundException
: Occurs when a specified *.dll* file can't be found.

DuplicateWaitObjectException
: Occurs when an object appears more than once in an array of synchronization objects.

EntryPointNotFoundException
: Occurs when the CLR can't find the requested method when calling methods in an unmanaged (that is, non-.NET) *.dll*.

ExecutionEngineException
: Occurs when there is an internal error in the CLR's execution engine.

FieldAccessException
: Occurs upon an attempt to access a private or protected field in a class, by code that is not permitted to do so.

FormatException
: Occurs when a method argument value is incorrectly formatted.

IndexOutOfRangeException
: Occurs when an array index is outside of the bounds of the array.

InvalidCastException
: Occurs when an invalid conversion of a reference type is attempted.

InvalidOperationException
: Occurs when a method call is invalid for the type's current state. This is the base class for the ObjectDisposedException class.

InvalidProgramException
: Occurs when a program contains invalid IL or metadata. This would only occur if there is a bug in the compiler—there is no combination of Visual Basic .NET statements that can produce invalid IL or metadata.

MemberAccessException
: Occurs when an attempt to access a type member fails. This is the base class for the FieldAccessException, MethodAccessException, and MissingMemberException classes.

MethodAccessException
: Occurs upon an attempt to access a private or protected method in a class, by code that is not permitted to do so.

MissingFieldException
: Occurs upon an attempt to access a nonexistent field through reflection.

MissingMemberException

Occurs upon an attempt to access a nonexistent member through reflection. This is the base class for the MissingFieldException and MissingMethodException classes.

MissingMethodException

Occurs upon an attempt to access a nonexistent method through reflection.

MulticastNotSupportedException

Occurs upon an attempt to combine two instances of a nonmulticast delegate.

NotFiniteNumberException

Occurs upon an attempt to use a nonfinite floating point number (`PositiveInfinity`, `NegativeInfinity`, or `NaN` [not a number]) in an expression that requires a finite number.

NotImplementedException

Occurs when a method stub exists, but the method's functionality has not yet been implemented.

NotSupportedException

Occurs upon an attempt to invoke functionality or features that are not supported by the current implementation or in the current program state.

NullReferenceException

Occurs upon an attempt to access a nonshared type member through an object reference that is set to `Nothing`.

ObjectDisposedException

Occurs upon an attempt to reuse an object whose Dispose method has been called, when that object doesn't support dynamically reallocating its resources.

OutOfMemoryException

Occurs when the program is unable to allocate needed memory.

OverflowException

Occurs when an arithmetic or conversion operation results in an overflow.

PlatformNotSupportedException

Occurs upon an attempt to use a feature that is not supported on the current platform.

RankException

Occurs when an array with the wrong number of dimensions is passed as a parameter in a method call.

StackOverflowException

Occurs when the program stack overflows.

SystemException

Represents the base class for all exception classes in the System namespace.

TypeInitializationException

Occurs when a class initializer throws an exception.

TypeLoadException
: Occurs when a type cannot be loaded. This is the base class for the DllNotFoundException and EntryPointNotFoundException classes.

TypeUnloadedException
: Occurs when an attempt is made to access an unloaded class.

UnauthorizedAccessException
: Occurs when an unauthorized attempt is made to access an operating-system resource.

UriFormatException
: Occurs when an invalid URI string is passed to the constructor of the Uri class (defined in the System namespace).

APPENDIX C

Cultures

The @ Page directive can include a Culture attribute that allows you to specify the language and culture for which the page is intended. This appendix lists the names of the cultures that can be supplied as arguments to the Culture attribute. A culture name has the general format

<languagecode>-<country/regioncode>

where *<languagecode>* is a lowercase code generally consisting of two letters that defines a language, and *<country/regioncode>* is an uppercase two-letter code defining the country or region in which that language is used. In a few cases, the Culture attribute takes the form

<charactercode>-<languagecode>-<countrycode>

where *<charactercode>* is a mixed case two-letter code (e.g., Cy for Cyrillic) indicating the character set, <languagecode> is a lowercase two-letter code indicating the language, and *<countrycode>* is an uppercase two-letter code defining the country in which that language and character set are used.

A culture name that takes the form *<languagecode>* only is a *neutral culture*; it is associated with a language, but not with a particular country or region.

Culture name	LCID	Culture display name
af	54	Afrikaans
af-ZA	1078	Afrikaans (South Africa)
ar	1	Arabic
ar-AE	14337	Arabic (U.A.E.)
ar-BH	15361	Arabic (Bahrain)
ar-DZ	5121	Arabic (Algeria)
ar-EG	3073	Arabic (Egypt)
ar-IQ	2049	Arabic (Iraq)
ar-JO	11265	Arabic (Jordan)

Culture name	LCID	Culture display name
ar-KW	13313	Arabic (Kuwait)
ar-LB	12289	Arabic (Lebanon)
ar-LY	4097	Arabic (Libya)
ar-MA	6145	Arabic (Morocco)
ar-OM	8193	Arabic (Oman)
ar-QA	16385	Arabic (Qatar)
ar-SA	1025	Arabic (Saudi Arabia)
ar-SY	10241	Arabic (Syria)
ar-TN	7169	Arabic (Tunisia)
ar-YE	9217	Arabic (Yemen)
az	44	Azeri
be	35	Belarusian
be-BY	1059	Belarusian (Belarus)
bg	2	Bulgarian
bg-BG	1026	Bulgarian (Bulgaria)
ca	3	Catalan
ca-ES	1027	Catalan (Spain)
cs	5	Czech
cs-CZ	1029	Czech (Czech Republic)
Cy-az-AZ	2092	Azeri (Cyrillic) (Azerbaijan)
Cy-sr-SP	3098	Serbian (Cyrillic) (Serbia)
Cy-uz-UZ	2115	Uzbek (Cyrillic) (Uzbekistan)
da	6	Danish
da-DK	1030	Danish (Denmark)
de	7	German
de-AT	3079	German (Austria)
de-CH	2055	German (Switzerland)
de-DE	1031	German (Germany)
de-LI	5127	German (Liechtenstein)
de-LU	4103	German (Luxembourg)
div	101	Divehi
div-MV	1125	Divehi (Maldives)
el	8	Greek
el-GR	1032	Greek (Greece)
en	9	English
en-AU	3081	English (Australia)
en-BZ	10249	English (Belize)

Culture name	LCID	Culture display name
en-CA	4105	English (Canada)
en-CB	9225	English (Caribbean)
en-GB	2057	English (United Kingdom)
en-IE	6153	English (Ireland)
en-JM	8201	English (Jamaica)
en-NZ	5129	English (New Zealand)
en-PH	13321	English (Republic of the Philippines)
en-TT	11273	English (Trinidad and Tobago)
en-US	1033	English (United States)
en-ZA	7177	English (South Africa)
en-ZW	12297	English (Zimbabwe)
es	10	Spanish
es-AR	11274	Spanish (Argentina)
es-BO	16394	Spanish (Bolivia)
es-CL	13322	Spanish (Chile)
es-CO	9226	Spanish (Colombia)
es-CR	5130	Spanish (Costa Rica)
es-DO	7178	Spanish (Dominican Republic)
es-EC	12298	Spanish (Ecuador)
es-ES	3082	Spanish (Spain)
es-GT	4106	Spanish (Guatemala)
es-HN	18442	Spanish (Honduras)
es-MX	2058	Spanish (Mexico)
es-NI	19466	Spanish (Nicaragua)
es-PA	6154	Spanish (Panama)
es-PE	10250	Spanish (Peru)
es-PR	20490	Spanish (Puerto Rico)
es-PY	15370	Spanish (Paraguay)
es-SV	17418	Spanish (El Salvador)
es-UY	14346	Spanish (Uruguay)
es-VE	8202	Spanish (Venezuela)
et	37	Estonian
et-EE	1061	Estonian (Estonia)
eu	45	Basque
eu-ES	1069	Basque (Spain)
fa	41	Farsi
fa-IR	1065	Farsi (Iran)

Culture name	LCID	Culture display name
fi	11	Finnish
fi-FI	1035	Finnish (Finland)
fo	56	Faeroese
fo-FO	1080	Faeroese (Faeroe Islands)
fr	12	French
fr-BE	2060	French (Belgium)
fr-CA	3084	French (Canada)
fr-CH	4108	French (Switzerland)
fr-FR	1036	French (France)
fr-LU	5132	French (Luxembourg)
fr-MC	6156	French (Principality of Monaco)
gl	86	Galician
gl-ES	1110	Galician (Spain)
gu	71	Gujarati
gu-IN	1095	Gujarati (India)
he	13	Hebrew
he-IL	1037	Hebrew (Israel)
hi	57	Hindi
hi-IN	1081	Hindi (India)
hr	26	Croatian
hr-HR	1050	Croatian (Croatia)
hu	14	Hungarian
hu-HU	1038	Hungarian (Hungary)
hy	43	Armenian
hy-AM	1067	Armenian (Armenia)
id	33	Indonesian
id-ID	1057	Indonesian (Indonesia)
is	15	Icelandic
is-IS	1039	Icelandic (Iceland)
it	16	Italian
it-CH	2064	Italian (Switzerland)
it-IT	1040	Italian (Italy)
ja	17	Japanese
ja-JP	1041	Japanese (Japan)
ka	55	Georgian
ka-GE	1079	Georgian (Georgia)
kk	63	Kazakh

Culture name	LCID	Culture display name
kk-KZ	1087	Kazakh (Kazakhstan)
kn	75	Kannada
kn-IN	1099	Kannada (India)
ko	18	Korean
kok	87	Konkani
kok-IN	1111	Konkani (India)
ko-KR	1042	Korean (Korea)
ky	64	Kyrgyz
ky-KZ	1088	Kyrgyz (Kyrgyzstan)
lt	39	Lithuanian
Lt-az-AZ	1068	Azeri (Latin) (Azerbaijan)
lt-LT	1063	Lithuanian (Lithuania)
Lt-sr-SP	2074	Serbian (Latin) (Serbia)
Lt-uz-UZ	1091	Uzbek (Latin) (Uzbekistan)
lv	38	Latvian
lv-LV	1062	Latvian (Latvia)
mk	47	FYRO Macedonian
mk-MK	1071	FYRO Macedonian (Former Yugoslav Republic of Macedonia)
mn	80	Mongolian
mn-MN	1104	Mongolian (Mongolia)
mr	78	Marathi
mr-IN	1102	Marathi (India)
ms	62	Malay
ms-BN	2110	Malay (Brunei Darussalam)
ms-MY	1086	Malay (Malaysia)
nb-NO	1044	Norwegian (Bokmål) (Norway)
nl	19	Dutch
nl-BE	2067	Dutch (Belgium)
nl-NL	1043	Dutch (Netherlands)
nn-NO	2068	Norwegian (Nynorsk) (Norway)
no	20	Norwegian
pa	70	Punjabi
pa-IN	1094	Punjabi (India)
pl	21	Polish
pl-PL	1045	Polish (Poland)
pt	22	Portuguese
pt-BR	1046	Portuguese (Brazil)

Culture name	LCID	Culture display name
pt-PT	2070	Portuguese (Portugal)
ro	24	Romanian
ro-RO	1048	Romanian (Romania)
ru	25	Russian
ru-RU	1049	Russian (Russia)
sa	79	Sanskrit
sa-IN	1103	Sanskrit (India)
sk	27	Slovak
sk-SK	1051	Slovak (Slovakia)
sl	36	Slovenian
sl-SI	1060	Slovenian (Slovenia)
sq	28	Albanian
sq-AL	1052	Albanian (Albania)
sv	29	Swedish
sv-FI	2077	Swedish (Finland)
sv-SE	1053	Swedish (Sweden)
sw	65	Swahili
sw-KE	1089	Swahili (Kenya)
syr	90	Syriac
syr-SY	1114	Syriac (Syria)
ta	73	Tamil
ta-IN	1097	Tamil (India)
te	74	Telugu
te-IN	1098	Telugu (India)
th	30	Thai
th-TH	1054	Thai (Thailand)
tr	31	Turkish
tr-TR	1055	Turkish (Turkey)
tt	68	Tatar
tt-TA	1092	Tatar (Tatarstan)
uk	34	Ukrainian
uk-UA	1058	Ukrainian (Ukraine)
ur	32	Urdu
ur-PK	1056	Urdu (Islamic Republic of Pakistan)
uz	67	Uzbek
vi	42	Vietnamese
vi-VN	1066	Vietnamese (Viet Nam)

Culture name	LCID	Culture display name
zh-CHS	4	Chinese (Simplified)
zh-CHT	31748	Chinese (Traditional)
zh-CN	2052	Chinese (People's Republic of China)
zh-HK	3076	Chinese (Hong Kong S.A.R.)
zh-MO	5124	Chinese (Macau S.A.R.)
zh-SG	4100	Chinese (Singapore)
zh-TW	1028	Chinese (Taiwan)
iv	127	Invariant Language (Invariant Country)

APPENDIX D

Resources for Developers

The amount of brainpower floating around in cyberspace is amazing. If you're stuck, you need never stay stuck for long. In this appendix, I list some of my favorite .NET hangouts on the Web—though it is by no means exhaustive.

The links shown here were verified at the time of printing, but of course, there is no guarantee that they will remain so.

.NET Information

Microsoft

http://www.microsoft.com/net/

This is the official home page for information about Microsoft's .NET initiative. On this page you will find links to:

- Definitions and overviews of .NET
- Information about *.NET My Services*, Microsoft's package of web-service offerings
- .NET books and articles
- .NET training
- Information about Visual Studio .NET
- .NET success stories

Microsoft Developer Network (MSDN)

http://msdn.microsoft.com/net/

This offeres complete .NET reference documentation online.

Microsoft's GotDotNet

http://www.gotdotnet.com

.NET articles, samples, and links are provided by Microsoft .NET team members, as well as users.

Microsoft's IBuySpy
: *http://www.ibuyspy.com*

  This is a reference implementation for a complete web site developed using ASP.NET. Complete source code is downloadable in Visual Basic .NET or C#.

O'Reilly
: *http://www.oreilly.com*

  O'Reilly has a large lineup of .NET books written by experts in the field.

Ron's VB Forum
: *http://vb.oreilly.com/ron/*

  O'Reilly editor, Ron Petrusha, hosts this column in which particularly interesting VB questions are answered.

DevX .NET Developer Resources
: *http://www.devx.com/dotnet/resources/*

  This is a great list of links to a huge number of .NET resources.

Discussion Lists

Discussion lists are one of the greatest resources on the Internet. These give you the opportunity to ask questions of tens, hundreds, or thousands of people who are in your field of interest. The web URLs listed here link to pages that provide instructions for subscribing to the lists.

Netiquette

If you've never before been a member of a discussion list, take care to note the concept of *netiquette*. This term refers to the rules of behavior expected from people who post messages to discussion lists. You will receive or be directed to a list of such expectations when you subscribe to a list, but they can be summed up as follows:

1. Monitor the discussion list a while before posting messages.
2. If available, search the list archives before posting a question.
3. Don't post questions that are outside of the list's discussion topic.
4. Be nice.
5. Answer the questions that you can.
6. Maximize your *signal-to-noise ratio*. (That means you should post more helpful answers than witty remarks.)

DevelopMentor's DOTNET List

http://discuss.develop.com/dotnet.html

This is my all-time favorite .NET hangout. There are many heavy hitters on this list, including Microsoft-development team members and program managers, as well as third-party experts who were learning and using .NET as much as a year or two before it's official release.

ASP Lists

http://www.asplists.com

This site is amazing for its breadth of coverage. There are over 400 highly focused, moderated lists available through this one site. Many of these are now . NET-related, and many are available in languages other than English.

Visual Basic List

http://peach.ease.lsoft.com/archives/visbas-l.html

The members of this list discuss everything related to Visual Basic, including Visual Basic .NET, as well as earlier versions. This is a large, very active list with developers of all skill levels. There are plenty of advanced Visual Basic developers on this list who are ready to lend a hand when they can. There are approximately 4,400 subscribers.

Visual Basic Beginner's List

http://peach.ease.lsoft.com/archives/visbas-beginners.html

For beginners who don't feel comfortable posting to the Visual Basic List, there is the Visual Basic Beginner's List. There are approximately 1,000 subscribers.

APPENDIX E

Math Functions

Math functions are provided by the members of the Math class (defined in the System namespace). All members of the Math class are shared, so it is not necessary to instantiate the class before accessing its members. Members are simply accessed through the class name. For example, the following line computes the cosine of 45:

```
Dim result As Double = Math.Cos(45)
```

The Math class exposes two constants:

`E` The base of natural logarithms.

`PI` The ratio of the circumference of a circle to its diameter.

The methods of the Math class are as follows. Note that the trigonometric functions consider all angle values to be in radians.

Abs
: Computes the absolute value of a number.

Acos
: Computes the angle whose cosine is the given number.

Asin
: Computes the angle whose sine is the given number.

Atan
: Computes the angle whose tangent is the given number.

Atan2
: Computes the angle whose tangent is equal to the quotient of the two given numbers.

Ceiling
: Computes the smallest whole number greater than or equal to the given number.

Cos
: Computes the cosine of a number.

Cosh
: Computers the hyperbolic cosine of a number.

Exp
: Computes `e` raised to a given power.

Floor
: Computes the largest whole number less than or equal to a given number.

IEEERemainder
: Calculates the remainder in the division of two numbers.

Log
: Calculates the logarithm of a number (either the natural logarithm or in a given base).

Log10
: Calculates the base 10 logarithm of a number.

Max
: Returns the larger of two numbers.

Min
: Returns the smaller of two numbers.

Pow
: Raises a given number to a given power.

Round
: Rounds a number to either a whole number or a specified decimal place.

Sign
: Returns `-1`, `0`, or `1` to indicate whether the argument is negative, zero, or positive, respectively.

Sin
: Calculates the sine of a number.

Sinh
: Calculates the hyperbolic sine of a number.

Sqrt
: Calculates the square root of a number.

Tan
: Calculates the tangent of a number.

Tanh
: Calculates the hyperbolic tangent of a number.

Index

Symbols

Numbers

A

We'd like to hear your suggestions for improving our indexes. Send email to *index@oreilly.com*.

B

C

D

E

F

G

H

I

J

K

L

N

O

P

Q

R

S

T

X

Z

About the Author

Dave Grundgeiger is a consultant at Tara Software, Inc., in Madison, Wisconsin, where he spends his days immersed in cool technologies. Dave specializes in the design and development of multitier vertical market business solutions using Visual Basic .NET, Visual C# .NET, IIS, COM+, and SQL Server. Dave's research interests include artificial intelligence (AI), with particular interests in both natural language processing and robotics. He is especially interested in AI techniques that facilitate human-like interaction with computers. Dave has written for *MSDN Magazine* and *C/C++ Users Journal*. *Programming Visual Basic .NET* is Dave's second O'Reilly book.

Colophon

Our look is the result of reader comments, our own experimentation, and feedback from distribution channels. Distinctive covers complement our distinctive approach to technical topics, breathing personality and life into potentially dry subjects.

The animal on the cover of *Programming Visual Basic .NET* is a catfish. Catfish can be found all over the world, most often in freshwater environments. Catfish are identified by their whiskers, called "barbels," as well by as their scaleless skin; fleshy, rayless posterior fins; and sharp, defensive spines in the dorsal and shoulder fins. Catfish have complex bones and sensitive hearing. They are omnivorous feeders and skilled scavengers. A marine catfish can taste with any part of its body.

Though most madtom species of catfish are no more than 5 inches in length, some Danube catfish (called wels or sheatfish) reach lengths of up to 13 feet and weighs as much as 400 pounds. Wels catfish (found mostly in the United Kingdom) are dark, flat, and black in color, with white bellies. They breed in the springtime in shallow areas near rivers and lakes. The females leave their eggs on plants for the males to guard. Two to three weeks later, the eggs hatch into tadpole-like fish, which grow quickly in size. The largest recorded wels catfish was 16 feet long and weighed 675 pounds.

Darren Kelly was the production editor, Jeffrey Holcomb was the copyeditor, and Rachel Wheeler was the proofreader for *Programming Visual Basic .NET*. Matt Hutchinson, Mary Anne Weeks Mayo, and Claire Cloutier provided quality control. Brenda Miller wrote the index. Interior composition was done by Philip Dangler. Linley Dolby wrote the colophon.

Pam Spremulli designed the cover of this book, based on a series design by Edie Freedman. The cover image is a 19th-century engraving from the Dover Pictorial Archive. Emma Colby produced the cover layout with QuarkXPress 4.1, using Adobe's ITC Garamond font.

Melanie Wang designed the interior layout, based on a series design by David Futato. Mihaela Maier converted the files from Microsoft Word to FrameMaker

5.5.6, using tools created by Mike Sierra. The text font is Linotype Birka; the heading font is Adobe Myriad Condensed; and the code font is LucasFont's TheSans Mono Condensed. The illustrations that appear in the book were produced by Robert Romano and Jessamyn Read, using Macromedia FreeHand 9 and Adobe Photoshop 6. The tip and warning icons were drawn by Christopher Bing.

Whenever possible, our books use a durable and flexible lay-flat binding.

More Titles from O'Reilly

Microsoft .NET Programming

VB .NET Language in a Nutshell

By Steven Roman, Ron Petrusha & Paul Lomax
1st Edition September 2001
636 pages, ISBN 0-596-00092-8

The VB documentation typically provides only the bare details for each language element; it doesn't provide the little tidbits of information that a programmer really needs to know to solve programming problems or to use a particular language element effectively. *VB .NET Language in a Nutshell* is a reference that aims to document the undocumented and present wisdom that comes from many years of experience.

Programming C#

By Jesse Liberty
1st Edition July 2001
680 pages, ISBN 0-596-00117-7

The goal of C# is to serve as a high-performance language for .NET development—one that is simple, safe, object-oriented, and Internet-centric. *Programming C#* teaches this new language in a way that experienced programmers will appreciate—by grounding its application firmly in the context of Microsoft's .NET platform and the development of desktop and Internet applications.

Programming ASP.NET

By Jesse Liberty & Dan Hurwitz
1st Edition January 2002 (est.)
600 pages (est.), ISBN 0-596-00171-1

Programming ASP.NET is aimed at experienced programmers and web developers, who have the desire to quickly create ASP.NET applications. Rudimentary topics such as language syntax, datatypes, and program control are treated concisely so greater attention can be devoted to applications development. By design, this book features many short examples, rather than a single, unmanageably large application, in order to show the widest range of constructs, both valid and invalid.

C# in a Nutshell

By Peter Drayton & Ben Albarhari
1st Edition September 2001 (est.)
650 pages (est.), ISBN 0-596-00181-9

C# is likely to become one of the most widely used languages for building .NET applications. *C# in a Nutshell* contains a concise introduction to the language and its syntax, plus brief tutorials used to accomplish common programming tasks. It also includes O'Reilly's classic-style, quick-reference material for all the types and members in core .NET namespaces, including System, System.Text, System.IO, and System.Collections.

ASP.NET in a Nutshell

By Andrew Duthie & Raja Mani
1st Edition December 2001 (est.)
600 pages (est.), ISBN 0-596-00116-9

As a quick reference, *ASP.NET in a Nutshell* goes beyond the published documentation by highlighting little-known details, stressing practical uses for particular features, and providing real-world examples. With only a quick introduction, this book then documents application and web service development, the creation of custom controls, data access, security, deployment, and error handling. It also presents an overview of the class libraries and provides information on migration from ASP to ASP.NET.

How to stay in touch with O'Reilly

1. Visit Our Award-Winning Web Site

http://www.oreilly.com/

★ "Top 100 Sites on the Web" —PC Magazine
★ "Top 5% Web sites" —Point Communications
★ "3-Star site" —The McKinley Group

Our web site contains a library of comprehensive product information (including book excerpts and tables of contents), downloadable software, background articles, interviews with technology leaders, links to relevant sites, book cover art, and more. File us in your Bookmarks or Hotlist!

2. Join Our Email Mailing Lists

New Product Releases

To receive automatic email with brief descriptions of all new O'Reilly products as they are released, send email to:
ora-news-subscribe@lists.oreilly.com
Put the following information in the first line of your message (not in the Subject field):
subscribe ora-news

O'Reilly Events

If you'd also like us to send information about trade show events, special promotions, and other O'Reilly events, send email to:
ora-news-subscribe@lists.oreilly.com
Put the following information in the first line of your message (not in the Subject field):
subscribe ora-events

3. Get Examples from Our Books via FTP

There are two ways to access an archive of example files from our books:

Regular FTP

- ftp to:
  ftp.oreilly.com
  (login: anonymous
  password: your email address)
- Point your web browser to:
  ftp://ftp.oreilly.com/

FTPMAIL

- Send an email message to:
  ftpmail@online.oreilly.com
  (Write "help" in the message body)

4. Contact Us via Email

order@oreilly.com
To place a book or software order online. Good for North American and international customers.

subscriptions@oreilly.com
To place an order for any of our newsletters or periodicals.

books@oreilly.com
General questions about any of our books.

cs@oreilly.com
For answers to problems regarding your order or our products.

booktech@oreilly.com
For book content technical questions or corrections.

proposals@oreilly.com
To submit new book or software proposals to our editors and product managers.

international@oreilly.com
For information about our international distributors or translation queries. For a list of our distributors outside of North America check out:
http://www.oreilly.com/distributors.html

5. Work with Us

Check out our website for current employment opportunites:
http://jobs.oreilly.com/

O'Reilly & Associates, Inc.
1005 Gravenstein Hwy North
Sebastopol, CA 95472 USA
TEL 707-829-0515 or 800-998-9938
(6am to 5pm PST)
FAX 707-829-0104

TO ORDER: ***800-998-9938 • order@oreilly.com • www.oreilly.com***
ONLINE EDITIONS OF MOST O'REILLY TITLES ARE AVAILABLE BY SUBSCRIPTION AT ***safari.oreilly.com***
ALSO AVAILABLE AT MOST RETAIL AND ONLINE BOOKSTORES

Titles from O'Reilly

Programming
C++: The Core Language
Practical C++ Programming
Practical C Programming, 3rd Ed.
High Performance Computing, 2nd Ed.
Programming Embedded Systems in C and C++
Mastering Algorithms in C
Advanced C++ Techniques
POSIX 4: Programming for the Real World
POSIX Programmer's Guide
Power Programming with RPC
UNIX Systems Programming for SVR4
Pthreads Programming
CVS Pocket Reference
Advanced Oracle PL/SQL
Oracle PL/SQL Guide to Oracle8i Features
Oracle PL/SQL Programming, 2nd Ed.
Oracle Built-in Packages
Oracle PL/SQL Developer's Workbook
Oracle Web Applications
Oracle PL/SQL Language Pocket Reference
Oracle PL/SQL Built-ins Pocket Reference
Oracle SQL*Plus: The Definitive Guide
Oracle SQL*Plus Pocket Reference
Oracle Essentials
Oracle Database Administration
Oracle Internal Services
Oracle SAP
Guide to Writing DCE Applications
Understanding DCE
Visual Basic Shell Programming
VB/VBA in a Nutshell: The Language
Access Database Design & Programming, 2nd Ed.
Writing Word Macros
Applying RCS and SCCS
Checking C Programs with Lint
VB Controls in a Nutshell
Developing Asp Components, 2nd Ed.
Learning WML & WMLScript
Writing Excel Macros
Windows 32 API Programming with Visual Basic
ADO: The Definitive Guide

Using the Internet
Internet in a Nutshell
Smileys
Managing Mailing Lists

Web
Apache: The Definitive Guide, 2nd Ed.
Apache Pocket Reference
ASP in a Nutshell, 2nd Ed.
Cascading Style Sheets
Designing Web Audio
Designing with JavaScript, 2nd Ed.
DocBook: The Definitive Guide
Dynamic HTML: The Definitive Reference
HTML Pocket Reference
Information Architecture for the WWW
JavaScript: The Definitive Guide, 3rd Ed.
Java & XML, 2nd Ed.
JavaScript Application Cookbook
JavaScript Pocket Reference
Practical Internet Groupware
PHP Pocket Reference
Programming Coldfusion
Photoshop for the Web, 2nd Ed.
Web Design in a Nutshell, 2nd Ed.
Webmaster in a Nutshell, 2nd Ed.
Web Navigation: Designing the User Experience
Web Performance Tuning
Web Security & Commerce
Writing Apache Modules with Perl and C

Unix
SCO UNIX in a Nutshell
Tcl/Tk in a Nutshell
The Unix CD Bookshelf, 2nd Ed.
UNIX in a Nutshell, System V Edition, 3rd Ed.
Learning the Unix Operating System, 4th Ed.
Learning vi, 6th Ed.
Learning the Korn Shell
Learning GNU Emacs, 2nd Ed.
Using csh & tcsh
Learning the bash Shell, 2nd Ed.
GNU Emacs Pocket Reference
Exploring Expect
Tcl/Tk Tools
Tcl/Tk in a Nutshell
Python Pocket Reference

Using Windows
Windows Me: The Missing Manual
PC Hardware in a Nutshell
Optimizing Windows for Games, Graphics, and Multimedia
Outlook 2000 in a Nutshell
Word 2000 in a Nutshell
Excel 2000 in a Nutshell
Windows 2000 Pro: The Missing Manual

Java Series
Developing Java Beans
Creating Effective JavaHelp
Enterprise JavaBeans, 3rd Ed.
Java Cryptography
Java Distributed Computing
Java Enterprise in a Nutshell
Java Examples in a Nutshell, 2nd Ed.
Java Foundation Classes in a Nutshell
Java in a Nutshell, 3rd Ed.
Java Internationalization
Java I/O
Java Native Methods
Java Network Programming, 2nd Ed.
Java Performance Tuning
Java Security
Java Servlet Programming
Java ServerPages
Java Threads, 2nd Ed.
Jini in a Nutshell
Learning Java

Graphics & Multimedia
MP3: The Definitive Guide
Director in a Nutshell
Lingo in a Nutshell

X Window
Vol. 1: Xlib Programming Manual
Vol. 2: Xlib Reference Manual
Vol. 4M: X Toolkit Intrinsics Programming Manual, Motif Ed.
Vol. 5: X Toolkit Intrinsics Reference Manual
Vol. 6A: Motif Programming Manual
Vol. 6B: Motif Reference Manual, 2nd Ed.

Perl
Advanced Perl Programming
CGI Programming with Perl, 2nd Ed.
Learning Perl, 2nd Ed.
Learning Perl for Win32 Systems
Learning Perl/Tk
Mastering Algorithms with Perl
Mastering Regular Expressions
Perl Cookbook
Perl in a Nutshell
Programming Perl, 3rd Ed.
Perl CD Bookshelf
Perl Resource Kit – Win32 Ed.
Perl/Tk Pocket Reference
Perl 5 Pocket Reference, 3rd Ed.

Mac
AppleScript in a Nutshell
AppleWorks 6: The Missing Manual
Crossing Platforms
iMovie: The Missing Manual
Mac OS in a Nutshell
Mac OS 9: The Missing Manual
REALbasic: The Definitive Guide

Linux
Learning Red Hat Linux
Linux Device Drivers, 2nd Ed.
Linux Network Administrator's Guide, 2nd Ed.
Running Linux, 3rd Ed.
Linux in a Nutshell, 3rd Ed.
Linux Multimedia Guide

System Administration
Practical UNIX & Internet Security, 2nd Ed.
Building Internet Firewalls, 2nd Ed.
PGP: Pretty Good Privacy
SSH, The Secure Shell: The Definitive Guide
DNS and BIND, 3rd Ed.
The Networking CD Bookshelf
Virtual Private Networks, 2nd Ed.
TCP/IP Network Administration, 2nd Ed.
sendmail Desktop Reference
Managing Usenet
Using & Managing PPP
Managing IP Networks with Cisco Routers
Networking Personal Computers with TCP/IP
Unix Backup & Recovery
Essential System Administration, 2nd Ed.
Perl for System Administration
Managing NFS and NIS
Vol. 8: X Window System Administrator's Guide
Using Samba
UNIX Power Tools, 2nd Ed.
DNS on Windows NT
Windows NT TCP/IP Network Administration
DHCP for Windows 2000
Essential Windows NT System Administration
Managing Windows NT Logons
Managing the Windows 2000 Registry

Other Titles
PalmPilot: The Ultimate Guide, 2nd Ed.
Palm Programming: The Developer's Guide

International Distributors

http://international.oreilly.com/distributors.html • *international@oreilly.com*

UK, Europe, Middle East, and Africa *(except France, Germany, Austria, Switzerland, Luxembourg, and Liechtenstein)*

INQUIRIES
O'Reilly UK Limited
4 Castle Street
Farnham
Surrey, GU9 7HS
United Kingdom
Telephone: 44-1252-711776
Fax: 44-1252-734211
Email: information@oreilly.co.uk

ORDERS
Wiley Distribution Services Ltd.
1 Oldlands Way
Bognor Regis
West Sussex PO22 9SA
United Kingdom
Telephone: 44-1243-843294
UK Freephone: 0800-243207
Fax: 44-1243-843302 (Europe/EU orders)
or 44-1243-843274 (Middle East/Africa)
Email: cs-books@wiley.co.uk

France

INQUIRIES & ORDERS
Éditions O'Reilly
18 rue Séguier
75006 Paris, France
Tel: 33-1-40-51-71-89
Fax: 33-1-40-51-72-26
Email: france@oreilly.fr

Germany, Switzerland, Austria, Luxembourg, and Liechtenstein

INQUIRIES & ORDERS
O'Reilly Verlag
Balthasarstr. 81
D-50670 Köln, Germany
Telephone: 49-221-973160-91
Fax: 49-221-973160-8
Email: anfragen@oreilly.de (inquiries)
Email: order@oreilly.de (orders)

Canada

(French language books)
Les Éditions Flammarion ltée
375, Avenue Laurier Ouest
Montréal (Québec) H2V 2K3
Tel: 1-514-277-8807
Fax: 1-514-278-2085
Email: info@flammarion.qc.ca

Hong Kong

City Discount Subscription Service, Ltd.
Unit A, 6th Floor, Yan's Tower
27 Wong Chuk Hang Road
Aberdeen, Hong Kong
Tel: 852-2580-3539
Fax: 852-2580-6463
Email: citydis@ppn.com.hk

Korea

Hanbit Media, Inc.
Chungmu Bldg. 210
Yonnam-dong 568-33
Mapo-gu
Seoul, Korea
Tel: 822-325-0397
Fax: 822-325-9697
Email: hant93@chollian.dacom.co.kr

Philippines

Global Publishing
G/F Benavides Garden
1186 Benavides Street
Manila, Philippines
Tel: 632-254-8949/632-252-2582
Fax: 632-734-5060/632-252-2733
Email: globalp@pacific.net.ph

Taiwan

O'Reilly Taiwan
1st Floor, No. 21, Lane 295
Section 1, Fu-Shing South Road
Taipei, 106 Taiwan
Tel: 886-2-27099669
Fax: 886-2-27038802
Email: mori@oreilly.com

India

Shroff Publishers & Distributors Pvt. Ltd.
12, "Roseland", 2nd Floor
180, Waterfield Road, Bandra (West)
Mumbai 400 050
Tel: 91-22-641-1800/643-9910
Fax: 91-22-643-2422
Email: spd@vsnl.com

China

O'Reilly Beijing
SIGMA Building, Suite B809
No. 49 Zhichun Road
Haidian District
Beijing, China PR 100080
Tel: 86-10-8809-7475
Fax: 86-10-8809-7463
Email: beijing@oreilly.com

Japan

O'Reilly Japan, Inc.
Yotsuya Y's Building
7 Banch 6, Honshio-cho
Shinjuku-ku
Tokyo 160-0003 Japan
Tel: 81-3-3356-5227
Fax: 81-3-3356-5261
Email: japan@oreilly.com

Singapore, Indonesia, Malaysia, and Thailand

TransQuest Publishers Pte Ltd
30 Old Toh Tuck Road #05-02
Sembawang Kimtrans Logistics Centre
Singapore 597654
Tel: 65-4623112
Fax: 65-4625761
Email: wendiw@transquest.com.sg

Australia

Woodslane Pty., Ltd.
7/5 Vuko Place
Warriewood NSW 2102
Australia
Tel: 61-2-9970-5111
Fax: 61-2-9970-5002
Email: info@woodslane.com.au

New Zealand

Woodslane New Zealand, Ltd.
21 Cooks Street (P.O. Box 575)
Waganui, New Zealand
Tel: 64-6-347-6543
Fax: 64-6-345-4840
Email: info@woodslane.com.au

Argentina

Distribuidora Cuspide
Suipacha 764
1008 Buenos Aires
Argentina
Phone: 54-11-4322-8868
Fax: 54-11-4322-3456
Email: libros@cuspide.com

All Other Countries

O'Reilly & Associates, Inc.
1005 Gravenstein Hwy North
Sebastopol, CA 95472 USA
Tel: 707-829-0515
Fax: 707-829-0104
Email: order@oreilly.com